The Life of
Villiers de l'Isle-Adam

The Life of
Villiers de l'Isle-Adam

A. W. RAITT

CLARENDON PRESS · OXFORD
1981

Oxford University Press, Walton Street, Oxford OX2 6DP

Oxford London Glasgow
New York Toronto Melbourne Wellington
Kuala Lumpur Singapore Jakarta Hong Kong Tokyo
Delhi Bombay Calcutta Madras Karachi
Nairobi Dar es Salaam Cape Town

Published in the United States by
Oxford University Press, New York
© A. W. Raitt 1981

British Library Cataloguing in Publication Data
Raitt, Alan William
The life of Villiers de l'Isle-Adam.
1. Villiers de l'Isle-Adam, Jean-Marie-Mathias
Philippe-Auguste, Comte de—Biography
2. Authors, French—19th century—Biography
I. Title
843'.8   PQ2476.V4Z/   80-41596
ISBN 0-19-815771-1

Text set in 11/12 pt Linotron 202 Garamond, printed and bound
in Great Britain at The Pitman Press, Bath

CONTENTS

PART I
THE YEARS OF PROMISE
page 1

Contents

Contents

LIST OF ILLUSTRATIONS

(between pages 238 and 239)

INTRODUCTION

Of all the great French writers of the nineteenth century, Villiers de l'Isle-Adam had perhaps the most extraordinary and fascinating life. But, even before his death, the reality of his existence had already become inextricably intertwined with legend (not least because he himself wished it to be so), and, in the time since then, the legend has come dangerously close to taking over altogether. There have of course been several attempts to recount his biography—the cheerful but inaccurate memoirs of his cousin Robert du Pontavice de Heussey in 1893, the austere, well-researched book by Édouard de Rougemont in 1910, the lively essay by Fernand Clerget in 1913, the comprehensive study by Max Daireaux in 1936, the more recent examinations of the man and his writings by André Lebois in 1952, Jacques-Henry Bornecque in 1974 and William T. Conroy Jr in 1978. But, despite the very real merits of all these works, there still exists no detailed and reliable account of how Villiers de l'Isle-Adam actually spent his time—so much so that one is tempted to echo the question that his great friend Stéphane Mallarmé asked shortly after he died: 'His life—I search for anything that corresponds to that expression: truly and in the ordinary sense, did he live?'

The present volume is an attempt to fill that remarkable gap. Having been concerned with Villiers for over quarter of a century, I have been more conscious than most of how much need there was for such a book, but it is also that experience that has emboldened me to undertake the daunting task of writing it. In particular, my involvement in producing an edition of his complete works for the Bibliothèque de la Pléiade has acquainted me with the vast amount of unpublished material there is in public and private collections in Paris, La Rochelle, Oxford, and elsewhere, much of it extremely valuable in establishing the true facts of a life often shrouded in mystery. Moreover, I have had occasion to consult a very wide range of recondite and neglected publications which have helped to clarify this or that obscure episode. I do not pretend that there are no longer any lacunae or any problems—on the contrary, I suspect that with Villiers there will always be unsolved riddles, and that is exactly what he would have wanted. But I think the time has now come when it is reasonable to believe that a coherent narrative can and should be put together.

I have tried so far as possible to construct that narrative on the basis of documentary evidence, both printed and manuscript, emanating either from Villiers or from his contemporaries, and I have largely relegated to footnotes discussion of erroneous, unsupported, or purely speculative assertions made by those who knew him or by more recent writers. To have included such arguments in the main text would have overburdened it intolerably, such is the weight of myth or sheer misstatement that has built up around Villiers. This system has meant that tributes to the discoveries of modern scholars have unfortunately also been confined to the notes. In fact, without these researches this book could never have been written. The contributions of men like Pierre-Georges Castex, Joseph Bollery, Jean-Marie Bellefroid, Alain Néry, and above all Émile Drougard have transformed our knowledge of Villiers in a relatively short space of time, and provide a foundation of solid information on which all future study of Villiers will rest.

As for Villiers's works, I have not tried to give anything approaching a full critical assessment of them. But, since Villiers lived so much in and for what he wrote, it would have falsified the whole picture of his life if they had been left aside, especially as many of them are not well known. I have therefore provided brief accounts of all his major writings, as well as of lesser publications where they were relevant to an understanding of the evolution of his art or of his career.

During the course of my researches on Villiers I have contracted an immense debt to many people who have given me unstinted help and encouragement in all sorts of different ways. Some of them, alas, are dead now, but I shall not forget their kindness towards me: Émile Drougard, who for many years carried almost single-handed the banner of Villiers studies and whose numerous articles are all marked by the same elegance of style and sureness of documentation; Édouard de Rougemont, author of the first serious biography of Villiers; Joseph Bollery, editor of Villiers's correspondence and assembler of a remarkable collection of Villieriana now housed in the Bibliothèque Municipale de La Rochelle; Mme Aline Pasquet, daughter of Villiers's close friend Jean Marras, who generously placed at my disposal the letters of Villiers to her father at a time when they were still unpublished; Max Daireaux, whose *Villiers de l'Isle-Adam* remains the best single work about him.

Professor P.-G. Castex, membre de l'Institut, has effected an outstanding revival of Villiers studies in the last two decades, and I personally owe to him more than I can ever say. His never-failing kindness to me, in opening his collection of unpublished manuscripts, in guiding my researches, in revising what I have written, and in setting such a marvellous example of rigorous scholarship, is something beyond praise. Professor Austin Gill, who originally awakened my interest in Villiers, has never ceased to concern himself with my work, and to him too I owe more than I can express. Henri Leclercq, son of the great Belgian bibliophile whose vigilance was responsible for the preservation of so many of Villiers's papers, has been a firm friend ever since, in 1954, he first allowed me to consult his father's collection with all its unexplored riches. I have had the privilege of collaborating closely with Jean-Marie Bellefroid, whose lively enthusiasm has led him to make many unexpected discoveries about Villiers. Alain Néry, whose excellent Sorbonne thesis on 'Les Idées politiques et sociales de Villiers de l'Isle-Adam' contains much new and exciting material, has been good enough to place his erudition at my disposal. Mlle O. de Saint-Affrique, former curator of the Bibliothèque Municipale de La Rochelle, has done much to facilitate my work on the Fonds Bollery which was under her care. The enterprise of my friend Giles Barber, librarian of the Taylor Institution in Oxford, has resulted in the acquisition of vital unknown manuscripts by Villiers, which have thrown surprising light on dark corners of his life.

On various points of detail, I have turned to friends and colleagues, who have all responded with admirable goodwill to my often importunate requests for help—or have indeed spontaneously supplied information which I would otherwise have missed: Dr David Bellos, Professor Lloyd Austin, Dr Jancis Clarke, Dr Jill Forbes, Mr M. Pakenham, Miss Hermia Oliver, and Chanoine J. Raison du Cleuziou. I am deeply grateful to all of them, as I am to my wife Lia for the many constructive comments she made while typing my manuscript.

My experience of many years of intimate frequentation of Villiers is that he never disappoints and that, the better one knows him, the more attractive and individual he appears. I hope that something of that sense will come through in the pages of this book. Anyone who has read *Axël, L'Ève future*, or *Contes cruels* will want to know what sort of man wrote those extraordinary works; anyone who has not will still find in Villiers's life what Mallarmé called 'an exceptional tale, at the extremity of which is the tomb'.

PART I
The Years of Promise

1

Jean-Marie-Mathias-Philippe-Auguste, Comte de Villiers de l'Isle-Adam, was born in Saint-Brieuc on the northern coast of Brittany on 7 November 1838. His sonorous name was to prove at one and the same time the pride and inspiration of his life and a crushingly heavy burden to bear.

It is hard to know whether his distant and illustrious forebears or the more recent lineage of impoverished and eccentric Breton nobles had the greater influence on him. He later claimed, no doubt over-optimistically, to be able to trace his ancestry back to the tenth century, and the great glories of the family were Jean de Villiers de l'Isle-Adam (1384–1437), Marshal of France, who captured Paris from the Armagnacs in the civil war in 1418, and then from the English in 1436, and Philippe-Auguste de Villiers de l'Isle-Adam (1464–1534), Grand Master of the Order of the Knights of St. John of Jerusalem, heroic defender of the island of Rhodes against the besieging armies of Suliman, and subsequently founder of the Order of the Knights of Malta. Lesser luminaries included Pierre de Villiers de l'Isle-Adam, Grand Standard-Bearer of France, who distinguished himself at the battle of Roosebeke against the Flemish in 1382. The line was thus one of the grandest in the annals of French history, and the poet never ceased to be conscious of the privileges and obligations which this laid on him in a world which no longer recognized the qualities it represented.

The designation 'de l'Isle-Adam' indicates that the family had originated in the region of Pontoise, north-west of Paris, where there is still a small town of that name. But, late in the seventeenth century, one branch had established itself in Brittany, when Jean de Villiers de l'Isle-Adam, son of a Parisian lawyer called Hiérosme, became a naval officer and settled in Brest. In fact, it is a moot point whether there is not a break in the line at this point; it was Jean who added 'de l'Isle-Adam' to his father's name Villiers, and the arms of their immediate predecessors were not those of the great family.[1] But, if there is some doubt over the attachment of the branch to the tree, there is none thereafter: from that

3

point on, the descent is firmly established. Unfortunately, during the same period the fortunes of the Villiers de l'Isle-Adams of Brittany went gradually from bad to worse.

Throughout the eighteenth century the male members of the family were either lawyers or naval officers, honest, conscientious, occasionally even attaining mild distinction in their careers, but facing increasing poverty as their meagre possessions were split up among numerous children. In 1712 the family acquired a manor-house at Penanhoas, near Lopérec at the western end of the peninsula, and later in the century they came by marriage into possession of a not very prosperous sugar plantation in the French colony of San Domingo, now Haiti. Otherwise their resources were modest, and, when Charles de Villiers de l'Isle-Adam, a naval lieutenant, died in 1768 at the age of twenty-four, his infant son Jean-Jérôme-Charles, the sole surviving member of the family, had little to inherit.

Jean-Jérôme-Charles, known as 'Lilly', was to grow into an extraordinary character, and, since his grandson the poet knew him in his childhood, it is worth taking a closer look at him.[2] When his father died, his widowed mother lived alternately with a great-aunt and at Morlaix with her grandfather, who had been at school with Voltaire and had literary interests. But in 1782 she married Comte Jégou du Laz, a widower with three children to whom she rapidly bore four more. From then on, Lilly seems scarcely to have fitted into the new family circle, which may help to account for the growing wildness of his behaviour. He was packed off to Paris to study mathematics with a view to his becoming a naval officer, but the young Breton priest who had been charged with keeping an eye on him reported: 'There is a residue of pride in our nature which we cannot get rid of. It will make us commit many mistakes. We are hardly capable of sustained study,'[3] and a little later: 'We continue to be remarkably scatterbrained.'[4] But it was only in 1784, when he accompanied the priest back to Saint-Pol-de-Léon in Brittany, that the trouble really started, leaving the Abbé aghast at the change in the youth's behaviour, which culminated in his fighting a duel at the age of fifteen. After that escapade, he was sent as a boarder to the royal military school at Beaumont to remove him from the temptations of too much freedom, though he himself seems to have felt that he was being exiled from the affections of his mother, the more so as he was even kept short of proper clothing.[5]

Two years later, in 1786, he embarked on the frigate *Calypso*, but without the coveted status of *garde-marine*, which put him in a position of inferiority compared with the other cadets. After three years in the East, he returned to France, still hopelessly short of shirts and still liable to upset people by his quick temper. By then the Revolution had already broken out, and he was soon in hot water with the new authorities. In December 1789 he wrote to his mother:

I have been summoned before their illustrious Council to account for the remarks I had made about the Assembly which gives France so much happiness, which maintains our privileges, and which has endowed us with such blessed tranquillity! I was asked for my declaration of faith; I replied that it was that of any decent man and that, if I had said I didn't give a fig for the States-General, it was apparently because I was in no position to judge their worthiness, but that I knew we had been declared to be *free* and that I therefore assumed that we were also free to speak our minds.[6]

But the remainder of the letter shows him to have been more severely shaken than such ironic bravado would make one think. He announced his intention of retiring to Penanhoas, saying he would have more than enough to lead the life of a hermit, with only an old maidservant and a dog: 'Moreover, I'll have another advantage: I shall be far from the rest of the world, and for me that is a certain guarantee of happiness!'[7]

But, instead of becoming a hermit, the impetuous young Lilly went off and joined the counter-revolutionary army of the Princes, then was wounded at Mons while serving with an Austro-Belgian regiment, made his way to Jersey and embarked for San Domingo, but was captured by the French, escaped into the interior of Brittany, fought with the Royalist Chouans, was badly wounded near Quintin, and was taken in by a widow, Mme Hamon de Treveno, whose daughter he married on 16 September 1796. In the meantime the manor at Penanhoas had been confiscated and sold as the property of an *émigré*, while the estate in San Domingo had been lost as a result of the slaves' revolt there. So, more bereft than ever, he took up his abode with his new wife at a humbler dwelling at Maël-Pestivien, in the wilds to the south of Guingamp. Though he was officially amnestied in August 1803, he continued to make a nuisance of himself to all and sundry—to the Republican authorities because he was still in touch with royalist conspirators, to the peasants who had bought Penanhoas, whom he bombarded with threatening letters, and to his own wife and mother-in-law, whom he was suspected of trying to poison. He was also alleged to have procured an abortion for a local girl whom he had got pregnant. Eventually in 1811 he was ordered to reside at Saint-Pol-de-Léon with his mother, Mme Jégou du Laz, and was only allowed to return to Kerrohou, the house at Maël-Pestivien, after the Restoration.[8]

Even then his situation remained critical, not least because his wife had given him eight children in quick succession between 1798 and 1817 (she died in 1820). In 1824 a document which seems to have been sent to the ecclesiastical authorities to try to obtain charity for the family shows that, while Lilly was away on the king's service, his eldest daughter Pauline had been left with nothing to live on but potatoes and beans—'and people do not always dare to offer her dinner, since she is so sensitive about anyone feeling sorry for her'.[9] Despite his zeal for the royal cause, Lilly scarcely endeared himself to the restored monarchy. He was even arrested in 1818 and condemned to three years' imprisonment for having threatened to kill the Duc Decazes, one of Louis XVIII's ministers. In fact, it turned out to be a case of mistaken identity, and he was released,[10] but the vigour and indiscretion of the missives he continuously directed at the government had obviously made him highly suspect. Sometimes it was to denounce the local priest, of whom he alleged that 'only self-interest can have made him exchange his red bonnet for a black skull-cap';[11] more often it was to demand the pension to which he regarded himself as entitled. This he did with such vehemence that the author of the already-quoted 1824 document noted: 'Everyone agrees that the father has a right to a pension. The poor man has often asked for one, but he makes such a nuisance of himself in everything he says and does that he puts people off giving him anything.'[12] To the wife of the Minister of War, who showed some interest in the family, he explained in 1825 that he was reduced to writing his complaints, 'having no pen, with a piece of wood shaped with a pen-knife'.[13] The idea that he had lost everything in the service of an ungrateful king had been aggravated when, in 1815, he had learnt that Louis XVIII had authorized a certain Joseph-Gabriel de Villiers Deschamps to add 'de l'Isle-Adam' to his name (it was the son of this man who three years later wrote the threatening letters that brought about Lilly's arrest).[14] In a letter to the Minister of Justice, as superbly sarcastic as it is badly spelled, Lilly wrote:

So M. de Villiers is called Villiers de l'Isle-Adam. That is my name; my father, my grandfather, etc., handed it down to me; I accept with gratitude the new kinsman that His Majesty has given me, and, in the hope that he will show *esprit de corps* and proper family loyalty, I make so bold as to ask Your Excellency to have his address sent to me so that I may pay him my compliments. If my name had not been so long already, I would have also asked His Majesty to add to it that of 'poor devil', and that is a name I really deserve.[15]

In the end, in 1826, Lilly was allocated the sum of 27,867 fr. 40 from the 'milliard des émigrés' which the government had set aside to recompense those whose property had been confiscated while they were in exile. But it seems unlikely that he ever received the indemnity he had demanded for the loss of the family estates in San Domingo, so that his fortunes remained precarious.[16] He eventually went to live with one of his married daughters, in whose house he was to die in 1846.

The difficulties he had in rearing his eight children—four boys and four girls—can be imagined. One of the boys died in infancy; the others all had to be provided for, and in ways not inconsistent with their rank. Pauline, the eldest girl, stayed at home to keep house after her mother's death; two others, Gabrielle and Julie, went into convents, but only Gabrielle became a nun, Julie, who was something of a handful, eventually leaving to wed a country gentleman. The fourth girl, Delphine, married a doctor. Of the boys, Philippe-Auguste became a lawyer; little is known of him save that he remained a bachelor and wrote a brochure in 1859 on a *Nouvelle Application de la vapeur à la navigation*.[17]

His older brother Victor had a curious career. Thanks to the local deputy, he was given a partial scholarship to the naval cadet school at Angoulême, but he evidently had to withdraw because the family could not afford to keep him there, and he was transferred to a Jesuit school at Montmorillon, where he proved a very successful pupil. In 1833 he became a teacher at Brest, but in the 1840s discovered a belated vocation and went off to Rome to study for the priesthood, spending six years there and returning with a doctorate in theology. He became rector of Kerpert in his native Brittany in 1853 and moved in 1864 to Ploumilliau on the north coast, where he remained until his death in 1889. He was a learned man and had a reputation for saintliness in his parish, but such letters of his as have survived show him as extremely narrow-minded and preoccupied above all with material things.[18]

However, it is the oldest boy, Joseph-Toussaint-Charles, who interests us most, not only because he was to be the father of the poet, but also because he was such an extraordinary figure in his own right. Born in 1802, he was destined for the priesthood and was sent to Paris to study at the Seminary of Saint-Sulpice. But in 1824 his father, the terrible Lilly, heard that he was having doubts and flew into a towering rage:

I have learnt, with deep grief and at the same time with great indignation, that his vocation is faltering. I gave him enough time to make up his mind. I have made sacrifices to send him to Paris, as well as for his education. I shall go on making them so long as he behaves properly, but if he turns into a weathercock, goodbye; be kind enough to tell him so and say that, if he leaves Saint-Sulpice, it is his own business what will become of him. It was my hope that he would be the support and the honour of his family, and I could not bear to see him, after being a burden on it, turning into its laughing-stock and its opprobrium.[19]

These objurgations produced their effect, and in 1828 Joseph was awarded a scholarship to continue his theological studies at the Seminary of Saint-Brieuc, where he took minor orders in March 1829. But the following year he finally decided to give up and resigned his scholarship. He nevertheless retained some of his ecclesiastical connections, and later, in 1840, was received into the Order of the Knights of Malta.[20] By then, however, the eccentricity of Joseph (or Joson as he was known in the family) had begun to assert itself in no uncertain fashion. The 1824 document speaks of 'a disposition more or less common to the whole family' and consisting of 'mental over-excitement, incoherence, oddities, failings, nothing stable or fixed':[21] Joseph obviously had more than his fair share of such quirks. He seems to have returned to Maël-Pestivien after giving up his prospective ordination, and it was probably then that he conceived the idea of setting up as a businessman.

But his notion of business was quite unlike anyone else's. He thought he could see two main ways of making a fortune. The first was to search for buried treasure in or near the castles and country-houses of Brittany, since he was convinced that in Revolutionary times many aristocrats had hidden their silver, their jewels, and their money, and then been unable to recover them; also it was likely that subsidies from the Princes had been spirited away; in addition, the Knights of Malta had perhaps somehow concealed their funds near Quintin. So there were untold riches scattered throughout the subsoil to his native province; all one had to do was to dig them up. Unfortunately, this involved buying the land and selling it again if the excavations proved unproductive, and that usually meant heavy losses. It is said that there were times when he was operating on as many as ten or twelve sites at once, but all he ever found was a dinner service at the Château de Chefdubois, near Lannion.[22]

The other main scheme was based on the belief that, after the Revolution, much land and property had got into the hands of people who had no right to it. He therefore went round offering his services to private individuals and, more especially, parish councils for the recovery of their lost wealth. This too developed into a large-scale if ineffectual operation: the Archives of Finistère contain twelve boxes of dossiers put together by him and by his collaborators, and there are still more in the Archives of the Côtes-du-Nord. He is known to have approached at least fifty parishes in this way, with the support of the Vicar-General of the diocese and of the local Prefect, proposing to take a third of any profits accruing from his investigations. By 1837 he had founded an 'Agence Villiers de l'Isle-Adam' to run his researches, and spent much time travelling round, burrowing into parish archives, pestering local notaries, demanding to see the records in town halls and so forth. Highly litigious by temperament and imbued with unconquerable self-confidence, he had some success in interesting people in his proposals, but since he only earned anything if a case came to a successful conclusion, all this frantic activity won him far more resentment than income.[23]

The Marquis (for such was the title he usually took, although on occasion he was also referred to as 'comte', 'baron' or even as 'duc') must have cut a strange figure on his peregrinations round Brittany. Tall and thin, with prominent cheekbones and piercing, dancing eyes under shaggy eyebrows, he had manners of great aristocratic distinction and a persuasive tongue, even if his conversation hopped unpredictably from one subject to another. In later years, when he was living in Saint-Brieuc, his lanky silhouette and fantastic garb (a long petersham cloak, a ruffled shirt, and trousers with foot-straps) used to excite the mirth of town urchins, whom he did not deign to notice, stopping only to take a pinch of snuff, with an elegant gesture, from an eighteenth-century snuff-box with a cameo on the lid.[24] As he grew older, his speculations became ever more ruinously crack-brained—raising the sunken galleons of Vigo,[25] opening up gold mines in Peru,[26] and the like—but he never lost either his unshakeable faith in the crock of gold at the end of the rainbow, or that grand air which made people imagine they could see in him some last reflection of medieval glories.[27]

It was in 1837 that the indefatigable Marquis came across a couple of women living quietly in Saint-Brieuc and began to press his suit on the younger of them. Marie-Françoise Le Nepvou de Carfort, then aged twenty-six, came from an ancient and noble Breton family which could trace its ancestry back to the Crusades. Though her parents and five brothers and sisters were still alive, Marie-Françoise, or Francine as she was called, had, for reasons which remain mysterious, been brought up and educated almost from birth by her maiden aunt, Marie-Félix Daniel de Kerinou, born in

1784 and a younger sister of the girl's mother.[28] In 1836 she had officially adopted Francine, who added the name Daniel de Kerinou to her own and thereby became something of an heiress. The two women lived in a large house in the rue Saint-Benoît, originally built in the seventeenth century to house the confessor of the nuns in a nearby convent, and it seems clear that Mlle de Kerinou was an active and lively woman who completely dominated her niece; perhaps the girl wondered why her mother, who seems to have had little affection for her, had abandoned her to her aunt. Mlle de Kerinou had her house to run, her charitable visits to undertake, her numerous relatives to see, and Mass to attend; Francine evidently preferred to stay at home.

When the Marquis came on the scene, it is said that Tante Kerinou was at once impressed by him and eager for the marriage to take place, whereas Francine was reticent, either because she did not care for him or because he was not rich enough. But, after one of his visits, a maid noticed that he had left his rosary on the mantlepiece, and, delighted by this proof of his piety, Tante Kerinou was able to persuade Francine to accept his proposal.[29] The couple were married on 1 June in the cathedral of Saint-Brieuc by the bishop, Mgr Mathias Le Groing de La Romagère, whose good graces the Marquis had won by his 'efforts' on behalf of the local parishes. Tante Kerinou, however, had no intention of allowing them to lead an independent life, and the marriage contract, which ensured that the newly-weds would have a joint estate, also included a remarkable clause whereby the old lady, who was more than comfortably off, undertook to give them and their children board and lodging for the rest of her life—on condition that they lived with her 'either in Saint-Brieuc or in any other place in which she might deem it expedient to take up her abode',[30] and that she be given absolute control of the education of any female children they might have.

Seventeen months later, in the house in the rue Saint-Benoît, Francine gave birth to Jean-Marie-Mathias-Philippe-Auguste, who was to be her only child.

2

Some idea of the family life led by Joseph, Francine, and Tante

Kerinou can be gleaned from the reminiscences of their little maid Héloïse Feuregard, who was interviewed about them many years later, when she was an old widow. The house was ancient, vast, and difficult to look after, the more so as there were only two servants, who also had to take charge of the farmyard—Héloïse used to take baby Mathias with her when she went to guard the cows in a field near the bishop's garden, in fear and trembling lest she dirtied the white pinny she had to wear at all times. 'Ah! you see, Mme de Kerinou wasn't always easy to get on with, and she would have given me a right telling-off.' According to her, those two self-willed characters the Marquis and Tante Kerinou were far from seeing eye to eye.

He wasn't a bad man at all, but talkative and very hot-tempered; there were times when you would have thought he wasn't quite right in the head. Often, he would jump down his aunt's throat, and she gave as good as she got. I've never seen such an active woman, but, oh dear me, so muddle-headed and bossy! ... She hardly ever gave in to her son-in-law, but he was a cunning devil, and he used to play lots of tricks on her.

And if the old lady noticed? 'Goodness me, then the storm started brewing ... gracious! Then everyone ran for cover ... do you understand?' As for Francine in the midst of the tumult, 'She was sad, naturally. All that was expected of her was to see nothing, keep her mouth shut, and above all do nothing. I don't think she was very happy, but she was the best of the lot of them!'[1]

By 1841 the Marquis was paying a clerk to assist him in his 'business',[2] but soon Brittany seemed too constricted a field for his financial enterprises, and in 1842 and 1843 he was operating in Paris from an address in the rue Mondovi.[3] It is not known whether his wife and child and Tante Kerinou were with him, but, as the house in the rue Saint-Benoît had been sold in 1841,[4] it is quite possible that they were. However, if Paris offered greater opportunities for the Marquis to indulge his get-rich-quick ambitions, it also contained even more people ready to divest him of his money and—more importantly—that of Tante Kerinou, who had somehow been induced to subsidize him. By 1843 they were inextricably embroiled in a lawsuit with three gentlemen with the unlikely names of Devey, Vilcoq, and Dugabé, who had been associated with the Marquis in some elaborate plan for the exploitation of farmland in Brittany and who, by playing on his credulity, had plunged him deeply into debt.[5] This was too much even for the meek Francine, who had never much wanted to marry him anyway, and on 8 August 1843 she started legal proceedings to have her estate separated from that of her husband. The document prefacing her request specifies that, 'since his marriage, M. Villiers de l'Isle-Adam has engaged in speculations in which he has contracted debts of over a hundred thousand francs, taking up all his fortune and fifty thousand francs over and above it'.[6]

It was three years before the courts finally accepted her petition, by which time Tante Kerinou had decided that it was prudent to beat a retreat back to Brittany, first renting and then buying a house on the Place du Marc'hallac'h at Lannion, taking the rest of the family with her. Her sister, Francine's mother, wrote to her on 10 March 1846 to express great relief at the news that the Marquis had at last become 'stationary' and that his affairs were prospering,[7] but her relief was short-lived, since Tante Kerinou promptly replied that Francine had just walked out. The sister's reaction is noticeably lacking in tenderness, considering that the person in question was her own daughter: 'That young woman has always had an eccentric character (. . .) I refuse to become involved again between you and your adopted daughter. When I tried to help last year, all I got out of it was reproaches from my husband.'[8] Evidently all was not sweetness and light in the Villiers de l'Isle-Adam household. Four months later the census returns showed that Francine had still not come back, and it is not known when she finally resigned herself to rejoining her incorrigible husband.

It can easily be imagined that such a chaotic situation scarcely provided a stable background for the upbringing of an only child. Tante Kerinou and the unfortunate Francine naturally lavished affection on him, and the Marquis seems soon to have regarded him as the predestined saviour of the family fortunes. Little Mathias (he was always Mathias in the family, but later signed Philippe-Auguste or, more often,

Auguste), who was precociously intelligent, obviously realized that the quarrels in the household could be exploited to
his advantage, and rapidly got used to having his own way in
everything. His schooling was quite extraordinarily hap-
hazard and interrupted, partly due no doubt to the family's
frequent changes of domicile, and partly due to his tendency
to get himself expelled from any school to which he was sent.
So far as the chequered course of his education can be traced,
he spent a term at the Petit Séminaire at Tréguier at the end of
1847, then ten months at the Collège Saint Vincent de Paul at
Rennes in 1848 and 1849, followed by eighteen months at the
Lycée de Laval, on the confines of Brittany and Normandy,
in 1849 and 1850. At this point, his father was apparently
living in Paris, at No. 39 rue Neuve Saint-Roch. Then for
some reason he was sent back to the Collège Saint Vincent de
Paul at Rennes, where he spent the last term of 1850. In May
1851 he became a boarder at the Collège Saint-François
Xavier at Vannes, on the south coast of Brittany, but his stay
there was brief and inglorious, and he seems to have gone to
the École Saint-Charles at Saint-Brieuc, perhaps as a day-
boy.[9] It is rumoured that, some time after 1853, he also
attended the Lycée de Saint-Brieuc, and that his parents went
to live in the rue Corbin at Rennes while he finished his
studies there; in addition, in the frequent intervals between
two schools, he was probably tutored at home by young
priests.[10] It comes as no surprise to discover that this
whirlwind medley of educational establishments left him
without any formal academic qualifications.

Not that Mathias was by any means a backward pupil:
quite the contrary. At the Lycée de Laval, in 1849 and 1850,
he won prizes for Greek, Latin, recitation, handwriting, and
religious instruction, and at Rennes in 1851 he left with a
complimentary report. But the register of the school at
Vannes reveals what kind of boy he was. His marks at first
were good, then degenerated rapidly, especially for behaviour, until, after only one term, the school wrote to ask his
mother to remove him. According to the school records, 'The
reason was first of all the child's health, which, in the opinion
of our doctor, needed special care, then the knowledge he had
acquired of reading matter far beyond his age, and the fact

that, with people outside, he had contacts forbidden by the school rules.'[11] The same indiscipline and desire to go his own way were apparent when he attended the École Saint Charles at Saint-Brieuc. Claude Gaultier de Kermoal, one of his school-fellows there, remember that he was not lazy, though it was over his own writings and not over his school work that he was prepared to take trouble. But, when Kermoal made fun of his literary pretensions, he retorted: 'That's enough! You really think I haven't enough stamina or method; think what you like, but you'll see that I can prove you wrong.'[12] He then set about composing (in class) an interminable story called *Les Chants du bossu*, sheet after sheet of which was stowed away in his desk, which he also used for rearing ladybirds, until such time as an irate master pounced on him.

Mathias did little to endear himself to children of his age. Several of them remembered him as a young gentleman imbued with his own importance, moody, full of idiotic obsessions, often haughty, and generally rather antipathetic.[13] He was also madly susceptible, and at the age of thirteen challenged another boy to a duel over some supposed insult (shades perhaps of his grandfather's youthful exploit?). But, when the appointed day came, Mathias found himself alone on the beach where they were due to fight: authority had prevailed with his opponent (the Marquis had allegedly been delighted to encourage his son to defend the family honour), and the duel never took place.[14] On another occasion, he so disconcerted one of his classmates by persistently staring at him that the boy complained to a master. When interrogated, Mathias manifested astonishment that he should have been discomfited: 'How can that be, sir? It gave me such great, such sweet joy, for he is the very image of a brother whom I adored and who now lives only in my memory!'[15] The invention of a non-existent brother was nothing to some of his other fantasies, though; in later years he claimed to have been carried off as a child by gypsies, and to have spent two years wandering through Central Europe. His cousin and first biographer Robert du Pontavice de Heussey said that in reality the gypsies had taken him no further than Brest, where he was recovered by his father a day or two later;[16] others allege that all that happened was that he was found wandering in the streets of Saint-Brieuc and taken home by some travelling showmen.[17]

Most often the riotous imagination was channelled into juvenile literary compositions, which not only the budding author but also his parents and great-aunt took with the greatest seriousness. Here is how he was remembered by a young female cousin called Sébert, whose family had a town house in Saint-Brieuc, as well as a country manor with the picturesque name of la Ville-Néant:

We didn't greatly care for Mathias; he would have so little to do with us, it was as if it humiliated him—children don't really count, do they? . . . I remember one day in particular at la Ville-Néant, where we used to go to spend time in the country, when he was especially surly . . . We did all we could to get him to join in our games, it was no use. There was no way we could stop him walking up and down the tree-lined avenues, whose highest branches he stared at lovingly, while he muttered to himself under his breath. 'Never mind! Let's leave him alone,' said one of the other girls, 'we'd only stop him thinking about his *Robinson des arbres*!' And when I looked amazed, she went on: 'What, didn't you know that it's a fine book he's working on?'[18]

If the Séberts went to visit the Villiers de l'Isle-Adams, it was the same thing: Mathias would fail to appear, and, if anyone asked after him, his mother would say: 'Mathias is well, thank you,' and Tante Kerinou would add in solemnly mysterious tones: 'Please excuse him; he's working!' One day the girl was horrified by an indescribable racket which suddenly started up on the floor above:

It was as if everything was dancing a wild jig. To the sound of furniture being pushed around, there were added at times moans or even mournful howls, and at others melodies reinforced by chords on the piano . . . all this punctuated by detonations which made me jump on my seat and drew from me little hoarse cries, despite all my desire to appear a well-bred young lady, just as poised as anyone else . . . I learnt that it was our great man composing! . . . Ah! What a chap![19]

For Mathias was a musician as well as a writer. He had in fact had extra singing and piano lessons at school at Rennes, and was a sufficiently accomplished pianist to accompany a local singer, one Courcoux, at public concerts in Saint-Brieuc. Courcoux recollected rehearsing in the Villiers de l'Isle-Adam house:

Suddenly I heard a kind of whimpering noise from the next room. At first, out of discretion, I pretended not to notice, but as there was a crescendo in the noise, I thought it right to stop. As for my friend, he had stood up, his brow furrowed, his face pale. Realizing how embarrassed I was, he said: 'Don't worry; it's my mother who isn't well, but it'll pass off quickly, so long as I go to her; I'm the only one who can calm her down, if I recite my poetry to her. Excuse me for a few minutes.'

Thereupon Mathias disappeared, and Courcoux sat down to wait, until it became clear that his friend had forgotten all about him, after which he quietly made off.[20]

According to Courcoux, Mathias was a good accompanist, read music with great facility, and was passionately interested in it. His love for music was to remain with him throughout his life; so was his taste for reciting his own works. But these latter performances did not have the same therapeutic effect on everyone as they did on his mother. The Sébert girl recalled that every now and then he would do them the honour of coming down from his room:

One would see him appear, pushing back with a lordly gesture the long fair locks which hung down over his shoulders, a silk scarf wrapped high around his neck, somewhat carelessly dressed, with a benevolent smile on his lips ... and soon he would be declaiming his latest lucubration ... One evening when we were having dinner together, we had to sit through some new thing or other; all I remember is that the reading on that occasion struck us as so macabre, so desperately arid ... that we all fell asleep.[21]

Clearly, young Villiers was assiduously cultivating the conventional image of the Romantic artist—full of inspiration, flouting convention, dreamy, and melancholy (though he also liked shooting, and left one of the houses in which they lived heavily scarred from his target practice).[22] But it is not impossible that at the same time he did in reality suffer the tragic disappointment in love without which no budding Romantic poet could feel himself properly equipped. According to his cousin Robert du Pontavice de Heussey, when he was seventeen he was in love at Rennes with a young girl who died, and, though Pontavice is much given to embellishing the facts, it is true that the poem which was to occupy the central position in his first volume of poetry is an elegy, entitled 'De profundis clamavi', on the death of a girl loved and lost.[23] Another early biographer, Louis Tiercelin, who derived much of his material from a close friend of the poet, claims that the true tragedy of these early years was not that spoken of by Pontavice, but the end of another love-affair with a girl 'whose fate was even more painful'.[24] One might infer, from the later indirect evidence of Villiers's works, that the mysterious fate worse than death was being forced to enter a convent without having a vocation, but this can be no more than speculation. All one can say with certainty is that two writers who were well placed to know both asserted that Villiers was marked for life by the loss in adolescence of a girl whom he dearly loved.

3

By the time Villiers had finished his peripatetic studies in the schools of Brittany, the family seems to have been dividing its time between Saint-Brieuc and Paris, no doubt according to the exigencies of the Marquis's affairs.[1] Apparently no effort was made to find a profession for the young man. With startling unanimity, the Marquis, his wife, and Tante Kerinou were agreed that he was going to be a writer, and a great one, so that, far from meeting the traditional parental opposition to an artistic career, he was actually encouraged in it. No one seems to have given much thought to the mundane business of earning a living, perhaps because Tante Kerinou's coffers were deemed to be inexhaustible, perhaps because it was supposed that such outstanding genius was bound to meet success with the suddenness of a thunderclap.

So in 1855 we find the young man installed in Paris, presumably in the company of his family, working on various dramas and spending a great deal of time in the Café de l'Ambigu (Villiers had a pronounced tendency to noctambulism, and was always as likely to be found in some café as at home). This particular café was a stamping-ground for ambitious young writers, among them Lemercier de Neuville, a few years older than Villiers, Breton like him, and already endowed with the prestige of having spent a month in prison for producing a satirical journal called *La Muselière* (not that the satire was political, but a captain in the National Guard had taken umbrage at being taxed with incompetence). Villiers and Lemercier at once struck up a close friendship, elaborating vast literary projects together; the letters Villiers wrote to him then (they are the earliest to have survived) demonstrate how intoxicated he was over the prospect of their imminent glory, with Lemercier, who had some slight acting experience, playing the lead in the plays his companion would write for him:

What is needed for the new age which is awakening, so to speak, lying on the tombs of the great writers and the great artists—is a creative genius who will revolutionize the threatre, and another dramatic genius on whom the poet's thought will be profoundly imprinted (. . .) Believe me, when Victor Hugo is snoring for ever in his winding-sheet of glory and immortality . . . I am certain that I will climb to the throne of thought where he is seated. It will have to be taken by storm![2]

For a seventeen-year-old who had just arrived in Paris from the fastnesses of one of the remotest provincial backwaters, the ambition is staggering—perhaps Hugo himself had helped to ignite it, since it has been plausibly asserted that Villiers had sent him some of his verses while he was still at school and had received in return one of those grandiloquently laudatory letters which the Master regularly dispatched to any neophyte who submitted his writings to him.[3] Exactly what works were supposed to achieve this effect in the ten years which the young man had modestly allowed himself is not known, but they include a *Faust* on which he worked for some time until he suddenly declared it inept, and a five-act drama in the style of Bouchardy, one of the popular authors of melodramas at the time—this, according to Villiers, was certain to be accepted at the Théâtre de la Porte Saint-Martin.[4] Obviously, he was already inclined to those spectacular constructions with metaphysical overtones which were to remain an obsession for the rest of his life; equally obviously, his expectations that these works would immediately hoist him on to the same level as Victor Hugo were completely unrealistic.

In the meantime he found it necessary to supplement whatever allowance his family was giving him, since he was about as irresponsible with money as his feckless father, and for this purpose too Lemercier was pressed into service. One of the other habitués of the Café de l'Ambigu was an ex-gendarme called Désiré Didier who had founded a society for young dramatists, and Lemercier, as secretary, was asked to provide Villiers with a certificate of membership, so that he could appeal to his parents for the mythical entry fee.[5] The theatre in fact so preoccupied him that at that time he had, wittingly or otherwise, adopted the diction and gait of the great actor Dumaine, who was his idol.[6] But in 1856 the family suddenly disappeared again from Paris. Lemercier, who had little contact with Villiers thereafter and who was himself to become famous as a puppet-master, said that they had gone on a journey,[7] but the truth was that in August of that year the Marquis had been sent to Clichy Prison for debts,[8] and Tante Kerinou no doubt thought it wise to return to Saint-Brieuc for the time being—the Villiers de l'Isle-Adams are recorded as having lived in three different houses in the town in 1856.[9]

It must have been something of a shock to young Villiers's dreams to be hauled off back to Brittany before he had had a chance to make his mark in the capital. Very little is known about what he and his family were doing in the next year or so—though one may be sure that, whatever happened, he would not have stopped writing. But, by the summer of 1857 they were back in Paris, living at No. 4 rue Richepanse, and had been there long enough for Villiers to get into hot water for the company he was keeping. The evidence is a letter the Marquis wrote on 4 June to the great Dom Guéranger, Abbot of the Benedictine Abbey of Solesmes, restorer of the Benedictine Order in France, author of many books and one of the most influential and respected priests in the country (Tante Kerinou knew Dom Gardereau, one of the monks there, who had been an army officer before taking orders). The Marquis had kept his faith even when he had decided not to become a priest, and was horrified at the dangers he saw his son running:

I have the honour to ask you to be good enough to receive into your House my son who is a young author of eighteen, perhaps destined for a bright future, as you may judge for yourself. My son, dear Father, has as a dramatist thrown himself into a dangerous milieu from which he is the first to feel he must escape without delay. The solitude of the monastery and the edifying conversations and instruction which he will have with you will bring him back to God. I therefore request you kindly to admit him for as long as you deem it necessary for his conversion.[10]

These drastic measures do not seem in fact to have been put into operation for the time being, and the errant Villiers was apparently allowed—on sufferance—to go on with his activities as a so-called dramatist.[11]

But his failure to get any plays produced or to make any impact on the literary life of the capital evidently threw him for a time into a deep depression, and the journalist and lawyer Victor Cochinat later recalled that in 1857 he had been one of the few who had tried to put new heart into the young man, 'on the verge of despair and on the point of giving up poetry, to follow the absurd and dispiriting advice of those who profess to despise verse'.[12] But Villiers's moods could change in the twinkling of an eye, and it is very doubtful whether his family, who attached such importance to his literary status, ever seriously begged him to turn to more bread-and-butter occupations.

On the other hand, they did continue to be extremely concerned about his spiritual welfare, and though the Solesmes plan had come to nothing, they arranged in 1858 for him to spend some time in the country in the company of a pious young lawyer named Amédée Le Menant des Chesnais, whose influence was thought likely to be salutary. The Marquis had met Le Menant in the course of one of his innumerable lawsuits, when the young man was head clerk to a Parisian lawyer, and had introduced him to his family. Villiers and Le Menant had become friends, and, when in 1858 the latter opted for the quieter life of a country notary in the village of Montfort-sur-Meu near Rennes, it was decided that it would be a good thing if Villiers went off to keep him company. Away from the temptations of Paris, the lawyer's sage counsels might help to restore his lost faith.[13]

The two of them lived together in rooms overlooking the village square. Le Menant would get up early and go off to his legal work; Villiers rose only at noon, to have a lunch of steak and cider. Then, when his friend returned at four o'clock, they would go for long country walks together, until it was time for dinner, which they took in the local hotel, at what was known as the 'functionaries' table'. After that they would sit and argue for hours, as Le Menant earnestly tried to make Villiers see the light again. At ten Le Menant took himself off to bed, whereas for his companion the night hours had always been, and were always to remain, the only ones in which he came truly to life. Villiers stayed for several months in Montfort, writing busily all the time, for he had now turned his attention from the theatre to lyric poetry, and was trying to accumulate enough poems to make a volume.[14] In July 1858 he brought out *Deux essais de poésie*, a privately-printed brochure containing only two poems, one an imitation of an anecdote he had found in Stendhal's *De l'amour*, the other a pompous and prolix denunciation of the English, apropos of a recent controversy over the payment of a legacy to a man suspected of having tried to assassinate Napoleon. Both poems are clumsy and mediocre, and their main interest lies in the fact that the second marks the beginning of a continuing patriotic fervour and was the only instance of his departing from the family's traditional royalism to express public support for the Second Empire.

But this was no more than a trial run, and Villiers's eyes were on more splendid things for his first substantial publication, which he wished to see dignified with suitably imposing and elegant typography. Consequently, he turned to the publisher Nicolas Scheuring, a German who had a high reputation for producing fine books, and in February 1859 he took out a passport at Montfort to enable him to travel to Lyon, where Scheuring worked.[15] Publication was agreed, at a cost to Villiers, so he later averred, of 3,000 francs,[16] and he returned to Montfort to correct the proofs—which were so extravagantly set out that Le Menant declared that the finished work would be 'phosphorescent'.[17] When the book eventually appeared in

December 1859, Villiers returned to Paris to publicize it. His success was scant: hardly any critics deigned to notice it at all, and in *Le Figaro* Alphonse Lemerre remarked that the magnificence of the edition was its only merit.[18] Villiers probably sent copies to those writers whom he most admired, but, if so, only one of their replies has survived, that from Joséphin Soulary, a correct and elegant minor poet also published by Scheuring.[19] The warmth of his congratulations must have helped to temper the disappointment caused by the general neglect of the volume: 'At the age of nineteen, you are a *good* poet; at twenty-five you will assuredly be a *great* poet.'[20]

Otherwise, the only known expression of enthusiasm for the *Premières Poésies* came in *La Causerie*, a weekly bearing the subtitle 'journal of the cafés and theatres', which was run by Lemercier's friend Victor Cochinat. There the editor not only published a highly laudatory article on the collection ('the most remarkable to have come, for a number of years, from the inspired pen of a twenty-year-old poet'), but also inserted a poem addressed to 'Auguste Villiers (de l'Isle-Adam)' by Albert Glatigny, himself no older than Villiers, and who died of tuberculosis in abject poverty a few years later. Moreover, Cochinat, who had met Villiers at the Opera after having lost sight of him since 1856, offered to employ him as *La Causerie*'s regular music critic, with the result that in the numbers of 11 and 18 December 1859 there appeared two reviews by him of performances of operas by Félicien David and Verdi.[21] These were his first published prose writings, but the collaboration ended there, either because he had to leave Paris again or because he was reluctant to apply himself to commissioned journalistic work rather than waiting for inspiration to strike him.

It is hardly to be wondered at that the *Premières Poésies* attracted so little attention.[22] Many of the poems are visibly derived from the great masters of Romantic lyricism; the volume is dedicated to Vigny, and imitations of the other Romantics abound, notably Hugo and Musset—two years earlier when Musset died, his housekeeper had been astounded to find on the doorstep in the middle of the night a youth in tears asking to see the body: it was Villiers. If the verse is remarkably fluent, it is also entirely conventional in its structure, and it is full of the clichés of local colour, disordered passion, Byronic irony, and the like. But it is redeemed by the total commitment with which it is written, especially in some of the longer poems in which Villiers uses the Don Juan legend to express his despair at being unable to find philosophical fulfilment in love, or in which, no doubt in partial response to Le Menant's sermonizing, he bewails the difficulty of belief in God after the ravages of modern thought. Many of the themes of his later work are already present, notably his violent pessimism, but they are expressed with so little originality that, a few years later, he dismissed the whole book as 'schoolboy verses' and vowed that he would destroy every copy he could find.[23]

4

We have two portraits of Villiers around 1859. One is the dry official description on the passport he took out to go to Lyon:

Age 20. 1 metre 70 tall. Light brown hair. Brown eyebrows. Wide forehead. Blue eyes. Short nose. Ordinary mouth. The beginnings of a beard. Square chin with a dimple. Pale complexion. Distinguishing marks: a scar on the lower part of the left cheek.

The other is a medallion by the sculptor Charles Matabon, executed in 1863, but probably based on an earlier drawing.[1] It shows a clean-shaven young man in profile (he was soon to grow a moustache and goatee) with tousled, untidy hair, a high forehead, prominent cheekbones, a slightly upturned, rather sharp nose and a somewhat sulky expression about the mouth. The head is thrust forward in an aggressive questing pose. One can well imagine the face to be that of a spoilt but talented child who had not yet completed the process of growing up—perhaps the secret of his art is in part that he never did.

The flyleaf of the *Premières Poésies* reveals the numerous projects that were either already started or under consideration (the fact that they are said to be 'about to appear' means nothing: throughout his life, Villiers was always anticipating on the completion of works of which not a word was written). The public was promised the first three cantos of *Séïd*, *Wilhelm de Strally*, *Faust*, and *La Tentation sur la montagne*. An unremarkable extract from *Séïd* did in fact figure in the *Premières Poésies*, as did a song from *Faust*, with an epigraph from the same work, which was evidently in dramatic form and in prose. Presumably Villiers had decided to resurrect the scheme on which he had worked a couple of years previously, and indeed the Faust myth was to haunt him until he died. Nothing is known of *La Tentation sur la montagne*, though its title indicates that it too would have dealt with lofty religious and philosophical themes. But the mention of *Wilhelm de Strally* indicates that Villiers already had the idea of *Isis*, an enormous metaphysical romance, of which only the first volume ever appeared in 1862. In 1860 the author wrote about it to a relative:

Wilhelm de Strally is about to appear. I am in the middle of the third and last volume of this study. (It is an application of the theory of the Ancients about the double soul). It is making the jester's bells of madness ring in my ears. I shall only start *La Tentation* with terror. I have vast constructions in my head. God knows what will become of them![2]

Clearly, all sorts of ambitious plans were jostling one another in his teeming imagination, and it is perhaps because they were so numerous that so little of them ever transpired on paper. One characteristic which they all seem to have in common, however, is their vast scale and their philosophical pretensions—the first three cantos of an epic, a reworking of the story of Faust, a three-volume novel with occult over-tones, and a religious work so awesome that it frightened even its potential progenitor. Besides such enormous enter-prises, a volume of occasional poems must have seemed very small beer, which may be why, with totally uncharacteristic modesty, Villiers said in the preface to the *Premières Poésies* (which he dated November 1858, to suggest that they already belonged to the past) that, as he was only nineteen, it was with a certain diffidence that he offered them to the public.

That he was turning more and more to forms which would permit him to develop elaborate philosophic meditations in symbolic garb may be attributable to his close association around 1859 with a much older man, a Breton like himself, Comte Hyacinthe du Pontavice de Heussey, whose son Robert was to become Villiers's first biographer. Hyacinthe du Pontavice, born in Tréguier in 1814, was a curious person.[3] The author of several collections of somewhat ponderous philosophical verse, he had read widely in several languages, particularly books on literature, history, and philosophy. Possessed of an unshakeable faith in progress, a committed democrat who had participated in the liberal agitation leading to the fall of the July Monarchy, an opponent of Louis-Napoléon's *coup d'état*, a freethinker and adversary of the Church, he represented in many ways the direct opposite of Villiers in his religious and political stance,[4] but he obviously attracted his younger colleague, to whom he was distantly and obscurely related. He divided his time between his country residences at Fougères and Saint-Quay-Portrieux in Brittany, where he had the reputation of being a dangerous eccentric who beat his wife,[5] and Paris, where, in rooms on the second floor of the Hôtel d'Orléans near the Palais-Royal, he held a literary and philosophical *salon*. It is said that Baudelaire was among his guests, although it does not seem that Villiers met the poet there; he was certainly a close friend of Marie d'Agoult, otherwise known as Daniel Stern, mistress of Liszt and mother by him of two remarkable daughters, one of whom, Blandine, married Émile Ollivier, last Prime Minister of the Second Empire, and the other of whom, Cosima, was wife successively to Hans von Bülow and Richard Wagner. The poet Léon Cladel was another of Hyacinthe du Pontavice's acquaintances, and it may be in part through him that Villiers was introduced to the more successful young writers of the day.

But if the *salon* did not contain many celebrities, its host, earnest, erudite, cultured, and charming, with his immense height and his prematurely silver hair, was endowed with much prestige in the eyes of Villiers. The two men engaged in interminable arguments, the one expounding his intransigent idealism, his detestation of modern life, and his ingrained pessimism, the other endeavouring to convert him to humanitarian action in the name of progress and socialism. The echo of these prolonged and vigorous debates can be heard not only in *Isis* and in the poems which Villiers wrote in 1862, but also in Pontavice's *Poèmes virils*, in which a long poem entitled 'Le Pèlerin' is dedicated 'to my friend Auguste Villiers de l'Isle-Adam'. In this heavily didactic work, the poet upbraids the pilgrim for wasting his time on the sterile pursuit of an imaginary ideal, until the young man recognizes the error of his ways and opts for the more utilitarian occupations of politics and social action.

In reality, Pontavice's persuasiveness was never enough to effect such a radical conversion, but his influence did force Villiers to think out his own position more clearly, to view the arguments of his opponents with more respect, and to extend his knowledge of modern thought. He is sometimes credited with arousing Villiers's interest in occultism, which is un-likely, given his dislike of all forms of revealed religion;[6] on the other hand, he may well have introduced him to Hegel, who had already become a kind of demigod for Villiers by the time of *Isis* in 1862, but, if he did, he can scarcely have suggested the highly idiosyncratic and subjectivized interpretation of Hege-lianism which Villiers later propagated.[7] Indeed, it was not to be long before many of Pontavice's ideas were to become the subject of caricatural transfiguration by Villiers, once he had finished working out his philosophical views and discovered the most effective way of expressing them. But in the meantime the disagreements were polite and fruitful, and Villiers's admiration for his mentor unfeigned, the more so as Pontavice encouraged his literary ambitions, entertained him in Brittany and lent him money on the all-too-frequent occasions when the young writer's funds ran out.

Their association did not last many years, since in 1862 Pontavice decided to retire from public life and withdraw to Brittany. Thereafter his only emergence from his privacy was to lead a company of irregulars against the Prussians in 1870. He died in London in 1876. But at a critical period he had acted as the young man's intellectual father, a role all the more necessary as the real father's irresponsibility became ever more marked, and Villiers probably owed Pontavice more than he ever fully realized.

More dramatic and lasting in its impact on Villiers's life and career was his meeting with Charles Baudelaire. After the trial for the alleged obscenity of *Les Fleurs du Mal* in 1857, Baudelaire was a scandalous figure, the opprobrium of all right-thinking and god-fearing people, an artist whose genius was hidden to all but a few friends and enthusiasts by the aura of perversity which hung around his person and his writings. The *Premières Poésies* show no sign at all that Villiers had read anything by him before 1859, but, once he did come into contact with him, it is no exaggeration to say that the effect was a total and permanent transformation. Exactly where and when they first met is not known. It could have been at Pontavice's rooms in the Hôtel d'Orléans; it could have been at the offices of *La Causerie* when Villiers was writing for Cochinat at the end of 1859, since Baudelaire also published in it. But the terms of Villiers's first letter to him, probably written in 1860, suggest that it was in a café, most likely the Brasserie des Martyrs, which both men are known to have frequented at that time.[8]

The letter is extremely respectful and extremely apologetic, for Villiers was uncomfortably aware that he was unlikely to have made a good impression: too much wine, too little sleep, and the excitement of seeing the man to whom he had long wanted to be introduced had made him tongue-tied or silly, and he was afraid Baudelaire might judge him by the disreputable company in which he had been seen. But Villiers's fears are a measure of his desire to please: 'Baudelaire is the most powerful, and consequently the most individual, of the despairing thinkers of this wretched age! He hits hard, he is alive, he sees things! So much the worse for those who can't understand!'[9] Baudelaire had the reputation of being remote, unapproachable, and unfriendly to prospective disciples, so that such unbridled declarations of admiration might well have elicited no more than a cynical smile or a shrug of indifference. But he seems to have divined Villiers's exceptional gifts, and the following year sent him a copy of his famous brochure on Wagner and *Tannhäuser*, despite the fact that Villiers's absence in Brittany must have hampered the development of their relationship.

Villiers's reply shows that his enthusiasm for Baudelaire's

poetry had if anything intensifed: 'You know, all that is royal. Sooner or later, people will absolutely have to recognize its humanity and its greatness'. He promised to send *Isis* when the first volumes came out: 'I assure you that what I am working on at the moment is beautiful, even very beautiful, and that you will perhaps not be displeased with it.'[10] He also announced that he intended to write a study on Baudelaire's work, but, like most of his plans to produce critical articles on the authors he admired, the project came to nothing. What Baudelaire himself thought of Villiers's work is not known. It is said that he wrote a letter of warm congratulations on *Isis*,[11] but unfortunately the letter has not survived, and one is reduced to conjecture. Villiers believed he detected friendship and benevolence in Baudelaire's attitude—'I guess that you are not too badly disposed towards me'—and the fact that they maintained cordial contacts for two or three years speaks for itself, since Baudelaire was not the man to tolerate importunate hero-worship from anyone he did not respect. Villiers was almost alone among his generation in being admitted to such intimacy with the great man; only his friends Catulle Mendès and Léon Cladel came anywhere near to achieving the same breakthrough in the protective wall of reserve with which Baudelaire surrounded himself.

Years after their meetings, Villiers remembered them with a kind of fearful fascination. He would wax vehemently indignant with anyone who dared to criticize Baudelaire,[12] whom he never ceased to regard as a very great writer, but there was an element of awe in his recollections, particularly of the poet's Satanism. As Henry Roujon said, 'Years later, Villiers was still haunted by Baudelaire's savage pleasantries, and felt the sort of remorse one feels after a disreputable encounter.'[13] He would relate how the two used to go see Meyerbeer's opera *Robert le Diable*, since it reassured them to think that that was how the general public conceived Satanism.[14] Another anecdote he used to tell concerned an evening in Baudelaire's rooms when one of the guests accidentally knocked a Japanese idol and a candle off the mantlepiece. As the idol broke and the room was plunged into darkness, Baudelaire was heard to say: 'Just suppose that was the true god!'[15] After Baudelaire's death, Villiers had a dog called Satin in part-ownership with the poet and inventor Charles Cros, and one day, when he was visiting some friends, Satin started sniffing round the basket where the hostess's dog was quietly dying. As soon as Satin came near it, the animal went into convulsions. 'There you are,' cried Villiers, 'Satin insinuated doubt into his mind! I've always suspected that Baudelaire's soul had gone to inhabit that dog; now I'm sure of it!'[16]

Probably Baudelaire had had a similar effect on Villiers, and his tormented scepticism may well have profoundly disturbed the younger man's religious sensibility. All sorts of things in Villiers's temperament and outlook seem to have been determined by the shock of his meetings with the poet of *Les Fleurs du Mal* – his taste for skirting dangerously close to blasphemy, his desire to flout conventional moral attitudes, his disdain for the common ruck of humanity, his sense of solitary superiority, his dandyism, his fiercely disconcerting irony, his misogyny, his revulsion at the idea of physical love. Even his artistic preferences were before long those which Baudelaire had proclaimed, and Poe and Wagner, after Baudelaire the two most vital influences in his evolution as a writer, were both artists whose cause Baudelaire had proudly championed. It was undoubtedly Baudelaire who freed Villiers from his allegiance to an already outmoded Romanticism and who gave him his predilection for originality and modernity in art; it was also Baudelaire who enabled him to find his identity as a man and as a writer. It was to be some time before the full consequences of these changes were to be apparent, but there can be no doubt that Baudelaire altered the whole course of Villiers's life.

In the meantime such dangerous acquaintances can have done little to allay his family's fears about the kind of company he was keeping, and if his father was too obsessed with his own extravagant financial dealings to care much, and his mother too timid and self-effacing to intervene, Tante Kerinou's assertive personality often made itself felt. No doubt it was primarily she who was responsible for keeping Villiers in Saint-Brieuc for so much of the time, since it was she who controlled the purse-strings, and, though he chafed at being kept away from Paris, 'that only city possible for me',[17] as he called it, he had to accept the situation, as he had no means of earning money of his own. Relations within the family were naturally somewhat uneasy, and in 1860 he wrote to a cousin: 'Papa is continually on the point of becoming a millionaire, and I like him a lot despite this formidable quirk. But I prefer to rely on my grandmother who really is a woman of inexhaustible goodness and the kind of Christian that one rarely meets'.[18] His affection for Tante Kerinou was such that he turned down invitations to go away on holiday in order not to leave her alone in Saint-Brieuc (presumably the Marquis had stayed in Paris with his long-suffering wife).[19] Late in 1860, after a visit to the capital, he announced that he had almost broken with his family, and seems to have been living with his cousins Sébert while waiting to accumulate enough money to return to Paris.[20]

In September 1861 he was complaining bitterly to Hyacinthe du Pontavice de Heussey that he was leading the life of a convict in Saint-Brieuc, in terms which may mean that he had been forced to work for his father.[21] That would also account for the fact that he was counting on being able to go back to Paris in six weeks' time with the very considerable sum of 5,000 francs in his pocket. Evidently Tante Kerinou obliged him to make lengthy stays in Brittany to keep him out of the way of temptation in the metropolis, and would only consent at intervals to provide him with leave and funds. By this stage he did not always live with his parents when he was allowed to be in Paris; he had come of age, and, when his resources were sufficient, he preferred to be free of any constraint, even if impecuniosity often forced him to lodge in whatever flat his parents happened to be occupying (they changed with startling frequency).

Robert du Pontavice de Heussey, Hyacinthe's son, has left these impressions of a visit he paid to the Villiers de l'Isle-Adams at the end of 1863:

I remember that the drawing-room was very big, very high-ceilinged, very sparsely furnished, and that the cold there made one shiver a little on that dark December day. The Marquise appeared to me like a shadow; dressed in black, she was pale, sad and gentle, with an air of distinction; when my father mentioned Mathias's name, her face lit up; she told us, with a faint smile, that the Marquis was about his affairs; she added that Tante Kerinou was ill in bed but wanted to see us. In a vast old bed, I caught sight of a tiny little old lady, whose rosy-cheeked face peeped out from an immense ruffled bonnet; she had a long twitching nose and little shining eyes and talked a lot; certain phrases which came again and again in her conversation struck me because they made my father laugh in spite of himself (...) 'You know, Hyacinthe, Mathias is a famous man—Mathias is going to be decorated—the Emperor wants to give Mathias a decoration!—Mathias is going to be given a decoration!'[22]

Others who knew the two women had a similar view of them. Fernand Calmettes saw Tante Kerinou as a woman of extraordinary liveliness, despite her great age; the famous ruffled bonnet was worn all day so that she might be ready to go out at any time.[23] Everyone paid tribute to her unquenchable faith in Villiers and to the sacrifices she was prepared to make for him—which he accepted as his due. In comparison, the Marquise, according to Le Menant des Chesnais,

seemed a very weak-willed woman, very gentle, rather preoccupied with social niceties, also with a deep love for Mathias, but in her own different way, a less stubborn love, a little vain and perhaps more concerned with her son as a member of the gentry than as an artist; a rather insignificant woman, but with an excellent kind heart.[24]

Calmettes is even more dismissive about her: 'A poor little pussy-cat who couldn't catch any mice'.[25] Their principal occupation was playing whist in the evenings, when Tante Kerinou's forgetfulness was liable to cause great irritation to her partner. When Villiers was short of pin-money, he did not disdain to join them, in the hope of picking up a few coppers.[26]

It was natural that the young man should have found this rather sepulchral atmosphere less congenial than the free-and-easy society of people of his own age and tastes, and it was about this time that he forged some of the most lasting friendships of his life, notably those with Catulle Mendès and Jean Marras. Mendès was born in Bordeaux in 1841, the son of a Jewish banker and his Catholic wife, but he had spent most of his youth in Toulouse before coming to Paris at the age of eighteen to try to make a name for himself in literature.[27] He may well have met Villiers at *La Causerie* in

1859, and when in February 1861, no doubt with money from his father, he founded the *Revue fantaisiste*, Villiers contributed a poem to the first number. Mendès was a strange mixture. Imbued with a very real love of art, he was also energetic and unscrupulous, full of worldly ambition, and equipped with a considerable gift for self-publicity. For nearly fifty years he managed to keep his name in front of the public, writing plays, novels, verse, and criticism with boundless fecundity, founding reviews and journals, always in company with the famous, constantly on the look-out for new opportunities to get into the limelight. His brashness and his deviousness made him many enemies, as did his notorious and compulsive womanizing, and little of what he wrote has stood the test of time—it almost invariably conveys the impression of being a brilliant but empty pastiche of someone else. But he also won the friendship of men of real value—not only Villiers, but Mallarmé, Verlaine, Flaubert, and Leconte de Lisle—even if his vanity and his lack of discretion were always liable to provoke quarrels.

Fair-haired and self-consciously handsome, Mendès was said by several contemporaries to look like a dissipated Christo,[28] and he certainly had no scruples about using his good looks to break as many hearts as he could. These habits may well have infected Villiers too, and, though Mendès's debauchery never had the overtones of a search for an ideal love always present in his friend's relations with the opposite sex, the two of them seem to have had an extraordinary penchant for being attracted to the same women, sometimes with disastrous consequences. In the early 1860s they were inseparable companions, sharing everything—their dwellings, their ideas, their artistic ambitions, their friends, and even their mistresses. But there was always a latent strain underlying their camaraderie: Mendès was obscurely jealous of the other's greater talent and more intense commitment to literature, and Villiers suspected the selfishness that was hidden under Mendès's ingratiating exterior. So in later years the disputes were frequent and violent, to the extent that Villiers was at times nearly obsessional about his dislike of the man, which was almost certainly a major factor in his professed anti-semitism.[29] Yet their paths went on crossing and there was never a complete break, so that some have even—and no doubt unfairly—seen Mendès as Villiers's evil genius.[30]

Jean Marras, whom Villiers met about the same time, was a totally different proposition. Born in Sète of Italian parents in 1837 or thereabouts, he worked in insurance in Paris, but later became assistant curator of the Palace of Fontainebleau and then curator of the state collections of marble statues in Paris.[31] He was passionately interested in literature, but wrote little himself, preferring to give other writers the benefit of his sage advice; both Leconte de Lisle and Villiers submitted all they wrote to him before publishing it. Small, squat, and swarthy, he had a strong personality and pronounced opinions, being both a staunch republican and a rabid anticlerical. Such views were in themselves unlikely to have endeared him to Villiers, but, apart from a brief cloud over the Commune, their friendship endured as a relationship of total trust and frankness for nearly thirty years. As devoted and disinterested in his dealings with Villiers as Mendès was egotistical, Marras often provided a much-needed pole of normality in his life, and Villiers relied on him absolutely, and never in vain, for financial help in hard times, for consolation in distress, and for encouragement in moments of depression.

Despite these new friendships and despite the frequent changes between Paris and Saint-Brieuc, Villiers never lost sight of the fact that the essential justification for his existence was that he was a writer, and between 1859 and 1862 work continued on his various projects, but more particularly on *Wilhelm de Strally*, later retitled *Isis*. Exactly how fast he got on with it is not known, since there is no evidence save his own statements, and he is a notoriously unreliable witness to the progress of his writings. But, having returned to Paris in November 1861, he felt that the first volume was sufficiently far advanced to start negotiations for its publication, and on 31 January 1862 the printer Poupart had lodged an official print order with the authorities, announcing a run of five hundred copies.[32] But the book had evidently not yet reached its definitive state, and a letter sent by Villiers to the publisher Dentu a few months later showed that he was still not

satisfied with what he had written and was making a lot of
corrections on the proofs[33] (this was to remain his invariable
habit until the end of his days, to the despair of every editor
and publisher with whom he ever worked). When the book
eventually appeared in August 1862, its format and the
number of pages had been changed, and the edition reduced
from five hundred to one hundred copies. Elegantly produced as it was, it must have cost Villiers a lot of money for
such a restricted edition (it was privately printed), particularly when one considers that, a quarter of a century later,
Dentu had only sold twenty-three copies, the remainder
having been handed over to either Villiers or Mendès, doubtless for free distribution to those deemed worthy to read it.[34]
Tante Kerinou must have been persuaded to put up the
necessary capital.

The volume bears the title *Prolégomènes*, and it is dedicated
to Hyacinthe du Pontavice de Heussey: 'Allow me, my dear
friend, to offer you this study in acknowledgement of the
feelings of friendship and admiration which you have inspired
in me.' Villiers goes on to explain what it is: 'ISIS is the title
of a collection of works which will appear, I hope, in swift
succession: it is the collective formula of a series of philosophical novels; it is the x of a problem and an ideal; it is the
great unknown. The Work will define itself, once it is
complete.' This grandiose if enigmatic pronouncement is not
of much help in interpreting the pages which it prefaces. The
action of the book is simple enough as far as it goes. In
Florence in the 1780s the mysterious and ravishingly beautiful Tullia Fabriana, a woman of immense intelligence and
occult gifts, is waiting to find the predestined young man
before embarking on a scheme apparently designed to win her
domination over the kingdom of Naples and thence perhaps
over the whole world. Wilhelm de Strally arrives, is chosen
by the heroine, and succumbs to a fantastic vision of delight
when he is ushered into her presence. There the novel breaks
off, and, since none of the continuation ever appeared, we are
reduced to guesswork if we want to know what happens next.
From various clues scattered in the text, it is possible to
divine that Tullia would have sought to put Wilhelm on the
throne of Naples, that her plot would almost have succeeded,

but that, having abdicated her superhuman invulnerability by falling in love with him, she would have been induced to wreck her own plan by being made to believe that he was betraying her.

So much for the plot, which clearly still owes much to the tradition of the Romantic historical novel and drama. But the work is filled out with an extraordinary series of disquisitions on all manner of subjects, so that the action almost disappears under the digressions. Physiognomy, the fallacy of Progress, the bankruptcy of science, Hegelian philosophy, the shortcomings of the modern world, how to get on in society, the transmigration of souls—Villiers lectures his reader volubly on almost anything that comes into his head, with superb self-assurance, considerable stylistic virtuosity, and no little pedantry (one footnote spreads itself over no fewer than ten pages). How these heterogeneous topics were intended to relate to one another it is impossible to deduce, in the absence of the sequel, and indeed it is more than likely that Villiers's own intentions in that respect were not entirely fixed. But it appears that his ultimate aim, in one form or another, was to provide in symbolic guise a synthesis of Christianity, Hegelianism, and occultism, each of which attracted him without satisfying him. That his knowledge of any of these systems was very deep may be doubted—Henry Roujon, who knew him well, said: 'he had skipped through a bit of everything and guessed the rest',[35] and some of the book's most pompously trumpeted erudition turns out to be second-hand. But everything in the work is vibrant with intellectual and emotional excitement, so that, even when Villiers is at his most comically clumsy, the reader is carried away by the sheer vigour of the writing and the sense of some tremendous event in gestation. Roujon was not far wrong when he commented: 'With *Isis*, Villiers thought he was going to shift the whole world.'[36]

Given that so few copies had been printed, it was scarcely to be expected that the world would notice what Villiers had wanted to do with it, and so indeed it proved. Apart from an enthusiastic article by Théodore de Banville, in which the poet declared that the novel bore 'the unmistakable clawmark of genius', the work was largely ignored. Only Catulle

Mendès did his duty by his friend, publishing not one but two reviews, the first in the same number of *Le Boulevard* as Banville's article, the other a few months later in the *Revue bibliographique*.[37] Both were obviously inspired by Villiers himself, and Mendès is visibly speaking for his friend when he says that Villiers attaches little importance to the success of his work, since, in the modern world, unpopularity is a glory in itself. No doubt it is also Villiers's voice that we hear when Mendès proclaims: 'The lofty divine and human problems, the frightening exigencies of life and death, of man and God, stripped of the cumbersome apparatus of philosophic terms, can present, and do in fact present, an admirable subject for the poetic dream and for the art which is its expression.' But few others took the trouble to recognize the existence of the new philosopher–novelist, and the publication of *Isis* hardly created a ripple on the surface of the great pond of French literature. Almost the only other recorded contemporary opinion came from the celebrated actor Rouvière, to whom Villiers had sent a copy (he was always fascinated by famous actors). When the two men eventually met at the Brasserie des Martyrs Rouvière was staggered by the writer's youth: 'It's not you; your book was written by a man of fifty; you're a monster.'[38]

5

Literature was not the only thing in which Villiers was taking an interest in the early 1860s. At that time he seems seriously to have believed that his name, his ancestry, and his talents entitled him to lay claim to an exalted position in the state, perhaps even the highest of all. In his works this preoccupation appears as an obsession with revolution, not for ideological reasons, but to give supreme power to an individual, portrayed, naturally, as his *alter ego*. But it also took more concrete forms in his own life. One of them was an undying fascination with monarchs, both real ones and those who with more or less plausibility pretended to be of royal blood. Another was his childish love of sporting bizarre medals and decorations, which he conferred on himself in some imagined role in the Order of the Knights of Malta. But the most extraordinary of all was the episode of his candidature for the throne of Greece.

This arose when, in October 1862, Otto I was deposed. Since the insurrectional leaders had no pretender to hand, it fell to Russia, England, and France as the protecting powers to suggest a suitable candidate to succeed him. Villiers's intervention in this situation has been variously recounted, and the truth is hard to establish. The tale, as first told by Pontavice,[1] was that a Provençal friend on whom Villiers had played a practical joke took his revenge by planting false rumours that the Emperor was considering putting the poet's name forward as the French candidate; Villiers and his family were taken in, the Marquis went off to arrange a loan from Rothschild, an audience with the Emperor was granted, and Villiers presented himself at the Tuileries, to be met by the Duc de Bassano, Napoleon III's Lord Chamberlain, who soon ushered him out again in the belief that he was mad—Villiers attributed his unfriendliness to the fact that he must have been won over to the cause of Prince George of Denmark, who was indeed ultimately designated. A number of other versions were also in circulation, emanating from different people who knew Villiers—Fernand Calmettes, Henry Roujon, and Émile Bergerat.[2]

However, according to some, the incident had never happened, and the whole thing was an invention of the Provençal friend, perhaps identifiable as Mendès.[3] Whether or not Villiers ever really believed that his name might be considered, and whether he actually sought an audience with the Emperor, we shall no doubt never know. But Stéphane Mallarmé noted shortly after his death that Villiers had never denied the story,[4] and there is in fact incontrovertible evidence that he put it about himself not long after the events had supposedly taken place. This is to be found in the Goncourt *Journal* for 12 September 1864. There the brothers record that Villiers joined them that evening at a café table and started to talk about his candidature: he had tried to launch it by means of a dispatch in *The Times*, which the French press would copy and which would impress Napoleon III—'After all, the Emperor believes what he reads in the papers like everyone else!' He had in the end succeeded in obtaining an audience, at which he had appeared bedecked with foreign decorations and with an air of dignified old age. The Emperor, so he said, had been 'bowled over', and had concluded the interview with the words: 'Monsieur le Comte, I shall think it over.'[5]

Had Villiers been the victim of a joke and decided to make the best of it by pretending that it had turned into reality? Or had he in truth deluded himself into imagining that he might really become King of Greece? What is certain is that he wished people to believe that he had been a candidate, and that he had just as much capacity for illusion as his father the Marquis, so the story was not inherently improbable. Perhaps he was already developing that technique of ambivalent self-parody that he was to practise so successfully and so disconcertingly in later years. Perhaps too he wanted to put himself in the public gaze and was prepared to be regarded as a buffoon provided that he drew attention to himself—that was a trick he also frequently employed. His obsession with actors was no coincidence: he was possessed of considerable histrionic talents, but alternated between acting out grand roles and farcical ones, and sometimes the two became confused.

But there was no play-acting in another adventure in which he became involved at about the same time. This was his liaison with Mme Louise Dyonnet. Not much is known about her life. She was older than Villiers, she was married or had been, she had two small sons, Jules and Jacques, she lived near Montparnasse, and she was at best a *demi-mondaine*. Villiers may have met her through Catulle Mendès, who was evidently also her lover at some point, and by 1863 at the latest he had installed her in a flat in the rue Grenelle-Saint-Germain. She obviously exercised a strong hold over him, and, though she caused him much distress by running up debts which he had to pay and by continuing to see other men, he was unable to break loose from her. The four letters he is known to have written to her in 1864 are extraordinary testimonies to the depth of his feelings for her, to the sufferings he went through, and to the difficulty he found in leaving her, despite his anger at her behaviour.

The first letter is a brief and cold note breaking off relations, without explanations and without a date.[6] The second, written on 14 July 1864, is also a letter of farewell, but it is much more

elaborate and betrays very mixed emotions. Apparently
Villiers knew that Louise had other lovers, and had decided
to put an end to their relationship, but not without regret.

If I had had a fortnight to spare, I would quite certainly have made
you love me. At least I hope so; but I don't have that much time.
That's right, I know I'm losing you, I know how much you are
worth when you are in love, but that's my misfortune.
  Let us stay friends. When I am rich, I can, perhaps, if you will
allow me, be useful to your children. Until then, do not try in any
way to look for me; you will never find me again. You didn't want
to understand; well, go on seeing your friends and those whom you
love, you have made a mistake, that's all.
  With no reproaches and with no rancour, I say goodbye: don't
have any regrets about me, it would be too late from now on: truly,
I no longer love you, but I still feel esteem and friendship for the
woman you used to be, I am sad and troubled not to understand
you any more, my dear Louise, and I don't want to receive your
pages of explanations: you don't need them to be, in my eyes, what
you are: a very sincere and very marvellous woman.

The letter ends by promises to pay her bills and injunctions
not to receive too many nocturnal guests during her remaining time in the rue Grenelle-Saint-Germain.[7]
  But two months later the affair was still not over, and on 11
September Villiers sent her a furious letter, complaining
bitterly about how poor she had made him, refusing to accept
further responsibility for her debts, and upbraiding her for
having cuckolded him. 'Enjoy yourself, since that is what
you want; bring whoever you like to the rue de Grenelle
tonight; understand my position and permit me not to accept
any more such debts.—Just remember that without me you
perhaps wouldn't be so gay at the moment, and let us say no
more about it.' The quarrel had clearly become very violent,
and Villiers goes on: 'Don't concern yourself with me or my
name; I shall not concern myself with you; but don't make
me lose my temper: it would do you no good and would cost
me time which has become precious because of the sorry
situation into which you have got me. Understand this: you
have threatened me; let it rest there.'[8]
  Even this diatribe did not mark the end of the contacts,
and a few days later he sent her a further missive from Lyon,

the tone of which is positively hysterical. There are incoherent references to a woman of remarkable intelligence and beauty in Lyon, and to his still being dazzled by the gold he had seen: from these one may infer that he had travelled to Lyon in the hope of marrying a rich heiress, but that something was going wrong, so that he might still end up poorer and more alone than ever before. He says he still wants to see Louise once more: 'Afterwards, if necessary, I'll put the seas between us, for I deserve better than what you have given me. I'll go so far that no one I know, except perhaps Catulle, will ever hear of me again.' After a paragraph of total despair, he tries to sum up what she has meant to him:

I adored you, Louise, and for a long time and amid frightful suffering; but bah! you are right: any deep affection must be sacrificed for a passable night. You have made me live through an accursed dream, but after all you are, you *must* be a very charming woman, or Catulle and I are two stupid fools, and that can't possibly be true!

And, despite everything, he asks her to meet him at the station on his return and have dinner with him.[9]

These letters mark the climax of what must always have been a singularly tempestuous relationship. Villiers had clearly thrown himself into it with even more than his customary violence, and, with his incorrigible tendency to go to emotional extremes, he had very nearly cracked under the strain. For a long time he had been alternating between despising her and loving her, and in August 1863 thought he had discovered the secret of her power over him, when he wrote to Marras: 'That excellent Mme Dyonnet—do you know what made me love her? A little box of cantharides that I found in her wardrobe! What a dirty trick! What a wretched woman! I forgive her. It's the best thing for me to do.'[10] But even this discovery had not set him free, and the storms had continued for at least a year longer. That Villiers was a turbulent, unstable, and emotional young man is clear, and it is no surprise that he should have become entangled with an older and more experienced woman, even if the involvement caused him as much pain as joy. But what sort of a person was Louise Dyonnet?

Despite the absence of factual information about her, it is possible to give a partial answer to that question on the basis of an incomplete letter found among Villiers's papers. Though the signature has disappeared, there can be little doubt that it was from Louise and that it constituted the 'pages of explanations' to which he referred so scornfully in July 1864. That he preserved it for a quarter of a century is some indication of how deeply it had affected him. It proves that, in addition to her presumed physical attractions, and whatever sort of life she led, Louise was a woman with a mind of her own, a strong personality, and no little originality of expression. Here is what she wrote to her young lover:

Do they have a soul, those unfortunate beings, do they feel anything in the words 'grief', 'unhappiness', 'despair', 'regret'? They only know one thing, their own self, and they only feel what concerns that stupid and insolent self of which they are so proud.

And to think that I have to smile graciously to those wretched idiots and that I have to make eyes at them, since that is the bird-lime in which they leave their feathers. But don't worry, what I give them is not the smile you love, nor the eyes you know. As you so rightly put it, such things are too good for them. I would regret all my life giving those vile *usurers of youth and love* a single one of those looks or smiles! . . . or the least little crumb of anything good or fine there is in me. There is still a tiny bit left, and I'm keeping it for you, Villiers, if you want it, as you are the only one in the world big enough and pure enough to understand it properly and not laugh at it. That's the whole secret of my crabbed and always bored existence. I am *proud* and everything *humiliates* me, *I love myself* and *I cannot get over it*! Oh! You see, all this will bring me to my grave a bit sooner. All the *shame* and the *pain* I suffer have brought me to the end of my tether.[11]

Though there may be an element of histrionics in it, the letter is remarkable both for its frankness and for its penetration. Louise does not deny that she is obliged to sell her charms to other men, but she claims that Villiers reigns alone in her heart, and that the humiliation of her situation is unbearable. One has the impression that she realizes the futility of dissembling with him, but that she clings desperately to him for the idealism and purity he brings to her. Perhaps Villiers had imagined himself in the stereotyped

Romantic role of the redeemer of the prostitute with a heart of gold; perhaps she too saw him as the one saving grace in a life which it sickened her to have to lead. Clearly she was an unusual person and she seems to have realized that there was something exceptional about Villiers. But so long as circumstances, or possibly a hidden inclination, forced her to live as she did, conflict was inevitable and irreconcilable. Villiers's idealism about love was far too extreme to allow him to accept half-measures or compromises; it had to be all or nothing, and with Louise neither was possible: he could not take her as she was, and he could not leave her.

To make matters worse, the troubles with Louise were not the only source of disturbance in Villiers's life at this period. Though the first volume of *Isis* had grandly announced the imminent proclamation of all sorts of philosophical certainties, Villiers was in fact passing through a religious crisis and on 28 August 1862, only a few weeks after signing the flamboyant preface to *Isis*, he turned up at the Abbey of Solesmes in a state of disarray. Maybe he had gone there at the behest of his parents and the anxious Tante Kerinou, as had nearly happened in 1857, but, according to what he told Dom Guéranger's secretary, the decision had been his own. By the secretary's account, after devouring the works of Kant, Fichte, Hegel, and Schelling, Villiers no longer knew what to believe, and, having been struck by some of the Abbot's articles in the Catholic newspaper *Le Monde*, 'when his mind no longer provided him with any resources against the scepticism which was invading him, he resolved to come to Solesmes to consult Dom Guéranger, whom he regarded, to use his own words, as a *man of strength*'.[12]

His arrival was however singularly hectic. On the way, at Chartres, he had felt he was starting a serious angina. During the first night at the Abbey, he was stricken by real or imaginary colic, thought he had been poisoned, and leapt out of bed to seek help from his neighbour, a worthy canon from Angers. The next day, before he had seen Dom Guéranger, he went off to Sablé, the nearest town, to cash a postal draft, decided to say the night in a hotel, and was twice tempted to leave forthwith for Le Mans. But instead he returned to the Abbey, and presented himself to the Abbot, who (still according to the secretary's notes) 'took an interest in this unfortunate and charming young man, so naïve, so shy and at times so violent, who wrote verse like Victor Hugo and prose like George Sand. There was something of the lion in him and something of the lamb.' A week was then spent in philosophical and theological conversations and in reading St. Thomas Aquinas. But the state of his health remained disquieting: the change in his way of life gave him such violent palpitations that he several times had to leave the refectory in the middle of dinner, and the Abbey doctor, supported by Dom Guéranger, advised him that the only cure was to stay away from Paris for at least a year. In the end, he took confession and communion, having seemingly recovered his lost faith.

But he still did not leave the Abbey, perhaps because he was interested in the presence of Raymond Brucker, at that time a well-known Catholic journalist in his late fifties, after a varied career as workman, poet, novelist, and lecturer. When eventually Villiers departed on 20 September, after three weeks in the Abbey, Dom Guéranger noted in his diary: 'Gratias Deo super inenarrabili dono ejus.' A week or two later Tante Kerinou wrote to express her heartfelt thanks for this 'miracle of kindness', assuring the Abbot that Villiers 'appreciated his good fortune and had depicted it in such glowing colours that it made us weep with joy'.[13] Villiers himself had promised the Abbot to come back at Christmas, and spoke of Solesmes as an 'earthly paradise'.[14] How far these protestations may be judged sincere is perhaps unsure in view of later developments, but there is no reason to doubt that the long stay in the Abbey and the prolonged contact with men of outstanding spirituality did much to reconcile Villiers with the faith of his forefathers.

But, once he got back to Paris, Louise Dyonnet was waiting for him, and it was not long before the vigilant Tante Kerinou decided that a second stay at Solesmes was essential to his salvation. So in August 1863 she reluctantly set pen to paper again and informed the Abbot of her adopted grandson's relapse, which she ascribed to a 'miserable creature' who had cast a spell over him; 'sometimes he would leave her, and sometimes he was her abject slave'. She insisted that he should be kept at Solesmes as long as might be necessary, without money or stamps so as to prevent him communicating with Louise, but, obviously fearing that rigorous asceticism might be excessive, she hinted that he would be unable to do without wine, coffee, and tobacco.[15] The letter, in its simplicity and its eccentric spelling, is a touching mixture of sternness and indulgence, and shows how tenderly the old lady loved her dear Mathias—and also how far she ruled the roost in the Villiers de l'Isle-Adam household.

If the young man's arrival was not this time attended with the same dramatic terrors as the previous year, it was nevertheless far from peaceful, largely because he hated the idea that he was being compelled to stay there against his will. On 26 August, when he had been in the Abbey for a little over a fortnight, he could stand it no longer, and wrote to Marras to beg him to send some money so that he could escape: 'I am a prisoner! and in a frightful situation!—I must get away from Solesmes, and people have arranged to cut off my source of livelihood so as to force me to go into retreat, confess myself, etc. I'm happy to do things voluntarily, but constraint exasperates me, and I don't think I deserve it.'[16] With profuse excuses for pestering his friend, he makes it clear that Marras is his only hope, that his situation is killing him, that it is enough to make him anti-Christian, that he is in a mood of intense irritation, and that he cannot bear to spend another day in the Abbey.[17]

The obliging Marras responded by return of post, addressing his letter to Sablé, *poste restante*, so as to avoid the eccesiastical censors, and enclosing the money required to facilitate his friend's departure. But, with one of his characteristic changes of mind, Villiers had suddenly decided that he was no longer particularly keen to leave. 'Frankly, I'm sorry to be going, and, if I hadn't caused you such trouble, I would perhaps have stayed, with the submissiveness which, as you know, is a fundamental part of my character.' He apologized for the strong terms in which he had written, explaining that he had been annoyed by the trick his parents had played on him, but adding contritely that it would have been more proper not to protest, 'especially since it was for my own good'.[18]

One reason for his unexpected docility was probably that the Abbey had some interesting visitors apart from himself. On the twenty-first Dom Guéranger had welcomed his old friend Louis Veuillot, the celebrated journalist and one of the most pugnacious Catholic polemicists of the time; *L'Univers*, the newspaper he edited, had just been suppressed by the Imperial government, and he wanted to rest and meditate in the Abbey. As it happened, Villiers had already tried to meet Veuillot in Paris, and the journalist was not exactly pleased to find him installed at Solesmes. Writing to a woman friend, he exclaimed:

Just imagine, Madam, the Abbey is full of savages; there are even building workers, there is even a poet! This poet is not unknown to me, in the past I had kept him at arm's length; now I have to go and find him here; and the worst of it is that he's converted, which is going to give him an excuse for coming straight up to me. I can see from the look in his eyes that he is getting ready to make his general confession to me. I just hope he doesn't have a religious poem in his pocket![19]

Evidently Veuillot managed to suppress his impatience, and Villiers told Marras: 'Veuillot has been charming with me.'[20] In fact Villiers was most impressed with him, and years later remembered with startling clarity the great man's conversation with Dom Guéranger as they all sat in the garden shelling peas. The Abbot reproved Veuillot gently for the vehemence of his writings, while the polemicist justified his hatred of positivists like Renan on the grounds that Christ had taken a whip to drive out the money-changers. Villiers took the lesson to heart, and his own later satirical writings are no more charitable than Veuillot's.[21] It was perhaps just as well that Veuillot had left on 24 August before the Abbey received a visit from two of the most prominent positivists of the time, the philosopher and critic Hippolyte Taine, Renan's great friend and ally, and Émile Littré, compiler of the famous dictionary. Presumably they came as tourists rather than pilgrims, and Villiers mentions their visit without comment, but Dom Guéranger's secretary cannot refrain from noting that Taine is 'Mr. Renan's colleague and emulator in their little war against the Church'.[22]

The monks themselves, notably Dom Guéranger, aroused much admiration and sympathy in Villiers. To Marras he wrote that he spent every evening discussing 'profound things' with the Abbot, whose character and learning he had already vaunted at length in a letter he had sent to Baudelaire shortly after returning from his first visit the year before.[23] All the monks, he told Marras, were 'admirable men',[24] and throughout his life he continued to feel envy and nostalgia for those who were strong enough to dedicate themselves to a life of asceticism which he saw as endowing them with extraordinary intellectual and spiritual powers.

By the end of his stay Villiers had once again become reconciled with the Church, and when he left Dom Guéranger's secretary recorded that 'his conversion has been strengthened, thanks to God and the Abbot'. In fact he had not taken immediate advantage of the money sent by Marras, and it was not until 29 August that he departed, using the pretext of a misfortune in his family. Though he often talked of returning, he never did, but his two sojourns at Solesmes had left a lasting impression on him, and all his friends knew that he had spent time at the Abbey—indeed, some of them believed that he had been educated there, and the legend is still not entirely dead today.[25] It is true that Villiers himself, unwilling to disclose that his presence there had not been entirely voluntary, was rather misleading about the reasons for his visits, and, in the article he wrote on Veuillot's death in 1883, he declared that he had gone 'for archaeological research'.[26] But, although his feelings about Solesmes at the time were much more mixed than the studious piety which predominated in his later recollections, the example of Dom Guéranger and the other monks had sunk deep into his mind, and was never wholly to leave him.

What with the turmoil of his affair with Louise Dyonnet and the vacillation of his religious opinions, Villiers had neither the time nor the peace of mind to get on with producing the sequel of *Isis* as quickly as he had hoped. To Baudelaire, just after the publication of the first volume, he wrote that he had taken a lot of useful notes in the magnificent library at Solesmes, which he proposed to use in *Samuèle*, as the next part was to be called. He added obscurely:

In short, I've got *Samuèle*, and, if my expectations are not tainted with silliness, I have really something which if not bigger (I'm speaking of the size of the volume) is at least as broad as the idea of

Faust. It's absolutely hair-raising that there's one thing that no one
has ever thought of, or, if they have thought of it, that it has never
been treated with amplitude and magnificence.[27]

But whatever this startling inspiration may have been, there is
little evidence that much of it was ever committed to paper,
though Villiers did attempt, without much success, to give a
reading from it at a banquet organized by the *Revue nouvelle*
towards the end of 1863.[28] On the rare occasions when he
later showed signs of taking it up again, it sounds as though
his intentions for it had changed completely, and in November 1865 he was talking about concluding it with a philosophical duel between Tullia Fabriana the Hegelian and a
Christian scholar, since at bottom he was a Christian and
viewed Hegel's work as 'an incomplete explanation of the
Gospel'. *Isis*, so he said, would be a metaphysical and poetic
work, and when a friend to whom he was talking objected
that such a mixture risked satisfying neither metaphysicians
nor poets, he replied blithely that for him poetry and
philosophy were the same thing.[29]

The truth probably is that the shifts in his opinions, the
upsets with Louise Dyonnet, and the impossible scale on
which the whole enterprise had been conceived, combined
to prevent him from writing much more of *Isis* at all. He did
pretend in later years that the manuscript of the sequel had
been completed and forgotten on top of a wardrobe when he
was moving house,[30] but that was probably no more than an
excuse to account for his failure to finish a work to which he
had publicly attached such vital importance. The troubled
years between 1862 and 1865 were in fact relatively barren.
A couple of mediocre philosophical poems, composed very
much under the influence of Pontavice de Heussey, one of
which he read at a meeting of the Saint-Brieuc literary
society in November 1862;[31] a long article celebrating Catulle Mendès's book of poems *Philoméla* in December 1863,
in which he expounds theories on the autonomy of art
visibly borrowed from Baudelaire; and that is about all.[32] It
was with some reason that late in 1865 Villiers compared
himself to a Sleeping Beauty who had been asleep for three
years.[33]

6

Though Villiers did not publish much in the years following *Isis*, that was nevertheless the period during which he established a brilliant reputation for himself among men of letters, if not with the public. His appearance on the Parisian literary scene was later remembered as an arrival of meteoric suddenness, and the legend has it that he and his parents burst upon the capital in 1857, ready to conquer the world with his writings. That the truth is not so dramatically simple is shown by the frequency with which he and his family alternated between Brittany and Paris, right from his childhood onward. There can therefore hardly have been a single specific occasion on which Villiers could be said to have 'arrived' so impressively from his native province, and most of the recollections of the electrifying impact he made probably relate to the time around 1864 and 1865 when he was making himself known to the young writers of his generation, particularly among the poets who were about to acquire the label of 'Parnassians'.

They all seem to have preserved the same image of a strange young Breton with unruly hair, wearing an overcoat with a fur collar, his pockets stuffed with manuscripts, convinced of his own genius and possessed of such personal magnetism that others became convinced of it too. Léon Cladel, who had probably met Villiers earlier than most, since he was an habitué of Pontavice de Heussey's *salon*, used to say: 'Villiers at the age of twenty was prodigious.'[1] Catulle Mendès described him as 'perhaps the only one of the men of our generation who had in him the spark of genius'.[2] Henry Roujon, essayist and museum administrator, rated him 'the most richly gifted young man of his generation'.[3] Stéphane Mallarmé (of whom more later) once said: 'The word "infinite" can only be proffered worthily by a young man looking like Louis XIII, wearing furs and with fair hair,' adding by way of explanation: 'That is how I first heard Villiers pronounce the word in my presence.'[4] The journalist Adolphe Racot recalled him reading his play *Morgane* before a distinguished audience in the *salon* of the Marquise de Ricard early in 1866:

Towards four in the morning, when we left the house, and when we found ourselves in the freezing, deserted boulevard, we were still under the spell of the ardent emotion aroused by *Morgane*, and we had no doubt, as François Coppée can confirm, that on the theatre-bills the name of Villiers de l'Isle-Adam would soon be saluted as that of a master.[5]

Of all the young writers who encountered Villiers at that time, the one for whom the meeting had the greatest meaning and who has evoked its overtones with the most delicate subtlety is Stéphane Mallarmé. In 1863, when they met, Mallarmé was a shy and sensitive young man of twenty-two, who had still not developed his own poetic manner, and he was at once subjugated by the effulgence of Villiers's genius, the prestige of his name, and the brilliance of his conversation. Thenceforward, Villiers symbolized for him the absolute figure of the Poet, and, as his own abstruse meditations on the nature of poetry led him deeper into the spiritual crisis of 1866–7 from which he was to emerge as a great writer, the image of Villiers and all he stood for was constantly present in his mind. It is no exaggeration to say that Villiers changed the whole course of Mallarmé's existence, both as a man and as a poet (not that the two can be separated in his case), and Mallarmé undoubtedly understood and loved Villiers more than any other contemporary did. Villiers too divined the exceptional qualities hidden in the reserved and diffident young poet, and there were forged the bonds of one of the most remarkable and moving literary friendships ever to have existed.

This is how Mallarmé, thirty years later, remembered the effect of stupor which Villiers produced on the rising generation of men of letters in the early 1860s:

I do not know, but I believe, as I reawaken these memories of early years, that in truth the arrival was extraordinary, or that we were mad! perhaps both, and I am proud to affirm it. He was also brandishing triumphal standards, very ancient, or future, those very ones which from the oblivion of the pillars drop their dimmed flame, still burning; I swear that we could see them. I think that what he who had appeared wanted was: to reign. (. . .) Nothing will disturb, for me, or in the minds of several others, adults now, dispersed, the vision of the man arriving. A lightning flash, yes, this reminiscence will remain in the memory of each (. . .) A genius! we understood him as such.[6]

Through the obscurities of Mallarmé's opaque prose style, one may glimpse something of the transcendental significance which Villiers assumed for him: Villiers was not just the man who was going to do things better than other writers, he was the man who would create something so radically and unimaginably different that the whole world might be transformed by it.

Of course not everyone could see so clearly past the outward eccentricities of Villiers into the depths of his heart and his mind. Even those who recognized his talent were often distracted by his disconcerting mannerisms, his unpredictable habits, or even his improbable and sonorous name. François Coppée, for instance, whose overt sentimentality was soon to alienate him from the other poets of the group, wrote that they all felt him to have 'a great but unbalanced intelligence, a sort of uneven and incomplete genius', and described thus the sudden appearances of Villiers in the poetic gatherings in Mendès's rooms in the rue de Douai: 'A young man with pale blue eyes and unsteady legs, chewing at a cigarette, throwing back his dishevelled hair and twisting his little blond moustache.'[7] Villiers would sit at the piano and sing, with an uncertain but magical voice, one of his settings of Baudelaire's poems, then break off abruptly and retire to a dark corner, rolling another cigarette and glancing suspiciously around at his stupefied audience. Likewise Xavier de Ricard, a poet whose early promise petered out and who eventually emigrated to South America: 'He passed among us like a sleep-walker, his eyes almost completely blank, talking to himself, with bursts of savage laughter. When someone spoke to him, it was as if they were waking him up, and sometimes he failed to respond, running his fingers through his hair.'[8] José-Maria de Heredia, the Cuban-born poet of *Les Trophées*, no doubt spoke for others beside himself when, in a letter to a friend in March 1865, he described Villiers as a 'very interesting madman'.[9]

Villiers naturally also gravitated into the *salon* of Leconte de Lisle, who was becoming recognized as the leader of the newer school of poets.[10] Twenty years older than Villiers, and with the volumes of *Poèmes antiques* and *Poèmes barbares* behind him, Leconte de Lisle already had an established reputation, reinforced by an imposing presence, a distant and haughty manner, and an air of intellectual authority and distinction. It is doubtful whether he particularly appreciated Villiers either as a man or as an artist (he once privately characterized him as 'a madman who can only conceive reasonably mediocre verses and who thinks they are extraordinary'),[11] but the two poets shared the same lofty conception of art, the same love of language for its own sake, and the same disdain for the crowd and for facile success, and Villiers was always well received when he appeared in Leconte de Lisle's flat. For his own part, he had a profound admiration for the marmorean art of his older colleague, whom he described as 'elevation, intelligence, and the *summum* of talent personified',[12] and the frequent references in his correspondence prove that he felt as much friendship as respect.

So by the mid-1860s Villiers's reputation was an enviable one. Not only did he appear to his contemporaries as perhaps the most outstanding man of his generation, he had also won the approbation of several of the most prominent older authors. Baudelaire had conferred on him the rare privilege of his friendship, Banville had publicly acclaimed him as a genius, Leconte de Lisle accorded him a conspicuous place in his poetic gatherings. In addition, as we shall see, he was cordially welcomed into the household of Théophile Gautier, who was then at the height of his fame; he was on good terms with Alexandre Dumas *fils*, the most famous dramatist of the day; and he made a sufficiently good impression on Gustave Flaubert for the novelist to come and call on him one day in 1864. (Villiers was very much afraid of the effect his 'august parents' might have had on Flaubert, in view of their ignorance of modern literature, and wrote to advise him not to visit their flat: 'Don't go there again, it's a thieves' alley: travellers get killed on the staircase.' But he was loud in his praise of Flaubert: 'I admire you and to my mind you are a colossal poet and one of the greatest writers who ever lived.')[13] It is clear that everything seemed set fair for him to become one of the leading writers of the century, perhaps even the greatest.

However, the wait for the missing volumes of *Isis* grew

longer and longer, until even Villiers felt that it was time that
he produced something else, even if he refused to admit that
Isis had been abandoned for good. So it is that, in 1864, we
find him working on a play to be entitled *Elën*. It is possible
that the original idea for it is much older, and even that the
first drafts went back several years, to the time when he was
primarily preoccupied with the theatre,[14] but there can be no
doubt that, when he set about producing the final text, what
was weighing most heavily on his mind was the anguish of
Louise Dyonnet's betrayal. Though the play is set in a
strongly and conventionally romanticized Germany, its action visibly transposes the peripeteia of Villiers's shattering
experiences with Louise. Samuel Wissler, a brilliant young
student leader and philosopher, is taken up by the courtesan
Elën, with whom he falls passionately in love, knowing
nothing of her past. But she dies in the middle of an orgy,
and, when Samuel realizes her true identity as the funeral
procession files past, he reviles her memory, flings his ring
and purse on to her coffin, and then departs for 'exile! prayer!
darkness!'[15]

The clumsiness of the construction, the obviousness of the
melodramatic devices, the schematic presentation of the
characters, the derivative nature of much of the material, with
constant reminiscences of Musset and Victor Hugo, all
combine to deprive the play of any real dramatic effectiveness
and to suggest that its conception is fairly juvenile.[16] But,
notwithstanding its glaring defects, the sufferings of Samuel
are expressed with such forthrightness, such intensity of
emotion, and such poetic vigour that the reader is moved in
spite of himself. One passage in particular has clearly been
worked out with special care: a long monologue in which
Samuel, recovering from a dose of opium, evokes the fantastic
dreams and visions to which he has been subjected. Here
Villiers breaks away from the old-fashioned Romanticism of
much of the rest of the drama and comes close to realizing a
new kind of Baudelairean prose for the theatre.[17]

Curiously enough, when he had finished the play, he did
not seek to give it maximum publicity, but arranged for it to
be published in a privately-printed edition of very few copies,
which were not offered for sale, So, when it came off the

press in January 1865, only Villiers's closest friends were
aware of its existence, apart from the theatre managers to
whom he may be presumed to have sent it, and, when he
decided to have a second edition printed in Saint-Brieuc the
following year (with a slightly revised text, a new dedication
to Théophile Gautier, and a prefatory poem 'A Elën', clearly
addressed in reality to Louise Dyonnet), he followed the
same procedure, with the result that both editions are equally
rare. It seems unlikely that this semi-secrecy was motivated
by undue modesty, of which Villiers was not often guilty, or
by the excessively personal character of much of what the
play contains. More probably, he was hoping to have the play
produced and thought it tactically preferable not to put the
text on sale too soon.

The present-day reader, for whom *Elën* is likely to have
interest mainly as a curiosity and as an unrestrained cry of
individual anguish, may well be surprised at the effect which
it produced among Villiers's friends. Stéphane Mallarmé,
writing to his friend Eugène Lefébure in February 1865,
extolled its 'divine beauty' and compared its author to
Shakespeare, Baudelaire, and Edgar Allan Poe: 'In a word,
the intellect, the feeling for art, the voluptuous desires of the
mind (even the most blasé) will find there a magnificent feast.
Savour this precious flagon drop by drop.'[18] Lefébure agreed,
and told Mallarmé that what he had written in his letter was
no more than Villiers deserved.[19] Another friend, Emmanuel
des Essarts, expressed minimal reserves: it might not, he said,
be quite as good as *Hamlet* and *Faust*, but it was well up to
Byron's *Manfred* and the German novelist Jean-Paul: 'In this
drama I felt I was present at a magnificent marriage between
transcendental philosophy and poetry. Everything is possible
to genius. It gave me a vision of a poetic Hegel, a tragic
Schelling, of something unheard of and inexpressible.'[20] A
few years later Paul Verlaine was to call it a 'magnificent
drama written and composed by a master, the performance of
which is greatly to be desired for the besmirched honour of
the French stage'.[21]

So, if the public knew nothing of *Elën*, at least it had
unstinted praise heaped on it by the circle of Villiers's literary
friends. But it is a relatively small-scale work in three acts,

and he doubtless felt that it did not have the scope to encompass his boundless ambitions. So, as soon as he had finished it, he set to work on another drama, more grandly planned, and more elaborately worked out. This was *Morgane*, which seems to have occupied him for most of 1865 (though it is not impossible that the idea of it is much older).[22] Before it was even completed, Villiers informed his friends that it had been accepted for performance at the Théâtre de la Gaîté in Paris.[23] No doubt he was exaggerating, but he had evidently received some encouragement from his hero the actor Dumaine, who had just taken over the management of the theatre and whom Villiers had in mind in writing the main part. A letter Villiers sent to Dumaine with his copy of the printed text reveals that the actor–manager had already written to him, and that his hopes had been raised: Villiers now asked for a sincere opinion on the finished article and on the part that had been written for him. 'Let me know if the role seems to be of a certain order . . . If you do not like it, tell me frankly, and I will write another one for you, quite simply. I already have another in my imagination. I want to associate my talent, if I have any, with one of your creations.' The following sentences display a quite remarkable degree of arrogance, not to say bumptiousness:

It will be no trouble to me to find a place for *Morgane* more or less where I like, even if I have to go right to the top to have it acted. As I am not enormously concerned about glory, I haven't really tried up to now. But seeing so many frightful imbeciles with no soul and no talent making a name for themselves, I am beginning to grow tired of my own disinterestedness.[24]

This confidence that theatre managers would leap at the chance of producing *Morgane* is manifest in the edition itself, which appeared in March 1866 with the same imprint of Francisque Guyon of Saint-Brieuc as the second edition of *Elën*. Only twenty-five copies were printed, and a pretentious little authorial note informed the reader that, pending a definitive edition, these were destined exclusively for the actors. But, perhaps because he was placing higher hopes in it than he had done in *Elën*, Villiers began to show a certain

nervousness as the moment of publication drew near. To
Mallarmé he averred that he was not very keen on the play,
but that there were a few passable scenes and a score of quite
good lines, together with two sublime epigrams that would
carry the rest; he also claimed that there would be a sensational preface, an idea which he subsequently dropped.[25] To
Heredia, he was even more categorical: 'I'm not going to send
you *Morgane*, which strikes me as idiotic and deadly, and
which I'm furiously disgusted with! Can I have spent nearly a
year clasping that rubbish to my heart; I could have written
some poetry; I was corrupted by the lure of lucre.'[26]

   Morgane is in fact a mixture of the very good and the very
bad. Set in Naples at the time of the French Revolution, it is a
spectacular cloak-and-dagger drama, dealing with an insurrection fomented by the adventuress Morgane, Duchess of
Poleastro, with the aim of deposing the Bourbon king in
favour of her protégé and lover Sergius, who happens to be a
legitimate claimant. The plans of the conspirators at first go
well, and Morgane seems to be on the point of defeating her
arch-rival Lady Hamilton, the real power behind the throne,
until she accidentally sees Sergius bestowing a chaste farewell
kiss on her young ward Sione. Misunderstanding its significance, and furious at her supposed betrayal, she destroys the
whole of her plot and allows the king's troops to arrest
Sergius and herself. The last of the five acts is a farrago of
implausibilities; Morgane drinks wine poisoned by Lady
Hamilton, and Sergius is shot while trying to escape after
disguising himself as a statue.

   The weaknesses of the play are all too apparent: a totally
unconvincing use of the supernatural in the shape of a
sorceress, a variety of melodramatic tricks which strain
credulity well beyond breaking-point, a plot which depends
essentially on coincidences and disguises, a ham-fisted insertion of comic scenes for light relief, and a general air of having
been resurrected from 1830. But, while Villiers's theatrical
inexperience and his overheated imagination mar the work,
they should not blind one to its very real merits. The
characters are infinitely more firmly and convincingly drawn
than those of *Elën*; there is a very fine sense of the dramatic in
the construction of some of the big scenes; the language is

constantly expressive and highly-wrought; and above all some of the most characteristic themes of Villiers's thought at last find a worthy form, notably the conflict between love and ambition which causes the downfall of the hero and heroine. Probably much of the play is based on materials amassed for the continuation of *Isis*, and the themes too are probably those which inspired the novel. It may be that their effectiveness in *Morgane* derives from the extent to which they are fundamental to Villiers's whole outlook on life. At all events, *Morgane* is a much more mature and a much more skilfully designed play than *Elën*, even if its imperfections seriously compromise its overall success, and it has a genuinely tragic ring to it.

All these literary activities and new friendships did not however mean that Villiers had finally been allowed to settle in Paris. The evidence suggests that he did live there for most of 1864 and 1865, sometimes in the flat he had taken for Louise Dyonnet in the rue Grenelle-Saint-Germain, sometimes in rooms at the Hotel du Brésil, Passage Dauphine, sometimes with his parents at No. 7 rue Saint-Roch, and sometimes just outside the capital with Catulle Mendès and the latter's father at Choisy-le-Roi. But towards the end of October 1865 he started out for Saint-Brieuc, only to miss his train connections at Le Mans and get into such a tangle, with his belongings in one place and himself in another, that both Marras and Heredia had to be called upon to bail him out.[27] Once back in Brittany he stayed there for some months, visiting his uncle Victor, the parish priest at Ploumilliau, and shooting woodcock with him—a trip which left an unmistakable mark on *L'Intersigne*, one of his greatest short stories, which he composed a couple of years later.[28] Being in Saint-Brieuc meant that he had fewer distractions from his writing, which enabled him to complete *Morgane*, despite its length, relatively quickly, but he was evidently also called upon to assist his father in his 'legal' work. The Marquis had been declared bankrupt in Paris in March 1864,[29] but back in Brittany was entertaining his usual high hopes of sudden riches, this time through an inheritance, which however was going to necessitate complicated researches and lawsuits—in May 1866 he wrote to tell

Marras that his son's presence in Saint-Brieuc was indispensable for these purposes.[30]

Villiers himself was almost as subject as his father to delusions of imminent wealth. According to Fernand Calmettes, the Marquis was easy prey for any enterprising confidence tricksters: 'When they offered him a deal, however brilliant they thought they could represent it as being without making it seem absurd, if they saw him hesitating, all they had to do was add a few more noughts; dazzled, Villiers's father would succumb.'[31] Once he was told that he was going to receive twenty-five millions on account—'and that's just the beginning,' he said to some friends. 'Perhaps you could rest contented with that,' one of them suggested. But the Marquis just rubbed his hands gleefully, adding: 'And I hope it will be the same thing every month.'[32] His son was hardly less gullibly optimistic, and the letters of the mid-1860s are full of confident pronouncements about a forthcoming change of fortune. To Marras he announced mysteriously in August 1863, just after leaving Solesmes: 'I think that you and I are about to see the end of our ill luck.'[33] A year later, as we have seen, he was talking to Louise Dyonnet about being dazzled by the gold he had seen, and of which he had not yet given up hope. At the beginning of 1866 he was far more categorical to Mallarmé: 'There is good reason to hope that I'm going to be rich, oh! madly! enough to make the fools and the so-called clever people turn pale,' and was cheerfully envisaging the possibility of being 'a millionaire a hundred times over, in three months from now'.[34] In September of the same year the forecast was just as glowing: 'I am still on the point of coming into an immense fortune, and I think it not completely pointless to take some trouble over it.'[35]

Like father, like son, obviously, although Villiers's expectations were not always based on the same sort of calculations. Inheritances may well have come into it (though where the Villiers de l'Isle-Adams thought they had fabulously rich relatives is far from clear), and of course literature, especially the theatre, offered large rewards to the right man—and Villiers had no doubt that he fulfilled that condition. Sometimes buried treasure was the lure, and the letters to Mallarmé attribute his impending enrichment to 'the escaped convict', whoever that may have been, and to the astuteness of Captain Kidd:[36] presumably he believed that he was on the track of the pirate's hoard. But the most tenacious and recurrent illusion was that he was about to marry some fantastically beautiful and immensely wealthy heiress. The trip to Lyon in 1864 seems to have been motivated by some such scheme, which naturally led to nothing, and it was only the first of many such tragic-comic adventures. If Fernand Calmettes is to be believed (and with Villiers, the most improbable answer is nearly always the right one), on more than thirty occasions,[37] he thought he was going to make such a match: his name and his genius were in his eyes always sufficient to ensure that the girl would fall madly in love with him. But, twenty-five years later, the final reality of marriage for Villiers was to be sadly different, and the dream of riches remained obstinately unrealized.

7

In the mid-1860s the young poets who foregathered under the aegis of Leconte de Lisle began to form a recognizable school, with shared ideals of the dignity and autonomy of art, the necessity for impeccable craftsmanship, avoidance of personal and confessional elements in poetry, concentration on visual and plastic values, and devotion to beauty as an alternative to the sordid realities of everyday modern life. Late in 1865 two of the more energetic and enterprising spirits among them, Catulle Mendès and Xavier de Ricard, conceived the idea of a poetic collection, to be entitled *Le Parnasse contemporain*, which would group a representative choice of their recent poetry. It was of course from this publication that the group subsequently acquired its nickname of 'Parnassians', with all its overtones of impersonality, frigid descriptive writing in imposing alexandrines, and ponderous displays of exoticism and erudition.

Leconte de Lisle was their recognized leader, and Théophile Gautier their patron saint. Among those who made their name while remaining more or less faithful to the Parnassian aesthetic were Mendès, Heredia, and Banville, already mentioned; Sully Prudhomme, who later won a Nobel Prize for Literature, and Léon Dierx, author of *Les Lèvres closes*, both of whom had become friendly with Villiers around 1865. But a more durable glory is attached to those members who later evolved away from their temporary allegiance to strict Parnassianism, notably Stéphane Mallarmé, Paul Verlaine, and Villiers de l'Isle-Adam, who were jointly to a large extent responsible for the direction which the next generation of poets would take. Villiers's own direct contribution to *Le Parnasse contemporain* was limited to three poems: 'Hélène', a reproduction of the poem 'A Elën' which also appeared in the second edition of the drama *Elën*; 'Esquisse à la manière de Goya', a mercifully shortened version of a bad poem about railways, first published in 1860; and 'A une enfant taciturne'. The modesty of this contribution is largely attributable to the fact that Villiers was no longer writing much verse; though he had intended to follow up *Premières Poésies* with further volumes of poetry, he had discovered, once he started work on *Isis*, that he was much more at ease in the more flexible rhythms of prose.

Indeed, one may wonder quite how much Villiers ever did have in common with the orthodox Parnassians. His deep admiration first for the Romantics and then for Baudelaire indicate that his underlying sympathies lay with a more flamboyant, a more intensely emotive, and a more individual-istic type of literature, even if he approved of many of the things the Parnassians were trying to do in opposition to the trivial, commercialized writings which dominated public taste during the Second Empire. It is significant that his closest friendship among his fellow-contributors to the *Parnasse*, apart from Mendès, was with Mallarmé (despite the fact that Mallarmé's posting to Tournon as a teacher prevented them from seeing much of one another) and that their literary association persisted long after Mallarmé's poetic style had followed its own idiosyncratic path into highly un-Parnassian obscurity.

But for the time being there was no doubt about Villiers's commitment to the Parnassian cause, and, when Mendès tried to organize a society for poetry readings, Villiers played a full and enthusiastic part as secretary, as is shown by the lively letter he wrote in September 1865 to ask for the support of Joséphin Soulary, the poet from Lyon. Among others invited to join in were Gautier, Baudelaire, Leconte de Lisle, and Gustave Flaubert, and Villiers joyously predicted an immense success for the enterprise, to which was to be adjoined a luxurious review. However, as so often happened, the young men had overreached themselves, and nothing came of the project.[1]

In the meantime Catulle Mendès's private life was developing in a way which was to prove fateful not only for him but also for Villiers. For some time past he had been paying assiduous court to Judith, the older of the two daughters whom Théophile Gautier had had by the singer Ernesta Grisi. Judith was a highly intelligent and attractive girl, born in 1845, with considerable talent as a writer, and she had fallen head over heels in love with the handsome and dashing Mendès. But Théophile was bitterly opposed to the marriage, having heard things about his daughter's suitor so detrimental that he refused to countenance the idea of having him as a son-in-law. What exactly this damaging information was is uncertain. It has been suggested that Gautier had been told that Mendès was a homosexual,[2] but that seems unlikely, given Mendès's incessant skirt-chasing. It is more probable that it had come to Gautier's ears that Mendès already had a mistress to whom he was much attached, and suspected him of wanting Judith as a wife primarily for the social and literary advantages it would bring him. But Judith was a strong-willed young woman, and, though her father made it clear that he would banish her from his house if she persisted in her intention of marrying Mendès, she waited until she had legally come of age and then did as she wished.

Gautier refused to be present at the wedding, though his friends persuaded him to give his written consent, and, out of respect for his feelings, Gustave Flaubert and Turcan, who were Judith's witnesses, declined to attend the reception. Mendès's witnesses were to be Leconte de Lisle and Villiers, but there was very nearly a hitch in the arrangements because of Villiers's mania for sporting improbable decorations on ceremonial occasions (once, when someone asked him who conferred such orders, he replied calmly: 'I do').[3] When

Villiers called on Leconte de Lisle to take him to the wedding, the older poet was stupefied to see him proudly open his overcoat to display a glittering row of enormous medals. When he was able to stop laughing, Leconte de Lisle said: 'But my dear friend, you look like a display-case. Please get rid of all that. Otherwise I should have to leave you in a shop-window.' And Villiers, evidently accustomed to such reactions, docilely stuffed them into his pocket, where they jangled for the rest of the day.[4]

Villiers may well have had mixed feelings about his friend's marriage. It seems that Mendès had already embarked on his long liaison with another remarkable woman, the young Irish-born musician Augusta Holmes (or Holmès, to use the spelling she adopted when she gallicized her name),[5] who lived in Versailles with her elderly father. Augusta was not only something of a child prodigy as singer, pianist, composer, and poetess, she was also a ravishing beauty with a great cascade of golden hair, and she had numerous admirers in the literary and musical *salon* which her father held. Of an independent and unconventional temperament, her love-affair with a Pole was causing gossip as early as 1863,[6] when she was only fifteen, and she was obviously a very attractive match for any of the eager young men who thronged the *salon* of the rue de l'Orangerie, including musicians like Saint-Saëns, painters like Henri Regnault, and novelists like André Theuriet, as well as poets like Mendès and Villiers. The fact that she was sole heiress to her father's considerable fortune naturally did not detract from her charms, and, with Villiers's incorrigible penchant for rich, cultured, and charming women, he must have considered himself a prime contender for her hand.

Indeed, it is not impossible that he also had hopes with Judith Gautier. She liked him, admired him, and understood him, and in later years was extremely good to him, and he felt at least great affection for her, if nothing more. Whether or not there was any conscious disappointment, he can hardly have failed to experience some muted envy when her choice fell on his friend Catulle. One can easily imagine how exacerbated such feelings must have become when he saw the same Catulle also carrying off Augusta Holmès. The sequence of events is anything but clear, and nobody knows for sure whether Augusta became Catulle's mistress before or after his marriage with Judith, but the two events were not far separated in time, and they began to put a severe strain on Villiers's friendship with Mendès, which from then on was subject to periodic interruptions and quarrels, sometimes of great violence. There had already been storms before, and as early as October 1865 Mallarmé's friend Cazalis had written to him: 'Villiers and Mendès apparently can't stand one another, even at the distance which separates them, the one being in Paris and the other in Brittany.'[7] By September Villiers himself told Mallarmé: 'I've quarrelled with Catulle; we gave up writing to each other six months ago. Well, you see, he's all right, but he's too cold.'[8]

However that may be, the example of Mendès's marriage caused Villiers to start thinking along similar lines. After all, Théophile Gautier had two daughters, and, though Judith might be the more talented, her younger sister Estelle was by no means unattractive. So by 1866, when Villiers was a regular visitor to Gautier's household, it came to be understood that he and Estelle were unofficially engaged. He was naturally proud at the prospect of becoming the poet's son-in-law, and he loved Estelle; she was pleased to accept the homage of a young man who, despite the oddities of his behaviour, was agreed to be the most promising man of letters of his generation and who, to boot, had a title and one of the most ancient and illustrious names in France; Gautier himself, having broken with one daughter over her choice of husband, saw no reason to object. All seemed to be plain sailing for what looked like an eminently suitable match.

Then an unexpected obstacle arose. Villiers's parents, doubtless prompted by Tante Kerinou, declared that they could never accept the idea of their son marrying the illegitimate daughter of a singer and author who was neither noble nor rich. Villiers insisted, but Tante Kerinou was inflexible: if he married Estelle, she would cut him off without a penny. She had subsidized the Marquis's follies, and she was prepared to allow Villiers enough money to enable him to pursue his career as an author, the only one which he would consider or for which he had any aptitude. But she adamantly refused to admit the possibility of what struck her as a grotesque *mésalliance*. Villiers's dilemma was agonizing. He knew the stubborn old lady would never change her mind, so there were only two courses open to him: to defy her edict and marry Estelle, knowing they would have nothing to live on, or to abandon Estelle when she had already signified that she was happy to be his bride.

How long his indecision lasted we do not know, but in the end he came to the conclusion that it would be wrong to inflict a life of poverty on Estelle, since, with more practicality than one might have given him credit for, he realized that his literary aspirations were so out of tune with the taste of the public at large that he could never hope to earn a steady living from his pen. It was one thing to devote himself to his calling and accept for himself all the hardships and sacrifices that might entail—with exemplary fortitude, he never shrank from that. But it was an entirely different matter to demand that someone else should share them, and in those circumstances a sober assessment of reality took over from his customary wild optimism. So on 3 January 1867, unable to bear the thought of confronting Estelle, he wrote in despair to her father to say that he was forced to give up the idea of marrying her.

The letter is desperately simple:

I am profoundly overcome with grief; but there is no way out, I am obliged to recognize the fact. Despite all my efforts, my family has refused me everything: their consent and the necessary money; I cannot earn my living with the sort of talent I have, in short there are obstacles and impossibilities everywhere. I do not want anything from anyone. I only wanted Estelle and a life of quiet. But since I cannot have it, I must withdraw. It is my duty towards her and towards myself.

After begging Gautier to try to find words to explain to Estelle and assuring him of his esteem and affection, he continues: 'As for me, I shall not go back on this decision. I shall keep the memory of the most loyal and good-hearted girl to whom a man could hope to give his name, his life, and his future. It is not my fault if I renounce this happiness; it is the bitterest necessity which absolutely compels me to it.'[9]

After the cataclysmic end to his affair with Louise Dyonnet

and the dashing of his hopes with the unnamed lady from
Lyon, the effect of having to give up Estelle can be imagined,
the more so as this marriage was not a pipe-dream, like so
many of his chimerical matrimonial enterprises. Estelle and
her father had both been willing, even eager; he saw her
regularly and knew her well; her sister was married to one of
his closest friends. To find at the last minute that his own
family, out of aristocratic prejudice, was irrevocably opposed
to the match must have been a terrible blow to him, and he
was certainly not exaggerating when he told Gautier: 'I am ill
and I have never been so sad in my life, and I have never
looked on things as I see them now.' It might be argued that,
if Villiers had loved Estelle as much as he claimed, he could
have followed the example of his friend Mallarmé and taken a
mundane job so as to earn enough for himself and his wife to
live on, reserving his literary activities for his spare time. But
that would be profoundly to misunderstand both his own
inability to adapt himself to the prosaic conditions of everyday life in nineteenth-century France and the imperiousness
of his artistic vocation. Right from his childhood he had
known with total certainty that there was only one thing to
which a Villiers de l'Isle-Adam could worthily devote his life
in the shambles of the modern world, and that was literature.
To make him abandon that position would have been to
destroy the whole justification of his existence, and it was
therefore unthinkable. To the end he was to remain, as
Mallarmé said, 'the man who refused to be anything but that
for which he had been born'.[10] So whatever it cost him in
pain, distress, and humiliation, the decision he took was the
only possible one for him under the circumstances.

How long it was before Villiers got over his disappointment is not known, nor how he managed to console himself:
his letter to Gautier breaking off the engagement is the only
surviving evidence about the whole affair. As for Estelle, six
years later she married Émile Bergerat, journalist and man of
letters. On that occasion no problems arose, despite Bergerat's apprehension when he went to ask Gautier for his
daughter's hand. He felt obliged to confess that he was a
natural son, but Gautier's only reply was to ask benevolently:
'Aren't we all?' But that was not the only revelation Bergerat

had to make: 'I think I ought to tell you that my mother lives with a priest.' 'Who better to live with?' said Gautier, and the marriage was agreed.[11]

But if literature had in a sense forced Villiers to give up his chance of happiness with Estelle, at least it offered him compensations, and, once *Elën* and *Morgane* had released the blockage caused by his inability to complete *Isis*, inspiration was not lacking. The nature of the inspiration however started to change at this time. In the *Premières Poésies*, the unfinished novel, and the two dramas, Villiers had shown himself firmly attached to the Romantic tradition of fiery passions, violent action, exotic settings, and stylistic pyrotechnics, all of which he had taken extremely seriously, even solemnly. Comedy, in so far as it was used at all, was introduced only in the Hugolian manner, to set off the sombre tragic colouring of the rest, with the result that these early works all had a certain tendency to pomposity and grandiloquence. By the mid-1860s he was beginning to experiment in an altogether different mode, realizing perhaps that those elements of his personality uncovered by his contacts with Baudelaire could not find adequate expression in the forms of the 1830s. The venom of the irony that Baudelaire directed at his own time certainly bit deep into him, and was reinforced by Flaubert's unmatchable contempt for the bourgeois; the production of terror by pseudo-scientific means had impressed him immensely when he met it in Edgar Allan Poe.

So, even before *Morgane* appeared, Villiers was showing signs of discontent with his exclusive allegiance to a Romantic ideal long since overtaken by events, and in November 1865 one finds Lefébure informing Mallarmé that their friend was about to start writing in the manner of Poe.[12] This desire to emulate the American short-story writer coalesced with a general wish to do something to shock and startle the bourgeoisie, already apparent in the way in which he wrote to Soulary in September of the same year about the proposed poetry-reading society: 'It will be a delight to terrify and astound that dear public which is eager to *see* and *hear* those rare animals which people call poets (. . .) we are determined to take our revenge on stupidity by plunging it into stupor.'[13]

Such aggressivity soon developed into a full-scale programme of literary terrorism, which he expounded in a long and excited letter he wrote to Mallarmé on 11 September 1866. By then the rapturous welcome accorded to readings of his satirical writings had convinced him that new perspectives were opening up before him, and he had resolved to make himself into the scourge of the bourgeois.

This is how he revealed his intentions to Mallarmé:

The fact is that, if I live long enough, I shall do for the bourgeois what Voltaire did for the 'clericals', Rousseau for the gentry, and Molière for doctors. It appears that I have a power in the field of the grotesque that I never knew about. Anyway, we'll have fun. I've been told that in comparison Daumier flatters them abjectly. And naturally, I look as though I love them and sing their praises, while I'm killing them like rabbits. You'll see my types, Bonhomet, Finassier, and Lefol: I cherish them and shape them with loving care. In short, I believe I've found the chink in their armour and that it will be unexpected.

The first fruits of these intentions had been made public at one of the Saturday evening gatherings in Leconte de Lisle's *salon*, in the presence of Louis Ménard, known as the 'Mystic Pagan' and one of the senior Parnassians; the results had been startling: 'I've had such success in provoking uncontrollable laughter at Leconte de Lisle's (Ménard was laughing so much that he hid behind the sofas, and the others made themselves ill) that my hopes are high.'[14] This sudden realization of his hitherto unsuspected comic and satirical gifts henceforward added an extra dimension to Villiers's writings. Though he never renounced his liking for the grand style of tragedy or the high-flown flights of lyricism, he also became one of the greatest, most insidious, and most incisive of French ironists.

At first Villiers thought he was going to be able to exploit this new vein in the press of the time, but he was indulging in his usual pastime of counting unhatched chickens. *Claire Lenoir*, so he said to Mallarmé in the 1866 letter, was 'a finished novel' that was going to appear in the newspaper *L'Époque*; in reality, neither was it finished, nor did it appear in *L'Époque*. In fact, Villiers's confidence over his relations with the press had very little foundation, despite his boasting to Mallarmé: 'I have two or three papers at my disposal: my work has been commissioned.'[15] The previous year he had already claimed to have published an article on Joséphin Soulary in *L'Epoque*[16] (one of his cousins was on the staff of the paper)[17] and a poem entitled 'Titanide' in *Le Publicateur*;[18] now he was announcing the imminent publication in the *Revue du XIXe siècle* of a set of verse and prose poems under the title 'Le Cantique nuptial', and in the satirical periodical *Le Nain jaune* that of his 'Réhabilitation du Tiers-État en France'—'a thing that will make the bourgeois jump with rage and surprise'. But nobody has ever been able to find any of these works, and there is no evidence that they were ever really written—Villiers was quite capable of persuading himself that he had completed and even published whole books of which not a line existed on paper. It is true that he did manage to get a couple of prose poems into print in *La Lune*, another satirical weekly, in August 1867,[19] and there is a reasonable presumption that in April or May of the same year he had published an article on the Persian exhibits at the Universal Exhibition in Paris. But the article is only known from a manuscript, and it looks as though he was prompted to compose it by Catulle Mendès and Judith Gautier, who were always anxious to persuade him to write and publish more regularly.[20] Otherwise few newspapers and periodicals were prepared to open their doors to him, and he was in any case temperamentally averse to allowing anything to be printed until he had rewritten it a sufficient number of times to satisfy his extremely demanding taste.

Frequently, of course, Villiers would try out works in gestation on any audience he could find, particularly in literary *salons*. He was a prodigiously exciting reader both of what he had written himself and of his favourites among other people's writings—we have already seen how a reading of *Morgane* in February 1866 had convinced those present that he was a theatrical genius and how he could convulse the normally staid atmosphere in Leconte de Lisle's *salon*. Paul Verlaine recalled how he used to arrive out of breath in the famous *entresol* of the Passage Choiseul where Lemerre published *Le Parnasse contemporain*, run his hand feverishly through his mop of hair, stroke his moustache hastily, then launch into the latest adventures of one of his heroes, before disappearing 'in a farewell as fantastic as the story he had told'.[21] Sometimes he would draw on his extraordinary memory to recite by heart, and without hesitation, 'the longest and most abstruse of Poe's novellas';[22] sometimes he would combine his musical and vocal talents to play and sing his own settings of Baudelaire's poems, notably 'La Mort des amants';[23] sometimes he would declaim Mallarmé's poetry (he read the prose poem 'Le Démon de l'analogie' at Leconte de Lisle's on 28 September 1867).[24] On one occasion his love of readings caused him to beat out a tattoo on a toy drum to summon his family and their cook to listen to a rendering of the sonnet 'Don du poème', which Mallarmé had just sent him in Saint-Brieuc.[25]

But the desire for human warmth and immediate approval which lay behind such readings was also a factor in making Villiers less keen to get into print, since the response then could only be delayed and remote, even if it was not hostile. For Villiers knew full well, at least in his more lucid moments, that the general public was never likely to take to the sort of literature he produced, and indeed he would not have wanted it to: in the preface he never wrote for *Morgane*, he had proposed to argue that 'an individual who writes for fame is not worthy, in the eyes of a poet, to be given a job as a nark in a properly run police-station'.[26] So his attitude to public acclaim was ambivalent: on the one hand, he always hankered after glory on a Hugolian scale, and, on the other, striving for popular success struck him as a degrading and futile pursuit. That such an attitude, coupled with an abiding contempt for bourgeois values and an uncompromising devotion to high ideals, should have made him suspect in the eyes of newspaper editors is wholly understandable, and it is one reason why he was neither able nor willing to publish more in the press of the time.

In such a situation there was of course one solution which never ceased to appeal to Villiers, as it appealed to so many of his contemporaries: to have his own review, in which he would be free to write what he liked and as he liked. For a brief spell this hope was to be realized; in the late summer of 1867 it was announced that a new periodical was about to appear: it was to be called the *Revue des Lettres et des Arts*, and its editor-in-chief was to be Villiers de l'Isle-Adam.

8

To found a review costs money, and Villiers had none, or at any rate not enough, after a series of legendary extravagances such as the supposed purchase of a carriage which had belonged to the Duke of Brunswick.[1] Nor was Tante Kerinou any longer in a position to hand over large subsidies: this was the time when the Marquis had embarked on a harebrained scheme to raise the galleons of Vigo with their bounty of gold, and the family resources must have been very severely depleted. But among the friends Villiers had made in the group around Leconte de Lisle was a young man named Armand Gouzien, born in 1839, who at first intended to be a painter but had then changed to music criticism and journalism,[2] and Gouzien had a brother Théophile, who must have been a wealthy and generous man, for it was he who put up the necessary funds. According to the official contract, signed by the Gouzien brothers and Villiers on 20 September 1867,[3] Théophile was to be the proprietor, Armand the director, and Villiers the editor-in-chief. But it was Villiers who was made responsible for preparing each number, and in practice he seems to have had more or less a free hand to run the review as he wished. Théophile evidently contented himself with being the financial backer, while Armand's functions were probably mainly administrative. The review was to appear weekly and was not to concern itself with politics or social economy; Théophile undertook to guarantee its existence for three months.

However unbusinesslike Villiers may have been, he took his responsibilities as editor of the *Revue des Lettres et des Arts* with the utmost seriousness and carried them out not unsuccessfully. In his ebullient way, he began in September 1867 to write to prospective collaborators and managed to assemble a remarkably brilliant team, largely chosen from among the poets of the *Parnasse contemporain*.[4] Among those who published prose or verse in the *Revue* were Leconte de Lisle, Théodore de Banville, José-Maria de Heredia, Léon

Dierx, Paul Verlaine, Stéphane Mallarmé, François Coppée, Xavier de Ricard, Catulle Mendès, Judith Gautier, Augusta Holmès, Dumas *fils*, and Mistral. Even Edmond and Jules de Goncourt were persuaded to send something, though they had a low opinion of Villiers and though their realistic novels were scarcely his kind of fiction. In addition, Villiers inserted substantial selections from Aloysius Bertrand's sequence of prose poems *Gaspard de la nuit*, to which Baudelaire had drawn his attention in *Le Spleen de Paris* but which were little known at the time; a number of translations of German poetry by Mendès; and regular articles on literature, painting, and music. When one looks through the contents of the twenty-five numbers which appeared, one is struck by the quantity of work signed by distinguished names, as compared to the relative scarcity of banal space-fillers. There are not many nineteenth-century literary reviews which maintained a comparable standard.

Villiers's own contributions are naturally given prominence. The first eight numbers contain a serialization of *Claire Lenoir*, the novel he said he had finished a year before; in fact, he told someone else it had been written as it was being published, in the rare moments of leisure left over from running the review.[5] The truth probably is that a partial or provisional version had been sketched out in 1866, but that each chapter was thoroughly revised before it was allowed to appear. *Claire Lenoir* was followed by another story, *L'Intersigne*, bearing the same general superscription of *Histoires moroses*, that figured in three numbers at the end of 1867 and the beginning of 1868. The only other major contribution from him was a tripartite serialization of *Elën*. The play had of course already had two editions in 1865 and 1866, but they had been so restricted in size that the publication in the *Revue* almost counted as the issue of a new work. Apart from that, he produced a couple of poems and two critical articles, one of them a eulogy of Shakespeare's *Hamlet*, a play for which he had an almost obsessive admiration, and the other a slashing condemnation of Émile Augier's *Paul Forestier*, which he took as the symbol of all that he detested in the contemporary bourgeois theatre.[6] It is also possible that some of the unsigned paragraphs of book reviews or general artistic gossip are by him, but there is no way of knowing which they might be. All in all, while he wrote more in the *Revue* than anyone else, it was by no means a one-man band (though no one else was allowed to serialize longer works); it was more a matter of *primus inter pares.*

There were of course some failures in his drive to recruit contributors. Baudelaire died on 31 August 1867 after a long illness, just before the review was launched, and, though Villiers wrote to his friend Charles Asselineau a few days later to see if there might be anything new in the poet's unpublished papers, he had in the end to be content with an article by Asselineau himself. He also had hoped that Flaubert would provide him with something, but failed to persuade him to interrupt his arduous labours on *L'Éducation sentimentale.* The absence of Gautier is unsurprising; no doubt Villiers was too embarrassed by the recent break with Estelle to invite him. As for Victor Hugo, since the *Revue* was avowedly non-political, it would hardly have done to solicit a contribution from the illustrious exile. Thus very few of Villiers's idols or friends are absent from the roll-call, which is in itself a tribute to the energy and tenacity with which he organized his team.

Apart from the distinction of those who wrote for it, the *Revue des Lettres et des Arts* has several claims to fame. The motto which appeared on its title-page was *faire penser*: to make people think, and that aim, so typical of Villiers, is one which it constantly attained. It was one of the first and most important reviews to support the Parnassian cause—almost every Parnassian of note contributed something to it—and, while nowadays Parnassianism conjures up the image of an art which is staid, stolid, and semi-official, in the 1860s it was anything but easily accepted. According to Mendès, cab-drivers used the term 'Parnassian!' as their ultimate insult,[7] and Barbey d'Aurevilly, in his lampoon *Trente-sept médaillonnets du Parnasse contemporain*, was particularly severe on Villiers: 'When someone has the honour to be called Villiers de l'Isle-Adam, he should imitate his ancestors, not M. Hugo.'[8] Villiers's review thus provided a rallying-point for what was then a progressive school of young poets, and, though it is not perhaps accurate to call it the first Parnassian review, it is certainly one of the most eminent and most influential.

Equally, it was one of the first periodicals to champion the cause of Wagner in France. Villiers had been a fervent admirer of Wagner for some years, even though he had probably not been present at the famous *Tannhäuser* scandal in 1861, as he later liked to pretend (his account of it was highly amusing).[9] That Baudelaire had taken up the cudgels on Wagner's behalf can only have increased his ardour, and he did indeed offer to play to Baudelaire piano arrangements of Wagnerian music, while several of his other friends were also deeply committed to defending Wagner against the virulent attacks to which the musical establishment was then subjecting him. Mendès had done all he could to get Wagner to write in the *Revue fantaisiste*, and, though the composer never gave him anything, he was duly grateful for Mendès's support; likewise Judith Gautier had had the courage to upbraid Berlioz in 1861 for his hostility to Wagner.[10] Since Armand Gouzien was primarily a music critic, it is not surprising that the *Revue des Lettres et des Arts* showed itself highly favourable to the still very unpopular music of Wagner. Not only is Wagner mentioned repeatedly and reverently in the columns devoted to music, but several pages of Villiers's *Claire Lenoir* are given over to extolling him as one of the leading representatives of idealism in art. Much more than *L'Esprit nouveau*, also founded by two French Wagnerians in 1867, the *Revue des Lettres et des Arts* deserves the distinction of being considered the first Wagnerian periodical in France, since it consistently sings his praises, whereas his name is not even mentioned in *L'Esprit nouveau*.[11]

Those of Villiers's own works which appeared in the *Revue* are another of its claims to distinction. Apart from the two brief articles on *Hamlet* and *Paul Forestier*, which are the first shots in Villiers's prolonged and determined campaign for the regeneration of the French theatre, *Claire Lenoir* and *L'Intersigne* are his main contribution, *Elën* having already been published elsewhere. The two works mark a decisive turning-point in his career as a writer, and both are among his outstanding achievements. *Claire Lenoir*, the longer and

more ambitious of the two, is an astonishing amalgam of
themes and techniques, all placed at the service of an intransigent philosophical idealism. The tale is related by Dr
Tribulat Bonhomet, in whom Villiers has incarnated everything he hated in the bourgeois mentality—positivism, philistinism, exclusive concentration on material things, petty-
minded distrust of art and the ideal, thoughtless adulation of
Progress, refusal to accept the existence of anything which
might upset blinkered smugness. But, whereas predecessors
like Henry Monnier's Joseph Prudhomme or the pharmacist
Homais in Flaubert's *Madame Bovary* had on the whole been
depicted as figures of fun, Tribulat Bonhomet is a creation of
monstrous grotesqueness, whom Villiers was to adopt for the
rest of his life as a butt and a scapegoat, constantly inventing
new sayings and adventures for him, both in conversation
and in print.

The story he tells us here is that of Claire Lenoir, who is
unhappily married to Césaire Lenoir; Bonhomet visits them
and tries to wean Césaire from his snuff-taking with such
violence that he kills him. A year later, he meets Claire again,
now blind; he has just heard that her former lover Sir Henry
Clifton has been killed by a native in the South Seas. As she
dies in his presence, Claire shrieks that she is being visited by
a horrifying vision, and, when Bonhomet inspects the pupils
of her eyes, he sees reflected there the image of a black savage
with Césaire Lenoir's features, holding in his hand the
severed head of Sir Henry. But on to this horrific and
implausible tale Villiers has grafted all sorts of philosophic
and artistic intentions. A long conversation between Bonhomet, Césaire, and Claire consists of a confrontation of
materialism, agnostic idealism, and a more religious if not
precisely Christian idealism, with a strong dash of occultism
thrown in for good measure. Patently Villiers still wants to
produce the synthesis of Hegelianism, Christianity, and
occultism which had obsessed him at the time of *Isis*, and, if
the result is somewhat confusing, it is nevertheless a brilliantly conceived and thought-provoking display.

The same conversation also serves as a pretext for Villiers
to expound his artistic preferences. Since it is Bonhomet who
is supposed to be writing, these are brought out mainly by

ironic antiphrasis, as the doctor is made to condemn Hugo, Wagner, and Poe in terms which only discredit his own mental processes. Further topics touched on include theories of metempsychosis, since Césaire's soul enters into the body of a savage, and the reality of visions, since what Claire alone could see has imprinted itself on her retina. *Claire Lenoir* is a complex and exciting work that operates on all sorts of different levels—arduous philosophical debate jostles with scenes of black comedy, pseudo-scientific Poe-esque devices contrast with the burning lyricism of some of Claire's speeches, a pugnacious and uncompromising idealism is supported by a rather penny-dreadful evocation of the supernatural. What predominates above all is intellectual verve, apparent as much in the delight with which Villiers creates a fantastic and angular style for Bonhomet as in the dexterity with which he juggles with metaphysical concepts, satirical epigrams, and aesthetic speculations.

L'Intersigne, while displaying the same aggressively idealistic stance, is much more sober in tone. The narrator, this time a double of Villiers himself, tells of a visit to a country priest in Brittany, during which he has a premonitory vision presaging the priest's death, which occurs a short time later. Its eerie atmosphere is no less disturbing than the subtle sophisms of *Claire Lenoir*, and demonstrates that Villiers has found his vocation as a short-story writer. From now on, the greater part of his writings will be in that form, but his mastery of it is already apparent in the gradation of effects in this cunningly-organized narration.

Both stories are clearly designed to *faire penser*, but the insidiousness with which they do it, particularly in the case of *Claire Lenoir*, is one of their most original features. Since Bonhomet relates the story himself, the unwary reader may find himself siding with the sinister doctor, and he will then become enmeshed in a web of disquieting contradictions and absurdities. This is no doubt the 'chink in the armour' of the bourgeois which Villiers claimed to have discovered, and the terms in which he wrote to Mallarmé reveal that it is all part of a deliberately conceived plan of intellectual subversion, in which the enigmas of Mallarmé's poetry would also play their part:

You know that as soon as we have a few subscriptions, we must drive the reader mad, and we have put our main hopes in you to reach this result and carry it to its ultimate conclusion. What a triumph, if we could make some subscribers end up in the lunatic asylum at Bicêtre! You must feel, as I do, the imperious necessity of it, and anyway you'll see, right from the first number, that I am not unworthy to work alongside you; yes, I flatter myself that I have found the way to the bourgeois's heart! I have incarnated him so as to kill him off at leisure and with greater certainty.[12]

To put it mildly, such a programme for a literary periodical is unusual and dangerous, and the remarkable thing is that the *Revue* survived as long as it did. Villiers had of course characteristically assumed that it was going to transform his life: 'The ill-luck that has pursued me in all I have attempted has been really matchless and I'm glad about it; from now on, things are, I hope, entering upon a more propitious sequence.'[13] In fact, the *Revue* must have had some success, for, although Théophile Gouzien had only guaranteed its existence for three months, it came out at regular weekly intervals from 13 October 1867 until 29 March 1868, with twenty-five numbers in all. But towards the end times were clearly becoming harder: the number of contributors was dropping off, famous names were cropping up less often, and Villiers himself evidently had no more major works to offer. He had taken to sleeping at the offices of the review in the rue de Choiseul, where Léon Dommartin, one of the regular contributors, acted as his assistant. This is how the scene was remembered by Louis de Gavrinis:

It was in the depths of winter; and there was no fire. In Villiers's little room, which did duty as the editor's office, the master would wait with wild impatience while the journal was being printed. And as soon as the printer delivered a few hundred copies, Villiers and Dommartin would make a bonfire of them, and warm themselves in front of it with indescribable pleasure. When night fell, Villiers would lie down on a bed—or, rather, a bedstead—pile up on himself all the clothes he had left, top off this meagre edifice with a chair to hold it down, and fall into a deep slumber, gently lulled by strange dreams, in which spectral fairies unveiled supreme visions for his ever-wakeful mind.[14]

The exact circumstances of the end are unclear. The

number dated 29 March 1868, the last to appear, announced
that the *Revue des Lettres et des Arts* was to be succeeded by
La Fronde. This new review, which still had the subtitle
Revue des Lettres et des Arts, was likewise owned by
Théophile Gouzien, but the editor was Georges Maillard,
and of the old team only Léon Dommartin remained. Moreover, its character was completely different, since it was
political and polemical, with a strong republican slant. It only
lasted for five numbers, and Villiers had nothing to do with
it. So it looks as though Théophile Gouzien, having had
enough of subsidizing his brother and Villiers, had decided to
make a clean break and try to get his money back with a
different type of weekly.[15] Once again, Villiers's hopes had
been dashed, and, despite its considerable achievements, he
had seen the *Revue* die on him without his having been able
to conquer the position in the world of letters which he
thought was his due.

9

The year 1868 began under bad auspices for Villiers, with the
disappearance of the *Revue* which had so excited him, and at
first sight it would seem to have continued equally unfavourably. All that he published that year after the end of the
Revue was a sequence of poems under the title 'Les Derniers
Soucis', in Arsène Houssaye's luxurious periodical *L'Artiste*,
and several of them were not new. Hardly any letters from
1868 have survived, mostly having to do with the difficulties
he was experiencing in paying bills at a *pension de famille* run
by a M. Garcias, a one-time banker who had fallen on evil
days, where he had lived for sometime in company with
Catulle Mendès and his wife Judith—there had even been
some question of his marrying a foreign heiress who also
boarded there, but at the last minute Villiers had taken fright
and withdrawn.[1] Relations with his closest friends were not
easy or satisfying. Stéphane Mallarmé was away in Besançon
teaching, and had plunged deep in the metaphysical and
psychological crisis which almost cost him his reason, but
from which he emerged with a startlingly new poetic system,
partly based on the meditations suggested to him by the

figure of Villiers. The latter reacted with solicitude when Mallarmé tried to explain to him the transmutation he was undergoing, though one may doubt the efficacy of the advice he tendered, which, as was to be expected from such a hypochondriac, centred mainly on things like rhubarb and iron pills.[2] As for Mendès, their friendship had become intermittent. At the time when he was founding the *Revue*, Villiers told Mallarmé that he had almost broken with Mendès and had had no news of him for six months; a few weeks later Mendès had become one of his most reliable collaborators and they were living in the same boarding-house; some time after that Mendès was brusquely refusing to help him out of his financial problems.[3] These must indeed have been considerable: as he was publishing nothing, he was earning nothing, and his family, whose circumstances were much straitened by then, only gave him a meagre and irregular allowance, with the result that the debts were piling up.

Yet, with remarkable resilience, Villiers was getting over the double blow of the loss of his fiancée and the demise of his review. It was now that he was given the chance to move in high society, which at first he seized with alacrity.[4] This came about because the thought crossed his mind that it would not be demeaning himself to accept a post in diplomacy, and one of his friends, an engineer named Michel Baronnet, managed to get him an introduction to the Duc de Marmier-Choiseul, whose daughter was married to the son of the Foreign Minister. The result was an invitation to a grand official ball at the Foreign Ministry, no doubt accorded to him because the Imperial regime would have been happy to enlist the support of someone with such an ancient and honourable name, hitherto devoted to the monarchy. It was arranged that his host's carriage would call for him at his rooms at the rue Royale, but Baronnet, wary of Villiers's unpredictable changes of mind, thought it prudent to check in advance that all was in order. To his horror, he found Villiers emerging from a bath with his hair in curlers (because his locks were so rebellious, it was his invariable habit to have them curled for ceremonial occasions), with the result that he looked like a demented poodle. Only after three-quarters of an hour's hard work was he reduced to respectability, after which he went off to the ball, where in fact he charmed everyone. But to appear regularly at such functions would have placed too much constraint on his fiercely independent spirit, and he neglected to follow up the opportunities which might have won him the posting to the London Embassy which he coveted.[5]

Villiers behaved with similar perversity when he was invited to an elegant party given by Arsène Houssaye, editor of *L'Artiste* and Director of Fine Arts. As was his wont, he sat down at the piano and was playing dreamily, when another guest came up to him and said: 'The ladies would be glad of a waltz.' He went on playing, and the guest insisted: 'The ladies would be grateful if you were so kind . . .' But Villiers just continued as though he had not noticed, until the guest stalked off in disgust. Someone else then told Villiers that his interlocutor was Jules Claretie, a leading critic and novelist, later to become an Academician and Director of the Théâtre Français, and added: 'You weren't very nice to Claretie. Be careful! He's a powerful man.' Villiers laughed and replied: 'So that was Claretie; I didn't know him . . . That's good! I'm not sorry.'[6] Perhaps it was a similar instinct that led him to accept repeated dinner invitations from the Duc de Cossé-Brissac, and then cry off at the last moment.[7] Despite his almost childish desire for honours and recognition, Villiers's non-conformism was so incorrigible that he nearly always behaved in a way that made it impossible for him to get them. No doubt the regularity with which he had suffered disappointments and frustrations was making him so fearful of failures that he would himself seek to provoke them in order to prevent his hopes rising too high.

These abortive excursions into a world into which Villiers might have been delighted to penetrate and where his friends thought he could have been a brilliant success did not have any immediate impact on his writing, though years later he was to use a glittering evocation of the ball at the Foreign Ministry as the setting for *L'Amour suprême*, one of his most moving tales. But he had no intention of abandoning literature, even if his publications temporarily dried up, and was indeed contemplating a bold new departure. Up to this point

Villiers had flown in the face of the general taste of his time, either harking back to the extravagances of the early Romantics, or supporting the stern new tenets of Parnassianism, or moving forward into the strange meanders of his disturbing irony, but always utterly rejecting the conventions of the realistic novel or the moralizing platitudes of the social dramas and comedies on which the theatre was at that time thriving. Now, however, his long succession of setbacks made him toy with the idea of adapting his manner to what the public wanted, and such was his faculty of mimetism that he had no doubt that he could easily outdo the practitioners of a genre he despised, if he only set his mind to it. In this he may have been encouraged by Alexandre Dumas *fils*, then the most famous and successful purveyor of social dramas, who had been one of his patrons for several years—little is known about their relationship, but they were probably introduced by Léon Margue, at one time Dumas's secretary and the man responsible for making Villiers known at the Brasserie des Martyrs around 1860.[8]

So, shortly after the collapse of the *Revue*, he began composing a play set in an upper-class modern *salon*, with realistic dialogue, recognizable characters, and a plausible action, turning on questions of intrigue and adultery. Only two acts of the play survive in manuscript, but that is probably all that was completed; they were not discovered and published until 1956,[9] and they were evidently written over a period of time, with at least one lengthy interruption—there are gaps in the plot, and the characters change names halfway through. It is not known how many acts Villiers intended to have in *La Tentation*, to give it the title bestowed on it in 1956, but the existing fragments, which are very carefully elaborated, are substantial enough to suggest that it was conceived on a large scale. So far as one can judge it in its unfinished state, it is an unexceptionable example of Second Empire social drama: the tone of elegant conversation is well caught, the characters are rounded and diverse, and there is a rather sententiously pointed moral lesson. Had the play been from the pen of anyone but Villiers, it would have been sound but unremarkable; what is extraordinary is that it should have been written by a man who, reviewing Augier's

Paul Forestier only a few months earlier, should have condemned out of hand the whole of that type of theatre. Indeed, the discrepancy between *La Tentation* and Villiers's usual view of drama no doubt explains why it was never completed. By an effort of will (and with considerable skill), Villiers had forced himself to adopt a manner quite foreign to his normal habits of thought and imagination, but the strain of keeping up the pretence eventually led him to abandon the attempt. On the other hand, if *La Tentation* remained an isolated moment in Villiers's theatre, he did not, as we shall see, give up the idea of using the norms of Second Empire drama for his own purposes, radically different though they may have been from bourgeois realism and moralizing. It must in fact have been almost immediately after deciding to drop *La Tentation* that he started work on another play, superficially of a similar nature, to be entitled *La Révolte*. This was to occupy him for some months and to involve him in one of the most crushing defeats of a life studded with disasters.

At the same time Villiers had been introduced into a new milieu, which for many years would be as near to becoming the centre of his life as anything ever was. This was the *salon* of Nina de Villard, one of the liveliest and most entertaining centres of Parisian artistic activity in the late 1860s and the 1870s. Born in Paris in 1843 as Anne-Marie Gaillard but always called Nina, she was a young woman bursting with talent and gaiety. Poet, painter, amateur actress, and an accomplished pianist, in 1864 she married Hector de Callias, a journalist and writer, but, though an amiable man, he was a hopeless drunkard, and they separated for good in 1867. Nina thenceforward kept the noble particle *de*, but took her mother's maiden name, with the result that she was regularly known as Nina de Villard. Pretty if somewhat plump, she loved the social whirl, and soon surrounded herself with a whole coterie of poets, painters, sculptors, and musicians, who became regular attenders at the soirées she gave in the different houses in which her parents lived before 1870. The atmosphere there was much more informal than in the rather starchy *salon* of Leconte de Lisle, though many of the same people went to both, and there was more than a touch of bohemianism about it (this became more pronounced later).

The occupations of the guests were diverse. Sometimes they would improvise and act comic plays; sometimes they would read verses; sometimes they would make music; sometimes they would devise practical jokes to shock the staid neighbours. Gradually Nina's *salon* became a kind of open house to impecunious artists and men of letters, who were always sure of a meal there, and even of a bed in case of dire necessity.

With all her different artistic skills, Nina was no fool, and was happy to lend her vigorous support to the most modern movements in art. She was a great admirer of Wagner, Manet was among her friends, and, if she had applauded the Parnasse in its early stages, once it had begun to ossify into officialdom she turned more and more to misunderstood dissidents. Politically she took up an aggressively advanced position, and like many of her friends was to be compromised under the Commune; she was a professed republican and a follower of Garibaldi. There was thus a strain of seriousness beneath the apparently carefree joys which Nina dispensed around her, and the uninhibited exchange of ideas which she encouraged benefited many young writers and artists.

Some of the visitors Villiers met there were of course people whom he knew already: Catulle Mendès, Augusta Holmès, Paul Verlaine, François Coppée among others. But there were also many new faces, and some who were to become very dear to him. One of the most picturesque among them was the poet, humorist, and inventor Charles Cros.[10] A few years younger than Villiers, he was Nina's lover and consequently a regular presence in her *salon*, where he recited his verses, showed off his drawings, and discussed his latest gadgets. Eccentric though some of these were, others anticipated major scientific discoveries, and he is credited with having had the idea of a phonograph before Edison and with having perfected a system of colour photography. There is no doubt that his wide interests and unorthodox scientific curiosity helped to open Villiers's eyes to new horizons and to set his imagination working on those ideas of improbable inventions which inspired so much of his later work, the great science-fiction novel *L'Ève future* as well as a number of joyous pseudo-scientific fantasies.

Then there were the artists and musicians. Though Villiers

was less interested in the visual arts than were many contemporary men of letters, he did become friendly enough with Édouard Manet to borrow money from him, at a time when Manet was still a figure of scandal to right-thinking art critics.[11] Among the musicians were the eccentric Ernest Cabaner, who probably gave him the idea for his comic extravaganza *Le Secret de l'ancienne musique*, Charles de Sivry, Verlaine's brother-in-law, and Henry Ghys, whom Villiers later asked to write incidental music for his plays. It was probably also through Nina's *salon* that Villiers was first brought into contact with left-wing thought, which soon began to attract him. If he had hitherto confined himself to a somewhat distant allegiance to his family's traditional monarchism and to benevolent neutrality towards the Second Empire, he rapidly found himself adopting extreme revolutionary attitudes, certainly not out of doctrinaire approval of socialism, but because he relished the thought of a cataclysmic upheaval which would destroy the bourgeois-dominated order that he abominated with ever-increasing violence. There were occultists too in Nina's *salon*, including the famous Henri Delaage, the author of numerous books on spiritualism, who enjoyed the protection of the Church because his theories were thought helpful in combating materialism.

For many years Villiers remained faithful to Nina de Villard's *salon*, and even came to be regarded as the great man of the house, entitled to a seat of honour at table, immediately after Charles Cros who, as her recognized lover, sat on her right.[12] For Villiers, it was not only a place where he could relax and enjoy himself in cultured but unstuffy company, it was also a kind of asylum where, at times of distress and poverty, he was sure of finding affection and understanding as well as the food and shelter which he so often lacked. With his own tendency to bohemianism and nocturnal peregrinations, it was much more congenial to him than the more formal gatherings where he was never able to feel wholly at ease, and for a long time almost all his activities relate in some way or other to Nina and her group. His frequentation of them undoubtedly influenced his thought and writings as well as his way of life, making them more nonconformist, more disrespectful and more capricious, and that he was very conscious of his debt is shown by the nostalgic article he wrote in 1888, entitled *Une soirée chez Nina de Villard*, in which he magically evokes the charm of the long-defunct *salon*.[13]

It has sometimes been said that Villiers was Nina's lover and that he exploited her generosity. That he spent a lot of time in her house and profited amply from her hospitality is undeniable; it is also true that Charles Cros was not her only lover. Prodigal with her favours, she gave herself to a number of other men, including Edmond Bazire, Anatole France, and the painter Franc-Lamy, so it is perfectly possible that at some time or other, either before or after her break with Cros in 1877, she was Villiers's mistress. Villiers himself poured scorn on the idea that he had taken advantage of her kind heart, and years later George Moore heard him say: 'What a fuss about a few chops!'[14] Certainly there is no reason to postulate anything like a love-affair between them, and Nina was quite sufficiently beneficent towards needy writers for her to have provided Villiers with occasional board and lodging without his having to seduce her first.

In fact, by late in 1868 Villiers was probably involved in an affair with a minor actress called Mathilde Leroy. Though she had been born in Elberfeld in Germany in 1846, she was of Belgian origin, and had joined the company of the Théâtre du Vaudeville in Paris, where she apparently never graduated above the role of maidservant. Maybe she met Villiers through his theatrical connections; maybe she was introduced to him by the pianist and composer Charles de Sivry, in whose company she was to be seen in Paris twenty-five years later. At all events, she gave birth to an illegitimate son, officially registered as Jules-Émile but known as Robert, on 9 September 1869, when she was living in the rue du Départ in Montparnasse. Since the child was illegitimate, the birth certificate did not bear the father's name, so that there is no direct evidence that Villiers was responsible, other than Mathilde Leroy's own declarations after his death. But there is some proof that she was close to him at one time: Villiers recommended her to a theatre manager in 1880,[15] she owned the manuscript of a prose poem by Villiers, Charles de Sivry believed her to have been his friend, and in 1895 she had no difficulty in convincing Léon Bloy that she really had had a child by Villiers. The son emigrated to the Belgian Congo in 1890, and returned to Europe twenty years later, dying in Brussels in 1911; Mathilde had died seven years earlier. There was also a grandson named André, born of Robert and a native mother; he was still alive and living on an island in the delta of the Congo in 1957. It is possible that this half-caste was the last of the Villiers de l'Isle-Adams, but the whole business is shrouded in such mystery that the truth will doubtless never be known. But even if Mathilde Leroy was briefly Villiers's mistress, it is unlikely that she occupied a large place in his life, since, apart from the 1880 letter, she is mentioned neither in his correspondence nor by any of the numerous friends who wrote reminiscences of him.[16]

In the meantime Villiers was working at two new projects. One was the play *La Révolte*, the idea of which had come to him as a result of his abortive experiment in the manner of the bourgeois drama, *La Tentation*. His intention this time was to keep outwardly to the style of a modern social play, while infiltrating into it an idealistic philosophy diametrically opposed to the bourgeois way of thought, and even designed to destroy it. This extension of the oblique manner already adopted in *Claire Lenoir* was a dangerous policy for the stage, where innovation in the face of entrenched convention is never easy, particularly when audiences are as sure of what they want as they were in the Second Empire. But Villiers had learnt his lesson from his failure to interest theatre managers in *Elën* and *Morgane*, and was determined to ensure that *La Révolte* was produced, both by pretending to conform to the theatrical norms of the day and by not allowing too much to become known about the play until he had found a taker for it. He went to Dumas *fils* for advice, and the playwright took the manuscript of *La Révolte* off to Puys, a fishing village near Dieppe where he owned two villas. Dumas's reaction to the play was very favourable, but he urged Villiers to discretion, begging him not to announce its performance until it was officially accepted. Dumas promised to read the manuscript to his friend Montigny, manager of the Théâtre du Gymnase, one of the most prosperous and prestigious theatres in Paris, where all his own plays were produced. The letter he sent Villiers in July 1869 concludes: 'In my opinion, your play is excellent. It will be produced, I promise you, but don't take too much notice of over-hasty friends. I shall be very happy to have it dedicated to me, and even more happy when it has the success that I once again forecast for you.'[17] So for the time being Villiers was obliged to curb his natural impetuousness and possess his soul in patience.

The other work, however, was something he succeeded in getting into print in a most unexpected place. This was a longish short story called *Azraël* (later retitled *L'Annonciateur*), which appeared on 26 June 1869 in *La Liberté*. *La Liberté* was one of the most influential and respectable of Parisian daily newspapers, and not at all the kind of journal in which one would expect to find some of Villiers's most ornate and idiosyncratic prose. Always inclined to a grandiose and elaborate style, Villiers has let himself go completely in *Azraël*, which is a variation on the old legend of the man who, seeing the Angel of Death approach, flees to the ends of the earth, only to discover that that is where the Angel was predestined to find him. But this simple anecdote is heavily overlaid with stylistic and linguistic decoration, so that one is far more conscious of external artifice than of any philosophic message, the more so as the tale has been set in Solomon's palace, which provides a pretext for a bizarre display of pseudo-Hebraic vocabulary. It is hardly surprising that Émile de Girardin, the magnate who owned *La Liberté*, did not invite Villiers to become a regular contributor. Indeed, the whole episode ended in embarrassment for Mendès, who had somehow managed to persuade the paper to accept the story, when M. Garcias, the boarding-house keeper, tried to stop Villiers receiving his fee because of his unpaid bills.[18]

But though this caused a brief unpleasantness between the two men, Mendès and Judith Gautier were in fact preparing to assist Villiers to what was to be one of the culminating experiences of his life as an artist: a meeting with Richard Wagner.[19] In 1868 Judith had written an adulatory letter to the composer, and, after a further exchange of correspondence, she had published in *La Liberté* a sort of manifesto which Wagner had sent her, together with an enthusiastic article on *Rienzi*, which was about to be performed at the Théâtre Lyrique. Villiers himself dedicated *Azraël* in the same newspaper to 'Richard Wagner, the prince of profound music', so clearly there was a concerted campaign afoot to try to persuade the recalcitrant public of Wagner's greatness. However, Wagner enthusiasts in France were severely hampered in their enjoyment of the master's music by the fact that, apart from *Tannhäuser* in 1861 and the untypical *Rienzi*, no complete Wagner opera had been performed in Paris, and only extracts were to be heard in concerts. To get a true idea of his art in all its amplitude, it was therefore necessary to go abroad, and in 1869 the incentive suddenly became greater with the news that the first performance of *Das Rheingold*, the introductory part of the still uncompleted *Ring*, was to be given in Munich by order of King Ludwig II of Bavaria, Wagner's royal patron, but against the wishes of the composer, who was bitterly opposed to any partial performance of his tetralogy. For Villiers, Catulle, and Judith, the problem was naturally one of finance: their own resources were insufficient, and the French press was so hostile to Wagner that there was little prospect of their being hired to report on his new opera. Happily, Catulle and Judith hit on the idea of offering their services as art critics for the Great Exhibition of painting which was to be held in Munich at the same time, and the three of them set about persuading editors to part with their money. At the same time Judith ascertained from Wagner that he would be willing to receive them at Tribschen, near Lucerne, where he was living at the time.

Villiers's excitement at this double change in his fortunes must have been intense. Not only was he about to have a play produced, but he was going to have the rare privilege of meeting the artist whom he most admired in the world. The setbacks he had suffered were forgotten: a new world was opening up before him.

10

The journalist Émile Bergerat came across the three would-be travellers at about this time, sitting in the waiting-room to the offices of the newspaper *Le Gaulois*, where Armand Gouzien had promised to try to obtain a subsidy for them. They were talking about their pilgrimage with great animation, and Villiers was the most voluble of the three: 'He could not keep still and leapt from one bench to another with the attitudes of a squirrel trying to crack a nut that someone wants to take from him'.[1] In the end Edmond Tarbé, the editor, came out with their railway passes and wished them *bon voyage*. The same scene must have been repeated in a number of newspapers, and by mid-July they had put together a respectable collection of commissions for articles—Catulle and Judith with greater ease than Villiers because they both already had a certain reputation as reporters on the arts, whereas Villiers's experience of such journalism was minimal. But he did succeed, again thanks to Gouzien, in extracting a promise of acceptance of five hundred lines from *L'Universel*, a not very prominent left-wing 'journal of agriculture, commerce, and industry', and vaguer indications of interest from *Le Rappel*, another radical organ, and the magazine *La Vogue parisienne*.[2]

In mid-July the pilgrims,[3] by now in a state of wild exaltation, set off by train for Switzerland. Their first stop was Basle, where Villiers, who had never been out of France before, was vastly intrigued by the steep streets leading down to the Rhine, the picturesque old houses with storks nesting on the chimneys, and the sound of a male-voice choir singing Wagner in a café.[4] The next day they travelled on to Lucerne, where Wagner was awaiting them on the platform, wearing a straw hat and exuding an impression of scarcely contained nervous energy.[5] After a highly emotive welcome, he took them off to the Hôtel du Lac, where rooms had been reserved for them, and returned to his villa at Tribschen to prepare to receive them. After changing, the French guests hired a boat to ferry them across the lake, and spent the evening with Wagner and Cosima von Bülow, Liszt's daughter, who had left her husband Hans von Bülow to devote herself to the composer. Their delight at such a cordial reception knew no bounds—or at least only those of hunger, since they were offered only tea and little biscuits, and arrived back at the hotel too late for dinner.

The next nine days were spent in close intimacy with the

Wagners, every evening from five o'clock onwards and sometimes during the day too, with the master discussing his music with them, playing the piano, explaining his current work on *Siegfried*, offering them pieces of manuscript, expounding his philosophy, and generally doing all in his considerable power to subjugate them completely to his service. He even insisted that they should all go off on a long excursion together to the Axenstein and Zug, where, to everyone's joy and astonishment, Villiers won a prize in the Swiss federal shooting championships, an exploit which covered him with pride and confusion.[6] Judith got on particularly well with Cosima, and Villiers, in his letters to Marras, was scarcely able to give coherent expression to his delight at being with Wagner:

He's an irresistible man. He never speaks ill of anyone, but he has a terrifying smile when he is scornful. He talks all the time, then he stops and listens, with his gaze on another world, and so *naturally* and so *calmly* that one is transfixed. (. . .) He has a piano which is a human soul, an orchestra, something incomparable: when he plays the prelude to *Lohengrin*, it's worse than the orchestra, it's more amazing than any instruments one can think of.[7]

The sessions of Wagnerian music sent them into ecstasies, and left them emotionally exhausted:

We have to tear him away from the piano (what a piano! muffled, sonorous, deep, billowy, magical, a crystal gong, a storm, a thunderclap, and so gentle, a divine whisper when he wishes!) We have to say to him: enough! because, after two hours, we are *really ill*. It's no longer a piano and a voice: it's a vision: the orchestra means nothing with him. One can't go any further, and we all start weeping and gambolling around the house.[8]

Villiers was naturally eager to please the master and made French puns to him, vaunted Hegel in their philosophical arguments, climbed trees with him, and played with his dog Russ. He had the impression that Wagner approved: 'I think I'm in his good books and that he likes me a bit, as I love him, as we all love him.'[9] In fact, overwhelmed by the occasion, he was behaving in an even more eccentric fashion than usual, and the Wagners were far from appreciating all his inexplicable oddities. When Villiers bruised his hand on the teeth of the dog Russ, he turned pale and insisted on being cauterized in Lucerne, which displeased Wagner, who, the next day, pretended to run away from him, shouting: 'He's got rabies! He's got rabies! Don't bite me!'[10] When he and Cosima tried to fathom Villiers's character by consulting his works, the result was not much better, and Cosima noted in her diary on 20 July: 'This morning, I read something of the books of young Villiers: not much that is edifying, a lot of strangeness.'[11] Catulle and Judith, more polished, more ingratiating, more tactful, were much more to their taste, especially as Judith showed great sympathy with Cosima's irregular marital situation.

But on the evening before their departure, Villiers had a surprise for the Wagners: a reading from the manuscript of *La Révolte*. Incoherent though his conversation may have been, he was usually an admirable reader, and on this occasion excelled himself. Judith Gautier noted: 'In a clear and well-regulated voice, he brought out the full value of the text with consummate art, and set the feelings and characters into relief quite remarkably.'[12] His audience listened in respectful silence, which Villiers took for unalloyed admiration, and he explained to them that Élisabeth, the heroine, was 'a female Prometheus, whose liver was being eaten by a goose'. But once the Wagners had got back to their room, they admitted that their real opinion was more mixed, as Cosima's diary reveals: 'The same man who we thought had no talent at all has found in reality the starting-point for a good play which he read to us with fabulous skill. In it, there are at least some situations, said Richard, and bad as they are, they do provide a picture.'[13] Still, a few days later, Cosima was much more complimentary when writing to Judith:

I must tell you that we have talked about M. de Villiers's play, and that we were agreed on the immense talent it reveals; it seems certain to me that, if the author casts on the ideal world, the world which is true because it is never real, the penetrating gaze which he has turned on the existing world, and if he has the ability to evoke characters as living as those which he presented to us, he is a very great poet. To look on ideal creatures in the way in which he has looked on the figures of our own society, that is what I should like to see him achieve.[14]

Though such praise seems to be based on the mistaken belief that *La Révolte* is an ordinary realistic bourgeois drama, Villiers must have been overjoyed by it, and he certainly took the Wagners' advice very much to heart.

When the travellers left for Munich on 25 July, Villiers was still exulting over his triumph the previous night: 'Hey! how he listened! . . . what an audience! . . . And how well I acted!'[15] Once they were installed in the Bavarian capital, they were introduced to various other Wagnerian fanatics, notably Hans Richter, who was due to conduct *Das Rheingold*, Franz Servais, a Belgian musician, and Édouard Schuré, who was to write some of the most important books about Wagner in French. At first they stayed in a hotel, but then they took rooms in the Maximilianstrasse, since the première of the opera was not scheduled until 29 August. In the meantime, in addition to attending a wide range of Wagner's other operas and participating in the social life of the city, they had to think about their articles in earnest. Fluent and practised, Catulle and Judith shot off a stream of travel notes and art criticism. Villiers was much less productive. By 1 August, he had sent to *L'Universel* an article on 'Richard Wagner à Lucerne', which was turned down and has never been found,[16] and a review of the Exhibition, which appeared on the ninth.[17] In addition, on 13 August *La Vogue parisienne* printed a short complimentary notice of Judith Gautier's recently published novel *Le Dragon impérial*.[18] A second review of the Exhibition, which resolves itself mainly into sketches of Munich, was to appear in *Le Rappel* on 21 August, having presumably been rejected by *L'Universel*.[19] The fact is that Villiers was privately bored by the paintings he saw,[20] and his boredom is all too visible in the articles, in which the general considerations on art are largely borrowed from Baudelaire.

Other occupations apart from this desultory writing included a tour to Nuremberg and Innsbruck, and regular attendance at rehearsals of *Das Rheingold*, to which they were admitted on Wagner's instructions. Villiers was bowled over by the majesty of the spectacle and the music: 'magnificent', 'sublime', 'frightening', and 'vertiginous' are the sort of epithets he uses in his letters to Marras.[21] The memory of

Wagner too was still glowing in his mind, and Villiers often lingered on the thought of the man who, in his eyes, was 'something like visible immortality, the other world become transparent, creative power carried to a fantastic degree, and at the same time, the sweat and the radiance of genius, the impression of the infinite around his head and in the naïve depths of his eyes. *He is terrifying.*'[22] Thanks to the Munich Wagnerians, they were all invited to a gala soirée given by the Countess von Schleinitz, wife of the Prussian minister, with Franz Liszt among the guests, which enabled Judith to start trying to reconcile him with his daughter Cosima, with whom he had broken off relations because of her liaison with Wagner. At the same evening Villiers was presented to the Countess Kalergis-Muchanoff, whose alabaster shoulders had inspired Théophile Gautier's famous 'Symphonie en blanc majeur'. She was so impressed by what Villiers told her of *La Révolte* at Tribschen that she at once asked him to read it in her drawing-room the following evening, which he accepted with alacrity, scenting the possibility of a new triumph.

But when the great moment arrived, things turned out very differently. With his hair curled like an astrakhan bonnet (a habit which had greatly alarmed the Wagners) and an enormous Cross of Malta on his chest, Villiers stood nervously by the grand piano waiting to begin. At first the reading went well, and the distinguished audience was captivated. But suddenly Villiers stopped in alarm, dropped his manuscript, unfastened the belt on his trousers, and jumped on to the piano with his legs dangling. Shock and consternation fell upon the guests; they did not know that, when Villiers had palpitations, he regarded it as a sovereign remedy to loosen his clothing and sit with his feet swinging in mid-air. His companions were much mortified by this strange spectacle, and, after he had gone, Servais exclaimed: 'Only one thing could have saved the situation, there could only have been one excuse for Villiers: death! . . . Yes, for the honour of all of us, he should have died!'[23]

In the meantime, though the early rehearsals of *Das Rheingold* had gone well, trouble arose at the dress rehearsal on 27 August, when the settings turned out to be a disaster.

Warning telegrams were sent to Wagner, Richter refused to conduct the work, and the theatre manager sacked him on the spot. Wagner himself then arrived incognito, and after a lot of argument it was agreed that the première should be put off until 21 September, after which Wagner returned, somewhat molli-fied, to Tribschen.[24] But the French visitors were rapidly running out of funds and could not wait much longer. On 13 September they left Munich and paid a second visit to Tribschen, along with Servais; Richter was already there, and the whole party joined in playing charades. Finally, on 18 September, they bade farewell to the Wagners and departed, having spent a total of sixteen days in the master's company and having thus acquired an insight into his work and his personality which had been vouchsafed to no other Frenchmen.

By then Villiers had composed his account of *Das Rheingold*, and it finally appeared in *L'Universel* on 21 September, preceded by a chilly editorial note disclaiming responsibility for the views expressed in it.[25] Villiers, well aware that Wagner's music had suffered in France because it was believed to be the cacophonous product of abstruse theorizing, carefully refrains from any abstractions and confines himself to trying to recreate for the reader the effect of being present at a performance. This he does by evoking the atmosphere of the darkened theatre and narrating the action of the work, interspersed with lyrical effusions—to very good effect. Here is how he presents the climax:

Freed now from the fear of the giants, the gods prepare to enter into their abode. The god of lightning begins a song of triumph, the stage is enshrouded in clouds, flashes zigzag through the harmony and tear into the heavy drums with great clashes of thunder, the storm runs through the violas and the brass; and the trumpet notes, borne off on the tempest of the violins like leaves torn away on the mountain-tops, whirl through space. The clouds clear, revealing the gods again. At their feet the rainbow leading from Earth to Valhalla curves away, radiant with sublime colours. Far off, in the distant sunset, there appear the towers of the immortal edifice, and Wotan, Frigga, Loge, Froh, Donner, Freya, the melancholy gods, walk ecstatically along the rainbow and make for the dwelling which they have wrested from the force of the world.

Villiers himself was very pleased with his piece, and wrote to

Marras: 'It's the best thing I've done, and it will please you, I promise.' He even intended to build a book on Wagner around it, a project which, alas, never came to anything.[26]

When the little group had left Tribschen, Catulle and Judith accepted an invitation to visit Brussels with Servais, and on 2 October they dined with Victor Hugo at the Hôtel du Grand Miroir.[27] But, though Villiers would dearly have loved to accompany them to meet the exiled poet, he had *La Révolte* to think about, and deemed it wiser to stay in Paris. On his return there, he had been saddened and discouraged to learn that Montigny of the Gymnase was making difficulties and wanted him to write a new scene for the play, which he was reluctant to do, unless Dumas thought it necessary. A comic letter to Mendès written in dog-Latin late in September informed him that a young lady named Clarisse was helping him to forget his anger about Montigny, but that he was hoping to join his friends in Belgium.[28] It is not known whether he did so, but it is quite likely that financial stringency prevented him. Indeed, a short time later, after Catulle and Judith got back, he was embarrassed when they saw him in the street in a new suit, new gloves, and a new shirt, and felt constrained to write to explain that, although he knew full well he owed them a thousand or two francs, he was not wasting his money but needed to be well-dressed for his 'business': 'I've seen ruin staring me in the face, and that has changed me somewhat; now I have an idea of what I am doing in the struggle.' Whether the promise in this contorted rigmarole that he would share his purse as soon as he had anything in it appeased Mendès is doubtful: lending money to Villiers was at best a risky business, and good intentions came more easily to him than restitution. On this occasion he clearly felt positive guilt, though there is some truth in the excuse he proffered: 'You know that what I lacked in Munich was not the desire to work, but the possibility of putting my work to any useful purpose.'[29]

Still, Dumas had a lot of influence over Montigny and was prepared to stake his reputation on getting *La Révolte* produced, so Villiers continued to harbour strong hopes with the Théâtre du Gymnase, despite the manager's hesitations. But, some time in October or November 1869, negotiations finally broke down, either because Villiers refused to make the alterations Montigny wanted, or because Montigny had come to the conclusion that the play was too harsh and too unusual for his public. For some time Dumas tried in vain to interest other managers in it, until it occurred to him to try a new tactic. This was to offer the leading role in the play to the famous actress Anaïs Fargueil, who worked at the Théâtre du Vaudeville. The Vaudeville was going through a lean time, with manager succeeding manager, and Dumas obviously hoped that, if Mlle Fargueil liked the part, her prestige would be sufficient to persuade the latest incumbent to put it on. The tactic was partly successful, in that Mlle Fargueil, who was used to acting in popular drama, was very impressed by the play and decided that Élisabeth was one of the major roles of the modern theatre, but unfortunately, Harmant, the new manager, was less convinced and hesitated just as Montigny had done.

So in January 1870 Dumas lost patience and wrote Villiers a letter designed to be communicated to the press, in which, after a few digs at Montigny, he threatened to take the play away from Harmant altogether. Villiers promptly passed the letter on to François Oswald, a friend who wrote the theatrical gossip column for *Le Gaulois*, where it was inserted on 20 January, with flattering commentaries. The letter itself is as forthright as it is cunning:

My dear friend,
I find the play excellent, superior, original, true, sound, and *novel.* It will be produced, *I promise you.* Do not worry about the obstacles. As he lay dying, Parny said to his nephew: 'Nephew, stupidity covers the world.'
Your play does indeed, as you say, lie outside all the conventions of the theatre; but this time it is an important experiment, which makes it all the more interesting. Do not change *anything!* The rehearsals will suffice to put a few details right. If, from the point of view of traditional theatre, a manager may raise objections on the grounds of this or that stage practice, do not give in. You are right from the point of view of ideas, and, as far as dramatic technique is concerned, the play is extremely solidly constructed.
I am going to take it myself to Mlle Fargueil.
Do not be impatient. If it does not suit her (which I cannot believe), I shall go to the Théâtre Français. If the Théâtre Français

does not like it, I shall go to the Odéon. In short, I shall do all that I can do and have to do for a work which I admire and which must see the light of day.

Believe me, what I am doing for you is something I find so agreeable that you can never be more grateful to me than I am myself.

Yours,
Dumas *fils*.[30]

Such a vehement open letter from the man who was indisputably the leading figure in the contemporary theatre cannot have failed to create a stir, the more so as Mlle Fargueil had obviously already been enlisted on Dumas's side.

The effects were sufficiently rapid for Villiers to write on 26 January to a creditor that things were going well for him and that he was due to give a reading a day or two later.[31] About the same time Villiers met a friendly journalist in Nina de Villard's *salon* who agreed to insert, over his own name, a brief note which the author himself had written, in the hope that this would clinch the deal and ensure that rehearsals began immediately. The note shows what Villiers valued most highly in *La Révolte:* 'It appears that *La Révolte* is a remarkably abrasive and novel play; we may expect to be given emotions of a quite abnormal kind.—The author of *Azraël* and *Morgane* is a poet and a hard worker; the play is bound to be living and audacious.'[32] But despite these pressures, Harmant was not to be hurried, and it took a further visit from Villiers towards the end of February before he at last overcame his hesitations and undertook to put the play on at the Vaudeville.

However, even when rehearsals had begun, no decision had been taken about the date when the play would actually be produced. *La Révolte* being a one-acter, though a relatively long one, it could not constitute a programme on its own; equally, it could only fit into a normal evening's entertainment with another work which was reasonably short. By 21 March, according to the faithful Oswald in *Le Gaulois*, all that had happened was that a plan to put it on with Théodore Barrière's *L'Héritage de M. Plumet* had been scrapped, because it would have meant making cuts in

Barrière's play, to which the actresses had objected strenuously.

At this point, with the play in rehearsal but with no signs of an imminent production, a new distraction arose through Villiers's continuing preoccupation with Wagner. It was announced that the Théâtre de la Monnaie in Brussels was going for the first time to produce *Lohengrin* in French, so that the three pilgrims of Tribschen at once decided to make the journey, apparently in the company of Charles de Sivry, and they all took a box at the première on 22 March.[33] By this time the coolness between Villiers and Mendès arising from the money problems in Munich had dissipated, and, when in February Mendès had nearly fought a duel with Hector de Callias over an imagined insult to Judith, Villiers had been quick to leap to his support.[34] Equally, Mendès and Judith were eager to incite Villiers to produce more—in July 1869 he had written to a friend: 'Villiers worries me. He talks too much and doesn't write enough.'[35] Both of them therefore supported any venture which seemed likely to result in something by Villiers being published. So the joint journey to Brussels was as much a way of getting more articles on Wagner in print as it was a way of seeing *Lohengrin* again (they had already seen it in Munich the previous year).

With the practised efficiency of professional journalists, Catulle and Judith had their reviews in the press on 26 March, Catulle's in a little satirical weekly called *Le Diable*, and Judith's in *La Liberté*. As usual it took much longer for Villiers to be satisfied with his prose, and, by the time it appeared on 6 April, the article was more than a little out of date, which can hardly have pleased the newspaper which had commissioned it. This was *Le Citoyen*, a newly-founded republican socialist daily where Villiers considered himself to be 'of some authority',[36] no doubt thanks to his friends on the extreme left, to which he had been leaning more and more, as we shall see. The article, long and dithyrambic, follows the same pattern as that on *Das Rheingold*: a narrative of the action of the opera, with impressionistic comments on the music, all in a carefully wrought and highly literary style, in which particular attention is lavished on the evocation of the prelude, doubtless in emulation of Baudelaire's famous paraphrase in his essay on Wagner. The conclusion is emphatic: 'To sum up, Richard Wagner has definitively won, in Belgium, the title that he will bear in the eyes of universal posterity, alongside the shades of Sebastian Bach and Beethoven.'

No doubt the trip was a very short one, since Villiers was anxious to put as much pressure as he could on the dilatory Harmant. This he did with the help of his friend and spokesman Oswald, who inserted the following note in *Le Gaulois* on 7 April: 'And what about M. Villiers de l'Isle-Adam's *Révolte*? It seems to me that by now the actors must know this much-praised play backwards. Surely M. Harmant will not be so cruel as to wait until the middle of July before putting on this first work by a young man who, according to M. Dumas *fils*, is so full of promise?' New but vague undertakings were forthcoming: *La Révolte* would be produced at the end of the month. In the meantime Villiers and his associates intensified their publicity campaign, even though the première was postponed yet again. On 3 May Oswald announced (interestingly but wrongly) that Wagner had sent some incidental music, and Mlle Fargueil gave an enthusiastic interview—she is even said to have declared: 'It's not *La Révolte*, it's the Revolution!'[37] On the day of the première Mendès trumpeted in *Le Diable*: 'Everywhere and in every age *La Révolte* will send a shiver down the spine of all those who hear it (. . .) The success will be immense and unanimous.'

Inevitably Villiers shared this opinion. If the public had not applauded *Elën* and *Morgane*, that was only because no theatre manager had been able to see what jewels they were. Now that *La Révolte* had been successfully read in private and publicly acclaimed by the most prominent living dramatist and one of the most popular actresses of the day, how could it possibly fail to delight the audience, the more so as it had been deliberately designed to fit in with the public's prejudices (at least outwardly) and had been elaborated with almost unbelievable meticulousness through no fewer than eight revisions?[38] Moreover, arrangements had been put in hand in March to have an edition of two thousand copies, a remarkably high number for a one-act play, published by

Lemerre, the regular publisher of the Parnassian poets, immediately after the première.[39] There can have been no doubt in Villiers's mind that he was at long last about to enjoy that vast triumph for which he had been thirsting ever since he had decided to devote himself to literature. To understand why things did not turn out like that, it is necessary to look not only at *La Révolte* itself, but at Villiers's reputation with the middle-class public and critics in 1870.

11

The action of *La Révolte* is simplicity itself. It begins with the businessman Félix going through his accounts one evening with his wife Élisabeth, who acts as his book-keeper. But, when the sound of a carriage is heard outside, she lays down her pen and announces that she is about to leave him—not with a lover, but alone, because her aspirations towards the ideal have been crushed by the materialistic, money-grubbing life he has forced her to lead. In the face of his stupefied incomprehension, she launches into an impassioned lyrical tirade in favour of dreams:

To dream is, first of all, to forget the omnipotence of inferior minds a thousand times more abject than Stupidity! It is to block one's ears to the irremediable cries of the eternal victims! It is to forget the humiliations which each one undergoes and everyone inflicts, and which you call social life! It is to forget those so-called duties which revolt one's conscience and which are nothing but the love of those base and immediate interests in the name of which it is permissible to ignore the misery of the disinherited! It is to contemplate, in one's secret thoughts, an occult world of which the external world is hardly even the reflection! . . . It is to strengthen the invincible hope in death, already imminent! It is to recover possession of oneself in the Imperishable! It is to feel oneself alone but eternal! It is to love ideal Beauty, freely, as the rivers run to the sea! And the other pastimes and duties are not worth a farthing in these accursed times in which I am forced to live. In the end, to dream is to die; but at least it is to die in silence and with a little bit of heaven in one's eyes![1]

Overcome, Félix faints as she goes out, and remains unconscious while the clock moves on several hours. Then, as dawn breaks. Élisabeth returns and in a pathetic monologue explains that, once alone, she had realized that it was already too late and that her soul had been destroyed by living with Félix. She sits down at her desk again, and when her husband comes to, endures his reproachful gloating in dutiful silence. The play ends with her looking at him 'with infinite compassion and melancholy' and saying: 'Poor man!'[2]

Though *La Révolte* has a modern middle-class setting and begins with domestic dialogue about financial matters, that is patently all it has in common with the social drama of the Second Empire. Its whole philosophy is indeed designed to subvert and condemn those very values that underpinned the society which dramatists like Dumas *fils* and Augier were depicting and for which they were acting as spokesmen. Elisabeth's torrential eloquence transcends by far the sort of marital problems which such playwrights so frequently treated: what is at issue is not the status of the married woman or what a good husband's duties and obligations are, but rather a symbolic confrontation between the ideal and the real, in which the whole basis of bourgeois society is rejected out of hand. It has been well said of Dumas *fils* that he 'shocks and reassures at the same time, but he reassures even more than he shocks',[3] and the same is true of all the successful practitioners of social drama in mid-nineteenth-century France. But Villiers has not the slightest intention of reassuring: quite the contrary. He is one of those writers to whom Félix refers with such distaste, and who only seek 'to upset decent people, by giving them emotions of some almost dangerous kind',[4] and *La Révolte* is the earliest and most distinguished forerunner of the idealist theatre of the 1880s and 1890s.

That *La Révolte* is a minor masterpiece is corroborated by its frequent revivals in recent times and its permanent presence in the repertoire of the Comédie Française, but it flies so hard in the face of everything that Second Empire theatre-goers stood for that they could hardly have been expected to take it to their hearts. It is a thoroughly uncomfortable work, as it is meant to be; an audience which valued its mental and material well-being above all else was not going to appreciate seeing itself humiliated and insulted in the person of Félix. The patronage of Dumas *fils* only added to the shock: what was he doing supporting a play so foreign to his normal tendencies?[5]

To those qualities in *La Révolte* inherently unlikely to endear it to a contemporary public must be added those features of Villiers's own reputation which singled him out as a dangerous man, to be discouraged and kept in order at all costs. Quite apart from his aristocratic name and his personal foibles, there were three things about him which were likely to alienate the sympathies of the ordinary theatre audience. The first of these is that he was avowedly a Parnassian, and that *La Révolte* was a deliberate attempt to translate certain aspects of Parnassianism on to the stage, notably its hatred of commercialism and its love of beautiful language. But to the man in the street, in so far as he was aware of them, the Parnassians were a haughty and pedantic bunch, much given to talking over the heads of ordinary folk and imbued with an excessive sense of their own importance. The fact that so many Parnassians took up the cudgels on behalf of *La Révolte* only exacerbated matters: if they saw in the play the first serious attempt to conquer the theatre in their name, their adversaries realized all too well that this was the thin end of the wedge. So much propaganda had been produced in its favour that Francisque Sarcey, the most influential bourgeois critic of the time, was clear that it was 'the manifesto of a school which is a great nuisance and which plays on the credulity of young people',[6] and he was not entirely wrong in his assessment. Those who disliked Parnassianism were therefore predisposed to dislike *La Révolte*.

Secondly, there was Villiers's well-publicized adherence to the Wagnerian cause. Wagner's name was still anathema to music critics and the average music-lover, and anyone who expressed public support for him was automatically thought to belong to some lunatic fringe. Just as the Parnassians were thought to want to do away with all the decent, comprehensible literature of the past and present, so Wagner was thought to want to do away with all decent, comprehensible music, and Villiers's name was high on the list of his notorious adherents. After his article on *Lohengrin* in April, Francis Magnard of *Le Figaro* had poured vituperative scorn on him:

Do you know why Richard Wagner, *Lohengrin*, and all the rest can never become acclimatized in France? It is because of the fanatics who have espoused his cause. After M. et Mme Mendès, M. Villiers de l'Isle-Adam wants to celebrate the famous prelude of *Lohengrin*, and he does so in terms of incomparable obscurity.

Magnard gives some tendentious quotations, and then concludes, more aptly than he knew: 'Music which specializes in producing processions of *ineffable* seraphim in the *immarcessible* azure (an old word meaning incorruptible)[7] has little chance of success in a time dominated by interests and entirely terrestrial passions.'[8] The rumour that Wagner had composed incidental music for *La Révolte* was the last straw. Those who detested Wagner were all set to detest *La Révolte*.

Finally, there was the suspicion that Villiers was a wild revolutionary. This was based not only on his friendship with left-wing figures and his contributions to left-wing journals; the figures were not well known and the contributions non-political. It arose also from the incredible events in which Villiers had been implicated a few months earlier when Prince Pierre Bonaparte, the Emperor's cousin, had shot and killed a republican journalist named Victor Noir who had gone with a friend to challenge him to a duel with Paschal Grousset, another journalist. Villiers was a friend of Noir, and on 10 January 1870, the day of his murder, was present when the body was brought back to the house where he lived. Horrified at what had happened, Villiers conceived the extraordinary project of starting an insurrection by taking the body through the streets of Paris, as the February Revolution in 1848 had been started by wheeling a cartload of corpses through the working-class areas. But, in order to get past the police, Villiers suggested that they should take a carriage, prop the corpse up on the front seat with a cigar clamped between its teeth, and drive out as though they were all going to a party. His plan was not adopted, but, given the popular indignation at the killing of a defenceless young man by a member of the Imperial family, it was not entirely fanciful. Indeed, when the funeral took place a couple of days later, there was an immense gathering of two hundred thousand people, and it would only have required a spark to ignite a conflagration. On this occasion too Villiers was very much to

the fore: the papers mentioned his presence at the windows of
Noir's house with members of the family as the cortège wound
past, and identified him at a later stage of the proceedings as one
of the pallbearers.[9] For Villiers to have figured so prominently
in a case which attracted vast publicity must have made many
people view him with great alarm: the political situation was
tense, both internally and externally, and here was a man
apparently ready and willing to start a revolution. For him then
to produce a play entitled, of all things, *La Révolte* was
bound to appear an act of foolhardy provocation.

   With all these factors counting against him, the success of *La
Révolte*, had he but known it, was very far indeed from being
assured. Many years later Catulle Mendès remembered the first
night on 6 May 1870: 'The play was performed in deep silence
from the auditorium (. . .) and drew to its close amid
astonishment and total incomprehension.'[10] When he found
himself alone with Jean Marras, Villiers could no longer contain
himself and broke down in tears.[11] The reviews made matters
even worse, though there was a sharp division of opinion among
the critics. Some of them, especially the Parnassians, praised it
to the skies. For Théodore de Banville, 'this terrible and sincere
and violent play' had 'burst on the world like a furious
thunderstorm'.[12] Other friends, Mendès,[13] Anatole France,[14]
Camille Pelletan,[15] Ernest d'Hervilly,[16] were equally laudatory, and Gautier, more cautiously, pronounced it
promising.[17] A few were hesitant, such as Arthur Ranc[18] and
Jules Claretie, who had been put off by Villiers's friends
exclaiming: 'You don't understand, it's as good as Shakespeare!' and 'It's sublime!'[19] But the majority, including most of
the great daily newspapers, were slashingly hostile—'insane',
'insignificant', 'pretentious', 'an enigma'. Edmond Tarbé of *Le
Gaulois*, like Claretie, attributed the play's failure in part to the
excessive claims made for it by the author's friends: 'Thanks to
them, the twenty Parnassians who were trying to obstruct the
corridors of the Vaudeville will make their friend pass for a
martyr, a victim of bourgeois cretinism'.[20] Seeing his worst
fears realized, Harmant took *La Révolte* off after only five
performances. Villiers's total share of the proceedings was
thirty francs.[21] It was the end of a dream.

   Yet with that extraordinary resilience which characterized

him, Villiers refused to take his defeat lying down, even though it scarred him for the rest of his life. He halted the publication of the play until he had time to write a superb, blistering preface in which he excoriated his critics and thanked his defenders. It is indeed noteworthy that the latter category included names like Wagner, Banville, Gautier, Leconte de Lisle, Dumas *fils*, Franz Liszt, Mendès, and Anatole France, whereas the detractors are almost completely forgotten. The exception is Barbey d'Aurevilly, one of the most flamboyant survivors of high Romanticism, who in many ways seems almost like an elder brother of Villiers. His hatred of anything which smacked of Parnassianism had led him to a wounding attack: 'M. Villiers de l'Isle-Adam! What a great name to do such little things!'[22] One can only subscribe to Villiers's judgement: 'How sad it is to see a wolf trying to bray with the asses!'[23] The climax of the preface is a resounding declaration of faith in the rebirth of serious drama in France: 'So justice will be done!—And we have the time to wait . . . Besides, what do we care even about justice? He who does not, from birth, carry his own glory in his heart will never know the meaning of the word'.[24] Even more than the play itself, the preface is a declaration of war on the theatrical routine of the day, and from then on Villiers was to devote much time and energy to satirizing and ridiculing popular plays and dramatists. His attitude to the theatre itself changed too. He had viewed *La Révolte* as the first attempt to break away from the stultifying conventions of the 'well-made' play, with its stereotyped characters, tawdry stage tricks, and predictable dialogue, and replace it by a drama of ideas. Now that the play had proved such a failure, he was no longer sure that it was worthwhile trying to change the ingrained habits of managers, public and critics; perhaps it was better to forget about performance and concentrate on writing for the theatre of the mind. Yet he never ceased to be haunted by his childhood vision of a stupendous success on the stage, with a consequent wavering in his attitude. The consequences of the dismal and undeserved fate of *La Révolte* were to echo through his works for the rest of his life.[25]

It is possible that they began immediately to affect a work which Villiers had started some time in 1869, after his return from Germany and Switzerland, although nothing of it was revealed to the public for several years. This was *Axël,* the vast symbolic drama that became the centre of his preoccupations and his most deeply cherished book for the rest of his life. Into it he was to put the distillation of all his thought, all his experience, and all his feelings, so that it became a kind of *Summa,* destined never to reach its definitive form but a constant companion for him, even at (or particularly at) the darkest moments of his existence. Constantly revised, rewritten, and altered over the next twenty years, in his eyes *Axël* was to be a mission and a justification, not merely another work eventually to be added to the list of his publications. It is probably to the first part of the first version of the play that he was referring when, late in 1869, he wrote to Mendès: 'I have written a new act, quite good, in *two scenes.* I shall read it on Saturday at Delisle's [*sic*].'[26] Xavier de Ricard later remembered hearing a reading of part of *Axël* in Leconte de Lisle's *salon,*[27] and this must have been the occasion. Though it was designed from the outset as a large-scale work, over which Villiers had every intention of taking his time, he probably wanted to get the first act finished without delay in order to demonstrate to Wagner that he had taken his advice about turning his gaze on to the ideal world. As it happened, the opportunity was soon to arise, and that knowledge may have provided a ray of consolation in the sombre disarray into which the failure of *La Révolte* had thrown him.

12

The new Wagnerian adventure came about for two reasons. One was the announcement that the Grand Duke of Saxe-Weimar was to offer a great Wagnerian festival in Weimar in June in honour of Tsar Alexander II of Russia, and the other was the news that Ludwig II of Bavaria was again overriding Wagner's objections and ordering the première of *Die Walküre* in Munich a few days later. So once more the trio of French Wagnerian writers started drumming up commissions from Parisian newspapers in order to finance the journey and once more they were successful in finding the support they needed.

So far as one can make out from the travel notes Mendès
sent back to *Le National*, they set out from Paris early in June
and stayed for a few days in the Rhineland, probably at
Koblenz, then, after making a few excursions to places like
Worms, Bad Ems, and Bacharach, travelled on to Weimar,
where they arrived about the seventeenth. Among the other
visitors awaiting the arrival of the Tsar was Franz Liszt, to
whom they had been introduced by Countess Kalergis-
Muchanoff the previous year, and he, knowing Villiers's
talents as a reader (notwithstanding the unfortunate incident
of the palpitations), arranged for a reading to take place in the
presence of the Grand Duke himself. This time Villiers
decided to offer an extract from *Claire Lenoir*, and proceeded
to read in front of an extremely distinguished company. Two
things made the reading memorable. One was the unbridled
laughter it provoked. Villiers later wrote:

This almost convulsive hilarity spread even to gravest personages in
the audience, to such an extent that etiquette was forgotten. I call
the guests to witness: the Grand Duke literally had tears in his eyes.
One austere officer of the Tsar's household, quaking with silent
mirth, was obliged to withdraw—and we could hear him in the
antechamber at last freely giving vent to monstrous gusts of
laughter.—It was fantastic.[1]

If we are to believe Pontavice, this hilarity was brought on by
the coincidental similarity between the caricature of Bonhomet and the craggy countenance of Franz Liszt, but
Pontavice was not there, so his testimony is suspect.[2]

The other incident, which nearly brought the reading to an
untimely end, has been related by an eye-witness—the
Franco-Polish sculptor Cyprien Godebski, who had already
been present at the previous year's interrupted reading of *La
Révolte*. This is his account:

At a certain moment, His Highness, at a very funny and very
Parisian joke, burst out laughing. Villiers de l'Isle-Adam, no doubt
stupefied that a foreigner should understand so well the subtleties of
our language and wanting probably to express his satisfaction,
slapped the Grand Duke on the stomach and cried: 'Ah! he
understood!' Immediately all the dignitaries rose as one man, ready
at the slightest order to throw him out of the window; the Grand

Duke, hardly able to get over his surprise, at length said to Villiers, who was somewhat taken aback at his own involuntary breach of manners: 'Oh yes . . . sir, I understood!' It looked as though events were about to take a tragic turn, when His Highness, with his usual benevolence, cast a look around the room; everyone sat down again, and Villiers concluded his reading without further incident. All's well that ends well.[3]

The following day the Grand Duke and his entourage went to Eisenach, where Villiers visited the Wartburg and in the evening saw massed choirs on the mountain give a spectacular rendering of the Pilgrims' Chorus from *Tannhäuser*. On the nineteenth the festival proper began in the Tsar's presence with a performance of *The Flying Dutchman* at which Villiers, Mendès, and Judith were seated in the box of Countess Kalergis-Muchanoff. On subsequent days they were able to see *Lohengrin, Tannhäuser,* and the *Meistersinger*. Villiers, always fascinated by royalty in whatever form it manifested itself, was particularly interested by the Tsar, and later claimed to have had a premonition of his fate when he saw him walking alone one night in the park.[4] Another character who impressed both Villiers and Mendès was a chamberlain, a tall, elderly man of Russo-Polish origin, eccentric demeanour and dress, and a portentous flow of conversation on world politics and famous personalities. This person so struck them that Mendès made him into one of the main characters in his *roman à clef Le Roi vierge*, under the name of Prince Flédro-Schemyl, while Villiers depicted him as Comte Phëdro in *Le Tzar et les grands-ducs*, the reminiscences of his visit to Weimar written thirteen years later. It is probable that the Commander in *Axël* owes much to him.[5]

Villiers even cherished hopes that he might find a permanent position at the Grand Duke's court, and, meeting him in the palace gardens one morning, started to recount *Axël* to him. The Grand Duke listened politely, and Villiers was already beginning to see himself as a latter-day Goethe when the conversation was interrupted by another Frenchman, one Charles de Lorbac, who combined being a music critic with trading in wine. The Grand Duke's attention was distracted, and the expected offer of a post never came. For years afterwards Villiers would wax furious at the thought of the importunate Lorbac, and would proclaim: 'That day, I missed the opportunity of a lifetime!'

The première of *Die Walküre* had in the meantime already taken place in Munich, so that there was no hurry to go there, and the travellers decided to go first to Dresden. For some unexplained reason, Mendès and Judith seem to have stayed on there while Villiers returned to Weimar, where he had ten days on his own.[7] But international events were now casting a dark shadow over their trip, with the announcement of the Hohenzollern candidacy for the throne of Spain on 5 July, the ensuing anger of the French, King Wilhelm's intervention on 11 July to persuade Prince Karl Anton to withdraw, the insistence by the French that there should be a formal renunciation of future claims on the throne, culminating in King Wilhelm's rebuff of the French Ambassador on 13 July and the dispatch of the Ems telegram, which Bismarck so manipulated as to precipitate the French into a declaration of war. The increasingly uncomfortable situation of the French citizens on German territory was not improved when Wagner wrote to them to forbid them absolutely to see *Die Walküre*. This ban caused them all considerable anguish, especially Villiers, who wrote Wagner a long, convoluted, and somewhat tactless letter on 15 July, full of elephantine hints that they would nonetheless love to see the opera and informing him that, because the 'excellent Prussians' were in Cologne, they intended to return home via Munich and Switzerland. Despite its clumsiness, the letter affords renewed proof of Villiers's admiration for Wagner. After bewailing the prohibition on seeing *Die Walküre*, Villiers goes on: 'But I love you more than a joy, even the kind of joy one has in Valhalla. I shall see the *Nibelung* before I die and then I shall be consoled for the past.' Alas, his prediction was never to be fulfilled. He also mentions his meeting with the Grand Duke: 'I told him, very calmly and in front of Liszt, that you are the only man who makes it worth while to be alive today.'[8]

As soon as Catulle and Judith got back from Dresden, they deemed it expedient to move on to Munich without delay, and, despite some disagreeable incidents on the trains when Villiers thought successively that he was going to be sent to prison and beaten up, they were able to stay just long enough to see *Die Walküre*, in defiance of Wagner's ban. Villiers's enthusiasm knew no bounds when at last he had the revelation of 'the most dazzling, the most colossal masterpiece one can dream of under the sun'. The conclusion in particular transported him:

The nine Valkyries, riding headlong through the shadows with their hair streaming out in the depths of Valhalla which swells and slides under the horses' hooves, on planes which move past beneath them, in the clouds, with the terrifying music, it explodes, it's full of mad vision and beauty; then the flames, on Wotan's order, surrounding Brunnhilde lying on the mountain top, the fiery forests, the whole theatre ablaze, flaming, whole trees burning on the stage, blinding, so terrifying that the women were fleeing aghast and we were sitting with our eyes rivetted to the stage in fright. And the music rising up as though it were all aflame too! In the end, the flames were shooting right up from the footlights to the rails. In short, sublime! sublime! hair-raising! streaming! nameless![9]

But when they left Munich to go to Tribschen, what they did not know was that Wagner, violently nationalistic and xenophobic, had already written to say that he did not wish to receive them. Villiers's feeble joke about the 'excellent Prussians' had made both him and Cosima furious, and he had explained vehemently that they were totally committed to the Prussian side. Unfortunately, because the French visitors had brought forward their departure, the letter did not arrive in time, and on 19 July, the very day of the declaration of war, they arrived in Lucerne. In addition to Villiers, Catulle, and Judith, the party now included Camille Saint-Saëns and the young composer Henri Duparc, a great admirer of both Wagner and Villiers (who is said to have inspired his well-known setting of Baudelaire's 'La Vie antérieure'). The situation was naturally tense, since neither Cosima nor her husband concealed their consternation at the untimely arrival of their French guests. When they came over to Tribschen from the Hôtel du Lac, Cosima told them outright her views on the war, which were tactfully received, especially by Mendès, but the atmosphere was only rendered bearable by a diversion to musical matters. Thus, on successive days, Wagner and Richter played *Sieg-*

fried, and Wagner sang *Die Walküre*, brilliantly accompanied by Saint-Saëns.[10]

But the tension kept returning, for instance when Saint-Saëns was ill-advised enough to say to Wagner that he owed it to the French to compose a *Charlemagne* for them, or when reports of minor French military successes provoked Wagner into an outburst in which he demanded that his guests should realize how much he and Cosima hated the characteristic traits of the French. Notwithstanding these clashes, the visitors remained at Lucerne and regularly went over to Tribschen, keeping the conversation so far as possible on musical topics. On 28 July Friedrich Nietzsche came from Axenstein to stay for two days before going on to the Maderanertal, but what may have passed between the authors of *Axël* and *Also sprach Zarathustra*, those works which have so much in common, will, alas, never be known. Then on the twenty-ninth came Nietzsche's sister, and Richard Pohl, composer, music critic, and poet, together with his wife. Villiers at least was as delighted with his stay as he had been the previous year:

Here, we are with Wagner night and day. We eat here, shout and listen to him. He is the same: immutable. With Richter, he played us *Götterdämmerung*, the prelude and all of *Siegfried*. Oh! it's unique: it is the Nibelungen, all the night of time. He is really the most amazing of men, and an incomparable genius, at every moment. He is formidable.[11]

However, the need to move on eventually made itself felt. The war clearly meant that there could be no question of sending back reviews of Wagnerian operas to the Paris papers, and the expense of staying at the Hôtel du Lac was too heavy to be borne indefinitely, quite apart from the fact that they could not impose much longer on Wagner's by now somewhat threadbare goodwill. The question was what to do next and how to replenish their depleted finances. One solution which struck Villiers was to turn himself into a war correspondent, since he had only just returned from the depths of enemy country and could draw on his experiences, such as they were, to submit dispatches to the home press. The first result of this scheme was an article dated from

Lucerne on 22 July, which appeared in *Le Constitutionnel* on the twenty-fifth. It is not a very inspired piece of reporting, largely because Villiers's journey from Weimar to Lucerne via Munich had taken him nowhere near the scene of action, with the result that all he could talk about was the mood of the people and a few banal, isolated incidents that he had witnessed—such as the near-brawl with soldiers on the train to Nuremberg, now suitably ennobled into a polite discussion between officers and gentlemen. At the end, Villiers announces that he intends to leave for Vienna,[12] and a letter to Marras confirms that such was indeed at one time his intention.[13]

This plan however posed problems, not least that of money, and, when it became clear that Mendès and Judith wanted to return to Paris by way of Avignon in order to visit Mallarmé, who was teaching there, Villiers decided that it would be safer to accompany them. So on the twenty-seventh Mendès wrote to tell Mallarmé that the three of them would be arriving in ten or twelve days' time, Wagner having expressed the desire to keep them with him for another week.[14] Mallarmé, who languished for lack of contacts with his Parisian literary friends, was delighted to hear the news and sent off instructions as to the best way to reach Avignon (including the practical advice that, on the Rhône steamer from Lyon, they should take second-class tickets, go into the first-class section, and then demand a reduction: 'They would sooner feed you than not have you').[15] But they probably never received the letter, since a sudden change of plan supervened, with a decision to leave on the thirty-first, perhaps because the situation with Wagner had become intolerable.[16]

In the meantime Villiers was continuing his career as a war correspondent, and on 1 August *Le Constitutionnel* published a second dispatch about conditions in Germany.[17] But there are several suspect features about this letter, which is dated: 'Augsburg, 24 July, in the evening'. In it he claims to have left Munich precipitately four days earlier because a chance word had led him to believe his life was in danger. This is in flagrant contradiction not only with the date of his first letter but also with the diaries of Cosima Wagner and

Hans Richter, all of which place him firmly in Lucerne on the twentieth. When one realizes that the second letter is even less visual than the first and that it repeats some of the details already used, and when one notices that Villiers specifies that he is obliged to send it through Switzerland, the truth becomes clear: he had hit on the idea of pretending to be still in Germany in order to be able to continue making a little money by sending fictitious accounts of life behind the enemy lines. The deception was harmless enough, but the literary result is unimpressive: the second letter contains little more than windy bluster about German weakness and his own desire to fight for his country: 'to be a man of the mind is something, I know; but there are times when one remembers that Aeschylus, who knew something about literature and dramatic poetry, did not want to have inscribed on his tomb: "Here lies Aeschylus who wrote *Prometheus*", but: "Here lies Aeschylus who fought at Salamina".'

Before leaving Lucerne there was one last rite which Villiers insisted on accomplishing. Remembering the success of his reading of *La Révolte* the year before, and wishing to demonstrate that he had followed Wagner's advice about turning to the ideal world, he read what existed of *Axël* to the assembled company. The result, whether he realized it or not, was an unmitigated disaster. Cosima noted in her diary:

Last dinner with the French; at the end of the evening great discussion between Catulle M. and R[ichard], following on a reading by Mr. Villiers, whose pretentious manner, bombastic presentation and histrionic performance truly filled us with indignation. R. pointed out to them how objectionable their rhetorical poetry is; he was listened to with great emotion and understanding by Catulle, whose fine sensitivity and high culture have made us really like him, whereas we find his friend ever more unbearable.[18]

Hans Richter's diary is no less dismissive (he detected a resemblance between the Archdeacon in the play and Molière's Tartuffe): 'In the evening departure of Catulle, Judith, Villiers. The latter boring reading of a play. (Tartuffe.) The Master very displeased about it.' So Villiers's parting from his idol took place in inauspicious circumstances, and, though the Wagners remained in touch with

Mendès and Judith, they thereafter showed little inclination to keep up contacts with Villiers. Henry Roujon, who often heard Villiers talking ecstatically about his friendship with them, guessed right when he wrote: 'In Villiers's lyrical accounts, I thought I could divine that he had impressed his hosts at Tribschen as being a funny sort of fellow, a bit crazy.'[20]

By the beginning of August the three French writers were on their way south to Avignon, perhaps stopping in Lyon to pay their respects to Joséphin Soulary. The journey did not pass off without incident, however, for, while wandering round a badly-lit railway station at night, Villiers contrived to injure his face, sustaining a severe gash near his eye. Far from being distressed by the scar (although, as he ruefully said, he was ugly enough without it), Villiers at once started thinking of ways of turning the accident to his advantage and decided to sue the railway company for damages, on the somewhat specious grounds that the injury had prevented him from continuing his series of dispatches from south Germany.[21] It was indeed his intention to go on writing them from Avignon, using his by now somewhat distant reminiscences and the German newspapers which Mallarmé's wife received (Marie Mallarmé was German by birth), but, given the speed with which events at the front were developing, it is not surprising that *Le Constitutionnel* turned out to be no longer interested in inserting them. Equally, his hopes of squeezing 10,000 francs out of the railway company soon faded, though, with the love of litigation inherited from his father, he persisted with the lawsuit for some time.

Since neither Villiers nor Mendès had seen Mallarmé for some years, they were both eager to know what sort of work he had been producing during the long and mysterious crisis he had been traversing. They were soon to find out, for, on their first evening in Avignon in early September, he took them into his study and began to read to them from a manuscript. According to Mendès's recollections over thirty years later:

It was a rather long tale from Germany, a kind of Rhenish legend, the title of which was—I think I am not mistaken—*Igitur d'Elbenone*. Right from the first lines, I was horrified, and Villiers sometimes consulted me with a furtive glance, and sometimes stared at the reader with his little eyes popping with astonishment.[22] At the end, so Mendès says, Villiers hid his embarrassment with snorts of admiration; Mendès himself retired to bed and left for Paris the next morning before Mallarmé could ask him his opinion. He also claims that Villiers subsequently regretted his feigned admiration. The anecdote however is suspect. That Mallarmé did read to them fragments of *Igitur* is not in doubt: he never finished the work and it was not published until twenty years after his death, but it is known that he had been elaborating it in 1869 and 1870. That *Igitur* is one of Mallarmé's most obscure writings is also obvious, so that a reading of it would indeed be a disconcerting experience, the more so as Mallarmé had none of Villiers's hypnotic gifts as a reader. But it is very doubtful whether Mendès and Judith left so abruptly, or whether Villiers's admiration was anything but genuine. Particularly with his deep affection for Mallarmé, he can hardly have failed to be touched by the symbolic tale of Igitur, whose fate, as well as that of his ancestors, will be determined by one crucial throw of the dice. For if Igitur is a disembodied double of Mallarmé, he is also a double of Villiers, conceived in part as a result of Mallarmé's long meditations on what his friend really represented in the world. The fact that Villiers stayed on in Avignon for several weeks speaks for itself, and gives the lie to Mendès's envious insinuations.

Villiers's occupations in Avignon during the month of August were diverse. Naturally he spent much time talking about poetry, not only with Mallarmé, but also with Frédéric Mistral and Théodore Aubanel, the Provençal poets of the Félibrige. No doubt philosophy was another subject of conversation. In the letter to Mallarmé announcing his arrival, Villiers had declared boldly: 'I've dropped Hegel.'[23] Whether the sudden abandonment of his one-time idol had been brought about by Wagner's championing of Kant and Schopenhauer we do not know, but he must certainly have wanted to discuss this new development in his thought with Mallarmé, on whom he had previously pressed Hegelianism with much zeal. It may be doubted whether this nominal renunciation of Hegel made much difference to Villiers in the event: he had never known much at first hand of the German philosopher's works, and he continued to use his own individual brand of idealism until the end of his life. But for the moment he obviously regarded it as a momentous decision.

Yet another activity was concocting fake dispatches for *Le Constitutionnel,* but to no avail; the paper was no longer interested. Then there was his case against the railway company, which he was preparing with zest. But he was also extremely worried about his family in Paris, since the first week of August had shown decisively that, contrary to all expectations, the French army was no match for the Prussians, and that a staggering defeat was in sight. As his aunt Gabrielle de Villiers de l'Isle-Adam was a nun in the Convent of the Sacred Heart in Avignon, [24] he managed to arrange with her that his mother and Tante Kerinou should be given shelter there, while he hoped to be able to send his father off to join the Abbé Victor at Ploumilliau in Brittany. But all that involved returning to Paris, and he did not even have the money for the fare, since no one would pay him for his articles. To complicate matters further, he enlisted in the Second Regiment of Light Cavalry, which was commanded by a distant relative, but contrived to get himself three weeks' leave before he actually joined them. [25] In the end he was forced to ask Mallarmé to advance him enough money to get back to the capital, [26] whither he made his way at the beginning of September.

By then the Emperor had surrendered after the catastrophe of Sedan, the Empire itself had been toppled, and it was only a matter of time before Paris was besieged. How and where Villiers spent the agonizing months of the siege is not known. Evidently he had given up the idea of evacuating his family to the provinces, perhaps because it was already too late for them to get away, so he probably lived with them at least some of the time. But he had also involved himself in military duties of some kind, though probably not with the Light Cavalry—at the prospect of serving with them, patriotism had vied with nervousness, and, while he contemplated with relative equanimity the idea of death in action, his lively imagination had painted some scarifying pictures: 'What I don't like is the horses trampling all over you.' [27] From time to time his friends would see him going about his obscure errands. Leconte de Lisle informed Heredia that everyone was well, including Villiers, 'who has been all over the town, wearing the strangest captain's uniform imaginable. No one has ever been able to find out what branch he belongs to.'[28] Sometimes he would turn up at the house of Mme Mauté, mother of Mme Paul Verlaine, whose kindness attracted many men of letters at that black time. There is even a story that on one such occasion there Villiers was indirectly responsible for the composition of Charles Cros's famous comic poem 'Le Hareng saur'. Villiers is supposed to have arrived at Mme Mauté's bearing the rare trophy of a salted herring and then, having spent the night on the ramparts, gone to sleep on her settee; finding him asleep, Cros hung the herring on a string above his head, and sat down to write the poem. One would like the story to be true.[29]

Other pictures of Villiers during the Siege are fragmentary and tantalizing. According to Pontavice de Heussey he joined a corps of irregulars with other artists and composed a number of warlike songs. Henry Roujon recollected that he had conferred on himself the euphonious title of 'Captain-General of the Waifs and Strays of La Villette'.[31] Gustave de Malherbe, who knew him in later life, reported that, accompanied by his father, he had turned up at the offices of a charitable organization run by Malherbe's mother to pick up some flannel shirts, 'resplendent in the uniform of a sub-lieutenant in the militia, with stripes halfway up his sleeve'.[32] Another document shows him in the role of 'Commanding Officer of the Scouts of the 147th Battalion of the National Guard' (the battalion was led by Louis Noir, brother of the murdered journalist Victor).[33] All these extraordinary titles and uniforms suggest that Villiers was playing some vast game of soldiers during the Siege; it satisfied the desire to act out flamboyant parts which was one of the guiding impulses of his life, and offered him an ideal opportunity for at least outwardly imitating the military glories of his forebears.

Villiers himself, in his rare and reticent autobiographical writings, makes only one allusion to his life at that time. This occurs in the article he wrote about Augusta Holmès in 1884, where he recalls an evening that he spent in Augusta's *salon* with Catulle Mendès and the young painter Henri Regnault, all three men wearing soldiers' capes. Regnault, who had a good tenor voice, sang songs by Augusta and Saint-Saëns, which so moved his companions that they were struck by a presentiment. The next day, 19 January 1871, Regnault's battalion was sent out to attack the Prussian positions at Buzenval in a vain attempt to break the encircling ring of iron, and Regnault never returned.[34]

13

At the end of January 1871, bowing to the inevitable, the French authorities signed an armistice with the Prussians. Elections were held, Adolphe Thiers became Head of the Executive, and the National Assembly was brought back from Bordeaux to Versailles. But, when in mid-March Thiers ordered the National Guard in Paris to return its guns, disturbances broke out, and on 26 March the Commune was declared. The remnants of the army under the orders of the Versailles government laid siege to Paris on 2 April, and in May began bombarding the fortifications of the city. On the twenty-first they succeeded in breaching the Communard defences, and for the next week street fighting raged in Paris, with buildings ablaze and merciless shootings on both sides. By the time resistance was finally crushed, the Communards had lost about twenty thousand dead.

If it is difficult to know what Villiers was doing during the siege, it is next to impossible to discover what he was up to under the Commune. Two things only seem clear: that he was actively in favour of the Commune in its early stages, and that he was actively against it by the time it was defeated. It is no surprise that he should have welcomed the Commune when it was first set up. He had always taken a keen interest in the whole idea of revolution, he had himself tried to foment one in 1870, he had many left-wing friends and connections with the left-wing press, and he loathed the whole structure of bourgeois society. Moreover, at the outset the Commune was not exclusively a socialist and communist preserve; the initial motivation for it was patriotic as much as social, and it only gradually assumed its distinctive political colouring. Many of Villiers's friends were involved in it: Jean

Marras, always a radical republican, who had to take refuge in Spain afterwards; Nina de Villard, who likewise fled to Geneva; Paul Verlaine, who accepted a job under the Communards at the Hôtel de Ville and later went into hiding; Charles de Sivry, who was arrested; Charles Cros, who acted as medical assistant to the troops of the Paris National Guard; Edmond Lepelletier, the journalist, who worked for it as a civil servant and an editor. Some of its leading figures were people whom Villiers had known at Nina de Villard's or elsewhere: Raoul Rigault was its Procurator General on 27 April; Gustave Flourens, one of its most prominent members, was killed in battle in May. Villiers's idealistic hope for a total regeneration of society, his sympathy with a certain romantic notion of revolution, the ties of friendship, even his position as an officer in the Paris National Guard, make it entirely comprehensible that he should at first have supported the Commune against the defeatist bourgeois conservatives of the Versailles regime.

There is little direct evidence of how far his participation went. The only person to provide eye-witness testimony is Émile Bergerat, who writes: 'I can still see Villiers, wearing the kepi of a captain in the National Guard (which was covered by a cardboard case), trying to rally the Parnassians to the federal cause.'[1] Bergerat adds that Verlaine, being more convinced, was a more effective proselytizer. Villiers himself provided some indirect evidence a few months later, when *Le Figaro* inserted the following paragraph: 'For a uniform or a few francs, some very noble men have for ever sullied their names by serving the Commune. It is said that among them there was a real Comte Villiers de l'Isle-Adam.' Instead of the thunderous riposte one might have expected from such a combative polemicist, this elicited only a very circumspect response, since Villiers's reply, printed on 1 October 1871, is confined to a quotation of the offending words, with this comment: 'I am the real Comte Villiers de l'Isle-Adam. During the insurrection, I neither wore a uniform nor received any pay. I request you to be so good as to publish this correction.'[2] The cautious restrictiveness of this denial speaks for itself: Villiers obviously knew that there were things he could not deny, and contented himself with rebutting the details while remaining silent on the substance of the charge. The embarrassment of his position at that time did not escape his friends, and Léon Dierx wrote on 11 October to the exiled Marras about the *Figaro's* denunciations:

Perhaps you saw there the hateful and perfidious insinuation about our poor friend Villiers. You can just imagine him shooting into towering rages, telling everyone all about it, enumerating the attitudes it would be fitting to strike, showing the crushing replies he has written, and in the end putting none of these intentions into effect, for the identity of the I and the non-I, of being and non-being, of intention and fact is absolutely proven.[3]

Though there is some ambiguity in the phrasing here, the general drift is that both Dierx and Marras knew perfectly well that Villiers was in no position to issue a categorical denial of any allegiance to the Commune.

But whether that allegiance went beyond declarations of general support in the early days is another matter altogether. Certainly, by 23 April Mallarmé, who knew his Villiers, was certain that he was not on the side of the Communards, when he wrote to Henri Cazalis, who was in Amsterdam: 'Imagine our momentary torment, believing you to be in Paris out of choice, when in fact you were being kept, along with Villiers, with Mendès, in the ranks of the insurrection. Our anxiety remains great for them. Have they too been able to leave the unfortunate city?[4] In fact, it seems likely that after the first week or two Villiers had become disillusioned and no longer supported the Commune in the extreme form it had assumed.

Indeed, Villiers went so far as to make contacts with the so-called 'Versaillais' and even took the dangerous step of travelling to Versailles. This is clear from a letter he wrote on 25 May, after the government troops had partially reoccupied Paris. His correspondent is a M. Langeron, who was evidently the secret representative in Paris of the Versailles forces, and the draft of Langeron's reply gives some corroboration of Villiers's account of what had happened. Forced to remain in Paris to look after his parents, Villiers had managed to make one trip to Versailles to offer his services to the authorities, who had put him in touch with Langeron. Perhaps this was before the clampdown of the siege, but, when he had tried to make a second journey, he was arrested and taken to the Hôtel de Ville, where only the intervention of Marras secured his release. Suspect to the Communard forces because he was regarded as a 'recalcitrant' who refused to bear arms on their behalf and because it was known that he had been to Versailles, he then awaited the arrival of the liberating army in some trepidation. His relief on the twenty-fifth seems genuine: 'At last we have been freed! Let us thank God. It is as if we had been unable to breathe!'[5]

It is true that, without Langeron's reply, which is sketched out on the back of Villiers's letter,[6] one might suspect that he is simply inventing in order to evade the responsibility of having backed the losing side—and, with all the denunciations and executions that were going on, such an attitude would have been very understandable. It is also true that there may well be some exaggeration for effect, as there usually is in Villiers, and that it is displeasing, to say the least, to find him referring to the person who had ensured his release as 'M. Marras (whom I spoke to you about and whom I am sorry to have known in the past as a man of letters)'. But since Langeron patently accepts his version of events and must have been in a position to know, it is clear that Villiers is basically telling the truth. That in turn means that he had turned against the Communard cause and had ended by supporting the Versaillais.

If this is so (and the only other interpretation would be the highly unlikely one that he was playing a game of quite remarkable duplicity), one must have the gravest doubts about the attribution to Villiers of a series of five articles entitled *Tableau de Paris*, which appeared in the Communard newspaper *Le Tribun du peuple* between 17 May and 24 May 1871, over the signature 'Marius'.[7] The supposed justification for the attribution is an affirmation by Victor-Émile Michelet in 1913 that in *Le Tribun du peuple* one might find 'an inflammatory article by Villiers in favour of the newborn Commune, "brandishing vengeance-coloured flags" '. Apparent confirmation comes from the editor of *Le Tribun du peuple*, Edmond Lepelletier, who, in his *Histoire de la Commune*, which also appeared in 1913, likewise quotes the phrase about 'vengeance-coloured flags' and refers it to

'Villiers de l'Isle-Adam in his *Tableau de Paris* published by the paper *Le Tribun du peuple*'. But these belated allegations, one of which is almost certainly copied from the other, are insufficient to establish authorship, especially at a distance of more than forty years. That Villiers may have had contacts with Lepelletier and other Communard newspapermen is entirely credible; that he may have committed something to paper in favour of the Commune in March or early April 1871 is not impossible; but that he should have penned five articles in loud praise of the Commune at a time when he had already avowedly broken with it and was acting on behalf of its Versailles adversaries is beyond belief. Stylistic differences, the fact that the incriminating phrase about the flags is not textually in the articles by 'Marius', Villiers's notorious inability to produce newspaper articles to order—all these things serve only to reinforce one conclusion: whoever wrote *Tableau de Paris*, it could not have been Villiers.

What is certain about Villiers and his family under the Commune is that they underwent severe hardship. There is no reason to doubt what he told Langeron:

We have suffered unspeakably. The farmers not paying any more, the notary in Brittany not answering, the war and the Commune having temporarily ruined us, my friends being in Versailles, we were reduced to the end of our resources for something to live on, and, if things had gone on in the same way, we would literally have died of starvation.

There was not even any possibility of earning money from writing for the press: Villiers's last articles had been the *Lettres d'Allemagne* in *Le Constitutionnel* in 1870, and he had difficulty in getting his fee for them. Cut off from their usual source of income in Brittany, the family could not rely on Tante Kerinou's money, so that their situation was even worse than that of the other inhabitants of the beleaguered city. The health of Tante Kerinou herself, now aged eighty-six, deteriorated rapidly as a result of these privations.

In these desperate straits Villiers bethought himself of his two favourite remedies: a rich marriage and a diplomatic post, if possible in combination. So, with breath-taking presumptuousness, on 26 June 1871 he sent off a letter to

Jules Favre, Thiers's Minister of Foreign Affairs, asking to be appointed as an attaché to the French Embassy in London. The qualifications he lists are simple: his 'special aptitudes' and 'the various works of science, literature, and history' he has written (quite which of his publications he has in mind is no doubt a question one ought not to ask). Somewhat naively, he goes on to disclose some of the real reasons behind his request:

The fact is that this title would open for me, at the age of thirty-two, a career in which I may sooner or later distinguish myself in the useful service of the interests of my country. The position which it would confer on me at the English Court would raise legitimate hopes of the sort of marriage which could save a great and ancient family from coming to an end in undeserved oblivion.

The conclusion of the letter is full of tranquil self-assurance: 'After due reflection I can find no reason why, in the eyes of a representative of the French Republic, there should be any motives for a refusal in the considerations which I have just set forth.'[8] It is hardly necessary to say that no nomination was forthcoming, since the Minister was unlikely to relish being used quite so blatantly as a matrimonial agent, but it is worth pointing out that even Villiers would scarcely have dared to put forward his resistance to the Commune as a reason for his employment if only a month before he had been publishing inflammatory articles in a Communard paper.[9]

There are even some grounds for thinking that his request was not rejected quite as brusquely as one might have expected, because, two months later, Villiers was saying that under Favre people had taken a lot of trouble to find him a consulate in all sorts of strange countries. Favre had in the meantime been replaced as Minister of Foreign Affairs by Charles de Rémusat, and this had heightened Villiers's hopes of a posting to London, 'since we are on rather good terms with the new minister who is a charming person and a man of letters'.[10] However, far from leaving later the same month as he was expecting, Villiers evidently heard nothing more.

But in another way August 1871 was to prove a fateful

month for Villiers. On the ninth the aged Tante Kerinou fell
ill, and four days later, at eight o'clock on the morning of the
thirteenth, she was dead.[11] The disappearance of the indomitable old lady hit Villiers very hard. Not only had he been
very attached to her, but it was her strength of character alone
that had lent some semblance of sanity and stability to his
home background. Now that she was gone, he realized that
henceforward he was in a sense on his own. His distress
shows in the letters he wrote to Amédée Le Menant des
Chesnais[12] and to Dom Guéranger asking them to pray for
her soul. The letter to Dom Guéranger is particularly moving: 'Madame Daniel de Kerinou, my grandmother, is dead. I
have asked for prayers for her. I believe that the monks at
Solesmes have a voice which is known to God, and that you
can speak her name at the requiem mass. She was called Félix.
I remain your very humble son and servant in Jesus Christ.'
Then, after sending greetings to some of the monks he had
met in 1862 and 1863, and expressing the hope that he would
soon return to the monastery, it is as if he could contain his
despair no longer, and in tiny handwriting at right angles to
the rest one reads: 'Ah! Father, if I didn't still have my
mother!'[13] Tante Kerinou's death moreover betokened more
than a bereavement: it also meant the end of the family's
slender resources, since her money, or what remained of it,
had been invested in life annuities which came to an end with
her death. No doubt the sale of such property as she had left
in Brittany provided some funds (the house in Lannion, for
example, was sold in 1872),[14] but for the Marquis to have his
hands on some capital was a recipe for disaster.

Up to 1871, though Villiers had very often been short of
money and though the family fortunes had been steadily
dwindling under the depredations of the spendthrift Marquis,
his poverty had been that of an improvident bohemian rather
than real and total destitution, the more so as occasional
generous gifts from Tante Kerinou had enabled him to have
the odd fling of wild extravagance. But, now that there was
no Tante Kerinou in the background, the situation was
completely different. Already over thirty and completely
devoid of aptitude for any mundane occupations, he only had
his pen to live on, and he knew full well from bitter

experience, especially after the catastrophe of *La Révolte*, that the public simply did not want the only kind of things he knew how to write. Even his friends were no longer there to help him: Marras was in exile in Spain, Mendès (who may have feared that he too had been compromised by the Commune) was keeping away from Paris, first in Normandy, then in England, Nina de Villard was in Switzerland, Verlaine had embarked on the first of his escapades with Rimbaud, Mallarmé was still in Avignon. From now on Villiers's plight was to be permanent and desperate.

PART II
The Years of Darkness

14

The period following Tante Kerinou's death is one during which Villiers almost disappeared from view. He published nothing, no letters that he may have written have survived, he seems to have little contact with his friends. Always secretive about his domicile, he may or may not have had rooms of his own; most probably he was living with his parents in what were less and less salubrious lodgings. When he went to the local *mairie* to register Tante Kerinou's death on the morning of 14 August 1871, he gave the same address for himself as for her: 49 Grande Rue des Batignolles, which is in a working-class quarter of the north of Paris, beyond Montmartre.[1] Clearly the family had come down in the world since the days when they had occupied expensive apartments near the Palais-Royal. By November, however, they had moved to another address in Batignolles, this time 3 rue Brochant,[2] and the following November they were still there—with the bailiff's men sequestering the Marquis's belongings because he owed 114 fr. 70 in tax.[3] The fact that Villiers signed the official papers as bailee indicates that he was living on the premises too, but his presence there was no doubt sporadic—some idea of the situation can be gleaned from what had happened when Mendès wanted him to be his second when he nearly had a duel with Hector de Callias early in 1870. Léon Barracand, the other second, had gone with a friend to the address they had been given:

We were shown into an austere, rather dark room hung with old tapestries, where, after a few minutes, an old gentleman appeared, our friend's father, and, with a calm smile, replied in answer to our questions: 'Auguste went out forty-eight hours ago and I haven't seen him since; I don't know where he is or what he is doing.'[4]

Occasionally he would surface unexpectedly, only to disappear again without trace. When Catulle Mendès's play *La Part du roi* was produced in June 1872, Villiers turned up at the première and startled everyone both by being unusually subdued and by announcing that he had a job. 'He is talking a lot less, and claims to be *Comptroller of the waggonage of the cattle transported from the South to Paris*! He's the only person who could have discovered this new profession, and the word *waggonage* (the loss in weight suffered by the above-mentioned cattle during their journey in the waggons!!!),' so Dierx informed Marras.[5] The latter seems to have judged it safe to return to Paris about then, since there is evidence that Villiers was present when he gave a reading of his play *La Famille d'Armelles* in the autumn of 1872.[6] Another of his appearances was at the performance of François Coppée's *Le Rendez-vous* at the Odéon in 1872, when he emerged so furious with the play's mawkish sentimentality that he loudly improvised an alexandrine that summed up what he thought Coppée really meant: 'Donnez-moi de l'argent puisque j'aime ma mère!'[7]

By now the elegance of his youthful dress was only a memory. His overcoat was worn and his shirts frayed. But he still retained such charm and distinction that he could carry off his shabbiness with style, and Fernand Calmettes noted that he could make women overlook his sartorial shortcomings—if someone pointed out how dilapidated his appearance was, they would say: 'True, but he is one of the very few men who can wear dirty clothes without one noticing.'[8] One society lady, when her attention was drawn to his grimy shirt, replied: 'Yes, but it looks so good on him!'[9] His face too was beginning to show the marks of his sufferings. This is how he struck Louis de Gavrinis:

At the sight of this puny figure, with his emaciated and almost livid face, constantly deep in a sort of mortal prostration, his eyes dull, his hair all over the place, his gestures slow and devilish, one might think one was looking at a sleepwalker or a simpleton. He is in fact nothing more nor less than a great writer—the word is exact—possessed with a passion for what is improbable and terrifying.[10]

Gone too were the heady days when he could appear at elegant balls in evening dress: both the invitations and the evening dress were lacking. Though he was able to resume his visits to Nina de Villard when she and her mother returned to Paris in mid-1872 and rented a house in the rue des Moines, and though he presumably saw Mallarmé more often since the latter had succeeded in getting himself transferred to a post in Paris in November 1871, he seems gradually to have deserted Leconte de Lisle's more formal *salon* and to have been less often in Catulle Mendès's company. Relations with Wagner had ceased completely, and, though Richard and Cosima, now married, were in regular correspondence with the Mendès couple, especially Judith, they no longer bothered even to ask for news of Villiers. The only remnant of his earlier prosperity, so Judith Gautier said, was part of an elaborate costume of black velvet and jade which he had had made for the role of Hamlet before the war[11] (according to Henry Roujon, he had worn it at the Great Exhibition of 1867, when he had entertained some whirling dervishes to dinner).[12] Hamlet, like Faust, was for Villiers one of the archetypal figures of all literature, and he had cherished the ambition of learning the part and acting it better than it had ever been acted. But now, anything that had any monetary value had long since found its way to the pawnbroker's.

So, if his friends saw him at all, it was mostly in cafés. Villiers had always tended to shun daylight and to sit up most of the night, talking or writing, and, as he also liked smoking and drinking, he became a regular frequenter of cafés as soon as he arrived in Paris. When he had been able to afford rooms of his own, or when his parents had inhabited large enough apartments, it had been possible for him to work at home when he wanted. Now that he was driven to share much more cramped quarters with his eccentric father and his brow-beaten mother, the urge to spend the night hours elsewhere must have been irresistible, so that one was always liable to find him seated at a café table, with a glass of beer in front of him and a half-smoked cigarette in his hand, scribbling away at his latest work and with other manuscripts poking out of his capacious pockets. But he delighted in finding company to whom he could declaim his writings or with whom he could discuss literature, so that composition was as often as not replaced by conversation.

Even his dreams of royalty had shrunk by this time. After having tried to become King of Greece, after having hob-nobbed with the Grand Duke of Saxe-Weimar and the Tsar of Russia, Villiers was reduced to frequenting the sort of crowned heads one might find in Parisian drinking haunts. In particular, he became a familiar of Antoine de Tounens, better known as Orélie-Antoine I, King of Patagonia and Araucania. This one-time lawyer from Périgord had taken it into his head to go to South America and set himself up as ruler of the Patagonians and Araucanians, who had not been touched by the Spanish conquest; this he succeeded in doing in 1861 and proceeded to endow his states with a constitution and legislation on the French model. But the Chilean army ambushed and imprisoned him, and he was only released after diplomatic intervention from France. A second expedition to reconquer his realm was a flop, and in 1871 he returned to France to distribute imaginary largesse to anyone willing to listen to him. Villiers was one such voluntary subject, and according to Henry Roujon probably occupied some honorary and theoretical post in his service for a time.[13]

These half-serious occupations and the lack of any new publications seem to have persuaded some of Villiers's friends and acquaintances that he was essentially a talker and not a writer, an accusation which never failed to raise his ire. It was about this time that, when someone taxed him with laziness, he undertook to write a play there and then, and in a few hours scrawled out *L'Évasion* on a café table.[14] The result, it must be admitted, is no masterpiece, and one can well understand why he made no effort to have it published for fifteen years. It is a badly-constructed and schematically presented little drama, full of lachrymose sentimentality, in which Pagnol, an escaped convict, allows himself to be recaptured because he does not have the heart to harm two newly-weds. The moral lesson is heavily underscored by a last line which is as unconvincing as all that has gone before: as the convict gives himself up, he says sententiously: 'It seems to me that it is now that I am escaping!'[15]

L'Évasion, mediocre as it is, betokens a return of interest for the modern social drama that Villiers had already experimented with in *La Tentation* and that he had attempted to transcend in *La Révolte*. Evidently he could not quite get rid of the feeling that, since such plays were the staple fodder of theatre audiences, he ought to be capable of exploiting the genre successfully, even if it was totally uncongenial to him. Several other dramatic fragments, all apparently dating from the early 1870s, attest his continuing preoccupation with the form—one has to do with a woman seduced during the war,[16] another with a rogue insinuating himself into the bosom of an honourable family,[17] but none of them seems to have gone beyond the stage of vague sketches. Whatever his desire to please the public (or at least to flatter its tastes), Villiers was incapable of forcing his nature into a mould which it would not fit, and his projected realistic dramas were consequently all stillborn.

Another abortive scheme from about the same period resulted from Judith Gautier's wish to help Villiers get down to some regular literary production. Since she was an extremely fluent writer, it occurred to her that she might collaborate with Villiers on an epistolary novel in which she would write the letters supposedly emanating from the young woman, while Villiers would be responsible for those from the hero. There was to be no plot; the work would simply grow and develop under its own impetus. Two of the letters Villiers wrote have survived;[18] they are couched in a lyrically melancholy tone, and the beauty of the prose makes one regret that the idea petered out. No doubt the absence of a fixed plot and the difficulties of keeping up such an improvised collaboration were the main reasons for its premature conclusion.

In fact, those who thought Villiers idle or unproductive could not have been more wrong. As Henry Roujon writes:

People have called him lazy; what an extraordinary thing! The peasant who, after a night of hail, harnesses the oxen to the plough again is not more full of stoical courage. Villiers laboured away, in his own time and in his own way, on a beer-house table, in a newspaper office, on the top of an omnibus, in furnished rooms, in the city, in the country, at night, even during the day, wherever he found a pen to hand, but his work was considerable. This artist, who carved his words one by one and put them in fine settings like jewels, left us ten volumes. In his mind he composed a hundred.[19]

The improvisations in cafés, the impromptu readings from tattered scraps of paper, the interminable tirades were not a substitute for writing, they were a rehearsal for it. Remy de Gourmont, one of those who knew him best towards the end of his life, has admirably defined the way his mind worked:

Villiers de l'Isle-Adam had, so far as I could judge, this method of
work: the idea came into his mind, and it happened that it would
come in suddenly, usually in the course of a conversation, for he
was a great talker and he profited from everything: the idea, having
come in first of all by the back door, invaded all the storehouses of
the unconscious, then from time to time surfaced in the conscious
mind and literally forced Villiers to bow to the obsession; at such
times, regardless of his interlocutor, he talked; he even talked when
he was alone; anyway, when he was talking out an idea, he always
talked as if he was alone.[20]

The apparently blank years of the early 1870s were in
reality anything but empty. The fact is that Villiers was
working extremely hard at what had in his eyes the proportions of a major work, even his life's work: *Axël.* The first act
of this lofty philosophical drama had been composed in 1869
and 1870 and read both to Leconte de Lisle[21] and to
Wagner;[22] certainly more of it had been drafted at the same
time, but probably not yet in full. A large-scale revision took
place after the war and the Commune, and it was about this
time that Edmond Lepelletier noted that Villiers had taken to
reciting long extracts from *Axël* in cafés.[23] Eventually, late in
1872, he deemed that the first act had reached a sufficiently
advanced stage to be revealed to the public gaze, and he
offered it to Émile Blémont for his review *La Renaissance
littéraire et artistique,* a weekly publication founded in April
1872 under the patronage of Victor Hugo, with the aim of
revivifying French literature, mainly through the poets of *Le
Parnasse contemporain.* The first instalment of *Axël* appeared
on 12 October with the subtitle 'Tragedy in three parts' and
preceded by this editorial note: 'We regret that the somewhat
restricted space available to the *Renaissance* does not allow us
to publish M. Villiers de l'Isle-Adam's work in its entirety.
We shall give all the first scene, which is a veritable prologue.'
But there was then an unexplained hiatus of two months
before the second and third instalments, which came out on 7
December and 14 December respectively, so clearly Villiers
had had second thoughts and decided to go in for yet another
session of extended revising. From this one may infer that the
editorial note was designed to disguise the fact that the work
was still incomplete. Indeed, when Villiers sent a poem to *La*

Renaissance in July 1873, the accompanying note to Blémont indicates that even then it was far from finished: 'I'm still working on *Axël*; it's taking a long time, but there you are! . . . I think it will not be wholly absurd.'[24]

As it stands in *La Renaissance*, the First Part is relatively simple. The action takes place in the Convent of St. Apollodora on Christmas Eve; the Abbess and the Archdeacon are preparing for Sara de Maupers to take the veil, as they fear her intelligence and covet her riches. The ceremony starts with a long sermon from the Archdeacon, but when he puts to Sara the ritual question: 'Do you accept Light, Life, and Hope?' she replies only: 'No', the one word she speaks during the whole act. The nuns flee in shock, and Sara, left alone with the Archdeacon, forces him to go down into the *in pace* in which he had intended to incarcerate her for her punishment. She then disappears into the night. Though the published text goes no further, it is possible to deduce how Villiers at that time intended the work to continue. The other two parts would have taken place in Axël's castle in Germany. Axël is studying occultism with his mysterious mentor Maître Janus and the moment of his final initiation is approaching. But an old servant reminds him that a vast treasure is hidden somewhere in the castle, and when, after a long discussion of mysticism, Janus asks him if he is willing to accept Light, Life, and Hope, he too replies: 'No'. In the meantime Sara, guided by an ancient parchment found in the convent, arrives at the castle. She and Axël meet in the crypt when she discovers the hiding-place of the treasure; they fall in love and passionately evoke the life of joy which the new-found hoard will enable them to lead. But Axël persuades Sara that realization of a dream can never equal an unrealized ideal, and instead they drink poison and die together as dawn breaks. A brief reappearance of Maître Janus would have indicated that they had been right to free themselves from the trammels of life.[25]

These dispositions were to be changed many times during the coming years, and the First Part itself was to undergo substantial rewriting, but the general outlines of the play, particularly in its philosophical import, were to remain largely unaltered. For the readers of 1872, of course, these outlines and their implications were still unknown. What they were confronted with was a sombre fragment, couched in a sumptuous style, and organized with a superb sense of dramatic effect. To have made a whole long act turn so decisively on a single monosyllable is a remarkable achievement, and the utilization of spectacle and music in the interrupted taking of the veil is not unworthy of the Wagnerian music-dramas that inspired it. What must have surprised many of Villiers's friends is the overt and violent anticlericalism which suffuses the act. The Abbess and the Archdeacon are portrayed as tyrannical, cruel, and grasping hypocrites, and Hans Richter was quite right to think of Tartuffe—except that Villiers's attack is even more clearly directed against the Church itself than Molière's. Later alterations were somewhat to mask the vigour of the onslaught, but the 1872 text leaves no room for ambiguity. Sara's rejection of Christian asceticism is categorical and is only partly motivated by her attraction to occultist doctrines: it is mainly directed against the authoritarianism of the Church, and it is even more complete and final than Tullia Fabriana's refusal to believe, in *Isis* ten years before. Her 'No' clearly precludes any synthesis of Christianity with other systems, of the kind which he had envisaged for a variant ending of *Isis* in 1865 and had attempted to attain in *Claire Lenoir* in 1867.

Perhaps this outburst of hostility to the Church sprang from memories of the childhood sweetheart who, less determined than Sara, was forced to enter into religion against her will (if that was indeed what happened): it is difficult to account for the vehemence of the resentment without some such personal grudge. It is even harder to square it with the devoutly respectful tone which Villiers had used (with obvious sincerity) in writing to Dom Guéranger only a few months before. But it is as well to remember what the Abbess says of Sara: 'I believe her to be endowed with the terrible gift of Intelligence.'[26] That was certainly Villiers's opinion of himself, and he never took kindly to being told what it was licit for him to think. Hence the ambivalence in his relations with priests noted by several of his friends. Henry Roujon recalled being told that Villiers had once found himself at table next to a country priest, whom he was urging to read

Salammbô, when the priest turned on him and asked: 'Have you read Beaumarchais?' On being told that he had, the priest then flabbergasted Villiers by adding: 'But did you understand him?' According to Roujon, he could never be in a priest's company without asking awkward questions and then furnishing his own monstrously heretical answers.[27] Villiers's relations with Christianity, and more particularly with the Church as an institution, were always compounded of contradictory elements, but nowhere is the negative side so much in evidence as in the First Part of *Axël*.

However, in *Axël* Villiers was always striving to say the things which meant most to him and to delve most deeply into the secrets of his own heart and mind. That is why the work remained with him for many years and why he was so reluctant to give it its definitive form. It also explains why the level of his personality from which it draws its substance is one which did not easily manifest itself in his day-to-day behaviour. In fact, Émile Blémont, the editor of *La Renaissance*, remembered a Villiers apparently quite unlike the author of the darkly splendid work he was publishing. This is his account of an evening spent in a private room in a restaurant with Villiers and two or three other friends:

Villiers, at first silent and dreamy, seemed to perk up at the harmonious sound of the first rhymes he heard. He stood up, took a few steps, as if he wanted to reflect, came back to the table, and started speaking in his turn, to fall silent no more, gripping everyone's attention with the unconscious plenitude of his own being, effortlessly impressing us all by the natural effect of the abundance, the strangeness, and sometimes the profundity of his ideas and his imagination, by the unexpected and picturesque boldness of his language, by the ardour and the enthusiasm of his gestures, by the conviction of his tone, by the strange sparkling flame in his eyes, by the astonishing authority of his inspired and visionary nature. He would shoot off headlong on some fine chimaera of his poetics or his philosophy, then would stop suddenly and laugh. At himself or at others? There was no way of knowing. He looked as though he was making fun of his own enthusiasm as much as of the open-mouthed amazement of his friends. His nervous, jerky, sarcastic, and mysterious laugh seemed as troubled as it was troubling, as painful as it was mocking, and it went from the sneer of Voltaire to the gaiety of Rabelais. One could feel in it something subtle and ingenuous which constantly dis-orientated one. And how this slim, pale, little man, with his thin drooping moustache, would pull himself up to his full height after having effaced himself! How he flung back his long fair hair! With what a hysterical neighing sound he reared up at his own hallucinations! How great, handsome, and superb he seemed in these sudden lyrical flights, around which rumbled and eventually exploded the thunderbolts of his despairing irony! He was at one and the same time Faust and Mephisto. His fancy, metaphysical and bantering, danced like David before the Ark, or fled away on a broomstick like a witch to the sabbath. He became dionysiac, he became apollonian; he went from Aesop to Socrates, from Aristophanes to Aristotle. A magus and a fakir.[28]

The evening ended memorably with Villiers sitting down at the piano and singing his own setting of poems by Ronsard and Baudelaire.

15

With *Axël* continuing to occupy all his time, 1873 was outwardly not much more productive for Villiers than the previous two years had been—a poem and a short story in *La Renaissance,* and that was all. In order to try to earn some money, it did occur to him that the time might have come to attempt once again to have one of his early plays produced, the more so as he still had enough regard for them to read them aloud when the occasion arose; there had been readings of both *Elën* and *Morgane* in the house of Paul Verlaine's mother-in-law shortly before the war.[1] So in April 1873 he submitted *Morgane* to Carvalho, the new manager of the Vaudeville, and persuaded *La Renaissance* to insert a little note in support of the play, praising its 'singular plot, vigour of style, and dramatic complications'.[2] Though he was evidently unwilling to take time off from *Axël* to rewrite the play, he was prepared to envisage some shortening of the text to make it more manageable, and negotiations with the theatre evidently went far enough for agreement to be reached on some of the cuts.[3] But in the end Carvalho decided against *Morgane*. Despite this negative outcome, Villiers had come near enough to success to make him feel that *Morgane* might after all be a viable theatrical proposition, and for some time to come he devoted considerable effort to getting it into production.

Another development in 1873 was a result of the political situation in the country as a whole, since it was in that year that the likelihood of a restoration of the monarchy first approached and then receded. With a monarchist majority in the National Assembly and some apparent prospect of agreement between Legitimists and Orleanists, it seemed in the summer as though the proclamation of the Comte de Chambord as Henri V was imminent. But on 27 October the Count wrote an open letter declaring his absolute refusal to sacrifice his honour by accepting any flag other than the white standard of the Bourbons. Henceforward the restoration was impossible. These events moved Villiers and stirred in him a royalism which up to that point had been largely dormant. It is more than likely that as a child he had been brought up in that somewhat independent and disrespectful fidelity to the king in which the Breton nobility and in particular his own family specialized, and in later years he claimed to have had nostalgic thoughts about 'the king in exile' during the Second Empire.[4] But nothing in his public acts or words had hitherto denoted any very real commitment to the royal cause—indeed, his flirtation with the extreme left around 1870 and 1871 would scarcely have been compatible with it. The nearness of the restoration and the Comte de Chambord's uncompromising stand however altered that, and he drafted a poem apostrophizing Henri V which, though he did not publish it, betokened a much livelier interest in the politics of legitimism. In the only two stanzas which survive, he calls on the king to return to his land but approves of his decision to stand by the traditional flag: typically, Villiers prefers the noble gesture to mundane political practicalities. But one isolated line gives a significant insight into his personal involvement with Chambord: 'We, your great barons, waiting in the shadows with folded arms'.[5] Only in a monarchy could the Villiers de l'Isle-Adams occupy their rightful place in society: the theme was to become ever more important for the rest of his life and to make him ever more active in politics.

As for his private life, the obsession with marrying a rich heiress had lost none of its potency, though there were no doubt other less prestigious and more transitory attachments in the meantime. Some time around 1869 or 1870 there had been an affair with a certain Marianne, about which nothing is known other than that Villiers wrote her an extremely charming letter breaking off relations,[6] and in the middle of 1873 there occurred a mysterious episode in which he pretended to be about to go to Brittany, in order to escape from some woman who, so he said, was pursuing him.[7] Fernand Calmettes relates that at one time he was inordinately proud to have won the favours of a fashionable Jewish courtesan, but suddenly stopped seeing her when someone pointed out to him that, if she became pregnant, the next Villiers de l'Isle-Adam would be half-Jewish.[8] The same prejudice likewise got in the way of some of the possible matches with heiresses, since several of them were Jewish. It may be that one such match was in the offing in the spring of 1872: that seems to be the implication a rather illiterate missive sent to him then by a gentleman who was evidently acting as some kind of intermediary.[9]

But the most extraordinary episode of this kind occurred at the end of 1873. The first signs of something afoot came when Villiers started writing round, early in December, to try to collect copies of the favourable reviews of *La Révolte* which had appeared in 1870. To Banville, he was portentous and vague:

The thing is this: *for a reason which is of absolute urgency and importance for me,* I need, but really need, the article which you wrote about me in the *Opinion* (. . .) My dear friend, it is *highly important and highly urgent, I assure you:* you must believe that I am very serious when I set my mind to it, and never more so than now! It is a matter, I confess, quite exceptionally vital for me.[10]

To a Mme Hennequin, a few days later, he was equally pressing and mysterious: 'Your article being one of the few and one of the best which took up my defence, I should be very happy to have it, and it just so happens that it would be to my very real advantage to have it today.'[11]

What Villiers was doing was in fact putting together his

credentials as a prospective husband. He took the view that he had two inestimable qualifications: his name and his genius. The one he could demonstrate with his family archives, and that is no doubt why he deposited them officially with his notary Me Pinguet on 19 November 1873.[12] The other could of course be shown by the brilliance of his conversation (secretly he had a low opinion of the intelligence of women, but he liked persuading them they were clever, by means of a display of his own talents); nevertheless, a few written proofs that his outstanding qualities had been recognized by others would not come amiss. Hence the desire to compile a dossier of articles praising *La Révolte*, which at that stage were about the only reviews of his work to have appeared in print.

The cause of all these preparations was an introduction to an Anglo-Irish heiress which had been arranged for him by a certain Comte de La Houssaye, who was either a professional or an amateur matrimonial agent and to whose wife Villiers believed himself to be related.[13] Little is known about La Houssaye other than what can be deduced from the contract which he entered into with Villiers and which must be one of the most incredible pacts since Faust's agreement with Mephistopheles. Its terms are known from the receipt which La Houssaye gave to Villiers on 23 December, the main part of which runs as follows:

I the undersigned acknowledge having received from the Comte de Villiers de l'Isle-Adam a signed promissory note for two hundred thousand francs, payable upon his marriage to the person to whom I am to introduce him, and in the event of the marriage not taking place, the note would be null and void and consequently could not be presented.

Having accepted this unbelievable document, Villiers suddenly had misgivings: supposing the girl turned out not to be so rich as La Houssaye alleged, would he not then be ruined? So La Houssaye generously penned an additional clause and duly signed it: 'The fortune of the wife of the Comte de Villiers will have to be at least three millions.'[14] Thus everyone's interest was safeguarded, and the preparations for the introduction could go ahead.

These preparations, apart from collecting the evidence of his ancestry and his talents, consisted of making himself more presentable, since both his clothing and his person were showing distinct signs of wear. La Houssaye, who obviously had a strong interest in sacrificing a number of sprats to catch a very large mackerel, advanced Villiers sufficient money for him to buy a repeating-watch and another of his favourite fur-trimmed overcoats, and to invest in a set of false teeth (for some time past, his teeth had been badly decayed, and he often kept his hand in front of his mouth to hide them when he was talking). Then there was the question of language. Villiers had not studied English at school, but his friend Mallarmé, who was one of the few people in the secret of his plans, taught English at the Lycée Condorcet, so he was pressed into service to give a couple of English lessons. When he ventured to point out that time was rather short, Villiers replied that they could simplify things: 'Since it's a matter of a wedding, I'll only learn the future tense of the verbs.'[15]

Then, towards the end of December, Villiers crossed the Channel, under the watchful eye of La Houssaye. Evidently there had been some previous correspondence with the young lady,[16] but the meeting itself was a revelation. His prospective fiancée was a Miss Anna Eyre Powell, doubtless connected with the Irish family of the Eyre Powells of Clonshavoy,[17] and her interest in things French (including husbands) derived from the fact that she had for some reason been brought up in a convent in Paris. She had also had some training as a singer in Italy, and in later years was to return to France as an opera singer and subsequently a magazine editor.[18] Whether she was really as rich as La Houssaye supposed is doubtful, but it seems that her father had estates in both England and Ireland, so there may well have been money in the background. According to Villiers, he was intent on his daughter marrying a man whom she did not love; it was therefore going to be necessary for her to wait until she was of age to marry without his consent, after which they would elope together.[19] Her subsequent career suggests that she had literary as well as musical interests; it also suggests that she was of unorthodox and independent temperament, but that she did not have the means to live without earning some money.

When Villiers first set eyes on her, the effect was immediate, as he confided to his best friend:

Dear Mallarmé, I have fallen in love very late in life and it's the first time that I've been in love. How can I compare what is incomparable? I love an Angel whose like is positively not to be found anywhere under the sun! She is the last one, my dear friend, there can never be anyone better! I love the only possible wife for me. It's all very fine about her millions, it's very fortunate and very splendid, but that's not the point at all now. It's quite natural that a star should have radiance, it's an admirable thing; but the star is a celestial body too, independently of the atmosphere that makes it shine.[20]

To Judith Gautier, he is almost as ecstatic. Pretending that both he and Judith are dead from boredom, he writes:

My dear Judith, there is a girl who is a dream from Ossian, who has never harmed anyone, who is as beautiful as the East and who will love you as if you existed! You will leave her that illusion, so that she may grow in the charm which you will spread through her soul, and we mustn't tell her that we are dead, in order that we may sometimes come to life again ourselves in the splendours of purity. I hope to bring her to see you one day, and you will see that Chance is a serious matter and that it's not for nothing that I am losing my head.[21]

What exactly Villiers did during his stay in England is not very clear. Mallarmé had given him the address of his friend John Payne, solicitor and poet, and Villiers called on him to discuss his affairs on 30 December and again on 2 January;[22] no doubt legal advice was both welcome and necessary, and Villiers was duly grateful for the help. When he was in London, he stayed at the Grosvenor Hotel at Victoria, but he also made two trips to Newcastle-under-Lyme (the Eyre Powell country house was evidently in Staffordshire),[23] and he talked about going to Dublin as well, although he perhaps did not do so in the end. What the purpose of this frenetic activity was cannot be guessed, but Villiers was extremely pleased with himself over it: 'The only important thing is to use one's will-power calmly and methodically, and I'm beginning to get down to it.' Miss Eyre Powell, whom Villiers affectionately referred to as 'R' because the French pronunciation of the letter is approximately that of 'Eyre', spent a lot of time with him in London, calling him, so he said, 'her own, own Auguste all day long'. They went to Hyde Park together, to the Crystal Palace, and to the Drury Lane Theatre, where they saw Mozart's *Don Giovanni*. But Villiers was in such an amorous daze that he was completely blind to his surroundings: 'She was there, that's all.'[24]

So, contrary to all expectations, the future seemed to be rosy. Miss Eyre Powell was going to have a French poet of noble lineage as her husband; Villiers was going to marry a beautiful heiress with whom he had fallen head-over-heels in love; the Comte de La Houssaye looked forward to collecting his 200,000 francs. Mallarmé was overjoyed at his friend's good fortune:

You cannot imagine what good your letter has done me: not for the many whispered details, which confirm me in my hopes (I have not the least doubt that you will carry everything to a successful conclusion), but because of an impression of freshness and rejuvenation which your pages contain. The nearness of happiness gives you completely back to yourself (. . .) At last! But no, one must not say: at last. All the past, bad as it was, never existed, cast it to the winds! That has nothing to do with you, and you have only forgetfulness for it.[25]

Villiers himself, accustomed to the most violent disappointments, hardly dared to believe what was happening. Telling Judith that the girl was the incarnation of a magnificent dream, he added firmly, 'and one that won't escape me',[26] but with Mallarmé he confessed to a feeling of 'mortal anguish'. Still, he said that Payne had noticed a 'transfiguration' in him, and he even persuaded himself that he had mastered the English language, though the few lines he ventured to write to Mallarmé throw doubts on his fluency: 'Aoh! That is the most elegant and lovely gentleman I never knew. It is possible that it was poor fellow called Villiers? Aoh! very strange! very curious, indeed! etc . . .'[27]

Then, without warning, something went drastically wrong. What exactly it was will probably never be known. John Payne, who was well placed to follow events, thought the girl was to blame, though he admitted, when writing to

Mallarmé, that he did not know the full circumstances: 'I fear (as I have always feared) that the unfortunate outcome is the fault of the girl, a somewhat hysterical young person and a *poseuse*. I took good care not to say a word to Villiers, but I think he realized what my opinion was on that score.'[28] Two other views have certainly the overtones of legend, but may well have some basis in fact. One comes from Henry Roujon and doubtless originates with Marras. In this version Villiers met his beloved in a box at Covent Garden:

He was vague and tumultuous. He recited his next book to the foreign girl, poured lyricism over her, and terrified her; she took him for a fugitive from Bedlam. That very evening, the young miss, still trembling, declared that she preferred eternal celibacy, and even the convent, to the countly coronet of l'Isle-Adam.[29]

Another version was given by Mallarmé himself to Gustave Kahn, who noted, correctly, that the matrimonial agent was called something like Lahoussaye or Lahousset, and added that he had the somewhat unsavoury reputation of having been in the slave trade and having then tried an unsuccessful act of piracy against the mailboat to India, after which he returned to obscure business deals between London and Paris. This is what Kahn writes:

The introduction took place in a box at Covent Garden; the next day the young lady left London without giving any indication about her movements. Lahousset accused Villiers of having spent his time on a scarifying lecture about Hegel. However, he did not give up, but his information was so imprecise that he had to abandon the idea of pursuing the girl.[30]

In both the Roujon and Kahn versions, once the prospect of a marriage vanished, so did La Houssaye, leaving Villiers alone in London, with his new false teeth, but without the fur coat or the repeating watch, which the indignant agent reclaimed as his property.

There is just enough concordance between these pieces of evidence for one to hazard a conjecture about what actually occurred. Anna Eyre Powell, or Anna Eyre, to give her the name under which she later went as a singer and journalist, was a romantically minded and rather unstable young lady, on bad terms with her father, and she was dazzled by the idea of marrying an author of considerable promise who also bore one of the most ancient and distinguished names in France. The initial impression, when she met him, was good, and there was a brief idyll during which they both decided they were made for one another. But then Villiers's excitability led him into ever greater excesses of incoherent volubility, after which Anna suddenly came to her senses and wondered whether she was not about to commit an act of folly. The consequence was an abrupt departure after an evening at Covent Garden; thereafter Villiers, having disappointed his rapacious matrimonial agent, was left to his own devices to make his way back to Paris as best he could, probably with assistance from the French Consulate. Whether or not this reconstitution is accurate, there is no doubt that the whole episode, comic as it may have seemed years later to those who had known Villiers, had marked him for life. For once, his extravagant hopes really had seemed to be on the point of realization, and sensible friends like Mallarmé, Judith Gautier, and John Payne had confirmed that he was not entirely deluding himself. Then, just as complete success had seemed to be within his grasp, the whole edifice had come crashing to the ground, and he found himself not only rejected by a woman who had appeared to love him, but humiliated by being abandoned without a penny in a foreign country.

One can of course take the view that the whole story is so wildly implausible that even Villiers can never have taken it seriously and that therefore the hurt from it was more imagined than real. But Villiers lived so much in a dream world, and his contacts with what others saw as reality were so intermittent, that his involvement with Anna Eyre was total and unconditional, the more so as the girl's own unpredictable and impressionable nature offered him every encouragement. Villiers's letters to Mallarmé and Judith Gautier, as well as John Payne's letters to Mallarmé, make it crystal clear that Villiers had thrown himself heart and soul into his projected marriage with Anna. That others may have thought the whole thing ridiculous, that La Houssaye may have been little better than a crook, that it would have been an extraordinary coincidence if Villiers and his prospective fiancée had seen eye to eye, all that is irrelevant. With all his faults of credulity and fantasy, Villiers lived out to the utmost degree of commitment every role in which he cast himself, and this ignominious collapse of his hopes was perhaps the cruellest blow he ever suffered.[31]

Yet once again his indomitable spirit enabled him to overcome his wounds, even if he could never forget them, and within days of his return to Paris he was once more trying to persuade theatre managers to take on *Morgane*. This time he turned to the Théâtre de la Porte Saint-Martin, famous for its spectacular productions of melodramas, and, after calling on the manager, sent him a dilapidated copy of the play, the last one he had, with a letter in which he vaunted the quality of the work:

In reality, it is a melodrama, in the manner of 1830, passably written, I believe, and which involved me in some rather curious historical research. I conceived it according to a dramatic system which is as yet little known: that is, certain exaggerations of style are deliberate, so that the actor may express them with the greatest simplicity and a minimum of gestures.[32]

But when he went back to the theatre, he found that no one had bothered to read the play, and, although Théodore Barrière, the popular playwright who had already helped him at the time of *La Révolte*, went with him to lend his support, the management was not sufficiently interested to allow him to give a reading. 'One needs a lot of courage in the face of so much stupidity, so much nameless silliness, and so many perpetual disappointments,' he wrote despondently to Fernand de Gantès, a journalist friend who was very close to him at the time and who had evidently suggested trying the Théâtre de la Porte Saint-Martin. Momentary bitterness and discouragement overcame him at the end of the letter:

I thank you all the same and from the bottom of my heart for the kind thought you had, my dear good Fernand, but you see how it is, the earth in itself dislikes me: it suspects me of being one of its oldest enemies, and the circumstances which I am constantly coming up against are nothing more than the manifestations of its hatred in the sphere of instinct, emanating from the people of the earth, even though they do not realize it.[33]

16

By this time Villiers had probably finished *Axël*. There exist several fragments of what had obviously once been a complete text of the play, very carefully copied out by the author in inks of different colours (the calligraphy of such manuscripts shows that, when he took the trouble, Villiers could still produce the elegant handwriting which had won him prizes at school), and it is likely that this was ready by 1874.[1] But the shape of the play had been altered since the publication of the First Part in 1872. Though it was still to have three parts, Villiers had introduced into the second a whole new development which was eventually to have a drastic effect on the nature of the work. This was to do with the way in which Axël was tempted by the treasure. In the original version Axël had been reminded of its existence by an old servant; now Villiers brought in a new character, a cousin of Axël called Gaspar, or the Commander, a grasping and unscrupulous visitor whose one aim is to get his hands on the gold, the secret of which he worms out of the old servant. Learning of his nefarious designs, Axël challenges him to a duel and kills him, after which the action proceeds as before, with the hero refusing to accept the initiation proffered him by Maître Janus. The advantages of this new departure were that it brought more life and movement into what was otherwise a somewhat static and cerebral section, it introduced a contrast of styles and personalities, and it presented an opportunity for a philosophic clash between idealism and materialism, impossible in the original conception. But it began to obscure the essential symmetry between the reunciations of Sara and Axël, and it brought an element of confusion into Axël's motivation, since his attitude to the recovery of the treasure became inconsistent—on the one hand, he killed the Commander in order that the treasure might remain buried for ever, and on the other he was himself tempted to retrieve it. This discrepancy was to trouble Villiers for years and to entrap him in much tortuous rewriting.

Whether Villiers made any effort to interest producers or publishers in *Axël* at this stage is unknown. If he did, it has not left any trace in his correspondence or in the memoirs of anyone who knew him, and it is quite likely that he wished to hold it in reserve until such time as he was able to present it to the world in conditions befitting his great work. Perhaps too he had veered away from any idea of allowing it to be staged. The text of the First Part as printed in *La Renaissance* in 1872 is undoubtedly intended for the theatre, but Villiers later came to feel that a philosophical drama of this kind, like *Faust*, was more suitable for reading. That may have deterred him from offering it to theatre managers, a breed about which he was in any case feeling increasingly cynical.

This cynicism about the modern world which was using him so badly was however turned to good account in a number of pseudo-scientific fantasies which Villiers composed at this time. The first of them appeared in *La Renaissance littéraire et artistique* on 30 November 1873 under the title *La Découverte de M. Grave*, which was later changed to *L'Affichage céleste*. It is an ironic eulogy of a supposed new invention which would enable the sky to be used for advertising purposes, under which guise Villiers satirizes the commercialism, the materialism, and the vulgarity of nineteenth-century France, with a sideswipe at republican politics and the adulation of progress. The first of Villiers's purely satirical tales, it is written with great verve, and obviously made him realize that there was a rich vein to be exploited. Not long after, he set about a companion-piece to be entitled *La Machine à gloire*, the invention this time being a device for automatic applause or boos in the theatre, which of course gives rise to a swingeing attack on the popular drama of the day, together with the managers, the critics, and the public who supported it. At first Villiers had begun the story with a list of other possible fantastic inventions, but he soon saw that several of them were capable of furnishing material for independent tales, and so excised them from *La Machine à gloire*, which was published in two numbers of *La Renaissance* in March 1874.[2] One of the offshoots thus created appeared as *L'Appareil du Dr Abeille Ê. Ê. pour l'analyse chimique du dernier soupir*, in which the idea is that of an apparatus by which children can learn to carry out a chemical analysis of the dying breath of their parents, thereby distracting their attention from any possible grief they might feel—one of Villier's regular complaints against the bourgeois mentality was that it was deeply afraid of genuine emotion.

One incident which marked the publication of *La Découverte de M. Grave* illustrates the dangers to which Villiers exposed himself by his inveterate habit of rehearsing his works verbally in cafés before publishing them. A few days after *La Renaissance* had printed the tale, an article signed 'Lousteau' appeared in *Le Gaulois*, beginning: 'Let us move on to something unpublished, or at any rate I believe that the following idea, which is really the property of Villiers de l'Isle-Adam, the whimsical poet, has never been published by him.' There then came what was very recognisably a version of *La Découverte de M. Grave*. Not unnaturally, the editor of *La Renaissance* reacted sharply: 'What do you think of this curious and irresponsible way of taking over other people's property? Not only do they steal from a journal, but they assert that it doesn't exist, that what appears in it has never been published. That is a very arbitrary refinement.' But in fact the lines with which 'Lousteau' concludes the article reveal what had happened: 'May Villiers forgive us for having perhaps rendered his idea very badly ... but even so, is it not an admirable fantasy?' Clearly, the journalist had heard Villiers spinning his story in some café and had simply borrowed it, with due acknowledgement, but without realizing that it had appeared in print in the meantime.

'Lousteau' may therefore be considered blameless. But not all such borrowings were so innocent, and Villiers's friends often waxed indignant at the way in which others did not hesitate to profit from the riches which he so casually and prodigally lavished on them in his nocturnal divagations. A café waiter remembered that, when Villiers arrived, people would sigh with pretended boredom, but that, when he started telling stories, some would turn aside and take notes.[3] It is said that, on one occasion, after a colleague had published under his own name one of Villiers's tales, Villiers raised his hand to stop him sitting at the same table the next day: 'Be on your way, you were given something yesterday.'[4] Gustave Guiches confirms that there were writers who did not scruple about making a note of the anecdotes he retailed, the projects he outlined, the plots he invented.[5] There is no way of knowing how many of his ideas were thus appropriated and plagarized by others, but some approximation can be gleaned from the number of his tales recorded and repeated by friends who did acknowledge their source.

Catulle Mendès for example preserved this apologue. A stone at the bottom of the sea off the coast of Brittany, covered with moss and seaweed, never moved for years and years. Then one day a saint who walked under the water to bless those who had drowned saw the motionless stone and asked it what it had been doing for so many years. The stone replied that it had been contemplating the most distant star and, whenever it disappeared, waiting for it to shine again. 'What a strange way of passing the time!' said the saint: 'What good has that done you?' 'Remove the moss and the seaweed that cover me,' answered the stone. The saint did as he was asked. Then he saw that the stone was all diamond and that it was shining as brightly as the most luminous constellation in the sky.[6] Other tales were more savage in tone. The scene is a room. A woman is writhing on the bed. Around her are all the paraphernalia of a birth: doctor, midwife, bottles, phials; a sickly smell. The child pokes its head out with difficulty, looks around, says: 'Is that what life is like? Oh!'—and goes back again.[7] Then there is this lightning drama. A man armed with a sword leaps furiously out of a cab, dashes up a staircase, breaks down a door. On the bed a couple are making love. With a shout of 'Wretches!' he runs them both through. Then he turns the corpses over, looks at them with stupefaction, and says: 'Oh! oh! ...': he is on the wrong floor.[8]

But by no means all such inventions were scattered to the winds. The success of the scientific fantasies published in late 1873 and early 1874 brought it home to Villiers that, pending the completion of his large-scale works, there was a market for the more restricted form of the short story, and though he had no access to the main daily press, he was increasingly ready to produce a tale when asked for a contribution to a literary magazine. So he gave stories to the short-lived *Revue du Monde nouveau* founded by his friend Charles Cros in February 1874, to the barely less ephemeral *Semaine pari-*

sienne which survived from March until July of the same year and of which Fernand de Gantès was editorial secretary, to *La Comédie française* which first appeared in December 1874 and lasted until the following March. There cannot have been much profit in writing for reviews of this kind, but they revived Villiers's vocation as a story-teller and helped him to cultivate a facet of his talent which he had perhaps been in danger of sacrificing to his ambitions as a dramatist.

These ambitions were however as strong as ever, and continued to focus on *Morgane*. But now Villiers was beginning to wonder whether the play might not have some inherent defects that were responsible for its lack of success with theatre managers. So some time in 1874 he sat down to revise it completely. By the end of December he was able to inform the general agent of the Society of Dramatists that he had in hand 'something serious' for the theatre and that 'to be able to finish and get something done is now only a matter of strict necessity'.[9] A month later he had submitted it to the Théâtre Lyrique-Dramatique, as the public were informed by a note in his friend François Oswald's gossip column in *Le Gaulois* on 29 January 1875: 'To arouse curiosity is already something; M. Villiers de l'Isle-Adam deserves attention at least from the literary point of view; let us wait and see'. A further item the next day gave the names of those who would take the leading parts if the play was acted: they included the actor–manager Castellano and Mlle Rousseil, one of the most famous star actresses of the time. At this stage the play was entitled *L'Aventurière*, but it was soon to be renamed *Le Prétendant*. Villiers wrote to thank Oswald for his help: 'I should have started with the theatre again sooner, at least that's what people tell me.' Then, remembering that Edmond Tarbé of *Le Gaulois* had been one of the severest critics of *La Révolte*, he added a wry postscript:

Without rancour towards your 'Editor', M. Tarbé, who will, I think and hope (for his sake and a bit for mine too), change his mind about my ineptitude as a playwright.—Ha! what had I done to him, in the dim and distant past, to give him the teeniest justification for the awful ire which he displayed towards me at the time of the unfortunate *Révolte*? But let us not revive those memories: *La Révolte* was just a prediction that came true two months later, that's all. It is like the person who was shouting: Disaster to the city! and was struck on the forehead by a stone while he was shouting. The stone didn't kill me; it perked me up; I'm all cheery and joyful!'[10]

However, even Oswald's calculated indiscretions did not produce the desired effect on Castellano, and a month later Villiers was negotiating with another manager, Émile Weinschenk, who had just taken over the Théâtre des Arts. Weinschenk's initial reaction was favourable, and on 25 February he wrote encouragingly to the author: 'I should be glad to re-open the theatre with your work in which I should ask for some changes, I warn you, but which I would put on in a lavish production that would bring back the splendours of Fournier's time, and you remember how well we used to do things.'[11] A month later all was still well, and Villiers was metaphorically rubbing his hands with glee when he wrote to Fernand de Gantès on 20 March: 'Never worry about Weinschenk: the deal between him and me is signed, sealed, and delivered. *Le Prétendant*, or rather *Morgane* (since with your usual tact you have guessed that it's the same thing, you rascal), will be the opening play of the season under his management.' Villiers was delighted that the enlargement of the stage would enhance the play's spectacular effects, and he was puffed up with pride at the impression the play had created when he read it to Weinschenk and his associates: 'Weinschenk was in tears, my friend! Would you believe it? Clèves and the others were positively thunderstruck. During the five and a half hours the reading lasted, my triumph just went on increasing.' The conclusion was naturally glowing: 'In a word, and not to have any unnecessary illusions, I think there will be a material success, a little fame, and twenty or thirty thousand francs (with the translations, the provinces and the book), and that is not to be sneezed at.'[12] A week later Oswald announced in *Le Gaulois* that the Théâtre des Arts would re-open with Villiers's play.

In fact *Le Prétendant* is a very different play from *Morgane*, Villiers's adaptation having been very skilfully done. He has eliminated the tiresome sorceress, he has given the conspiracy a much more convincing political content, he has lengthened and strengthened Lady Hamilton's role, he has tightened up the organization of the plot, and he has rewritten the absurd last act so that it becomes a magnificently taut piece of suspense. The play is thus made into an extremely powerful drama from which all the original defects have disappeared, leaving only its very real qualities. That in its new form it should have exerted a strong appeal to an enterprising director like Weinschenk is entirely comprehensible: its strongly-drawn characters, its lively and varied action, its dazzling lyricism, its strong sense of the spectacular, its subtle political discussions, and its truly tragic ring make it a very good play indeed.

So Villiers's hopes were once again running high, the more so as *Le Prétendant* was not the only iron he had in the fire. In the early months of 1875 there had been a rumour that there was to be a competition for a play to celebrate the centenary of the American Declaration of Independence the following year, and, though the official announcement did not come until 21 April, it was common knowledge before then that the competition was to be a very important and prestigious affair. The effect which this had on Villiers was nothing short of electrifying, as one can judge from his letter to Fernand de Gantès, which was obviously written in a state of exhilaration, not to say intoxication:

I come to the point, capital and grave for me beyond all expression. Stretch your retinas (without squinting, though! without squinting, Fernand, do you hear me?) and run your eyes feverishly over the following lines: 'The Legation of the United States . . .' Get it into your brain that everything on earth is futile except this, my child: 'The Legation of the United States has just instituted a competition in France on the occasion of the Centenary of American Independence (1876).'

After outlining the conditions, Villiers goes on in an ever more excited tone:

The prize of 10,000 francs is nothing, the royalties are enormous and themselves are nothing in comparison to victory. Performed in Philadelphia in April 1876, with a production costing 300,000 francs at the Exhibition, then throughout America and in all the capitals of Europe, the same month, in twenty-five translations. Special contracts, voyage with the American embassy: over there, lectures at 100 francs a ticket, 5 or 10 dollars a head, like anything! Well, if I cared about that sort of thing, the money alone would be worth it, but apart from the formidable pleasure of constructing and writing such a universal drama if ever there was one, the finest possible modern subject, there is renown, glory itself instantly conquered in the whole wide world![13]

It is hard to believe that all this excitement was taking place in the aftermath of yet another disappointment in love, but that is how it was. The catastrophe with Anna Eyre had come about with dramatic suddenness, in a matter of days after Villiers had first met her; the latest blow was the culmination of a much longer process. For a number of years past the beautiful Augusta Holmès had been Catulle Mendès's mistress, and had borne him more than one child—a fervent Wagnerian, she had frequently been the travelling companion of Catulle and Judith on their musical journeys across Europe, notably to Munich in 1869. Indeed she may have become pregnant while she was there, since it was rumoured that there would have been a terrible family scandal had her father not died later that year before the child was born.[14] Judith can scarcely have been aware of her husband's infidelity but seems to have decided to make the best of the situation. Then, in 1873, Catulle's behaviour towards her became so boorish that a break was inevitable. He and Judith had gone to Vienna to report on the Exhibition there, with Augusta as usual in tow, when Judith fell so seriously ill with cholera that she had to be sent back to Paris. But Catulle, who had installed Augusta in a better apartment than the one he had rented for his wife, refused to accompany her, and she had to be taken home by a friend.[15] Though she was deeply wounded by this callousness and at first thought of leaving him, there was a reconciliation in the late summer,[16] and they continued to live together for several months more. However, by May 1874 the situation, which was public knowledge, had become so intolerable that Catulle, whether voluntarily or not, left Judith and went to live with Augusta, thus making their long-standing liaison quasi-official (there was no divorce in France at the time, and the legal separation did not come until 1878; divorce eventually followed in 1896).

At first sight it would not seem that Villiers should have

been particularly affected by what happened in 1874. He obviously knew that Augusta was Catulle's mistress and had had children by him, so one might suppose that any hopes he might once have had with her would have died long since. Yet the evidence is that, until Catulle actually went to live permanently with her, he nourished the delusion that she might eventually prefer him to his friend. A deformed echo of this situation is to be heard in the reminiscences of Baude de Maurceley, who met both men in Nina de Villard's *salon* a year or two later, and, though the details he gives are obviously wrong, it is clear that Nina and her friends knew roughly what had happened. Baude is describing an evening in the house in the rue des Moines:

Villiers and Mendès had drawn near to Augusta Holmès. The two men were friends, but there was little love lost between them, since they had always been more or less jealous of one another. They were together at Bayreuth, at the theatre which King Ludwig II of Bavaria had built for the performance of Wagner's work, when they first met Augusta Holmès, then at the height of her youthful beauty: that is where they got to know her, and they soon fell in love with her. There arose an ardent and assiduous rivalry, but Villiers, the irresponsible bohemian genius, intrigued Augusta but did not appeal to her, while Mendès, exceedingly romantic and dashing, passionately committed, like her, to Wagnerian music, struck her as the most seductive of poets. Resigned to his defeat, Villiers was painfully hurt by it, but he managed to hide the fact, and contented himself with remaining the friend of the young couple whose radiant and triumphal love filled the pilgrims of Bayreuth with wonder.[17]

All the references to Bayreuth in this story are so patently wide of the mark that there might be a temptation to dismiss it as so much invention, were it not that Mallarmé's correspondence provides corroboration of its basic truth. Shortly after Catulle had gone to live with Augusta, Mallarmé spent an evening in their house, and on 20 May 1874 sent Catulle a letter in which he wrote: 'Several times it was on the tip of my tongue yesterday evening, when I was sleepy after the cigarettes, to say that you ought to invite Villiers and talk to him: not to do so would be distressing for him, and even wounding.'[18] Obviously it was embarrassment and not absent-mindedness which had held Mallarmé back from speaking. With his usual delicacy and his incomparable understanding of Villiers, he wanted Mendès to realize that the new situation with Augusta would deeply hurt Villiers and that it was his duty to palliate the shock as much as he could. But if he thought it important to do that, he must have known how much Augusta still meant to his friend.

Subsequent events can have done nothing to lessen Villiers's hurt. Augusta had five children by Catulle, one of whom died; he rapidly ran through her fortune, and she soon realized the defects of his character. After Villiers's death they separated for good, and Augusta, who was reduced to making a living by giving piano lessons, used thereafter to refer to her years with Catulle as her 'life of unhappiness'.[19] In addition to knowing that Mendès was making Augusta miserable, Villiers must also have felt very sorry for the unfortunate Judith, who had been so good to him and for whom he had so much affection. Even so, he continued to frequent Mendès's Wednesday evening gatherings, but it must have been with mixed feelings. Their friendship, never tranquil, now became much more distant, and Villiers's epigrams about Catulle were ever more savagely barbed.

But there was always the prospect of seeing *Le Prétendant* produced at last and of winning the prize for the American play, so there were artistic consolations for the failures in his private life. These consolations also included contacts with two of his idols, Victor Hugo and Gustave Flaubert. Villiers was introduced to Hugo on 8 August 1874, and, when he learnt that the old poet had agreed to be president of the jury for the American competition, he called on him again: 'He isn't entering himself, of course, otherwise it would have been grave, not to say frightful. He told me himself and said: 'Go ahead!'' '[20] Though nothing more is known of what passed between the two men, it must have been an enormous privilege for Villiers at last to meet the writer whom he had admired for so long and who was universally recognized as the greatest living French poet. The extent to which Hugo's poetry went to his heart can be gauged by an incident witnessed a couple of years later by the painter

Franc-Lamy. He was passing in front of the Taverne Pousset when he saw a man bent over the new *Légende des siècles*, and greeted him:

'Hello, Villiers how are things?' Villiers straightened up. Two tears were trickling down his cheeks. 'Listen!' he said with a sob. Then he read a passage:
Vautour, qu'apportes-tu?—Les morts de la bataille . . .
He was there, amid the customers, as much alone with his thoughts and his impressions as if he had been in a desert. And he said, still shaken with emotion: 'It's good! Oh! It's good! . . .'[21]

Gustave Flaubert he had of course met ten years previously, but for some reason he had not kept up relations with him, and so a renewed meeting in 1874 was a great joy. In fact, Villiers sprang to Flaubert's defence twice in that year, with a eulogy of *La Tentation de saint Antoine*, which had just been published, and with a vindication of his play *Le Candidat*, which was a total failure when it was produced at the Vaudeville, where *La Révolte* had crashed so resoundingly four years previously. The article on *La Tentation*, despite its praise for the work, reveals some reservations of a religious nature, since Villiers argues, not without justification, that Flaubert's Antoine is not a real saint, having none of the childish warmth and spontaneity that characterize true Christian feeling. But with *Le Candidat*, a black comedy satirizing republican politics, Villiers's sympathy is total, and he takes the opportunity to produce a bitter denunciation of current theatrical practice as well as an eloquent proclamation of faith in the future of true drama, of which *Le Candidat* is for him an example. It is worth noting that Villiers's article is almost the only favourable notice the play received, as the professional critics were unanimous in damning it.

The actual occasion when Villiers met Flaubert again is graphically described by Henry Roujon, who was present. It happened in Catulle Mendès's flat, just after the publication of *La Tentation*:

It was like the burgrave Magnus among the little counts Gorlois. With the moustache of a Scandinavian pirate and the bulging eyes of a peasant, he resembled some legendary ogre. While he devoured fiercely and affectionately the magnificent dishes that Mendès's marvellous cook had prepared, he kept saying formidable things. We hung on his words as if they were oracles—enormous pieces of gossip, illustrious memories, exaltations, anathemas, the whole gamut of his joys, his resentments, and his furies. He went away early, leaving us terrified and subjugated. And while one of us read out again the dialogue between the Sphinx and the Chimaera, the spiritual presence of the kindly master hovered over the empty seat in which his gigantic frame had spread itself. Villiers, in his corner, was weeping with enthusiasm. We went to bed at dawn, drunk on style and exhausted with admiration.[22]

One of Villiers's most endearing qualities was his capacity for surrendering himself totally to the art and the artists he loved. Who could say, when his most beloved creators were Baudelaire, Wagner, Hugo, and Flaubert, that he was wrong to do so?

17

At the beginning of 1875, with the production of *Le Prétendant* imminent and the American competition on the horizon, Villiers's most urgent need was for peace and quiet so that he could get on with his writing undisturbed. In Paris, this was hardly possible. His address was still in Batignolles, though rue Clairaut now rather than rue Brochant; presumably he was still living with his parents, in so far as he had a fixed address at all, and that cannot have been conducive to calm and meditation. Fortunately Fernand de Gantès, whom he considered to be a distant relative (anyone with a 'de' to his name was bound to be at least a cousin) as well as a friend and colleague, was fiercely loyal to him and had a family which was prepared to give him full support. An aunt of Gantès seems to have owned a house near Nantes called Les Roches-Grises, and she too was devoted to Villiers, together with another member of the family called Eugène. These are the sort of terms in which she wrote to Villiers:

Do not be discouraged. You will succeed in spite of *everything* and *everyone*. Fernand tells me something of what you are doing. This is a last testing-time, I hope, and you will come out of it triumphantly. *God is just*, so do not doubt, and be of good heart (. . .) Don't count on anyone in future except *yourself* and *us three*.

Fernand is the tenderest and most loving brother to you. If you only heard him when anyone dares to make the least remark in front of him that isn't to your advantage! The other evening I thought I was going to have to leave, he had been so violent.[1]

These were the loyal friends who in March 1875 offered to put Villiers up in Brittany for as long as he liked.

Since the time-limit for the competition meant that he had only six months in which to research and write his American drama, Villiers was eager to accept, even though it meant borrowing more money to pay the train fare. His departure was several times postponed for different reasons—the necessity to do a minimum of research on American history, the hope of selling the foreign rights on *Le Prétendant*, the need to see Peragallo from the Society of Dramatists to try to get a further subsidy from him—but at the beginning of the second week in April he was on his way. His spirits were high: Weinschenk was still favourably disposed to *Le Prétendant*, he was convinced that he had an excellent chance of winning the prize in the competition, and he was planning a collected edition of his short stories with etchings by Manet. He had already sketched out the play in his head and taken most of the notes he needed, with the help of friends who consulted English-speaking experts on various legal and technical details, and he was filled with enthusiasm for the subject, 'the vital question of the races of mankind', as he called it. His determination to get down to it was such that he warned Gantès that he would accept no invitations and talk to no one: 'I must, I must *win the prize*, do you hear, and that's all there is to it, that is to say, being positive, self-disciplined, hard-working in the six-o'clock-in-the-morning sense of the word, powerful, robust, forthright and imaginative.' The idea of failure did not enter his head: 'Don't laugh too much if I speak to you as though I had already won the prize, since, *even if I don't get it*, my play will still be produced in Paris during the American Exhibition in admirable conditions'.[2]

Unfortunately, later in April things began to go wrong. First of all, Weinschenk started changing his mind about the feasibility of producing *Le Prétendant*. As the great actress Agar was on tour in Nantes, Villiers thought that he would try to persuade her to take one of the leading roles in the play, in which case Weinschenk might change his mind again. So, after writing to her to put his case,[3] he went to the theatre with Gantès in the hope of talking to her in the interval, bearing with him a copy of *Morgane* inscribed with a flattering dedication.[4] Agar was not uninterested in the idea, but in the end Weinschenk decided to give up the Théâtre des Arts and instead went off to America. That, for the time being, put an end to any hopes of seeing *Le Prétendant* on the stage. Then, on 21 April, the newspapers published the official rules of the American competition, the detailed organization of which had been placed in the hands of an international impresario called Théodore Michaëlis. While the rewards were alluring (the first prize consisted of 5,000 francs, a specially commissioned bronze plaque, a gold medal, a third of the royalties, and a luxury edition by Lemerre), the conditions were extremely restrictive: the play had to be essentially moral, contain only noble passions, have a young and sympathetic hero and heroine, provide a comic character for light relief, show historical figures in peripheral roles, give rise to outbursts of patriotism, and offend neither the English nor the Americans. The general verdict was that these rules were totally stupid, and Villiers wrote to his friend Henry Roujon, Marras's brother-in-law, journalist, and future Academician, to say that he was not going to enter after all. But Roujon (and no doubt Gantès) managed to convince him that the programme was just as much of a nuisance to all the other competitors and that it would be pointless to give up.[5]

Villiers did not after all remain in Brittany as long as he had intended, either because he needed Parisian libraries for his work on the American play or because he was unable to do without the stimulus of life in the capital. But even after his return he continued to work away extremely hard, and on 20 June, when Nina de Villard invited him to a party at her house, she clearly thought he needed to take some time off.[6] However, that was not in his nature when he was in the grip of inspiration, and one evening at Nina's (perhaps on that same occasion), when dinner was served he was nowhere to be found. Eventually he was discovered in a corner rewriting one of the major scenes of the play, and was only persuaded to come to table when he had finished the last word.[7]

The entertainment to which Nina had invited him was a performance of Charles Cros's little farce *La Machine à changer le caractère des femmes*. A week or two later the play was acted again, with Villiers himself in one of the leading roles. On that evening, one of the journalists present, probably Richard Lesclide, bumped into Villiers on the staircase, still in costume, with a wig, a feathered hat, and lace ruffles. Villiers was in a state of high indignation and could only be calmed down with difficulty. He was talking about taking the owners of the Théâtre du Châtelet to court and about writing 'letters to the papers', all because his ancestor the Marshal was portrayed in an unfavourable light in a melodrama entitled *Perrinet Leclerc*.[8] With anyone else, this might have been a source of passing ill-humour; with Villiers, it was to become an affair that occupied him for years and absorbed much of the energy that might otherwise have gone into literature. Even now, despite the urgency of finishing the American play, it immediately embroiled him in time-consuming complications.[9]

Perrinet Leclerc itself was anything but a novelty. It had been cobbled together in 1835 by Anicet-Bourgeois and Édouard Lockroy, two of the most prolific purveyors of melodramas, and it purported to tell the story of young Perrinet Leclerc who, in 1418, in order to avenge himself for an affront suffered at the hands of the Comte d'Armagnac, opened the gates of Paris to the besieging Burgundian army. Jean de Villiers de l'Isle-Adam does not in fact play a particularly prominent part in the action of the play, which is complex, episodic, and violent: he does not appear until Act III, when he offers his services to the Queen, and he then vanishes apart from a couple of scenes in which he is seen leading the Burgundian troops into Paris. He is presented as not being a very admirable character, but the truth is that he comes off no worse than the other protagonists in a plot where murder, treachery, insolence, and adultery abound. When one reads the text of the play, it is difficult to believe that Villiers took seriously the charge that his ancestor was being traduced—apart from the fact that it is the kind of melodrama that no one takes very seriously anyway, Jean is certainly not singled out for any special opprobrium and is in no sense the villain of the piece.[10]

Perrinet Leclerc had been reprinted several times since 1835 and had been revived in the summer of 1862, at a time when

Villiers was in Paris, so the play was almost certainly not new to him. Indeed, he claimed later that he had done all he could to prevent it being produced again in 1875 at the Châtelet. But the first night took place on 13 July and on the fourteenth he sent off a long letter, obviously prepared in advance, to the press. *Le Figaro* shortened it somewhat, but reproduced most of it on the sixteenth. In it Villiers rehearses the martial exploits of his ancestor and demands to know why, in the play, he is represented as having sold his country, as being a coward, and as having betrayed his king. He then goes on to a rather tortuous parallel between Maréchal Jean besieging Paris in 1418 and Maréchal MacMahon as commander-in-chief of the Versaillais troops besieging it at the time of the Commune in 1871 (in 1875 MacMahon was President of the Republic, so the comparison is more than a little tendentious). The letter concludes: 'He who insults the one insults the other. That is all I have to say. Now I am returning to my literature.'[11]

As far as it goes, the letter is a firm but dignified protest, even if what provoked it might seem extremely slight, and its closing words apparently indicated that for Villiers that was the end of the matter. In the event, it proved to be only the beginning. On 16 August, the ever-obliging François Oswald inserted in his theatrical column in *Le Gaulois* a paragraph announcing that Villiers had taken out writs over the alleged defamation of his ancestor's memory in *Perrinet Leclerc*, not only against the authors or their representatives but also against the directors of the theatre and against the publisher.[12] How and why Villiers took this step is not clear, particularly since money was involved and he had none. Probably, as Fernand Calmettes suggests, he was adroit enough to persuade a solicitor and a barrister, Me Milliot and Me Doumerc, that the case would be fought in a blaze of publicity and managed to extract subsidies from them.[13] As for his motives, they were doubtless mixed. He was of course accused of having started the whole affair simply for self-advertisement, and, given its slender pretext, there must be some truth in that—especially as *Perrinet Leclerc* was taken off at about the time the writs were issued. On the other hand, he was deeply proud of the great deeds of his forebears, and may have had a genuine wish to clear Jean's name of even the most minimal stain—everything one knows about Villiers proves beyond question that he was capable of the most quixotic and disinterested gestures. Certainly there was no hope of financial gain, since all he was asking for was the suppression or correction of the offending passages and the insertion of the judgement in ten newspapers: he made no attempt to seek damages. It is also possible that he found himself trapped by a train of events which he had not foreseen: he later let it be known that, in view of the cessation of performances of *Perrinet Leclerc*, he would have withdrawn his action, had it not been for the fact that there were insinuations that he had no right at all to the name Villiers de l'Isle-Adam. He may therefore have been forced to continue a prosecution which he had perhaps never intended to be more than a threat.

When the case was first announced, it was said to be a matter of urgency, due to be settled within a fortnight. In the event nothing more was heard of it for two years. No doubt the disappearance of *Perrinet Leclerc* removed some of the need for haste, but a more important reason for delay was the necessity for long research to establish both the truth about the Marshal's conduct in the fifteenth century and Villiers's own status as a genuine descendant. For when he first started protesting about the play, Villiers was in reality not very well informed about either his own genealogy or the Marshal's life, with the result that he was unable to take the case any further until he had put together the detailed documentation he needed. According to Henry Roujon, he set to work with joy:

First of all, at the Bibliothèque Nationale, he threw himself into all the histories of France he could lay his hands on, talked only of Burgundians, Armagnacs, and Cabochiens, discovered the fourteenth century and amused himself with it like a child. He was seen dashing from solicitor to solicitor, with genealogies under his arm. There was an absolute shower of ancestors. He was delighted at the idea that an officer of the court was 'acting on his behalf'. 'I must be off,' he would say. 'I've just got time to see the procurator who's acting on my behalf.'[14]

This sudden flurry of activity naturally interfered with his work on the American play, and, when the deadline came on 1 October, his text was still not ready, and he had to prevail on Michaëlis to grant him a twelve-day extension before he submitted it.[15] Once *Le Nouveau-Monde*, for this was the title he gave to the work, was handed in, all he could do was wait until the complicated process of judging was complete. About a hundred dramatists had entered the competition, and a first jury was given the task of effecting a preliminary sorting out, which it did in a strange manner. The members were so shocked by the number of manuscripts that it proved very difficult to get them to meet, and in the end the three most conscientious among them each took a pile and chose one or two plays from among it. Francisque Sarcey, the dramatic critic, opted for *Un grand citoyen*, the work of Armand d'Artois, a well-known popular playwright, in collaboration with Gabriel Laffaille; Édouard Fournier, author and theatre critic, chose *L'Amérique libre*, by Adolphe Michel; the American representative, Mr Greenville Murray, proposed Villiers's *Le Nouveau-Monde*: a couple more plays were thrown in as makeweights.[16] This happened at the beginning of January 1876, and soon everyone, including Villiers, knew the titles of the plays still in contention.

Since the final choice was going to depend on Victor Hugo as president of the second jury, Villiers became assiduous in cultivating his good graces, calling on him on the eighth, sending him on the ninth a fulsome letter in which he compared him to Christ, and dining with him the same evening, which was when Michaëlis was due to deliver the manuscripts to him.[17] Whether these importunities influenced the Master's decision is not known: it is said that he could not be bothered to read any of the plays and contented himself with pronouncing them all equally worthy.[18] At all events, on 22 January the result was made public: there was to be no first prize, the second prize was to be divided equally between *Le Nouveau-Monde* and *Un grand citoyen*, and the third prize was to go to *L'Amérique libre*. Why there was no first prize was never explained, but rumour had it that Michaëlis was behind the decision, since it enabled him to make considerable economies on the original prize money.[19] All the interested parties signed a contract on 3 February, by which Villiers, like d'Artois and Laffaille, had 2,000 francs prize money assigned to him, while Michel received 1,000 francs: by now there was no mention of plaques, medals, or luxury editions.[20]

Still, even if Michaëlis had whittled down the original rewards, Villiers could nevertheless claim to have won the competition, since he was named first in defiance of alphabetical order, and he was naturally overjoyed to find that at long last his old dreams of a tremendous success in the theatre were about to be realized in a glare of publicity, enhanced by all the imminent celebrations of the Centenary of the Declaration of Independence. The great expectations of the lyrical letters to Gantès no longer appeared idle speculation: the prize-money was in his pocket, his name was on everyone's lips, and it only remained for him to make his choice of Parisian theatres and to attend to the American end of the operation, which he reckoned was going to necessitate travelling to Philadelphia in order to arrange for the simultaneous production of his play all over the United States.[21] Had Villiers looked at the small print of his contract with Michaëlis, he might have been a little less sanguine: the impresario reserved the right to authorize production of the plays everywhere except Paris, and the authors were forbidden to publish for three years. However, flushed with triumph, Villiers was not worried about such details: this time, surely, nothing could go wrong.

Villiers could probably at that stage have had his pick of any Paris theatre for *Le Nouveau-Monde*, such was the fame which resulted from the competition. In fact, the theatre to which he decided to give it immediately after the announcement of the prize was the Ambigu, at first sight a logical choice since it had a long tradition of spectacular historical drama and was managed by Hippolyte Hostein, a celebrity since the July Monarchy when he used to put on Dumas *père*'s plays. Hostein, who had only just taken over the Ambigu after two successive managers had resigned in 1875, was no doubt delighted to have what looked like a ready-made success on his hands, and set in motion everything needed for a lavish and expensive production. Thanks to François Oswald in *Le Gaulois*, one can follow what went on almost day by day, since Villiers was obviously feeding him with titbits of information. On 11 February he announced that the great Mlle Rousseil was going to take one of the leading parts, and the next day inserted a letter from Villiers denying the rumour, but so half-heartedly that it was equivalent to confirming it.[22] On the nineteenth Oswald informed his readers that rehearsals had started, with Jean Richepin, actor, poet, lover of Sarah Bernhardt, and a friend of Villiers from Nina's *salon*, in the role of the hero.

But already difficulties were beginning to arise, and a few days later Richepin had withdrawn. There were also arguments over the text of the play. Hostein wanted it shortened and made substantial cuts; Villiers demanded that the missing scenes should be restored. On 21 February, *La Patrie* reported that the discussions were so violent that Villiers had threatened to take his play away from the Ambigu altogether. Still, preparations went ahead, and Villiers became involved in negotiations with the Franco-American Committee which was at that time collecting money for the erection of the Statue of Liberty.[23] On 25 February Oswald announced that Villiers, with typical generosity, had offered to donate the takings of the first night and of the best night thereafter. By 10 March, still according to Oswald, the settings had been ordered, and by the twenty-seventh it had been decided that *Le Nouveau-Monde* would be put on immediately after *La Berline de l'émigré*. However, Hostein was beginning to find, like his immediate predecessors, that the Ambigu was very difficult to run successfully, and early in May he surrendered his lease.

Nevertheless, there was no reason to think that this was any more than a temporary setback. The centenary was still to come, the settings and costumes were ready, and there was still every chance that *Le Nouveau-Monde* would be the success that everyone expected. Consequently, when F. Roques, who had already leased the Ambigu in 1875, took over the theatre again, he firmly intended to produce Villiers's play. But he immediately ran into problems with the proprietor, a widow named Chabrié, who maintained that he still owed her money from his previous occupancy. The case came before the courts, which ordered on 27 August that

Roques should be expelled, but he at once announced that he proposed to appeal. At this stage Villiers decided that he had had enough of the Ambigu and sent a brief note to the press, inserted in several papers at the end of August, specifying that he had withdrawn his play. This did not please Roques, who replied forthwith to say that he was still in possession of the manuscript of *Le Nouveau-Monde* and had every intention of putting it on as soon as he won his case. A full-blooded riposte was forthcoming from Villiers a few days later, and was published in *Le Pays* on 12 September. After an ironic reference to Roques's desire to hang on to the drama at all costs, Villiers launches into a violent diatribe at the stupidity of managers who had forced him to rewrite *Le Nouveau-Monde* several times in order to deprive it of its originality, since everything had to conform to convention.

Thus it is that the public finds itself condemned perpetually to see only the same spectacle beneath the apparent variety of the play-bills. We are impertinent enough to think little of the second-hand moulds which turn out successful plays according to a formula. Even were we to be regarded as conceited, presumptuous, etc., we do not care to knuckle under to those derisory laws whose puerile trammels are causing the sacred genius of the nation to atrophy. And—since I seem to remember that what is at issue is my drama—if the management of the Ambigu arrogates to itself the right to keep it, which I still dispute, at least people will know that it is against my will.[24]

In the end Roques was forced out and the Ambigu remained closed, which meant that Villiers was once again free to dispose of his play as he wished. By now, of course, the actual date of the centenary had come and gone, and the competition was becoming a rather distant memory, but *Le Nouveau-Monde* was still an attractive proposition, so that in October 1876 negotiations had opened with another theatre, possibly the Porte Saint-Martin, involving yet more revision of the text.[25] In addition, Villiers was hoping to see some Americans from Philadelphia, and was confident that all would be well: 'This time I have excellent, perfect news. All the troubles will be over very shortly, in ten days or a fortnight, perhaps. I have faith in that and, henceforth, the best-founded and firmest faith.'[26]

18

In the meantime the prize money had long since vanished, and times continued to be very hard. In April Villiers was signing promissory notes on behalf of his father and himself to the value of more than 4,000 francs.[1] A lady called Mme Perry, about whom nothing is known, was providing him with subsidies that even Villiers could not pretend he would ever be able to repay; they were on such a scale that he referred to her 'truly supernatural affection' and 'saintly devotion'.[2] There were of course small fees for the shorter works he published in reviews, and they had been more numerous recently—a couple of new tales, *A s'y méprendre!* and *L'Inconnue* in *Le Spectateur* in December 1875 and June 1876, and four others between January 1876 and June 1877 in Catulle Mendès's *République des lettres*, together with a number of reproductions, including one of *La Révolte*, in an ephemeral fortnightly called *La Quinzaine*, and an article on the mural paintings in Garnier's great new Opéra in the *Gazette musicale*.[3] He was also commissioned in 1876 to write portraits of three famous women—Hypermnestra, Lady Hamilton, and Isabeau de Bavière—for a series planned by the Belgian editor Albert Lacroix, but, though he delivered his manuscripts, the plan was dropped, and the texts were only rediscovered and published in 1896.[4] These were very slender resources indeed, especially as a part had to go to help out his parents—the Marquis was now well over seventy, his wife was not much younger, and they presumably had no income to speak of—even though the old man's ardour for financial speculations was undimmed.

There was admittedly the eternal hope of marrying an heiress, and not even the débâcle with Anna Eyre could cure Villiers of his fixed idea that sooner or later some radiantly beautiful girl was going to drop millions in his lap.[5] An undated letter to a matrimonial agent suggests only that his disappointments were inducing him to rate his qualifications higher and higher—in this curious missive, the exuberance of his verbosity leads to the most fantastic claims: statues and paintings of his ancestors occupy whole rooms at Versailles,

two of his great-uncles ranked as sovereigns and minted
money with their effigy on it, he is a prince of the Holy
Roman Empire and a grandee of Spain, he is a count
twenty-two times over, he has the Grand Cross of the Order
of the Knights of Malta. Even grandfather Lilly acquires
unsuspected status: an income of 300,000 francs, the title of
Governor of San Domingo, and the rank of brigadier-
general. These wild assertions are clearly a compensation for
him: 'I tell you that it is an absolutely inconceivable thing that
I should be in my present situation, thanks to some rather
excessive acts of imprudence on the part of my father.'⁶ The
truth was that sometimes he had to choose between smoking
a cigarette and putting a stamp on a letter, since he did not
have enough money to do both.⁷

It must have been dire necessity that drove Villiers to one
extraordinary transaction at this time. Among his acquaintances was a journalist who went under the sonorous name of
Baron Godefroy van der Dussen d'Herpent but also called
himself Jules de Clerville: under one name or the other he ran
both *La Semaine parisienne* and *Le Spectateur*, in which
Villiers published a number of tales, one of which is dedicated
to him 'as a sign of our strong and sincere friendship'. He
held extreme right-wing views and glorified himself with the
title of 'officer of the general staff of the royal armies'. Those
who knew him did not take him very seriously: one has the
impression of a noisy and pretentious showman with nothing
much in his head. At the time when he and Villiers were
seeing one another regularly, hopes of having *Le Prétendant*
staged had not entirely died after the near-miss with Weinschenk, and it occurred to the enterprising d'Herpent that he
might be able to cash in on the potential success of the play
with little cost or effort. So, on 1 August 1876, in the middle
of all the negotiations about *Le Nouveau-Monde*, he drew up
a contract which he induced Villiers to sign. This incredible
document states that Villiers has provided the scenario of a
five-act drama entitled *Le Prétendant*—a premiss which is
entirely false, since there had been in existence for sixteen
months a complete manuscript of the play, copied out by a
professional copyist. But d'Herpent had his reasons for using
the word 'scenario', since the idea of the contract was that he

was going to devote himself to 'the definitive execution' of
the play and 'activate its performance' by means of 'his work,
his relations, his influence, and the negotiations he would
undertake'. D'Herpent bound himself to pay Villiers 50
francs on the signature of the contract and 20 francs a week
for four months; in return, Villiers agreed to give d'Herpent
50 per cent of any royalties and signed away his ownership of
the play which he would only be able to recover two years
later on payment of an indemnity of 25,000 francs.[8]

Clearly, Villiers was in the hands of a bare-faced adven-
turer. D'Herpent had realized that, with all the publicity
around *Le Nouveau-Monde* and the prospect of its imminent
production, another play by Villiers might easily turn out to
be a very valuable property, and he had seen a way of
acquiring a half-share in the profits at a time when Villiers
was so short of funds that, simply in order to live, he would
do almost anything for ready cash. As for his contribution to
the work, his main activity was to shorten it by cutting out
discussions, incidents, speeches, phrases, but also to attenu-
ate stylistic eccentricities—and to indicate his royalist sympathies by censoring the word 'liberty' in the speech Sergius
makes to the conspirators. Though many of his cuts are
reasonably judicious, they represent no more than a few
hours' work and come nowhere near justifying his position as
co-author and his half-share of the royalties. Whether his
vaunted relations and influence were set in motion is not
known; at all events *Le Prétendant* was not produced, and no
further mention of it occurs in Villiers's correspondence. It is
perhaps the existence of the legally binding contract which
prevented Villiers from ever publishing it, since he would
either have had to name d'Herpent as his collaborator or pay
him 25,000 francs, and there was as little chance of his
accepting the one as there was of his affording the other. *Le
Prétendant* thus remained in manuscript among his papers
and did not finally appear in print until 1965, more than
three-quarters of a century after the author's death. As for the
d'Herpent–Villiers partnership, it broke up in acrimony at
some unknown time, with the courts ordering d'Herpent to
pay Villiers 500 francs; perhaps he had not handed over even
the meagre rewards he had dangled before his colleague.

The years of privation and poverty had begun to take their toll on Villiers's appearance, as Robert du Pontavice de Heussey, Hyacinthe's son, noted when he returned to Paris in 1876 after completing his studies in England. Having vainly sought Villiers in all the boulevard cafés, he was forced by a shower to take shelter in a passage-way. Suddenly he caught sight of his cousin:

He was coming from the far end of the passage, a fat roll of manuscripts under his arm, with little hurried steps, and that gait, at once springy and hesitant, that I remembered so well, walking along with that busy yet startled look he wore in crowds. To judge by a top hat so worn that it was red, a thin and threadbare overcoat hiding his shirt, trousers with frayed edges, fortune seemed to have favoured him with sovereign disdain. But no matter: as he drew near, I could detect in his ageing features neither despair nor discouragement; his pale blue eyes vaguely pursued their dream, and his ironic mouth was smiling at some inner vision. Certainly at that moment he was not on the earth; among those soaked, muddy, vulgar passers-by shaking themselves and puffing and blowing, there was something proud and noble in the thinker's haughty indifference to the populace that he went through blindly, like the waking sleeper of an oriental tale.[9]

Pontavice was of course at once caught up in the peripeteia of Villiers's two main preoccupations: finding a theatre for *Le Nouveau-Monde* and winning the case over *Perrinet Leclerc*. The proposed deals with the Théâtre de la Porte Saint-Martin and the visiting Philadelphians fell through in the autumn of 1876, but, when a new manager, one L. P. Laforêt, took over the Ambigu in December 1876, Villiers turned once more to the theatre he had originally thought of. Laforêt's response could not have been more forthcoming; on 6 February 1877 he wrote to Villiers: 'I have just finished reading your vast drama *Le Nouveau-Monde*, and I do not want to make you wait a moment longer for the reply you are expecting. I shall be proud to stage this strong, generous and powerfully inspired work.'[10] Yet again everything seemed to be plain sailing; but yet again the Ambigu was to prove too much for its new manager, and in June Laforêt gave up in despair. The Ambigu closed its doors, and the future of *Le Nouveau-Monde* was once more in jeopardy.

As for the lawsuit, the long months of study in libraries and archives was beginning to bear fruit, and Villiers handed over to his lawyers a whole series of texts. One was eighty large pages of carefully copied extracts from medieval chroniclers, modern historians, and encyclopaedias.[11] Another was an authenticated copy of some of the family papers he had deposited with Me Pinguet at the time of the Anna Eyre adventure. A third was a vehemently polemical *Notice généalogique*, ten pages long, in which Villiers argued with passionate conviction that those historians who had declared the family of Villiers de l'Isle-Adam to be extinct were simply ignorant of the existence of the Breton branch.[12] Armed with these substantial documents, which represented the outcome of many hours of arid work for which Villiers had had no training, the lawyers were at last able to bring the case to court. Villiers's own attitude towards them was suspicious. He plainly thought he was better qualified than they were, in terms of conviction, erudition, and eloquence, and some of the papers he presented to them were in effect the text of the speeches he expected them to make. Moreover, he was shocked by the casualness with which they were liable to treat an affair which had assumed vital proportions for him. Henry Roujon met him one day as he was leaving his lawyer's office:

His face was a greenish hue and he was showing symptoms of phobia. A clerk had just greeted him with a familiar slap on the shoulder and had said in a brutal, half-mocking tone: 'Here, I say! They claim we aren't descendants at all!' This 'we' had struck Villiers, unfamiliar with legal language, as the sort of revolting pleasantry one might expect from a pettifogger. 'Ah!' he cried, brandishing his bundles of papers, 'we'll soon see whether we are descendants or not!'[13]

The case was heard before the Tribunal civil de la Seine on Wednesday 25 July 1877. Me Doumerc appeared for Villiers; against him were arrayed Me Cléry for the authors, Me Bonnier-Ortolan for the theatre managers, and M^e Le Senne for the publisher. Me Doumerc opened his case by arguing that, since Villers was indisputably descended from the Marshal, he was entitled to bring the suit. This issue had by now taken on capital importance in Villiers's eyes, and, whether or not that had been his original intention, the case had come to be a public proof that he was indeed a true Villiers de l'Isle-Adam. Me Doumerc thus produced a whole series of genealogical arguments designed to establish his client's family tree. He then went on to the second part of his argument, the rehabilitation of the Marshal. This involved a long and complex discussion of the civil war between Burgundians and Armagnacs, of the part played by the English and of the exploits of the Marshal, notably his capture of Paris from the English in 1436. The tactic in both parts of the case was not so much to lay out a mass of detailed evidence as to rely on the prestige of established authorities. M^e Le Senne then spoke on behalf of the defendants. He put it to the court that, if some historians regarded the Marshal as a hero, others had heavily criticized his conduct; he also noted that there appeared to be an insufficiently explained gap in Villier's supposed lineage in the sixteenth century. He concluded his case by a slighting reference to Villiers's modest reputation and by alleging that he had only brought the case to 'bring himself publicity' and to get the court to deliver a 'certificate' of his nobility. The other defence lawyers indicated that they had nothing to add, after which Me Doumerc made a brief concluding speech, in which he argued that, after winning the prize for *Le Nouveau-Monde*, Villiers had no need of publicity, and that his lineage was so thoroughly proven by the documents in his possession as to render any new certificate superfluous. The state attorney intervened to put the point that *Perrinet Leclerc* was not the kind of work that could cause any appreciable damage either to the memory of the Marshal or to Villiers himself; on the other hand, he opined that the court ought to take cognizance of the official documents produced by the plaintiff. The court reserved its judgment until the following Wednesday, 1 August.

The wait must have been agonizing for Villiers. Was the court going to recognize his claim to be a genuine Villiers de l'Isle-Adam and establish once and for all his right to the name and ancestry which had been publicly challenged? Was the Marshal's name to be cleared of the slur which he claimed had been cast on it? Or was the whole affair to end in humiliation? When the judgment was finally given, it realized almost his worst fears. On the question of his ancestry, the court simply eluded the issue by ruling that, since there was no case to answer on the substance of the action, the matter of his status did not arise. On the question of the way in which *Perrinet Leclerc* portrayed the Marshal, the court deemed that a work of imagination was not subject to the same constraints as a historical study and that, since a contemporary writer had accused the Marshal of treason, the dramatists had the right to base their work in that view without taking into account the contrary opinion. Consequently, the case was dismissed and costs were awarded against Villiers.[14]

Perhaps this result had been predictable from the outset, at least as far as the alleged libel against the Marshal was concerned. It certainly seems very far-fetched to suppose that any court of justice could have taken seriously the idea of defamation of someone who had been dead for four centuries, and, had the principle been admitted, one can imagine the endless flow of litigation that would have ensued. Yet it was not necessarily a foregone conclusion, since the state of the law on the question was anything but clear. Villiers may indeed have known that in 1864 a certain Bigault de Préfontaine had won a case against Dumas *père* and his publisher for having maligned Préfontaine's grandfather in the novel *La Route de Varennes*, the action of which takes place in 1791, although he may not have realized that the Court of Appeal had overturned the judgment the following year.[15] Moreover, he had so convinced a lawyer of his chances that the lawyer, so it has plausibly been said, was actually paying him rather than the other way round.[16] In the event, the legal position was not settled until 1881, when a new law on the press specified that the memory of someone deceased could only be defended at law by an heir if the heir could prove that his own interests were affected by the libel—it may indeed have been partly the example of Villiers's case that had demonstrated the necessity for some such measure. Certainly the Tribunal civil de la Seine had carefully avoided discussing the question of principle, which means that, had the defence lawyers not been able to cite contemporary accusations against the Marshal, the decision could conceivably have gone in his favour. So the case was not necessarily as futile as it may have looked.

On the question of Villiers's status as a legitimate descendant, while he undoubtedly came to attach great importance to having it recognized by the court, it is doubtful whether that formed a very important part of the object of the exercise at the beginning. In the outline of the case which he submitted to his solicitor Mᵉ Milliot in 1875,[17] it occupies only a few lines in several long pages, and he later claimed that he had only produced the proofs of his genealogy because the defence lawyers had required him to—a reasonable assertion, given that Mᵉ Le Senne had taken the trouble to attack them in court, which shows that the defence rested partly on the contention that he was not descended from the Marshal. It was therefore not only legitimate but essential for him to ask the Court to pronounce upon the question of his lineage, not for external reasons but because his case could otherwise have no possible validity.

At all events, the verdict as it stood was a disastrous one for him. The stain on the Marshal's escutcheon was still there; the matter of his ancestry was left unresolved; and he had been saddled with the no doubt considerable expenses of his adversaries in addition to his own. Needless to say, there was not the slightest prospect of his being able to pay, and indeed nobody seems to have tried to have the court order enforced, no doubt because they knew his poverty made it pointless. His reaction to the verdict was one of total fury, and, far from licking his wounds in silence, he loudly proclaimed his defiance. A long and emphatic letter was sent off to the papers, after a lot of very careful drafting, and it is not without pertinence and nobility. Villiers refutes the allegation that he had only brought the case to establish his filiation by pointing out that he had never worried about it for the last thirty-eight years and that in any case it was the defence which had obliged him to do so. As for the supposed lacuna in his genealogy, he vigorously denied its existence and once more repeated his authorities.

I descend from Jean de l'Isle-Adam as directly as the average man descends from his father (. . .) People ask me what good it did me to get irritated about a play in which his pure and holy memory is insulted, and they claim that I was only using the opportunity to 'bring myself publicity'. A man is only the thought he has. My sole reply is to beg those who have had that thought to guard it preciously. They are worthy of it, and I shall take good care not to solicit their esteem or their sympathy.

After a renewed listing of his authorities, he concludes: 'What do you expect a court to pronounce upon or not to pronounce upon in that? What verbiage in the press could affect it? There are centuries there. It is a little late in the day. The thing exists.'[18]

But all the publicity around the *Perrinet Leclerc* affair had alerted another claimant to the name Villiers de l'Isle-Adam, and he too decided that the time had come to assert his rights. This was Georges de Villiers de l'Isle-Adam, the grandson of the Vicomte Joseph-Gabriel de Villiers Deschamps whose adoption of the name de l'Isle-Adam in 1815 had so enraged Lilly. In fact, the name had very nearly not been transmitted much further because the Vicomte's eldest son had turned out to be such a bad character that the father had unsuccessfully tried to change his name a second time. But the grandson, now in civilian life after an honourable career as an army officer, had no intention of allowing his status as a member of the illustrious family to be impugned, and wrote a letter, which *Le Figaro* published on 13 August, and in which he declared that his grandfather had been authorized by royal decree in September 1815 to take the name Villiers de l'Isle-Adam, as being the sole survivor of the family and consequently the only person permitted to use it. 'I am very surprised that a person to whom reference has been made in your paper, and who calls himself "Villiers de l'Isle-Adam" and not "de Villiers de l'Isle-Adam", should have been able to claim the slightest degree of kinship with the family to which I have the honour to belong.'[19]

Villiers had probably seen this letter, dated 10 August, before it was actually printed, because his own indignant reply, which had been elaborated with great care, appeared in *Le Figaro* on the fourteenth, the day after the protest. He had taken the trouble to verify in the state archives the precise tenor of the document authorizing the change of name in 1815 and reproduced it with this commentary:

I think that is sufficient.—It may be unbelievable, but I have copied it word for word. No man, no letter, no king has the right to dispose of my name, which is the property of my family. It is not enough that amid the troubles of 1815 anyone should come hurrying along to pretend that our family is extinct for them to take possession of our name. In that case, I do not see why everyone called Villiers should not have done the same.

He goes on to insinuate that the usurpers had also tried to steal his grandfather's money and had continued to use the name Villiers de l'Isle-Adam even when they knew they had no right to it; he further hints darkly that his rival is quite capable of pocketing the archival evidence unless it is kept under lock and key. After these deliberate (and quite unjustified) provocations, he makes it clear that he thinks a duel is the only honourable way to settle matters.[20]

In that, Villiers soon had his wish. Georges sought him out at the café Le Rat mort, and things went far enough for a duel to be rranged on the outskirts of Paris. Shortly before it was due to take place, Villiers wrote to a friend a letter which, not untypically, is at the same time theatrical and moving: 'If I had an accident, do you hear, I charge you with avenging my name and my memory, with saying clearly and simply who I was, and, if I was guilty of being too carefree in this world, with saying that too, without attenuating my mistake, so that it may serve as a salutary example to those who might imitate me.' After asking the friend to look after his parents, he goes on:

Listen, at this very moment, from afar, if through the things of the past there subsist any genuine rights, by this sword that I am about to wield in the name of old Jehan, I embrace you tightly, and (don't laugh, old friend, I have the heart of a king) I personally make you a knight!—Seal this letter with my old coat-of-arms that has shone so brightly! The last of the Villiers de l'Isle-Adams, even if he is poor, can at least send you this benediction.[21]

Such dramatics however turned out to be superfluous, and the two men succeeded in persuading one another that each of them had a different right to the name Villiers de l'Isle-Adam. Georges wrote to Villiers on 16 August to say that he was now entirely convinced of the authenticity of Villiers's descent from the family of Villiers de l'Isle-Adam, 'whose name is engraved in such glorious letters on the pages of our history and in whose ranks figures Marshal JEAN, whose memory, whatever people may have said, will always remain pure of any stain'. But he added that his own right to the name was equally indisputable, and indicated that, if Villiers still wished to fight, he was at his disposal.[22] A day or two later amicable agreement was reached, and it was evidently decided that each of them would write to the press recognizing the legitimacy of the claims of the other.[23] It is not known whether the letters were printed, and the two men did not remain in touch thereafter, though the homonymy went on causing confusion—Villiers has had attributed to him not only the misdeeds of Georges's scalliwag of an uncle[24] but also Georges's military career[25] and even his writings, since Georges too was a poet with right-wing and patriotic leanings.[26]

19

In the meantime Villiers had notified all and sundry of his intention of appealing against the court's decision. He claimed that the hearing had been too hasty, that the court had not examined the documents adduced by Me Doumerc, that the alleged break in his lineage was attributable only to the faulty transcription of a document, that the court had neglected its duty to take cognizance of the papers he had laid before it, and so on. That he was perfectly serious in this intention is shown by the rapidity and conscientiousness with which he set about further work. But in order to have some peace and quiet for it and to recover from the excitement of the case and the near-duel, he decided to accept an invitation from Robert du Pontavice de Heussey, who was spending the summer at a little rented cottage called Le Pin-Galant at Mérignac, a few miles outside Bordeaux. Pontavice had a clear recollection of Villiers appearing unannounced in mid-August:

It was one of those torrid afternoons that are unique to that region: Villiers arrived on foot from the neighbouring village, whither he had been brought by an omnibus from Bordeaux. He was simply dressed in trousers of black kerseymere, a straight-cut grey overcoat trimmed with fur (!) and a shiny, battered top-hat, and he was triumphantly twirling an enormous stick. The large pockets of his overcoat, which appeared to be cocking a snook at the incandescent sun, struck me as bulging so much that they raised fears they would burst at any time. At first I imagined that he was using them as an overnight bag, since there was no sign of any other sort of luggage about him. My mistake only lasted a few moments; scarcely had the poet come in, after the first cordially expansive greetings, when he drew from his vast pockets five thick bound exercise-books and, putting them one on top of another, with a pontifical air, he waved his hand, as white as that of a prelate, in a vague sign of benediction, saying: 'As in days of yore Columbus with his Spanish sovereign, I lay at the feet of your cousinly Majesty *Le Nouveau-Monde*.'[1]

Villiers probably stayed for several weeks in the relaxed atmosphere of the Bordeaux countryside, and Pontavice found him a different man away from the stresses and strains of the capital. They talked of the lawsuit, of the tribulations of *Le Nouveau-Monde*, of Baudelaire, of Wagner, of Poe, of women, of childhood, and they walked through the pine-forests, along the banks of the Gironde, past the vineyards— particularly at night, for Villiers remained faithful to his habits of noctambulism, even far from Paris. At other times he went off to Bordeaux to work in libraries and archives on a more complete and better documented version of his geneal- ogy,[2] or stayed at home and got on with revising *Axël*.[3] There had been some question the previous year of his publishing it with Richard Lesclide, but, still dissatisfied with the form of the work, he never delivered the manuscript.[4] No doubt in the rare intervals of work on *Le Nouveau-Monde*, his tales, and his lawsuit, he had taken it up again. However, the peacefulness of his sojourn in the south-west did not last long, and his restless, combative temperament soon reas- serted itself.

One of the motives behind Villiers's visit to Le Pin-Galant had been to see whether he would have better luck with *Le Nouveau-Monde* at a provincial theatre than he had had in Paris, and, as soon as he had arrived, he had recounted the misfortunes of which his play had been the victim: 'So straightaway I thought of you, of the provinces, of revenge; I've been dreaming of murder and decentralization!'[5] Ponta- vice knew Godfrin, manager of the Théâtre-Français at Bordeaux, and so was able to arrange an interview with Villiers. This took place in Godfrin's office in the presence of

Aimée Tessandier, later a famous actress but at that time a young member of Godfrin's company. Villiers, his hair freshly curled and his moustache waxed, was in a state of high nervousness and settled down silently in a dark corner, with a gloomy, suspicious, and frightened look, rolling a cigarette between his fingers. Then the reading began: Villiers started with the stage directions but soon leapt up:

With the intention of explaining to Godfrin the arrangement of the setting, he started jumping around the room, knocking over seats, pulling armchairs about, snatching down the swords from a little panoply hanging on the wall and accompanying his wild gestures with a stream of disconnected phrases and incomprehensible words.

Then he caught sight of the piano, struck a few chords, and started singing and reciting in a sepulchral voice. Godfrin was greatly alarmed at this performance; Aimée Tessandier buried her head in her hands to hide her laughter. Villiers then stopped long enough to ask Godfrin if he was following the symbolism, and the manager found the courage to ask him to read more calmly. Mortally offended, Villiers said to his cousin: 'Are you coming?' and made for the door with a backward look of withering contempt at the unfortunate Godfrin. In the end Pontavice prevailed on him to sit down and finished the reading himself, after which Godfrin declared that he was prepared to make any sacrifice in order to put the play on.[6]

Villiers's reaction was not quite as enthusiastic as might have been supposed, and he wrote off-handedly to a friend: 'I answered that I would have no objection to such an exhibition, if more important tasks did not prevent me from disposing of my time at present, that is to say, of the time which would be taken up by the rehearsals. At this, great agitation. I'm taking no notice.'[7] In the end he appears to have given his consent, but with some reluctance, both because he refused to believe that any of his plays could be properly produced if he was not present at the rehearsals and because he could not quite reconcile himself to the idea of *Le Nouveau-Monde* being staged anywhere other than Paris.

In the end, after about a month in the country, the call of the capital became too strong, and Villiers once more took himself off to Paris. No doubt he was anxious to get back to the libraries and archives so as to complete the proofs of his genealogy and the rehabilitation of the Marshal. This latter, according to his own view, was going to be 'an unexpected, curious, and solid piece of work'. He claimed to have collected quotations from 122 historians:

It is no longer going to be a rudimentary jumble, but a full and unified work that a child could read with pleasure, and in which I am not using the literary resources that I could have used, but where I am making the clarity and order of a historical composition work towards the ultimate goal I have set myself and to which every word I use is subservient.[8]

Presumably this is a text headed *Histoire du Maréchal Jean de Villiers de l'Isle-Adam, racontée ligne pour ligne par les Historiens anciens et modernes*, and consisting of twenty large manuscript pages in two columns: the left-hand side is a series of quotations and the right-hand side presents Villiers's commentaries.[9] Despite the title, it is concerned only with the period covered by *Perrinet Leclerc*, though he later planned to write a more complete life of his ancestor.

Work on this text, which is clearly intended for judicial purposes, must have occupied Villiers in 1877 and 1878; at the same time he was trying to elaborate a more detailed and better supported version of his genealogy.[10] But, despite the considerable labours which all this entailed, he had not forgotten his allegiance to imaginative literature, and in October 1877, taking up again the idea of a collected edition of his tales adumbrated in 1875, he submitted to the publisher Calmann Lévy a manuscript consisting of a score of short stories which had appeared in various periodicals. But Calmann Lévy turned it down on the grounds that not all the pieces were real narratives, that business was too slack to take on new commitments, and that Villiers had hitherto dealt with other publishers.[11] Still, there remained *Le Nouveau-Monde*, and, though he had a promise from Godfrin, he could not accustom himself to the thought that it would be staged in what he regarded as the back of beyond rather than Paris, with the result that he eventually lost patience and, to Godfrin's despair, demanded that the manuscript be returned to him.[12] This was singularly ill-advised, for when he took it to

Duquesnel, manager of the Odéon, he was told that they were too busy to look at it, with the result that it never even got as far as the reading committee. The bird in the hand had been allowed to fly away, and the bird in the bush remained obstinately out of reach.

However, Villiers refused to give up, and sought out a journalist acquaintance, Georges Duval, dramatic critic of *L'Événement*, in the hope that he might know some manager on the look-out for a new play. Duval read the manuscript and was impressed, so when, on the very same day, his friend Henri Chabrillat came to tell him that he was taking over the Ambigu, the critic was able to say to him: 'Well, old chap, you're really in luck. I'm going to give you the chance to open with a masterpiece,' and handed over *Le Nouveau-Monde*.[13] The next day Chabrillat wrote to say he was accepting the play, agreement on terms was reached in mid-May, and on the twentieth he summoned Villiers and the artist responsible for the settings to discuss the production.[14] But, since he had also been offered the stage adaptation of Zola's great *succès de scandale L'Assommoir*, he decided to open with that rather than with Villiers's drama, which meant another frustrating wait, since it would have been too risky to withdraw it in the hope of finding another theatre.

The manuscript submitted to Chabrillat was at least the sixth version of the play since it had been awarded the prize two years before. Although Villiers had originally intended to write five acts, the prize-winning text only had four and a number of the characters had not been given their definitive shape. Ever since he had been worrying about how to bring it up to the five acts he regarded as appropriate to such a lofty subject, and had considered various ways in which an extra act might be interpolated in the middle.[15] This had now been done, and the play was to keep its form, apart from minor alterations, for some years to come. The manuscript,[16] which is the work of a professional copyist, is prefaced by handwritten notes by Villiers designed to make it a more attractive proposition—Michaëlis would be prepared to give a subsidy of 10,000 francs, the designer would wait to be paid until there had been thirty performances, the censor had already passed it, the settings and costumes had been prepared, the

Franco-American Committee would supply an illuminated reproduction of the Statue of Liberty, and so on. Chabrillat, however, though willing to produce the play, went through it with a pencil and informed Villiers that, pending the production, he could get on with making alterations to it, since it would otherwise be too unwieldy. Had he known his Villiers better, he would have realized that what he was asking was equivalent to demanding improvements in the Holy Scriptures.

Indeed, Villiers was at that very time embroiled in a violent quarrel over just such an issue. This arose from a work entitled *Le Secret de l'ancienne musique* which Villiers had written in 1876 for the actor Ernest Coquelin *cadet* of the Comédie Française, who had since 1870 specialized in giving monologues at private entertainments. This was very lucrative for him, since he charged huge fees, but much less so for his authors, who only received a small royalty when the works were eventually published. Two such volumes had been published by Tresse in 1877; a third was projected in 1878, and in March Villiers received the modest sum of 40 francs for his contribution, which is an extremely amusing fantasy about an old player of that forgotten percussion instrument the Chinese hat. But Mme Tresse had the unfortunate habit of entrusting Coquelin with total editorial responsibility for the books, with the result that the actor often used the texts as he had altered them for recitation. When Villiers realized that Coquelin had tampered with *Le Secret de l'ancienne musique*, the effect was explosive, as Mme Tresse found to her cost.

I must tell you that, working as I have done for twenty years exclusively out of love for that absurdity called literary art, I cannot accept that anyone should take the liberty of asking the advice of professionals to check or modify what I write—even when I take it into my head to write trifles; moreover, it is not now (or tomorrow) that I intend to allow people to print under my name things for which I cannot accept responsibility. In a word, I will not be spoken to like that. I refuse to give permission for it to be printed: *Le Secret de l'ancienne musique* will be sent to me *or it will not appear.* I did not ask for it to be published!! I do not write dictations; I do not accept advice from anyone. That may be so much the worse for me, but that is how it is. What I produce is definitive and it must be read as I write it. It seems to me that I have suffered enough mistreatment in my life to be spared that of being 'corrected' by any Tom, Dick, or Harry.

To this thunderous missive Mme Tresse replied curtly that she would withdraw the story (retitled *Le Chapeau chinois* by Coquelin) but that she wanted her 40 francs back. Villiers not only accepted by return of post, though stipulating that he would only return the money when he was able to publish the tale elsewhere, but was even generous enough to offer to pay for the proof corrections which Coquelin had made. Considering his extreme poverty, such a gesture went well beyond what even the most punctilious correctness could demand.

However, Mme Tresse then discovered that the part of the volume containing Villiers's work was already printed, and so offered him an extra 60 francs to be allowed to keep it. Villiers's reply is a model of courtesy. He begins:

I only felt justified irritation because of the contempt with which all writers with any respect for their craft were being treated in my person, in that one of them could see one of his works, however insignificant, printed with cuts and additions that distorted its meaning and its style, and that without his even being allowed to see a single proof. It was because of this abnormal state of affairs that I protested—as you would have done yourself in my place. But now that it is clear to me that you are in no way responsible for having treated me like that, and that you were even willing to recompense me for the misunderstanding—that is a quite different matter:—if it is the case that I cannot prevent what has been done without harming innocent people, I bow to a misfortune, that is all.

He refuses absolutely the extra payment, which he says it would be unfair and indelicate of him to accept; on the other hand, he suggests that, since Coquelin made the proof corrections, Coquelin should pay for them. He then quotes the end of Mme Tresse's letter, in which she had said that, since it was not in his interest to harm her, she hoped he would accept her proposition.

Even if it were very much in my interest to harm you, please believe that I would not do so, since it would be unjust. I leave it to others, more 'practical' than I am, to do harm out of self-interest to people who have not deserved it. When I have done my duty and my conscience is clear, whatever ill may come out of it for me, I am so strangely constituted that I am always *satisfied* and that I even wish, from the bottom of my heart, that those who have harmed me should be as satisfied as I am.

No exchange of letters better illustrates both Villiers's extreme pride and susceptibility as a man of letters and his total disinterestedness.[17]

At this time Villiers was living with his parents, who had taken two modest rooms, sparsely furnished, in the Avenue Malakoff—or at any rate that was the address he sometimes gave.[18] But frequently he seems to have had no fixed abode at all, and such addresses as he used were often only to pick up correspondence. Where he actually slept was a mystery to everyone; it has even been said that at one stage he was reduced to sleeping rough in a building under construction.[19] Frequently his friends would not see him for weeks on end, until he suddenly reappeared. Mallarmé describes the phenomenon: 'He lived, in Paris, in some lofty non-existent ruin, with an eye on the heraldic sunset (none visited him) and descended from it at his moments, to come, go, and stand out from the hubbub only at the sight of a face known or half-remembered.'[20] People only met him in the street or in cafés, and even then unpredictably. The only place where he appeared regularly was Nina de Villard's house in the rue des Moines. There he was very much in evidence, collaborating with Nina and her friends in the farces they wrote, acting in them, playing and singing Wagner and his own compositions, reading his work in manuscript, declaiming his one-line poems (a genre in which he specialized), and joining in the practical jokes which were a feature of the evenings.

One of the people who started going to Nina's at this time was Baude de Maurceley, and he remembered Villiers vividly, years after:

His strangely anxious appearance aroused curiosity: with his head in constant motion, his grey-blue, yellow-streaked eyes staring, a tortured expression on his face, he would make a sudden feverish gesture with his hand to push back a mutinous lock of hair that immediately fell back across his forehead—that forehead where so many storms had raged and which had never known peace. His frame was supple and vigorous. He practised walking and boxing, and when he grew animated, he became prodigious, inspired by the constant power of his thoughts; all the words he spoke were masterly, fashioned with loving care. When, in a passionate discussion of literature or art, Villiers impetuously poured out all that was in his mind, it was as if his whole being was giving birth at the same time. Dressed as best he could, very simply but neatly, he wore his shabby clothes with as much careless elegance as if the magnificent cloak of his ancestors had been draped over his wide shoulders.[21]

If a distinguished visitor turned up at Nina's, Villiers would be particularly sparkling: that happened one evening when Ivan Turgeniev came to a dinner organized in honour of Guy de Maupassant. But if, as sometimes occurred, a respectable citizen strayed there, Villiers would lead the others in teasing him unmercifully until he left, baffled and resentful. The temptation to shock the bourgeois was always there, and on one occasion, when he joined Baude de Maurceley on the terrace of the famous Café Tortoni before going to Nina's, he looked around to see who was listening and then gave his order: 'Waiter, you will bring me some vermouth into which you will let fall, *as if by accident*, a few drops of syrup.' Then came another look to see what effect he had produced.[22] Nina's *salon* had in fact acquired an unjustifiably lurid reputation in the eyes of those who had never been there—Edmond de Goncourt saw it as a 'workshop for ruining minds',

where from dinner until late at night, a group of young intellects in revolt, lashed into a frenzy by alcohol, wallowed in every debauch of thought, every circus-turn of language, juggling with the boldest paradoxes and the most subversive aesthetic views, in a state of nervous excitement presided over by a pretty woman and a slightly mad Muse.[23]

20

Villiers's means of subsistence were as mysterious and hazardous as his dwelling-places. Every now and then a review would give him a few francs for one of his stories; friends would make him loans that they knew would never be repaid;

the occasional patron may have advanced him small sums. Another potential source of income was the literary competition, not on the scale of the Michaëlis prize for the American centenary, but minor affairs with very modest rewards. In 1875 a café-concert called the Eldorado offered 500 francs for a patriotic song; it attracted 600 competitors, among them Villiers and Catulle Mendès. But, when the results were announced in January 1876, the winner was a practised popular lyric-writer, and, though honourable mentions were accorded to both Villiers and Catulle, their works were not given prizes because they were adjudged to be odes of too literary a tone.[1] 'Ave Mater victa', Villiers's poem, is indeed far too elevated for a café-concert, as he well knew—he commented ironically: 'The sort of song that would best suit the licentious customers of that establishment would have to be patri-erotic!'[2] Similarly, in 1878 a society called La Pomme, for Normans and Bretons in Paris, offered a silver medal for a verse eulogy of Chateaubriand. Once again Villiers entered, all the more keenly since he was a great admirer of the Breton compatriot whose prose his own so often resembles. Only three verses of his poem have survived in manuscript, but it did not win the prize: as had happened with *Le Nouveau-Monde*, no prize was awarded and Villiers had to be content with another honourable mention.[3]

The more glittering prize of a rich marriage likewise continued to elude his grasp. In 1878 he believed himself to have found a suitable bride in the person of a Mlle de Solsona, whom he was due to marry in Rome and whose fortune would be sufficient to endow him with a 'terrible power' which he proposed to use on behalf of the Church and the King. Writing to some unidentified relative whose help he was requesting, Villiers said that, if the marriage did not come off, he would join the Pontifical Zouaves and send his mother to an old people's home. But naturally there was no possibility of failure: 'Put me in a position to bear our name in Rome. Do not worry: I shall succeed. It is all agreed; I am certain of success; but I should not be sorry to be able to prove to my future wife that I really do have a right to my name and that the Church holds it in high regard.'[4] This project went the way of so many others of a similar kind, and no more was heard of Mlle de Solsona.

The advice offered by his parents was not much more

practical. His father informed him in July 1878 that a M.
Nestor Caumel had set up an organization for 'the exploitation of the universal publicity of commerce', which would be
done 'very honourably as well-written prospectuses explain
in detail', and on which Villiers was going to be invited to
co-operate 'with many advantages'.[5] About the same time the
poor Marquise sent him a pathetic letter suggesting that he
could publish anonymous extracts from his work on the
fourteenth century and offering to give him an umbrella. But
this was only pending his marriage with someone who may
have been Mlle de Solsona: his mother, whose spelling was
highly eccentric, wrote with anxious affection:

I must tell you that the young Spannish widow who has more than
90 million is 26 she got married at 15, and sinse lost Her husband
the grief it is thought has afected her lungs her doctor has ordered
her to go to Nice untill January she went there before coming to
Paris with her aunt the duchess, you could join her there but she is
too ill at present Ill keep you informed.[6]

As for the work on the fourteenth century to which the
Marquise refers, it was growing in size and scope. The idea of
an appeal against the 1877 judgement was beginning to recede
into the distance, as there was no prospect of finding sufficient funds to meet the costs, but that did not mean that
Villiers was prepared to drop his design of proving his
genealogy and clearing the Marshal's name. It simply meant
that the materials he had accumulated would be used for
books rather than lawyers' briefs, and that the books would
be historical studies, not polemical refutations of *Perrinet
Leclerc* or vehement defences of his genealogical claims. With
this new aim in view, he widened his intentions so as to
encompass both a complete history of the Villiers de l'Isle-
Adam family and a biography of the Marshal,[7] which necessitated a further set of long and complicated researches, on
which progress was inevitably slow. The piles of notes and
drafts went on growing, as Villiers continued to write and
rewrite with indefatigable patience. But apart from a lively
but not very accurate evocation of Queen Isabeau de Bavière,
wife of the mad king Charles VI, which he had tried
unsuccessfully to have published back in 1876,[8] he was

evidently not interested in fragmenting his work as his mother thought he should, so that the outside world knew nothing of these occupations—hence, in part, his undeserved reputation for laziness.

In fact, another major literary project came into his mind in 1878, and that too consumed much time and energy. Some time previously (no one has ever discovered when), he had published a short story entitled *Miss Hadaly Habal*, in the vein of his other scientific fantasies, about the manufacture of an automaton which was an infinite improvement on a real woman.[9] It now occurred to him to use this as the nucleus of a full-scale novel, the first he had attempted since *Isis* in 1862. Into it he would incorporate all the misogynistic bitterness which the unhappy adventure with Anna Eyre had inspired in him. The plot of the novel would be simple. The inventor Thomas Alva Edison has an English friend called Lord Lyonnel (the name was later changed to Lord Ewald) who is on the point of killing himself because he is hopelessly in love with Alicia Clary, a singer of admirable beauty and total stupidity (Anna Eyre was visibly in his mind). Edison offers to save him by constructing an automaton which will exactly reproduce Alicia's physique but will, by various occult and phonographic devices, be equipped with a soul to match her appearance. Sceptical at first, Lyonnel, without realizing what is happening, ends up by falling in love with the automaton, the so-called Andréïde. Whether Villiers had decided on the ending is not sure; he may not have made up his mind how to round the story off. At all events, the action would be surrounded by all sorts of philosophical considerations: on the nature of reality, on perception, on love, on women, and on a hundred other topics.

Once Villiers hit on the inspiration for the novel, which was at that time given the title *L'Andréïde paradoxale d'Edison*, he worked at it incessantly in the winter of 1878–9, often in conditions of the most desperate hardship. According to Gustave Guiches, who became a close friend a few years later, 'in the icy horror of a room in the rue de Maubeuge, which had been emptied of its furniture, lying on the floor flat on his stomach and diluting in water his last drops of ink, he wrote long chapters of *L'Ève future*'[10] (that was the novel's definitive title). In later years he looked back on the composition of the work as a 'descent into Hell'.[11] By February 1879 he had written enough to proclaim triumphantly to Jean Marras, whom he had not seen for some time, that the novel was almost finished:

It's a work whose publication will, I believe, create something of a sensation, since, for the first time in my life, I am in earnest (. . .) Here, listen: it is an avenging and brilliant book, which will chill the blood and storm all the citadels of dreams! Never, never would I have believed myself capable of so much perseverance in the analyses!—of so much homogeneity in the composition, of so much astounding imagination, things, the new and magnificent evocation of which no one before me, do you hear, has dared to attempt. You can take my word for it, it is an exciting thing, a winner.[12]

Without false modesty, he says it will have as much success as *Don Quixote*.

In reality, the novel was probably much further from being finished than he pretended to Marras: no one more often mistook the wish for the deed than Villiers. In the meantime there was *Le Nouveau-Monde* to think of, and he was becoming worried about Chabrillat's intentions. The manager was refusing to advance him any money, and *L'Assommoir* was still pulling in the crowds at the Ambigu, so that there was no prospect of anything happening in the immediate future. Unfortunately, Villiers was unable to contain his impatience, as Georges Duval, who had introduced him to Chabrillat, relates:

He thought it his duty never to leave Chabrillat or the Ambigu alone. He came every afternoon, proposing changes, adding speeches—including the fine tirade on the star-spangled banner—none of which is particularly upsetting, but also, apparently, breaking out in such excesses of language and gestures that one morning Chabrillat rang my doorbell to tell me that it was impossible for him to stage a play by a man 'whose madness terrified him'.[13]

Villiers was by now exasperated by the number of managers who had promised to put on *Le Nouveau-Monde* and then changed their mind that he even thought of turning it into a novel and got as far as writing the first few pages before he lost heart.[14]

Villiers was just as liable to enrage publishers as to frighten theatre managers. At about the same time as he was ruining his chances with Chabrillat, he was reducing Richard Lesclide to impotent fury. Lesclide, who combined journalism and publishing, wanted to produce a luxury edition of *Azraël*, the story Villiers had published in *La Liberté* some ten years before. Villiers agreed and completely rewrote it. The work was announced in Lesclide's catalogue in May 1876, with illustrations by Frédéric Chevalier. Three months later ironic notes were appearing in the press to say that Villiers was busy correcting what was variously described as the seventeenth and the twentieth set of proofs, and Villiers himself was trying to pacify Lesclide: 'Do we want to produce a fine book, yes or no, and will one day more or less be so important that all will be lost if it isn't printed helter-skelter!'[15] Another three months passed, and Lesclide's review *Paris à l'eau-forte* included a limited edition of *Azraël* in its list of latest publications. Villiers himself later described *Azraël* as having been published by Lesclide in 1878. Yet only one copy of it has ever been discovered, and that does not bear the author's signature as had been promised. It is within the bounds of possibility that the work was printed but not put on sale; it is far more likely that only one trial copy was made, and that Lesclide gave up in despair at Villiers's costly dilatoriness and unending corrections.[16]

In 1879 Robert du Pontavice de Heussey came back to live in Paris, and he is one of the few people to have seen something of Villiers's domestic arrangements at this time, since he lived not far from the tenth-rate boarding-house in the rue de Maubeuge where Villiers had the simplest of rooms: 'mahogany bedstead, table and chest of drawers, cheap carpet, and lastly the inevitable wardrobe with a mirror. When the door swung open, there was no linen or clothes to be seen, only, on every shelf, piles of manuscripts, proofs, newspapers, and reviews.' Pontavice usually called on him between three and four in the afternoon:

I generally found him sitting in his bed, propped up by pillows, working away and stopping writing only to roll a cigarette which more often than not he did not bother to light. On the eiderdown that covered his knees, there was a pouch of Maryland tobacco, for which he had a particular fondness, packets of Job cigarette papers and, piled one on top of another, sheets of paper covered in his fine, ornate handwriting: he never used anything except pencil to write with, which made life extremely difficult for the copyists, the more so as, when he reread what he had written, he usually changed one word in five.[17]

Often he did not notice Pontavice's presence for ten minutes; then he would jump out of bed and fling the window wide open, regardless of the weather, causing the manuscripts and the cigarette papers to fly around the room. The two cousins would talk until about six o'clock, after which Pontavice would persuade Villiers to come out.

In the street he was a vastly entertaining companion, full of stories about the people they saw, the houses they passed, the different cafés they visited. Sometimes Villiers would go back to Pontavice's flat for dinner, partly for company, partly for some decent solid food, partly because he loved the view from the top-floor balcony, and partly because Pontavice had a Pleyel piano which he delighted to play. The balcony, with Paris far below and the night sky above, excited Villiers and he would recite the most moving passages of *L'Ève future* by heart to Pontavice:

His exaltation grew at the sound of his own words, his eyes became fixed in a sort of ecstasy, his gestures rose up towards God; he no longer belonged to the earth; I listened, struck dumb with admiration, and, when at last he fell silent, it seemed to me that a light had just been extinguished and that the whole world around me had grown darker.[18]

Villiers was (or had become) very indifferent to his sordid surroundings, to his inadequate diet, and to his worn-out clothing, but friends like Pontavice and Léon Dierx were all too well aware of the extreme hardship he was suffering and did what they could to alleviate it—unobtrusively, because Villiers was highly susceptible. They had for instance arranged that every day at noon a waiter should take in to him a big bowl of soup with a roll crumbled into it. If Villiers was still asleep the waiter would leave the soup on his bedside table and go away. But the poet, if he was awake, would say threateningly: 'What's this?' and the waiter would reply: 'It's your lunch, sir!' and disappear before any questions could be asked.[19] As for clothes, they used the services of a woman who lived in the same building and had attached herself to Villiers with such dog-like subservience that they called her 'the devoted one'.[20] She was Marie-Élisabeth Dantine, a charwoman and former midwife in her thirties, born in a part of Luxemburg that had become Belgian territory, widow of a coachman called Joseph Brégeras, and mother of a young son named Albert.[21] Though she was almost illiterate, she had developed a kind of hero-worship for Villiers and meekly bore his snubs, his mockery, and his rages in order to have the privilege of serving him, and in the end she came to be indispensable to him. Since she used to let herself into Villiers's room at night to wash and mend his clothing while he was out on his nocturnal peregrinations, Pontavice would sometimes give her a new shirt or a jacket that he no longer needed in order that she might substitute them for Villiers's worn-out garments. They both knew that he would never notice the difference, so there was no risk of offending him.

It was in 1879 that Villiers started to take a more active interest in politics. For some time past he had been doing his best to get a foothold in one or other of the great Parisian newspapers, which of course paid very much better than the ephemeral literary reviews where he usually published. But, despite his efforts with *Le Petit Parisien* and *L'Événement* and his hopes with a new paper to be called *Le Commerce*, no breakthrough had ever come. Then, in April 1879, he suddenly became powerful in another new journal entitled *La Croix et l'épée*. An editorial in the first number on 19 April expounded the nature of the mission adumbrated in the title: to defend the Church and conservative principles in the army, the paper being especially addressed to soldiers. It came out weekly on Saturdays, and by the third number it had begun to fly more openly royalist colours. But after the fifth issue, on 17 May, it disappeared without trace.

What exactly Villiers's functions were in it is obscure. According to Pontavice, who gives a highly inaccurate account of the whole affair, Villiers was everything except proprietor: editor, reporter, critic, columnist.[22] But the paper never mentions him in any official capacity. On the other hand, it did on 19 and 26 April devote a large amount of space to a greatly expanded version of *Azraël* and to a dithyrambic poem by one A. Saget addressed to the 'Grand Master Villiers de l'Isle-Adam', which is in reality a paean of praise to Villiers himself, and the numbers of 3 and 10 May contain a reproduction of *Impatience de la foule*, a tale which had first appeared in 1876. The editorials and most of the articles are unsigned, so there is no means of knowing whether any of them are from his pen: their general political line makes it possible that they are, though their style seems flatter than his normal flamboyance. At all events, the prominence accorded to him during the paper's brief existence suggests that Pontavice was not entirely wrong in attributing to him a great deal of influence behind the scenes.[23] Very possibly there is a connection between *La Croix et l'épée* and an undated letter in which Villiers, trying to borrow 10 francs from a woman friend, declares that he is on good terms with royalist society and that on all sides he is being offered funds to found newspapers to defend the cause (the 10 francs are necessary in the meantime, he explains, because it is the seven years of the lean kine, which in his case have preceded the others).[24] But if *La Croix et l'épée* brought him neither fame nor riches, it did implant in his mind the idea of a political career, and from this time onwards Villiers became an increasingly committed writer, with a strongly marked prejudice in favour of Church and Throne.

The year 1879 inevitably also brought its hope of a rich marriage. This time the presumptive fiancée was a Mlle E. to whom Villiers was going to be introduced by Mme Chesneau, a friend of the family; her fortune was alleged to be fifty million francs. But on 28 November Villiers's hopes were brought to such a brutal end that he went straight out to a beer-house and spent ten precious francs getting himself thoroughly drunk. The next day, when he woke up, he was so ashamed to realize that Marras had seen him in that condition that he sat down to write an abject apology:

That young woman that I told you about, you know, Mlle E., that I was supposed to take tea with at Mme Chesneau's within the next fortnight, well, I heard yesterday that she has a lover, a big Parisian banker, who *won't marry her*. She has five or six millions, and not fifty. But anyway the millions don't matter now since she has the lover and since there can't now be any question of marrying her. All that leaves its mark on my soul and makes me *a worse person than I really am*.[25]

The same month also nearly saw a duel with Mendès. In the early hours one Monday morning, Mendès, Marras, and Villiers were sitting drinking and arguing in a café, when Villiers made some kind of reproach to his old friend. Mendès reacted angrily and called Villiers names, and the party broke up. At first Villiers did nothing, on the grounds that they had known each other for years and that Mendès would undoubtedly come and apologize. But the next day, when Villiers was sitting in a café, Mendès came in, laughed, and walked away. Villiers gave him another two days' grace, and then, hearing nothing more, sent a formal and carefully phrased letter to Marras, asking him to find out whether Mendès was willing to retract his insults, or whether they were going to have to settle the matter by more bellicose means.[26] Presumably Marras succeeded either in extracting an apology from Mendès or in calming Villiers, since the duel seems not to have taken place.

But from then on Villiers had little to do with his erstwhile friend. Indeed, his epigrams about Mendès became legendary. He used to say: 'We were walking along side by side, and I was talking. Then, after a while, surprised by his silence, I turned towards him and saw there was nothing there any more . . . just a little blue flame disappearing down a drain.'[27] On another occasion he knocked on Mendès's door; when Mendès appeared and invited him in, he pretended to hesitate, then fled in mock terror, crying: 'No, not this evening, I have some money on me!'[28] He compared Mendès to a model frigate in a bottle: 'No one knows how it got inside, but it's there.'[29] But his most effective satirical performance was a kind of mime, usually acted at a café table, to the words 'Abraham Catulle Mendès'. For 'Abraham', with the 'h' pronounced as a rasping guttural, he would writhe and crook his fingers like a miser with his hoard, then with outspread arms gradually gather in all the glasses on the table, casting suspicious glances around him and with his little beard making him look like Shylock. Then came 'Catulle', when he would beam amiably, puff out his cheeks, roll his eyes, and generally give the impression of a mother hen defendng her chicks. Suddenly he would rap out 'Mendès!', spring up and, with a d'Artagnan-like gesture, pretend to whip out his rapier, make the folds of his cloak stream out behind him, and flutter the long plumes in his hat. Gustave de Malherbe, who tells the story, adds: 'For the movement of the cloak and the spurs, he needed five metres of clear floor space in front of him.'[30]

21

Although Villiers was still revising *Axël*, writing the novel about Edison, and continuing his historical researches, he had not given up his obstinate determination to get *Le Nouveau-Monde* produced, and in 1880 he was able to try a new tactic. The contract with Michaëlis had deprived him of the right to publish the play for three years, but that delay had now expired, so he set off in search of a publisher. Persuasive as he could be when he set his mind to it, he not only found one, but even induced him to undertake the publication of his complete works. It was not one of the big firms, but a certain Richard, whose offices were in the Passage de l'Opéra, and in the end his resources proved unequal to the task. In the meantime the fact that the play was at last in print revived hopes that the much-postponed production might after all take place. He had submitted it again to the Odéon, where a new director, Charles de La Rounat, had succeeded Duquesnel, and tried to mobilize his friends in its support, writing both to the influential journalist and man-about-town Aurélien Scholl[1] and to Alphonse Daudet[2] to beg them to help. He was also in touch with a London theatre agent named Edmund Gerson, who thought he could sell *Le Nouveau-Monde* in England.[3] Even Ernest Legouvé, one of the members of the original jury, recommended it to his friends, with the result that H. Ballande, an old and experienced director about to take over the Théâtre des Nations, set out to find Villiers and negotiate with him—not an easy task, as a note to the poet from his mother reveals:

A gentleman from M. Ballande has been desparately trying to find you for ages and he has tried everything to get your address, finally at his wits end he went to all the places we have lived in; he is on the point of signing for the théâtre des Nations—he is waiting for your play because he wants to be sure of it before commiting himself—he asks you to go and see him as soon as possible from 8 to 10 and even at any time—Mr legouvé spoke very highly to him about your play and urged him, this is the second time you have missed the chance because we dont know your address.[4]

Now that *Le Nouveau-Monde* seemed yet again to be about to triumph, the public could at last see what sort of work had won the centenary prize. It is the story of Ruth Moore, a woman torn between two men—Lord Cecil, her husband, whom she had married out of duty and had never loved, and Stephen Ashwell, a dashing young idealist. As the play opens, Ruth is about to obtain a divorce from Lord Cecil, who has magnanimously agreed to release her, when the ritual is interrupted by the mysterious and sinister figure of Mistress Andrews who, because she loves Stephen, wishes to ensure that Ruth never becomes free to marry him. In the second act we are transported to America, where Lord Cecil is one of the British leaders and Stephen an insurgent chief. An attempt by Mistress Andrews to kidnap Ruth at sea is foiled. Thereafter, in an increasingly complicated action, as the revolution progresses, Mistress Andrews tries to compromise Ruth as a British spy, Washington and Franklin intervene, various Indians, Puritans, colonists, soldiers, French aristocrats, crooked Italians, and others become involved, forests are burnt down, pitched battles are fought, and patriotic or revolutionary speeches made. In the last of the five acts, the American rebels are storming Boston and Lord Cecil is in charge of a desperate last stand. Ruth is his prisoner but resists his moving appeal to return to him, and then escapes a last attempt on her life by Mistress Andrews, who is herself killed. As Stephen bursts in at the head of the rebels to be reunited with Ruth, Lord Cecil dies nobly.

Le Nouveau-Monde is a very uneven play. The plot is confused and episodic, the characters stereotyped and unmemorable, the spectacular effects somewhat gratuitous, and the style occasionally tips over into bombast. Yet there are genuinely touching moments, there is a good deal of suspense, much of the language is elevated and poetic, and Villiers generates the exciting sense of the birth of a nation while at the same time paying tribute to the feudal and aristocratic values represented by Lord Cecil. Considered alongside other historical dramas of the period, it is a very worthy example of the genre; considered as one of Villiers's works, it lacks the intensity of philosophic idealism or the savagery of bitter irony that characterize him at his best. He has dispersed the interest in too many directions to be entirely convincing in any one of them, and the second act, interpolated at a late stage into an existing plot, is an uncomfortably irrelevant excrescence. That makes it in one way or another inferior to *La Révolte, Le Prétendant*, and *Axël*, but it is far from being a negligible work.

But once again his hopes had been raised in vain. La Rounat appears not have deigned to reply; Ballande, who had told Villiers that it was a 'magnificent play' and could have 'a very great success', decided that it would be so costly to put on that he would not do it unless the Americans put up two-thirds of the money;[5] Gerson's Englishmen lost interest. Even a plaintive little note in the edition failed to entice any prospective backers:

The vocal and orchestral score of this drama is already composed, the settings and costumes designed. So if the manager of an English or American theatre wishes to produce the work, he is requested to inform the author by letter, in Paris, addressing it care of Messrs Richard et Cie., 33 passage de l'Opéra, who will forward it.

Even the edition itself met an ignominious fate, and sold so badly that Richard, who was on the verge of bankruptcy, passed the copies on to his wife, who sold them off in her sweet shop in the rue de Rivoli at the reduced price of 25 centimes.[6] This time even Villiers grew discouraged, and for some time laid the play aside in favour of other things.

Some of these other things are indicated on the flyleaf of *Le Nouveau-Monde*, where Villiers lists the components of the projected edition of his complete works that Richard's financial difficulties soon brought to a halt. Apart from the texts already published—*Premières Poésies, Isis, Elën, Morgane, Claire Lenoir, Azraël,* and *La Révolte*—he proposed to print

L'Évasion for the first time and also the Edison novel and to collect his shorter works as *Poésies nouvelles, Histoires philosophiques,* and *Méditations littéraires.* This ambitious programme would eventually be extended by *Axël, L'Adoration des Mages,* and *Le Vieux de la Montagne* (though the fact that the latter two titles are not followed by the words '1 vol.' appears to signify that they were still only vague plans awaiting execution).[7] Strangely, his historical writings do not figure on the list; maybe he was still toying with the idea of an appeal prior to publication.

The appearance in print of *Le Nouveau-Monde* had seemed momentarily to push open the door to public recognition that had so far been closed to him. Then, just as that door was slammed shut again, another one unexpectedly opened up. With *L'Ève nouvelle,* as the Edison novel was now called, he at last made the breakthrough for which he had been hoping for years: one of the big Parisian dailies decided to serialize it. This was Arthur Meyer's paper *Le Gaulois,* and Villiers may have owed his opportunity to his friends François Oswald and Armand Gouzien, both of whom were on its staff. At all events, for the first time since *Azraël* had been published in *La Liberté* in 1869, the readers of the great middle-class press were to be given the chance to appreciate Villiers's talent.

At the beginning of September 1880 *Le Gaulois* heralded the impending publication of Villiers's novel with great—and justifiable—emphasis on its strangeness, and the first episode duly appeared in the issue of 4 September. A letter from Villiers to Marras on the eleventh reveals not only that Meyer had given him an advance of 500 francs but also that he was exhausted from the effort of rewriting the work as he went along.[8] Evidently (and predictably) the form and style of the novel as it then existed did not satisfy him, and, as so often happened, he had sought help and advice from Marras.

The idea of being published in *Le Gaulois* cheered him up greatly, and he went off to celebrate at La Grand'Pinte, an artists' café in Montmartre. The Swiss novelist Édouard Rod saw him there:

'You know, they're at last going to publish my novel *L'Ève nouvelle* . . . Yes, *Le Gaulois* . . . I've just been to see the cashier . . . I asked him for some money . . . "How much do you

want?"—"Twenty-five louis!"—"Here you are!"—So I said:
"Fifty"—"There you are . . ." So, you see, I really had to drink some
champagne."

And he went on as if he was talking to himself, with an *inner* voice that
I could hardly hear, even though I was all ears.

'Yes, the novel's going to appear! and the others after it. . . the others
. . . that are waiting their turn. . . And I'm going to write lots of books,
now I'm going to . . . The bourgeois are always asking me why I don't
produce anything. . . Why I don't produce anything, good God!. . .'

And suddenly standing bolt upright and raising his arms, he cried in a
truly tragic outburst: 'And what about poverty! . . .'[9]

The euphoria of seeing his name every day in the columns of a
great newspaper did not last long. After the instalment of 18
September *Le Gaulois* suddenly suspended publication of the
novel, without a word of warning or explanation. No one
knows what had happened: most probably the readers had
signified that they did not like a novel so different from their
usual diet of undemanding adventure stories or historical
romances, and Meyer had decided to cut his losses by
substituting another work before he lost more subscribers. So
L'Ève nouvelle met the same fate as *Le Nouveau-Monde:*
apparent acceptance, soon followed by total withdrawal.

Villiers's courage in the face of such disappointments was
remarkable. Fernand Calmettes reports that the words most
often on his lips were: 'We'll see next winter. . . a good fire. . .
good wing-chairs',[10] and his letters (especially to his creditors)
confirm his irrepressible optimism: 'I'll be successful, before
winter comes',[11] 'a few more days' work and I'll be home and
dry', 'you'll see, I'll succeed',[13] 'count on me when I win
through', 'as for me, everything will turn out well. It's a matter
of resilience, and thank heaven (literally) God has not totally
deprived me of that',[15] 'I'm used to these misfortunes that don't
affect me any more; I'm sorry about fate, but I don't complain
about it'.[16] Yet, in order to feed his parents and to keep body and
soul together, he was reduced to the most desperate expedients,
whose eccentricity was as legendary as their ingenuity. Writing
to Marras at the beginning of 1879, he described his life with
total lack of rancour: 'My lessons have saved me, along with my
family. I earn 40 francs a week all told, that is, 5 francs a day.
That's what the three of us have to live on; I only go out once

every six weeks. Give me a chop or a frankfurter or a hard-boiled egg, a cup of coffee, and I'm as happy as a king'.[17] But what lessons was he giving? The answer is almost certainly boxing lessons as a sparring-partner in a gymnasium. Villiers was very proud of his skills as a boxer, which he regularly attributed to the heroes of his tales, and the story of his boxing lessons has been repeated by too many of his contemporaries (including the sober Mallarmé) for it to be without foundation.[18]

But boxing instructor was far from being the oddest occupation of the one-time Comptroller of the Waggonage of the Cattle transported from the south to Paris. Henry Roujon mentions that he was reputed to have worked for an undertaker,[19] and that would have suited his macabre sense of humour, though there is no other evidence to confirm the rumour. One thing he almost certainly did do is even more bizarre. Around 1880 Villiers made the acquaintance of a Dr Latino, who ran a medical practice specializing in mental patients in the Avenue de l'Opéra and who also dabbled in spiritualism (Villiers used a séance held in his house as the basis of an eerie unfinished tale of the supernatural in 1884).[20] Their friendship was close enough for Latino to offer him a room in his house in the spring of 1881, but the probability is that Villiers paid in kind for his keep—his job was to sit in the waiting-room and play the part of the 'cured madman', assuring prospective patients that the doctor's professional skills had worked wonders in his own case.[21] Clearly, if Villiers took on such extraordinary jobs (and he was never prepared to consider ordinary ones), it was to demonstrate to the world at large to what degrading extremities a serious writer was driven in modern society.

Yet Villiers could never quite bring himself to despise the distinctions distributed by that society, even if they were insignificant in comparison to the thrones and premierships to which he had once aspired, and in 1878 or 1879 he thought it would be pleasant to add to his collection of exotic decorations the more modest but homegrown one of the *palmes académiques* awarded for literary and intellectual distinction. It was of course obvious to him that all he had to do was ask and it would be granted him, so he duly submitted his request and sat back to await receipt of his medal. What in fact he eventually received was his own dossier back again, with the one word 'unknown' scrawled across the cover.[22] Officialdom was nevertheless slowly beginning to become aware of Villiers's existence. The Marquis informed him in July 1878 that there had been a letter from the Minister of Fine Arts asking him to call at the ministry to make arrangements about a grant,[23] and, though on this occasion nothing may have come of it, in 1880 the Minister was sufficiently aware both of Villiers's achievements and of his plight to give him 500 francs from the fund for the encouragement of letters.[24]

If the Ministry of Education had not heard of Villiers at the end of the 1870s, it was not entirely their fault. The *Premières Poésies* twenty years earlier had passed unnoticed; *Isis*, *Elën*, and *Morgane* had been printed in such tiny editions that only a handful of people knew of their existence; *La Révolte* had appeared just as the Franco-Prussian War broke out, and since then, despite the Centenary prize of 1876, no new volume of his had been published. Only his closest friends and those who followed what went on in little literary reviews, had any idea of how much he had been writing in the meantime. When the young poet Gustave Kahn called on Stéphane Mallarmé in 1879, he had to admit that he had read nothing of Villiers. Mallarmé was shocked but understanding: 'It pained him, but in those days it took more than good will to discover Villiers, it took erudition. Fortunately, Mallarmé owned what was then a unique complete set of Villiers's works, made up of out-of-print volumes and pages cut out of reviews, that I took away with me.'[25] Those who were less lucky than Kahn had no such opportunity to find out what sort of a writer Villiers really was. They knew him from chance meetings in cafés, from often malicious paragraphs in gossip columns, from the innumerable more or less credible anecdotes that circulated about him, from occasional sudden appearances in the limelight like the American Centenary prize or the *Perrinet Leclerc* case, but very few were in any position to judge whether he was a misunderstood genius or an empty fraud with a talent for self-advertisement. The legend (assiduously fostered by Villiers) was gradually taking over from the man himself.

Another improbable element in that legend was heralded

when late in 1880 Villiers started behaving in a mysterious fashion which alarmed cousin Pontavice's old Breton servant Mar'Yvonne. One day Pontavice returned home to find Villiers rummaging through his drawers while Mar'Yvonne clucked in agitation in the background. 'Ties, serious ties, very serious ties' was what he said he was looking for, and in the end he departed with three white ties carefully wrapped in an old newspaper. Mar'Yvonne reported that he had also brought her a white shirt to iron, insisting that it should be impeccably smart. Pontavice and his maid concluded that he was either on the matrimonial trail again or had been invited into high society where his usual mode of dress would have been unacceptable[26]—there was an embarrassing incident about the same time when Villiers had been unable to borrow any gloves to attend an elegant evening party and turned up bare-handed; one of the lady guests, looking pointedly at his hands, said: 'Those are very fine gloves you have there, Villiers!' only to receive the reply: 'A present from my mother, madam!'[27] But on this occasion they were wrong. Villiers needed to look his best because he had decided to present himself as a candidate in the forthcoming elections to the Municipal Council of Paris.

Since the time of *La Croix et l'épée*, Villiers had been frequenting royalist circles, and at the end of 1880, with the elections due in January, he put his name forward to the legitimist Protest Committee that had just been formed to fight against the republican majority on the Council. His offer seems not to have been taken up with any great eagerness, since he was not on the first list of the Committee's candidates published on 4 January 1881, but he figured in a supplementary list published on the seventh as the official candidate for the Ternes district in the XVIIth Arrondissement in the north-west of Paris.[28] He had two opponents, the sitting councillor Severiano de Heredia, a Cuban-born left-wing republican who later became a minister, and a fringe 'collectivist' called Couturat. Since Heredia's majority was such that he was sure of re-election, Villiers never stood a real chance and was doubtless only adopted as a means of showing the royalist flag. He himself, with his usual contempt for democratic institutions, later wrote: 'The result of such elections nowadays being well-known in advance, I had accepted only for the honour of defeat.'[29]

This attitude seems to indicate that Villiers did not take the election entirely seriously, which may well be true: it would be in character for him to try to discredit an electoral process of which he disapproved by showing how easily it could be ridiculed. If we are to believe Pontavice, his electoral programme included the demolition, on aesthetic grounds, of the Opéra, Saint-Sulpice, and the Panthéon, and the revival of the debtors' prison as a sanctuary for men of letters.[30] Villiers himself records that he had notified his intention of trying to have Augusta Holmès made a member of the jury of the Musical Competition of the City of Paris, an idea which caused roars of laughter among male councillors but which was in fact adopted not long after.[31] But these may have been no more than jokes for private consumption, and there is no reliable evidence about what his campaign actually contained. In any case, it was very brief, since the elections took place on the tenth. In the ward for which Villiers stood, there were no surprises, and these were the results:

Heredia	2147
Villiers	593
Couturat	112

The fact that Villiers did not come bottom of the poll shows that his candidature was not wholly frivolous, and he thought that he had done well enough to go further in his political career, declaring to Pontavice: 'After all, I agree with Bulwer: the really strong personality should begin with literature, go on to public life, and end up in power!'[32]

22

Villiers's private life was undergoing drastic changes about this time. His father, now almost eighty, had a stroke in the summer of 1880 and was at death's door. His mother wrote in panic: 'Your father has had a relapse, he has been in bed for the last two days; the doctor told me to write to you. I am very worried indeed. Come back as soon as you can when you get my letter. I would have sent you a telegram if I had known your address. Come back quickly.'[1] Villiers found his father half-paralysed and apparently dying in a miserable room in a boarding-house. But the old man had not changed, and, while his son was out, said haltingly to a friend: 'This is the end for me, but I await death with serenity; I have realized my life's dream; I am leaving Mathias a fortune equal to that of the greatest princely families in the world.' The friend, to humour him, mentioned fifty millions, which he thought a suitably imposing figure. But the Marquis grimaced with disdain: 'Fifty millions? Chickenfeed!'[2] In the end, the Marquis was tough enough, even after years of privation, to recover and pursue his more and more lunatic dreams for several years to come.

The illness was nevertheless severe and costly, which strained even further the family's almost non-existent resources, and Villiers's mother was obliged to turn to her brother-in-law the Abbé Victor for help. His reply from Ploumilliau on 20 November 1880 is a tart and revealing document:

I am extremely sorry about the cruel situation to which your husband has reduced you. If I had been rich, I would have sent you a few hundred francs; I am far from rich, however, and, as I always feel it my duty to honour my obligations, I can only send you fifty—this I give to you very gladly. As for your husband who has never been capable of doing anything except lying, he will never get a sou from me. He has done nothing but harm to his family: he is the embodiment of selfishness and lies. I am convinced that without him his son could have made a decent marriage; with him it is very difficult. Farewell, my dear sister-in-law, and may God console you![3]

The saintly and charitable priest venerated by his parishioners (as he is said to have been) is not much in evidence in this missive, any more than it is in the one he sent Villiers in December of the same year, having had a copy of *Le Nouveau-Monde* presented to him. The Abbé begins by disclaiming any competence to judge the play, but adds: 'Since you were preferred to your rivals, that is a proof that your work was better.' After this parsimonious praise, he proceeds to express all manner of reservations—Washington is not seen enough, the female characters are dull, and of course a woman who wants a divorce is beneath contempt. Then he comes to the nub of the matter, in a way which shows him much less different from his errant brother than he would have liked to believe:

Anyway, my dear nephew, I am happy to learn that this work has brought you honour and money, which does not stop me fearing that you will never make your fortune with literature. Your father was supposed to marry you to a millionairess, that is what I should like to see and what I wish for you with all my heart. That would be better than Plays.[4]

It is a pity that we do not have Villiers's reaction to his venerable uncle's curt dismissal of all that he held dear; it would have been worth reading.

The extra burdens laid on Villiers by the failing health of his parents were not however the most serious responsibility he had to assume. On 10 January 1881, at a quarter to two in the afternoon, Marie Dantine, the widowed charwoman who had been caring for him, gave birth to a son who was given the names Victor-Philippe-Auguste. Six weeks later he was baptized at the Church of La Trinité, receiving more names: Marie-Joseph-Alphonse-Victor-Philippe-Auguste; his god-father and godmother were two people who lived at the same address as his mother, 64 rue de Larochefoucauld.[5] Villiers now had a son, a boy who could not bear his illustrious name because he was illegitimate, and whose mother was a humble working-woman who could not write and could barely read printed characters. But whatever the truth about the son which Mathilde Leroy claimed to have borne him twelve years earlier, Villiers had no intention of treating Victor as anything but his child. Of marriage there could be no question: there is no evidence that he loved Marie in the full sense of the word, and the discrepancy in name and intellect was simply too great for him to consider making her his equal. She had come to have a place in his singularly cheerless existence, but, so far as one can judge, the relationship was more that of master and servant than that of husband and wife or lover and mistress. How indeed could it have been otherwise when he lived so much for things of the mind that were totally beyond her comprehension? But Victor (or Totor, as he was known) was different. Villiers cherished him and loved him (in his own idiosyncratic way), and the whole direction of his life gradually changed as a result of the child's existence.

Whether he was actually living with Marie at this stage is unclear; probably he only moved in with her later. But he certainly felt obliged to do his best to provide for her and for her two children (Albert, her son by her first husband, was probably still at school; later he became an apprentice typographer, but died young of tuberculosis). To his friends, he was as reticent about his progeny as he always had been about his dwelling-places. He let it be known 'that this child had been brought to him in a basket, at his home, on behalf of a genuine princess, of superhuman beauty, whom he had met and who had given herself to him in a conservatory, during a reception at Princess Ratazzi's'.[6] Probably the Marquise never learnt that she had a grandson; if the Marquis found out, it was only later. So the effects of Victor's birth were not immediate, except for the increased urgency of finding more money.

No doubt it was this which made Villiers so assiduous in his attentions to the national press. The fact that *Le Gaulois* had suspended publication of *L'Ève nouvelle* after only fourteen instalments did not deter him from offering it to other papers, and, no doubt to his surprise, he was successful in finding a taker within a matter of weeks. This was in a new paper called *L'Étoile française* which was being launched by a journalist friend, Ed. Taine. Its political colouring cannot have been wholly sympathetic to Villiers, since it was aggressively republican, and the stark contrast between his avowed royalism and *L'Étoile française*'s campaign in favour of Gambetta, the politician whom he hated the most, was a source of friction. Nevertheless, when the first number of the paper appeared on 14 December, Villiers's novel was chosen to inaugurate its serials, always a vital ingredient in the circulation of French dailies in the nineteenth century. In addition to the serialization of *L'Ève nouvelle*, *L'Étoile française* at different times over the next eighteen months published reproductions of no fewer than eight of Villiers's tales or poems and, on 11 April 1881, an article on the shooting of Victor Noir, inspired by the death of his killer, Prince Pierre Bonaparte, which is perhaps his most brilliant piece of journalism in its vituperative irony and its dramatic vividness.[7]

But, despite Taine's personal benevolence towards Villiers, some of the other members of the paper's staff found it hard to stomach the fact that he was actually standing for the Municipal Council against Heredia, the candidate whom the paper was actively supporting. The result was that, on the day when the election results were announced, the instalment of *L'Ève nouvelle* was held over and Villiers's name was not mentioned in the voting for the XVIIth Arrondissement. Indeed, it seems as though the influence of Taine's colleagues almost forced him to give up serializing the novel altogether, and the prominence which Villiers gives in his article on Victor Noir to two obscure journalists on the staff of *L'Étoile française* suggests that he found it expedient to flatter them—the whole idea of resurrecting this episode of his revolutionary past may not have been unconnected with the need for keeping in with the more militant republicans on the paper. Despite these difficulties, *L'Étoile française* persisted with *L'Ève nouvelle* and by 4 February 1881 had published forty-six instalments, taking the novel to within three chapters of the end. Then, on the fifth, there appeared this announcement: 'Pressure on space compels us to postpone until tomorrow the end of the interesting novel of our colleague VILLIERS DE L'ISLE-ADAM: L'ÈVE NOUVELLE, that powerful and dramatic work which has had such a great and deserved success with our readers.'[8] But the next day nothing appeared, and the paper never mentioned *L'Ève nouvelle* again.

There are two possible explanations for this sudden cessation. One is that *L'Étoile française* was entering into a new phase of its activity, which it proclaimed on every page: 'we want to adapt ourselves more to the requirements of our subscribers', 'we shall affirm our republican ideas more loudly', 'our readers want to be amused and entertained'. It also reduced its price, so the new policy was clearly designed to make it more attractive to less educated and more politically committed readers, and it may have been felt that the subtle metaphysical speculations produced by a royalist and an aristocrat had become too incongruous to be tolerated any longer. On the other hand, one has some difficulty in believing that a newspaper which had been serializing a novel for nearly two months should abruptly have taken against it so violently that it discontinued it when it was within a few pages of the end:[9] some readers at least would be frustrated to be deprived of the conclusion. Moreover, the fact that no new serial started for several days demonstrates that the editor had no substitute to hand, so why not let it run its course?

This leads one to examine the second possible explanation: that Villiers himself failed to provide the end, or withdrew it at the last moment to alter it. It should be borne in mind that the *Étoile française* text of *L'Ève nouvelle* is a much more violent and Faustian work than the definitive version, in which the theme of human revolt against a divine order considered no longer bearable is much attenuated: indeed, in 1886 the chapters missing in 1881 show divine intervention defeating the revolt. But Villiers may well not have originally intended the novel to end in that way, or he may have been undecided about how best to bring it to a conclusion.[10] So it is quite possible that last-minute scruples may have brought about a sudden change of mind. Exactly this was to happen with *Axël* when it was being serialized in 1886: overcome with doubts about the audacity of its irreligious ending, he suddenly took his manuscript back in order completely to rewrite the last scene. But, whereas the monthly review in which *Axël* was appearing may have been able to accept such delays, a daily paper which depended on continuity would have felt that an interruption of more than a day or two was intolerable. It seems therefore on balance more likely that it was hesitation on Villiers's part, for doctrinal or aesthetic reasons, that led to the untimely suspension of *L'Ève nouvelle* in *L'Étoile française*.

The novel's partial appearance in the two papers cannot have done very much for Villiers's reputation. *Le Gaulois*, it is true, was an important and well-established daily, but the serialization there lasted only a fortnight and produced only a sixth of the text. As for *L'Étoile française*, it was a very small-circulation affair, founded essentially to fight the 1881 elections and no doubt not expected to survive much beyond them—in the event, it broke off publication in May 1881 and was only revived, as *L'Étoile de France*, after a gap of several months. In 1880 another approach to a publisher, this time Charpentier, for a volume of short stories entitled *Histoires énigmatiques*[11] came to nothing, despite the support of Coquelin, so Villiers was still largely unknown to the public.

But he was laying deep plans of his own to secure his position, and gave much thought to ways of breaking down the wall of silence which seemed to surround his writings. The first step in this new strategy came when he approached Ed. Taine with a scheme for founding his own paper, just before *L'Étoile française* was launched. Taine was impressed with the idea and offered his services without reservation:

I have studied and analysed the idea of your newspaper-review *Le Verdict* patiently and at length. I find it excellent, and, to prove it, I am putting at your disposal the offices, premises, administrative staff, printing works, and typography of my daily *L'Étoile française*, 16 rue de la Grange-Batelière, above *Le Gaulois*. Moreover, you are assured of the paper's support since we shall collaborate on it.[12]

Despite this generosity, it does not seem that *Le Verdict* ever saw the light of day, no doubt for lack of financial backing.

A man so accustomed to setbacks was however not easily deflected from his purpose, and in April or May 1881 he drew up, with minute attention to detail, an extraordinary document designed to attract funds for the foundation of another paper, this time to be called *L'Éclaireur*.[13] Under the heading *Important Considerations*, Villiers sets out the financial advantages of owning a newspaper: 'When a paper is founded, when its readership is established, when it is enjoyed and appreciated by the public, the property which it represents cannot but become a flourishing industrial enterprise.' There follows a series of examples of contemporary newspapers which, from modest beginnings, have become veritable gold-mines (the figures may be suspect, but Villiers has clearly taken a great deal of trouble over them). The peroration of this section vaunts the peculiar virtues of *L'Éclaireur*:

The newspaper *L'Éclaireur*, by the exceptional choice of its collaborators, whose names have been the making of several dailies and whose recognized and undisputed talent ensures immediate sales,—by the three or four quite special points of novelty and curiosity which it offers to the public,—by the independence and honesty of its political line,—by the reliability of the news items of varying degrees of importance with which it will be *first* in the field,—by its elegant and interesting appearance;—by the care taken over its layout and the general impression of *interest* which it will at once arouse,—by the excellent time of the year at which it will appear (the elections and the holiday period),—presents absolutely positive and *abnormal* guarantees and chances of success.

That is not all. Villiers then proceeds to a detailed breakdown of the daily cost of producing the paper, with a run of 10,000 copies: administrative costs of 867 francs per day, and editorial costs of 633 francs, plus an outlay of 14,000 francs for buying a printing-works, which would be covered in four months. The daily cost would then be 1,500 francs; the income would be at first only 820 francs. So there would be an apparent monthly loss of 20,900 francs, in fact calculable as 16,650 francs because of economies on printing. However, with increased sales and advertising revenue, this would soon be a profit of 24,000 francs a month, so that, at the end of a year, the fortunate proprietor would have a clear profit of 288,000 francs, and he would own both a printing-works and a powerful organ of public opinion. After these dazzling calculations, Villiers proceeds to enumerate the *Elements of Success* in a paper, for which, in his view, there are three possibilities: the paper may correspond to a particular public interest, or it may have an editor with star quality, or it may have a team of exceptional contributors. Needless to say, *L'Éclaireur* combines these three possibilities. The conclusion of all this is something of an anti-climax: 'Although it is very difficult to give an impression of a work other than by the work itself, we shall try to prove succinctly what we have postulated.' But at this point Villiers's courage fails him, and he ends lamely: 'If the deal is accepted in principle,—ensuring the existence of the paper for six months, that is, 250,000 francs—the proofs in question will be supplied.'

Villiers rarely thought it worth angling for trivial amounts, and clearly it would have taken nothing less than a benevolent millionaire to launch *L'Éclaireur* on the scale which he envisaged. Even so, and however suspect his sums may be, he was not wrong in arguing that a successful newspaper could be a very profitable business, once the inevitable initial losses had been recouped. But obviously, if *L'Éclaireur* was to stand any chance of establishing itself, it had to have a character and identity of its own, and, in this respect, *Our Programme* is not the least strange and surprising part of the whole document. This is how Villiers defines the paper's political line:

L'ÉCLAIREUR is the organ of that Spirit of transition and synthesis which, today, taking precedence over all the ulterior motives of political parties, is closely borne in upon everyone's conscience—and MUST therefore, in the legitimate interests of all, influence acts of a State. Let us be more precise.
1.—To defend the fair points in all opinions, while at the same time clarifying them.
2.—To change, through deep study and new analysis, the minds of those people whose views are formed in good faith and are befogged only by too strong prejudices, too exclusive beliefs.
3.—To support the efforts being made towards equitable reconciliations.
4.—To blunt, when occasion arises, the too sharp edges of reactionary, determined, and mocking spirits, if possible with the blade of a more sagacious irony.
5.—To rouse stagnant, suspicious, and doubting minds to new reflections which are always salutary, to prescribe new steps to be taken, to indicate corrective measures, pointing out past errors, and finally to fight for the good of society.
6.—To maintain, in all circumstances and in every different field, the honesty of our polemics with the most steadfast energy.
7.—To be the clearsighted Admonisher (at the risk of being importunate) of the great Indifference of the public. Such is the line which the newspaper *L'Éclaireur* proposes to follow on home politics, and which it will follow so long as I have control over it.

The contrast between this fog of vague and meaningless verbiage and the meticulousness of the financial calculations is very remarkable. It is as if Villiers, normally so trenchant in expressing his views, was trying to concoct a programme which sounded vigorous and impressive without in fact being specific about anything at all. A prospective backer would have been hard put to it to see what line, if any, *L'Éclaireur* was going to follow, other than a misty, shifting goodwill towards everyone. Certainly it is difficult to see a newspaper creating an identity for itself with such a fuzzy set of guidelines, in which even Villiers's normally powerful and individual style degenerates into inane verbosity. At first sight the contradiction between the ardent desire to found a newspaper and the total obscurity of its direction seems inexplicable; on examination it proves, however, to be part of a positively Machiavellian strategy.

The clue to the mystery is to be found in a letter which Villiers sent on 17 May, at almost exactly the same time as he was preparing his dossier on *L'Éclaireur,* to Comte Bretonneau de Moydier, who was one of the legitimist leaders in the XVIIth Arrondissement. The letter, which was accompanied by a copy of *Le Nouveau-Monde,* reveals unexpected ambitions on Villiers's part:

At the time of the last municipal elections in Paris, I accepted nomination from our committee. Today, I should like to throw myself completely into the struggle and win the confidence of a Département, for I believe I represent our cause with firmness. At the present juncture, goodwill is no longer enough. A certain knowledge of current questions, combined with some energy of mind, is indispensable. Now, do you not think as I do, Monsieur le Comte, that it is rather odd that the very men who have in every respect the qualities needed to hold in check those whose threats are well on the way to being carried out,—that men capable of defending, of filling a post of honour usefully, reliably, productively—that men whose whole past, ancestral as well as personal, guarantees the future—should be literally the last of whom their party ever thinks? I should be very eager to take a few moments of your time to discuss this matter, Monsieur le Comte, and I should be grateful if you would be kind enough to let me know when I might have the honour of calling on you.[14]

The tactic of *L'Éclaireur* becomes clear in the light of this letter. Villiers had decided that he would like to be a monarchist deputy and was angling for a constituency nomination in the general election which was due to take place later that year. In order to increase his chances of being returned, he had come to the conclusion that it would be extremely useful to have his own newspaper, and that was to be the function of *L'Éclaireur*. That is why, among the calculations about the sale of the paper, one finds the unusual item of 'electoral review', which is explained thus: 'That is, until October, an average of 10,000 copies a week bought outright by a candidate supported by *L'Éclaireur*.' The candidate was to be none other then Villiers himself, and the ambivalence of the paper's programme was designed to mask its total allegiance to himself and his party until such time as it became expedient to reveal it. In this way, potential backers would not know that they were financing a legitimist journal until it was too late, and the paper would in the meantime have acquired a spurious air of political independence. If the paper collapsed or the backer withdrew after the election, it would not matter. In fact, Villiers was planning to repeat something of the policy followed by *La Croix et l'épée*, which began with a more generally conservative line before openly nailing its royalist colours to the mast.

The whole plan is a curious mixture of cunning and naïveté. The cunning is evident in the care with which the tactics have been worked out, the minuteness of the financial calculations, the obfuscation of the real purpose of the paper, and the dangling of the bait of untold wealth as a possible return on the investment. But the naïveté is just as apparent in Villiers's inability to be specific about the journal's real policies, in his coyness about mentioning collaborators other than himself, in his avoidance of anything precise about the paper's contents, all of which amount to trying to sell an exceedingly expensive pig in a poke. There is also a certain naïveté in the tone of irritation that creeps into his letter to Bretonneau de Moydier, when he appears to be hinting that he has some kind of divine right to a high place in legitimist councils and that it is very wrong of the party not to have given spontaneous recognition to his superior qualities. But his attitude to the monarchists, even Henri V himself, was never exempt from a certain sense of resentment at their lifelessness and their failure to seize power.

Bretonneau de Moydier evidently did interview Villiers, but neither the newspaper not the candidacy came to fruition, not least because there was still some unfinished business left over from Villiers's January campaign for the Municipal Council. This concerned unpaid bills for distributing leaflets and posters, and the letter from Bretonneau de Moydier just after his meeting with the poet shows that that was uppermost in his mind. He reminds Villiers of his promise to settle the matter and goes on:

I should be very grateful if you would inform me of what has happened and put my mind at rest by assuring me of a final quittance; for, although it does not concern me directly, as far as responsibility is concerned, you will understand that, in my position, it is important for me to know that the honour of the party and its candidates is intact.[15]

But in September Villiers had still not paid off the distributors, and Bretonneau de Moydier found himself threatened with being sued for costs. This brought an angry letter from him:

Allow me, Monsieur le Comte, to express surprise that you should not yet have honoured the word you gave me as a gentleman the other day, and put an end to these complaints which are really taking on a more than unfortunate character. I trust that you will see the urgency of bringing matters to a conclusion, that you will do it promptly, and will then inform me.[16]

No doubt the legitimist party was not keen on having as standardbearer a man who was liable to leave a trail of unpaid bills behind him, and that may be one reason why Villiers did not stand in the general election of August 1881 (which in any case was disastrous for the monarchists). Villiers himself took a different view, and the day after the election wrote to Henry Mayol de Lupé, editor of the legitimist paper *L'Union*, to give his version of the reasons for his abstention. He begins by a reminder of his candidacy in January: 'Without any illusions about the outcome of the struggle, I accepted out of devotion to duty—being in any case one of those people who, indifferent by tradition to easy victories, never refuse the honour of a combat in which defeat is certain.' Then he goes on to say that his failure to stand in August may have caused surprise and explains (none too clearly) what had motivated his decision and that of certain others:

In a conflict of this nature, everyone has his prescribed duty, and inaction is sometimes by no means the least burdensome task to fulfil. Always mindful of a higher but temporarily misunderstood right, strictly loyal to our faith which has been constantly strengthened by adversity, we have been obliged to sacrifice our adventurous impatience to the categorical decisions of an august will. Such are the motives at least behind our personal abstention in a constituency where, out of twenty thousand electors, my only opponent could muster no more than three thousand votes. But if it has pleased the king to invite unshakeably devoted servants to keep silent for a brief space of time, it is because he knows he will soon have to use them for a decisive victory.[17]

On the face of it, this means that the Comte de Chambord had instructed some of his most ardent supporters, among them Villiers, not to stand in the general election. But in fact the circular sent out in Chambord's name to royalist committees in February had only given orders for the exclusion of half-hearted opportunists. What therefore did lie behind Villiers's abstention is obscure. At all events, by writing a letter which he presumably expected to see inserted in *L'Union,* he obviously intended to safeguard his position as a committed royalist, possibly also to scotch rumours that he was unacceptable as a candidate because of the unpaid bills, and perhaps even to hint that the shock troops of the monarchy were being held in reserve for something more serious than the solemn farce of parliamentary elections. All these tortuous manoeuvrings at least had the effect of giving Villiers the public status of an active and fervent upholder of what he called 'the Christian and monarchical cause', even if his way of defending that cause lent some justification to Henry Roujon's ironic description of him: 'distinguishing marks: blaspheming Christian and disrespectful royalist'.[18]

23

In various ways the background to Villiers's life was changing in the early 1880s. For some time past Nina de Villard's *salon* had been losing its brilliance. Fewer people came there, the evenings were less gay, and the atmosphere became progressively heavier as Nina herself, prematurely aged and grotesquely obese, showed more and more signs of nervous instability. In the end her mother was obliged to close the *salon,* and, not long after, Nina had to be interned in an asylum: when people asked her how she was, she would reply: 'I am not, since I am dead.'[1] Her physical death did not occur until 22 July 1884, but she had been cut off from her friends for two or three years, and, though Villiers appears to have remained in touch with her mother,[2] he had probably not seen Nina since the beginning of the decade.

The closure of the *salon* in the rue des Moines must have left a great gap in Villiers's life. For many years he had gone there regularly, had met his friends, had had a lively and sympathetic audience for his readings and his interminable conversations, and had always been sure of something to eat and somewhere to sleep. But, fortunately, just as Nina's *salon* came to an end, so another one started, which was to play an equally important part in his life. This was the Tuesday evening gathering which Stéphane Mallarmé inaugurated in his flat in the rue de Rome in 1880. It was not until about 1884 that this became established as perhaps the most important centre of poetic thought in Paris, but Villiers, with friends like Marras and Roujon, was among the first to take advantage of Mallarmé's hospitality. Though Villiers's appearances were sporadic and unpredictable, the *mardis* became one of his main channels of communication with the younger poets who had come to recognize Mallarmé as a master.

Another old friend who reappeared in Villiers's life was Paul Verlaine. After his affair with Rimbaud which had ended with the shooting in Brussels and eighteen months in prison, he had spent a couple of years teaching in England and had then returned to France to try to run a farm with a young man with whom he had fallen in love. The business failed in 1882, and Verlaine started appearing in Paris again, alternating between maudlin piety and alcoholic debauchery. He and Villiers had not seen each other for years, and some friends took Verlaine to a café late one evening, where they found Villiers. J.-K. Huysmans witnessed the meeting:

At the Brasserie Pousset, there was a succession of effusions, culminating in the relation of those extraordinary stories that only

Villiers could tell. And I can still see Verlaine, with a meditative expression in his little eyes, as he watched the ebullience of his friend, shaking a lock of hair out of his eyes, drawing back as if to give himself space, then raising his arms in the air as he leant right over the table between them.[3]

But if the 1880s saw Villiers and Mallarmé drawing ever closer, contacts with Verlaine remained occasional and infrequent. Of the other friends of earlier years, Marras was as faithful as ever, and Mendès was still sometimes to be found in Villiers's company, despite the violence of their quarrels. The one-time group of the Parnasse had however long since dispersed, as such aesthetic cohesion as it had ever had vanished altogether. Villiers no longer frequented Leconte de Lisle, now a lonely Olympian figure, he had years ago manifested his disdain for François Coppée's sentimental populism, and he had largely lost touch with such respectable personalities as José-Maria de Heredia and Sully Prudhomme. Léon Dierx, quiet, discreet, and calm, had remained close to him, and, because Dierx had never become a public figure, Villiers trusted him more than some one-time colleagues who had turned into portentous celebrities. Once, when Dierx was complaining that a publisher was taking advantage of him, Villiers looked at him in astonishment: 'I thought . . . that your poetry . . . had brought you . . . a lot of money . . . as much as François Coppée . . .'[4]

In addition to the old friends, there were however some new ones, significantly men of a younger generation. Throughout the 1870s Villers had been swimming against the main current of French literature. He had nothing but scorn both for popular novels and dramas that provided nothing but entertainment, and for the increasingly dominant forces of Realism, for whom the essential aim of art was to reflect life as it is—Élisabeth in *La Révolte* speaks for him when she exclaims: 'As the world has no meaning other than that given to it by the words which translate it or the eyes which gaze upon it, I believe that to consider all things from a higher viewpoint than their reality is the true Knowledge of life, of the only human greatness, of Happiness and of Peace'.[5] Even his association with the Parnasse had done little to alleviate this isolation, partly because he had more or less given up writing poetry, and partly because of the disintegration of the original group. So, apart from the idealism which he shared with Mallarmé and a few kindred spirits, he had for a decade or more been fighting an extremely lonely battle. At the beginning of the 1880s, however, one or two younger men were starting to take an interest in those writers whom their fathers had disdained, and they were the sort of people who were now discovering Villiers.

Among the first of such men was Henri Lavedan, born in 1859, who later achieved fame as a witty, satirical novelist and dramatist (he became a member of the Academy in 1899). He met Villiers in 1880, and nearly thirty years later wrote: 'It is one of the honours and blessings of my youth that from 1880 to 1889 I knew him well, was often with him and loved him greatly.' Like so many others, Lavedan was fascinated by Villiers's extraordinary gifts as a conversationalist, and he particularly recalled one occasion:

For a whole hour, more visionary and inspired than ever, he gave us a splendid and unforgettable picture of the crusaders arriving before Damietta . . . I could not retrace it after him (and would not even wish to try), but those spoken pages, which were spewed out in a magnificent eruption of eloquence and poetry, are among the finest things of Villiers that I know . . . and that he never wrote down! . . . for, once the delirium was over, he could no longer remember, or only vaguely.[6]

Another young man who was attracted to Villiers by the brilliance of his monologues in cafés was Gustave de Malherbe, who at that time was a civil servant in the Ministry of Finance, before going into publishing. He used to go along to Tortoni's or the Café de Madrid specially to listen to Villiers:

His general appearance in those days, if one observed him at rest, was that of a working upholsterer. He appeared ill at ease in his black overcoat, like a manual labourer in his Sunday best. He wore a top-hat with a flat brim; the ends of his moustache were carefully waxed. If when he was at rest he had that slightly awkward air, as soon as he grew animated, one immediately had the impression of being confronted by a great man with a marvellous command of language.

One day Villiers suddenly turned up in Malherbe's office at

the Ministry to ask him to be his second in a duel to be fought in Belgium the next day: 'I must ask you to be inflexible. A man must die. It perhaps won't be easy, but I am going to kill my opponent.' He promised Malherbe that his boss would give him leave and that money would be provided for the journey. So the next day Malherbe got out of bed two hours earlier than usual and waited . . . and waited . . . Villiers never appeared and never referred to the duel again.[7]

The fact is that Villiers was often mixed up in duels, but never seems actually to have fought one himself. There had been his abortive duel with a schoolfellow on the beach when he was thirteen; in 1866 he had been making threatening noises about pulling someone's ears and if necessary going off to Belgium to stick a sword in him;[8] in 1877 he had been within an ace of crossing swords with his namesake Georges de Villiers de l'Isle-Adam; also in 1877 he had sent his seconds to someone on the staff of the Ambigu;[9] in 1879 he had been ready to challenge Mendès (who was himself a frequent duellist). But there is no record of any of these brushes ever having ended in a real duel. On the other hand, he was often in demand as a second: for Albert Glatigny in 1863,[10] for Mendès in 1870,[11] for Robert du Pontavice de Heussey in 1879,[12] for Ed. Taine in 1881,[13] for his young friend Rodolphe Darzens in 1887.[14] His unimpeachable integrity and sense of honour made him an obvious choice when any of his friends felt that an insult had to be avenged in blood. But he could be belligerent in less formal circumstances too. One day, going down the rue La Bruyère in Montmartre with a friend, Villiers heard screams coming from a house. When they went to investigate, they found the concierge beating his wife, so Villiers laid him out with a single punch. The police arrived and took them all off to the station, where the concierge complained that he had a black eye because Villiers had treacherously taken him by surprise. Villiers, who had been very calm up to then, suddenly turned pale and, adopting the classical stance of a boxer, shouted: 'Ah! do you want me to black your other eye to show the inspector in what a "cowardly" way I attacked you?' The concierge took refuge behind the inspector's desk, and all ended peacefully.[15]

Notoriety in cafés and chivalrous behaviour however did

nothing to solve his financial problems, and it was still only the minor periodicals run by friends that welcomed him as a contributor. One story reproduced in *L'École des femmes* in 1879; one old one and one new one in *Beaumarchais* in 1880; some previously published poems in *La Comédie française* in 1880; another reproduction in *La Comédie humaine* in 1881; a handful more of previously published tales in *La Vie populaire* in 1880 and 1881: apart from what appeared in *L'Étoile française*, these are all the known publications of shorter works around the turn of the decade (though there were certainly others in even more ephemeral journals that have never been traced).[16] *L'Ève nouvelle* had not run its course in either *Le Gaulois* or *L'Étoile française*; *Le Nouveau-Monde* had met with so many disasters that it had been laid aside after its publication had failed to lead to a production; *Axël* was still not ready to be revealed to the public gaze. There remained *Le Prétendant*, and Villiers decided to have one last try with that. Knowing that the play contained two magnificent female parts, he began by approaching Augustine Brohan, who in her day had been one of the great stars of the national theatre. She was sufficiently impressed to pass the play on to the Comédie Française, but it never got as far as the committee, since the preliminary reader dismissed it out of hand, as looking like a parody of the historical melodramas of 1840:

This type of melodrama calls for a special sort of topography. You need state prisons within a few feet of the frontier, with doors opening on to every road, sentries who sleep all the time, trapdoors that open and close as the prisoners wish, warders and governors who invite the prisoners to supper, noble ladies who obtain entry into the fortresses, who fall madly in love with the mysterious and handsome prisoner locked up there, and who elope with him.[17]

Now more than ever Villiers needed money to support himself and his increased family, and, with so little coming in from his writing, he was naturally eager to get what help he could from patrons. The beneficent Mme Perry continued to advance him money, though not without some suspicious grumblings about his failure to improve his situation,[18] and a M. Bettenant, who had been his creditor since 1874 at least, was pressed into service again.[19] But a new benefactor appeared in the person of Benjamin Daymonaz, a lawyer, mystic, and legitimist who was known to have generous habits and a fortune to go with them. Daymonaz lived in Ghent, and his relations with Villiers may have been entirely epistolary, but they seem to have been quite close in 1881 and 1882. Daymonaz was an author of sorts and sent his books to Villiers in the hope that they would be reviewed, but he never received anything more concrete than flattery and promises:

I spend my time reading and rereading your *astonishing* book. I say astonishing because there is so much clarity, logic, and goodwill in it, in a word it makes such a good impression,—that I believe it to be one of the most salutary of our times.—One can feel that you are a Christian and a believer. It is extraordinary that I have not yet written anything on these weighty pages (however little my opinion counts). I SHALL SET ABOUT IT THIS EVENING.[20]

But two months later he was still making excuses.

The pious Daymonaz was eager to engage Villiers in abstruse theological discussion and also to assure himself that his correspondent was leading a proper Christian life: 'Are you not putting obstacles in the way of your own success? Are you really a believing and practising Catholic? Have you broken off all dangerous relations? Have you renounced every habit contrary to order?'[21] If Daymonaz was so concerned about Villiers's morality, it was because another poverty-stricken writer called Jules Feuillade, in the hope of attracting largesse for himself, was busily blackening Villiers's name to their potential benefactor. After telling Daymonaz of the failing health of Villiers's aged parents, he goes on:

As for the son, in two months, he has changed his lodgings ten times. Forty-four years old, he could, with his name and his fluency, have made a situation for himself, particularly in the last ten years. Unfortunately bad company has been his undoing. He has long since given up all religious observances. Getting up late, smoking a lot, drinking like a fish, his nights are sleepless and his days agitated. God alone can bring him back to the fold. Let us pray for him!

Feuillade's accusations may have been partly actuated by

malice, but description of the desperate straits of the family seems accurate and well-informed:

The father has been ill for a fortnight, which means he will have to go into hospital. You can imagine: eighty years old and ten years of privation . . . The mother, aged seventy-two, is not in a much better state. They are going to try to get her into an old people's home (. . .) The father and mother, with 40 francs rent a month, have not been able to manage. They owe four months in arrears and have no resources except a few vouchers from charitable organizations and from the Conférences de St. Vincent de Paul.[22]

What Villiers says to Daymonaz tells a similar story: 'So it is that I wander from place to place until I can earn enough for a bed, a table, and a chair. I hope it will not last much longer, for, even if they are never undeserved, trials that are a little too hard end up by overwhelming one, and our weak nature no longer feels them to be blessings.'[23] The somewhat uncharacteristic piousness of the last remark is obviously directed at Daymonaz's particular susceptibilities, as are pointed references to his having prayed and cut down on smoking and drinking.

One of Villiers's few new publications around this time would certainly have gladdened Daymonaz's conservative heart. This was a virulent satire against Gambetta, published in February 1882 as a separate brochure under the auspices of the weekly *La Comédie humaine*, which was run by Villiers's old friend Fernand de Gantès. Villiers had probably known Gambetta before the Franco-Prussian War and had disliked him, so that *Maison Gambade Père et Fils Succ^{rs}* is in some ways a highly personalized attack on a politician whose whole being offended him—his Italian parentage, his childhood in a grocery store, his vulgarity, his conceit, his ambition, his anticlericalism, his famous flight from Paris in a balloon during the Siege. But beyond the caricature of an individual, Villiers is condemning a whole political system and the men it produced: the regime of the Third Republic, with its venality, its hypocrisy, its materialism, and its demagogy. *Maison Gambade* is not a distinguished piece of work—its humour is laborious, heavy-handed, and repetitive—but its pugnacious antirepublicanism carries on the campaign which Villiers had inaugurated with his electoral adventures in 1881 and which he was to keep up for the rest of his life.

The unrelieved bleakness of 1882 was increased when on 12 April Villiers's mother died, after a brief illness and without suffering. Two short notes informed Mallarmé and Marras. To the former Villiers wrote: 'I haven't needed any money. I don't ask you to come round. You know what we are like, we people who are all alone, but the heart is all there.'[24] The loss of his mother was a grievous blow to him. The Marquise may have been a rather stupid woman, but she had loved her son with all her heart and watched over him with anxious solicitude. In her eyes he could do no wrong and he was still the great man she had always believed him to be. For all the vagaries of his behaviour, Villiers remained a dutiful son, all the more attached to his mother because both he and she knew what ravages the irresponsibility of the half-mad Marquis had wrought in their lives. She had perhaps never been in love with her husband and had nearly left him in her youth; Villiers liked his father in some ways (they were kindred spirits in their refusal to bow to prosaic reality) but he deeply resented the ruin he had brought on the family. So the bond between mother and son had been an unusually close one, even if there could be little intellectual contact, and, just as Villiers had realized on Tante Kerinou's death that his mother was the only person he could rely on, now he must have felt totally isolated. The fact that the last restraining influence on his father had been removed made matters even worse: if the old man had been a nuisance to Villiers before, he now became a positive pest, as he produced a steady stream of querulous, threatening, and half-crazy missives to his son.

The announcement of the Marquise's death which Villiers sent out to friends and relations is an extraordinary document:

The Marquis JOSEPH DE VILLIERS DE L'ISLE-ADAM, Doyen of the Knights of Malta of the Language of France; the Comte MATHIAS PHILIPPE-AUGUSTE DE VILLIERS DE L'ISLE-ADAM; the Abbé VICTOR DE VILLIERS DE L'ISLE-ADAM, Rector of Ploumilliau, in Lower Brittany; Sister GABRIELLE DE VILLIERS DE L'ISLE-ADAM, Lady of the

Sacred Heart of Avignon; the Comte and the Vicomte LE NEP-
VOU DE CARFORT, naval officers, and their families; Monsig-
nor Cardinal DE BONNECHOSE and the Marquis DE
COËTLES, as well as their family; the Marquis and the Marquise
DE COSSÉ-BRISSAC, née BOUCHARD DE MONT-
MORENCY, and their family; the Comte DE BLOIS and his
family; the Marquis GAUCHER DE CHATILLON and his
family; the Prince DE CLERMONT-TONNERRE, the Duc and
the Duchesse DE PRATULO and the Comtesse ADOLPHE DU
LAZ, née DE SAISY, and their family; the Comtesse DE GUISE,
née DE COURSON-VILLENEUVE, as well as the Comte
ALFRED DE COURSON-VILLENEUVE and their families; the
Marquis DE MIRABEAU and his family; the Comte DU MAIN
DE KÉROUZIEN, the Comte DU MAIN DE LA JAILLE and
their families; the Comte LOUIS DE KERSTRAT and the Com-
tesse DE KERSTRAT, née DE CATHELINEAU, and their
families; the Baron HINGANT DE SAINT-MAUR and his
family; the Comte DU RUMAIN; the Marquis and the Marquise
DE KÉROUART and their family; the Marquis DE MONTBOU-
CHER and his family; the Comte CHARLES HAY DES
NÉTUMIÈRES DE BRECQUIGNY and his family; the Baron
EPHREM HOUEL, Officer of the Legion of Honour, and the
Baronne HOUEL, née DE KERSTRAT; the Comte and the
Comtesse DE RODELLEC DE PORZIC and their family;
   Husband, son, brother-in-law, sister-in-law, nephews and great-
nephews, cousins by marriage, first cousins, and second cousins,
   Are grieved to inform you of the death of
        Marie-Francine LE NEPVOU DE CARFORT
        MARQUISE DE VILLIERS DE L'ISLE-ADAM,
Lady Patroness-Foundress of the Cathedral of Moulins, deceased,
with the Sacraments of the Church, in the holy faith of Our Lord
Jesus Christ, on 12 April 1882, in Paris, rue Saint-Roch, in her
seventy-second year.
        LUX PERPETUA LUCET EI.
Paris, 25 April 1882

On behalf of the Comte DE VILLIERS DE L'ISLE-ADAM, her
son, 38 rue de Bruxelles.

   It must have been some consolation to Villiers to pen this
sonorous list of the cream of the French aristocracy, with its
rolling titles and interminable names, evoking an age of feudal
splendour, wealth, and power, even if many of the people
concerned would have been surprised to discover that they

had the slightest connection with the Villiers de l'Isle-Adam family. As so often, the incantatory power of words served to soften the unbearable harshness of reality. Anatole France said of him: 'He loved the art of writing with all his heart. There is no love without superstitition. He believed in the virtue of words. Certain terms had for him, like runes, secret powers.'[25] Particularly when he started writing about his ancestry, he was seized by a kind of verbal delirium, and the torrent of noble names and titles which he pours out here has replaced in his mind the terrible truth of his mother's death in some squalid furnished rooms. In fact, he did not even have enough money to buy a permanent grave for her.

24

The year 1882 was one of the bleakest of Villiers's life. He had a mistress and a child to support, as well as a senile father; he had no fixed address; what little he published came out only in obscure periodicals that hardly anyone read; creditors were baying at his heels; nobody would produce his plays; his own health was weakened by years of undernourishment; and, as Remy de Gourmont pointed out,[1] his name was less well known than it had been fifteen years earlier. Never can he have been nearer to feeling that his whole existence had been a failure, that all the dedication and hardship had been in vain, that fate had finally got the better of him. But, as the year wore on, one or two unexpected rays of light broke through the clouds that hovered over him.

The first came on 19 August, when he received a letter from the publisher Calmann Lévy, to whom he had re-submitted the volume of tales he had vainly been hawking round since 1875. Calmann Lévy had already turned it down in 1877, and in the meantime it had also been rejected by Charpentier and probably Hetzel too. But over the years its composition had changed considerably, as Villiers published more and more tales and revised those that had already appeared, so that it was both a larger and a more homogeneous collection than it had been originally. Perhaps this is why Calmann Lévy was now more forthcoming: 'If on Tuesday or Wednesday you are free in the morning, I should be grateful if you would come and see me about the volume which you have offered me and which I have now had a chance to read.'[2] Villiers accepted with alacrity, and Lévy was able to drive a hard bargain: he would publish the book if Villiers sold him all his rights in it outright for 375 francs.[3] Glad to have a sum of money in his pocket, however derisory it might seem, Villiers agreed, and the printers set to work on what was to be the *Contes cruels*.

It may have been this success that enabled him to have a further extract from *Axël* published in *La Vie artistique* in October, where it was preceded by this note:

M. de Villiers de l'Isle-Adam, whose *Contes cruels* are due to be published by Calmann Lévy at the end of this month, has been kind enough to send us a scene from an important work, conceived on the scale of the German *Faust*, and which is to be published after the *Contes cruels*. We are happy to offer our readers this scene which impresses us as being of a most extraordinary metaphysical profundity.

Ten years had elapsed since the First Part had appeared in *La Renaissance littéraire et artistique*; what Villiers now revealed to the public was most of the Third Part (the play now having been enlarged to have four parts), that is to say, the long discussion between Axël and Maître Janus, at the end of which Axël refuses the possibility of initiation as a magus offered to him by his mysterious mentor. Probably this section of the play was what had varied least since the original conception—at any rate relatively few of the extant early manuscript fragments are connected with it—but Villiers still did not regard it as a definitive text, since it bears the sub-title *Étude*. In the event, though he lengthened it greatly in subsequent revisions, he did not change its general outlines or its basic tenor, contenting himself with extending and deepening the already subtle and complex philosophical debate of which it consists.

This was the first indication anyone had had for a decade that *Axël* was a reality and not a figment of Villiers's imagination. In the world of letters, it was known that he had once projected such a work, but it was generally thought that it was just another of those chimerical enterprises in which his brain was so fertile, and that nothing would ever come of it. Now, at last, Villiers was able to produce evidence that he had never ceased to labour at the work, and the loftiness of the confrontation between Axël and Janus proved that it was the most ambitious thing he had ever attempted, surpassing even *L'Ève nouvelle.*

La Vie artistique was a new publication, which had just been founded in August 1882 by Émile Delarue. It was a luxurious illustrated monthly with several contributors well known to Villiers, including Catulle Mendès and Charles de Sivry. But prominent among them was a man whom Villiers had not met before, half-politician and half-author, the Comte Charles d'Osmoy. Born in 1829 of an old Norman family, d'Osmoy had become the centre-left deputy for Pont-Audemer in 1871 and had been regularly re-elected ever since (he was elevated to the Senate in 1885). He had also been a close friend of Flaubert and Louis Bouilhet and, having previously had some of his own plays produced in boulevard theatres, had collaborated with them in writing their joint work *Le Château des cœurs* in 1863. His interest in literature had not diminished with the years and, as he was a man of substantial means, Villiers began to wonder if there might not be some possibility of persuading him to subsidize a production of *Le Nouveau-Monde.*

A young painter and journalist called J. E. S. Jeanès was introduced to Villiers at this time, and remembered his anxious expectations about *Le Nouveau-Monde* on the evening when they met. Jeanès was sitting in the back room of a café called Le Nègre on the Boulevard Saint-Denis with Jules de Brayer and Alexandre Georges, both musicians, when Villiers came in.

There he was at the door of the café: a wide-brimmed felt hat, an Inverness cape, a white muffler. He walked through the first room, with a certain solemnity, and came to a stop beside us. He unwound the interminable silk scarf that hid his moustache and his little beard . . . and appeared to me: very handsome, calm, austere, despairing, very different from what I had imagined, but I recognized him at once.

At first, everything about his attitude and his tone of voice expressed despondency.

'Will we get the money?' Such was his first sentence. He sat on the

bench seat, ordered a beer, looked slowly round at us, appeared
surprised at my presence, and then listened, with his light-coloured
eyes gazing fixedly ahead, to the long and cordial objurgations
which his friends inflicted on him in order to whip up his courage
and reawaken his hopes. At first he scarcely replied, but gradually
he became excited and produced his arguments. 'Don't they
understand that the whole future of America is perhaps contained in
this play, which symbolizes both the break with the Old World and
a pact of alliance? Don't they understand anything? Not even what
they are? Certainly they have no idea how far the power of the
word goes, and yet they were born of a word, like everything that
exists . . . A cataclysm that raises a million tons of rock—what is
that compared to a word that falls into the minds of men? . . . It
echoes down the centuries in the depths of their soul, until it comes
to pass . . . Verily! . . . Verily.'

The tirade became ever more frenetic:

'If we get the money, it'll be very big business. The play is sure to
be a success. All the English and the Americans will recognize
themselves, their crimes, and their virtues as well. With the
marvellous music of my dear friend Alexandre Georges, how could
anyone remain indifferent? They'll see, they'll hear, they'll be
convinced. And then, it's decently written, that play, not badly
written at all! But we need the money . . .'

Then came dark mutterings about how England had done
him out of his due, how the English were afraid of his drama,
how English interests were prejudicing the Americans against
it, how he regretted ever having become involved in the
competition. 'Thank heavens! there are still theatres and
actors in France, to proclaim the truth. And the truth is
rather moving . . . What I bring is a beam of light.'[4]
   In fact, at this stage, it was not Alexandre Georges that
Villiers had in mind for the incidental music, but another
friend, Henry Ghys, likewise a composer. By early November Villiers was sufficiently hopeful of success to have talked
to Ghys's wife about the need for an overture, but it turned
out that for some reason Ghys was in prison, so the idea fell
through.[5] What Villiers wanted was to rent the Théâtre des
Nations, where Ballande had been manager since 1880, when
Le Nouveau-Monde had nearly been produced there; it was
known that Ballande intended to retire and might be prepared

to sublet until the theatre was taken over by Damala, Sarah Bernhardt's husband. Apart from d'Osmoy, a number of other people were also becoming interested in this idea. One of them was Eugène Lalouette, a bookseller and publisher in the rue de Tournon; another was Frédéric Gilbert, born in 1843, a journalist and novelist who wrote under the name of Yveling Rambaud; a third was Victor-Henry Pop, an actor at the Théâtre du Châtelet. By December 1882 the rumours that the production was imminent had grown so strong that actors were writing in to Villiers to ask for parts in the play.[6]

How the deal was finally concluded is recounted by Villiers himself in a manuscript which he never published. The tale as he tells it may be somewhat simplified or embellished, but other contemporary accounts confirm that, however unlikely it may sound, it is basically accurate.

One evening, at Brébant's, three months ago, I made the acquaintance of a publisher, M. Eugène Lalouette. He asked me why my play *Le Nouveau-Monde* had never been performed, despite its having been accepted by MM. Hostein, Laforêt, and Chabrillat, and rehearsals started. 'It's because it will take eighty thousand francs to put it on,' I told him.—Some time later, in the presence of one of my closest friends, the Comte d'Osmoy, the conversation was resumed. M. d'Osmoy having offered to lend me twelve thousand francs or so to rent M. Ballande's theatre, M. Lalouette, in a most noble movement of enthusiasm in favour of the type of dramatic literature for which I stand, declared that he cared little whether he gained or lost by it but that it was a matter of honour for him to stage the play. 'When?' I asked him. 'If you will come with me,' he replied, 'we will go straight to the director and I will rent his theatre; we will order the settings tomorrow; the day after, you will read the play to your actors, and it will open on 10 February.' We took a carriage. Two hours later, the contract was signed. As MM. Iveling [*sic*] Rambaud, and Victor Pop, two young friends of mine, happened to be present, we asked them to take over the management, to which they were graciously pleased to agree.[7]

There seems little doubt that Lalouette, the main backer of the play, had been mesmerized by Villiers's persuasive eloquence and was genuinely prepared to sink an enormous sum in the play. As for the involvement of Rambaud, he too wrote for *La Vie artistique* and so very probably already knew d'Osmoy. Indeed, as the musician Alexandre Georges was d'Osmoy's secretary in addition to being a friend of Villiers, one has the impression that there was a nucleus of committed supporters of the poet behind the enterprise, of whom Pop may have been one (little is known of him), and that, when Lalouette came along brandishing his money, or at least his promises, everyone at once combined to take him at his word and make him agree to back the production to the hilt, before he had a chance to change his mind. Certainly Rambaud, at least, regarded him as rather a fool and was even indiscreet and ungrateful enough to say so publicly before the play was produced. Villiers was more charitable: 'You may say: a publisher straight out of the Arabian Nights' Tales! Maybe: but I cannot conceive how it is that those who profess to write should not have paid to this very noble movement of enthusiasm for a cause we should all defend the honour and the tribute which I now give to it.'[8]

At all events, the contract was signed just before Christmas, and Rambaud and Pop took over the Théâtre des Nations from Ballande for a period of three months, the lease to begin when the current play, *La Fille des chiffonniers*, ended its run. The rent was 15,000 francs. According to Maurice Ordonneau in *Le Gaulois* on 23 December, negotiations were started with well-known actors, the settings were ordered from three artists, MM. Robecchi, Lavastre, and Chapron, and the first night was fixed for 1 February. The cast which the directors envisaged was as illustrious as could well be imagined. For the male leads, they wanted three well-known actors from the Comédie Française, Lafontaine, Baillet, and Volny; for Ruth Moore, they had in mind Léonide Leblanc, the star of the Gymnase, celebrated for her liaisons with Prince Napoleon, the Duc d'Aumale, and Clemenceau; and for Mistress Andrews, they turned to Mlle Rousseil, notorious for her temper and her illusions that she was a poetess as well as for her talents as an actress—she had nearly been engaged for the same part at the Ambigu in 1876.

But difficulties started arising forthwith. First of all, Villiers, who rightly believed himself to be a gifted performer and who attached enormous importance to reading the play to the actors, started suffering from a sore throat, and began to fear that he would be unable to do the reading. Consequently, he sent an urgent message to call in Marras.[9] Marras had been very busy directing the rehearsals of his own play *La Famille d'Armelles* at the Odéon, but found himself in dispute with the management, with the result that rehearsals were suspended and the production postponed (it did not take place until October 1883, the author having threatened to sue the director unless he fulfilled his contractual obligations). With his usual fidelity, he at once responded to the call and took Villiers's place, assisted by Rambaud and the actor Charpentier, who was going to play Stephen Ashwell. Thereafter, in addition to Villiers, there were three producers to the play, Rambaud, Marras, and Pop, all equally inexperienced, which greatly amused the press, who referred to them as 'the republic', or 'the governing body', or 'the joint managers'. Though the practical Marras, with his strong personality, may have helped to stop the proceedings getting totally out of hand, Villiers was convinced that his inability to read the play to the cast was nothing short of a disaster.

In the event, few of the actors originally approached could be engaged. Baillet and Volny turned down the offer, and Lafontaine, who had at first been disposed to accept, ended up by deciding that he was too old for the part of Lord Cecil (he was in his fifties). As for Léonide Leblanc, she would have been delighted to participate, but discovered that her contract with Koning of the Gymnase would not allow her to. She wrote to Ballande to express her regrets: the part of Ruth was 'superb' and 'the last scene with Mlle Rousseil marvellous'. She asked Ballande to pass on her sincerest thanks to Villiers and added: 'I shall give *Le Nouveau-Monde* pride of place on my bookshelves.'[10] Mlle Rousseil was the only one to keep her part, but she had reason to do so: when there was a report that she was going on a tour of the provinces, Rambaud wrote to *Le Gaulois* on 3 January to deny it: 'Mlle Rousseil has signed with us for *Le Nouveau-Monde* at a forfeit of 20,000 francs, and she is not thinking of leaving us so soon.' But although a few days later the *Gil Blas* quoted her as saying that Mistress Andrews would be 'the most extraordinary creation of her life', she had really wanted the more important and more sympathetic role of Ruth, with the result that she became increasingly ill-disposed towards the whole business.

Throughout January the cast kept changing. After Volny turned down the part of the Chevalier de Vaudreuil, Stephen Ashwell's French lieutenant, Pop thought of taking it on himself, then tried to engage Angélo, and finally gave it to Rosambeau. The two comic characters, Moscone and Bob Upfill, changed hands just as frequently: Moscone's part was assigned successively to Montbars, Brémond, and Legrenay, and Upfill's to Vivier and Monza. To make matters worse, Delessart, formerly of the Comédie Française, who had succeeded Lafontaine as Lord Cecil, fell ill with typhoid, of which he died shortly after, so that he had to be replaced only a few days before the première was due to take place. All this chopping and changing naturally added to the unease which the actors already felt at being in the hands of a collective production team none of whom had ever produced a play before.

Then it turned out that Lalouette's assurances of unlimited funds were not as solid as they had seemed, and, instead of producing the vast sums needed, he was only able to make advances on account. This was particularly serious as far as the settings were concerned, since by now there were no fewer than five designers involved, each of them with luxurious and costly sets; some of the suppliers refused to hand over a single scenery flat until they were paid in full. The actors too were forced to wait for their pay, which must have been particularly irksome to Mlle Rousseil, whose demands were becoming daily more exorbitant: she was asking for a hundred francs for every rehearsal and three hundred for every performance.[11] Since d'Osmoy's financial commitment had come to an end after he had paid the rent for the theatre, and since none of the other participants except Lalouette had any money at all, it was growing increasingly clear that the whole enterprise was an enormous risk, and that, with Lalouette's coffers rapidly emptying, the only hope was to press on in the hope that the play would have a very long run with a packed house every night.

The music created its own problems. As far back as 1880 Villiers had prepared some incidental music of his own composition,[12] but, because his training was insufficient to enable him to write it down, it existed only in his head. When Ghys had to

refuse his commission, Villiers turned to his young friend
Alexandre Georges, d'Osmoy's secretary, and Georges composed a score incorporating some of Villiers's own melodies.
Georges was not an amateur, having been musical director at
Sainte-Clotilde and teacher of harmony at the École Nieder-
meyer, but he had no more experience of the theatre than his
associates. That was bad enough as far as the composition of
the music was concerned; it was even worse when Cresson-
nois, the conductor of the orchestra at the Théâtre des
Nations, had to leave his post early in February to go to the
south of France for health reasons (he died not long after).
There being no one else, Georges was drafted to replace him.

The atmosphere during the rehearsals became more and
more tense and more and more anxious, particularly as they
coincided with a series of deaths—Gambetta, General
Chanzy, Delessart who was to have played Lord Cecil, and
Albert Larmet, an actor at the Théâtre des Nations, who was
burnt alive in his bed on 9 February. This is Villiers's own
account of the gathering storm-clouds:

The contract was signed two days before Christmas. We met with a
series of obstacles, of all kinds, for the rehearsals. Christmas Eve
parties, the end of the year, New Year's Day, present-giving,
crowded streets, holidays, Twelfth Night, rent-day, quarter day,
the deaths of Delessart and Larmet—to say nothing of those of
more illustrious men whose funeral processions filled the thorough-
fares.—Moreover, M. Eugène Lalouette, having had to meet particularly large commitments at the end of the year, found himself
obliged to give money only by large payments on account, which
frightened the suppliers, given that the directors were temporary
and that people were very unwilling to accept orders from them.
One of them, M. Pop, on a day when I was not there, was struck in
the face by an actor, in the middle of a rehearsal. To crown it all,
right from the day of the reading I lost my voice unbearably, for
three weeks. That was, I believe, an accident of which only authors
can understand the importance. It was MM. Marras, Rambaud, and
Charpentier who read in my place. This meant that it was impossible for me to give the intonations and the nature of the different
characters, so as to render the whole thing intelligible.[13]

The business of missing the reading was an especially sore
point.

Once the rehearsals have started, it is too late: no one can change the intonation that an actor has hit upon, nor a word that he has pronounced three times. Such a task is beyond the power of man. And without the proper intonations, which, I am sorry to say, are not in agreement with those given by the actors,—not only does the feeling of novelty no longer exist, but the play becomes incomprehensible; any depth, any attempt at real grandeur, is turned into a gross travesty. But provided they can squeeze the last drop out of the simplest words until those words lose all sense, what do they care? The failure of the play becomes inevitable; what do they care?[14]

Despite these forebodings, a glare of publicity focussed on the play. The unusual circumstances of the production, the prize that *Le Nouveau-Monde* had won, Villiers's notoriety as a character about town, the rumours that floated out about the lavishness of the spectacle kept the press buzzing for weeks on end. Every journalist produced his favourite Villiers story, respectfully or otherwise; the papers reported continuously on the progress of the rehearsals; an enormous amount of public interest and curiosity was created and maintained. In the *Gil Blas* on 16 January Christian de Trogoff passed on these enthusiastic accounts obviously supplied by Villiers:

The sets by MM. Lavastre, Carpezat, and Fromont (. . .) are marvels, and, to judge by the designs, the production will be of exceptional magnificence. The statue of King George III, for the episode of the Bloodstained Hand, is copied from the one smashed at Bunker-Hill [*sic*]. M. Lemoine has lent his Scottish greyhounds for the black pageboys at the castle of Swinmore; the arms of the Cecil family have been painted by Stern. The beautiful Mlle Cassan (Dahu) will wear Indian costume, one of M. Gray's masterpieces, like a vision of the Pennsylvanian prairies (. . .) We have read in an article by Théodore de Banville that one had to go back to *Marie Tudor* and to certain scenes of Shakespeare to find anything in dramatic literature comparable to the dialogue which opens the fifth act of *Le Nouveau-Monde*. Mmes Rousseil and Jeanne Pazza say they are determined to make the public share this view (. . .) so, there are no two ways about it: we can look forward to a first night of a sort rarely seen at that theatre!

All kinds of advertising devices were conjured up. A

rumour was started, no doubt deliberately, that the Marquis of Salisbury (whom Villiers regarded as his ally) was coming from England specially for the première, in honour of his fictitious ancestor Lord Cecil. On 2 February Dom Blazius of *L'Intransigeant* announced that the directors had ordered from the moulder Bouillon, the man who had executed Falguière's group on the Arc de Triomphe, a reproduction of the Statue of Liberty, ten metres high, with an oxyhydric torch which would blaze out over Paris, from the top of the theatre, every night while the play was on.

In the meantime, in addition to the other problems faced by the directors, the text of *Le Nouveau-Monde* itself was proving a headache. At the outset, the intention had been to perform the play as it had been published in 1880, with five acts and forty-three characters. But as soon as rehearsals began, it became apparent that it was far too long and unwieldy to fit into a normal evening at the theatre. So by mid-January a number of minor roles had already been excised to shorten it. These cuts however proved insufficient, and Marras realized that, if there was to be any chance of success, further drastic pruning was essential: he therefore suggested to Villiers that he had no option but to make substantial reductions. Needless to say, the reaction was violent: the play was his work and had to be acted exactly as he had written it. For the time being, Villiers's will prevailed, but it was clear to the other directors that he was being unrealistic and that, sooner or later, he would have to acquiesce in reductions. In the end they persuaded him to accept some shortening of the second act, which had not been part of the original design and which had never wholly satisfied him.

But that in turn infuriated some of the actors, whose parts would have been reduced in importance as a consequence, and they obviously realized that, with directors who were very unsure of themselves, there were ways and means of manipulating the situation to their advantage. The rehearsal on 14 February was chaotic. Charpentier, who was playing Ashwell, and Rosambeau, who was playing Vaudreuil, professed to be unable to work out what was required of them, and everything broke down. The next day Charpentier wrote a hypocritically crawling letter to Villiers to apologize, but adding: 'Now, I cannot insist too much on the extent to which I deplore the amputation of that poor second act, and I *beg* of you, if the decision is not irrevocable, to put it back again, in your own interest even more than in mine.'[15] These supplications were in vain. On the seventeenth Villiers at last gave in to his friends, and reluctantly authorized Marras to do as he wished: 'I give my friend Marras full power to carry out those cuts which he and I have agreed today in the common interest.'[16] The second act was then finally suppressed, which solved the problem of length, but left the action difficult to follow and the actors angry and resentful.

It did not help much when Villiers himself suddenly had bright ideas. This is what 'Choufleuri' told the readers of *Le Gaulois* on 20 February:

Always a poet, M. Villiers de l'Isle-Adam wanted real monkeys and real birds to be released in the virgin forests of the second and third acts. It was a terrible job to make him give up the idea. Only when it was pointed out to him that the monkeys would inevitably go and sit on the knees of the critics and that this might have unfortunate repercussions on the Monday morning reviews did he decide to abandon it.

A week before *Le Gaulois* had presented another anecdote which is no doubt exaggerated but is nevertheless typical of the fantastical care Villiers was taking over the production.

There is talk of a magnificent setting in a virgin forest for one of the main scenes of the play. The success of this scene happens to depend on three humble girls, who only have a few words to say. But there's the rub. They have to speak them and not *chant* them. And the three little speeches would need exceptional actresses who, naturally, would never agree to accept the parts. How many theatres have been visited by M. Villiers who is, as everyone knows, a very highly-strung poet, how many auditions he has given, how many young actresses he has inspected, in order to find, among the players of bit parts, those rare birds—the story can never be told: it is the recital of a long martyrdom. Now he has found what he wants—or to be more exact, every day he is busy inculcating the spirit of his vital scene into a few docile maidens.

25

But what was going through Villiers's mind during these hectic weeks? On the one hand, the extraordinary generosity of d'Osmoy and Lalouette was the realization of a dream. For once in his life, someone had come along out of the blue and had put what seemed to be unlimited funds at his disposal, so that *Le Nouveau-Monde,* the work by which he set so much store, could at last be produced. Hitherto, only *La Révolte,* with its modest dimensions, had been put to the test. Now, a major drama was to be revealed to the public amid a blaze of publicity, and the publication of the *Contes cruels,* his first commercially produced book for general sale, had been timed so as to coincide with the première. So it all amounted to an ideal opportunity. On the other hand, so much was at stake that there was something terrifying in the situation, the more so as, clearly, the production was not going at all smoothly. All his life, through all the adversities he had encountered, Villiers had been sustained by one fixed idea: he had a destiny as a writer, and sooner or later it would be fulfilled. If this had not happened so far, it was the fault of circumstances—of the stupidity of theatre managers, of the malevolence of critics, of lack of resources, of sheer bad luck. But with *Le Nouveau-Monde* the moment of truth had come. For the first time, he was to present himself to the world as he was. What if the world still laughed at him?

Hence, with his nervous and excitable temperament, Villiers passed rapidly from the extremities of elation to the extremities of depression, and back again, sometimes almost experiencing both simultaneously. He wanted to throw himself into it heart and soul, since it was his great chance and could never be repeated; but at the same time he wanted to keep a certain detachment from it, so that in the event of failure he would not be utterly destroyed. Sometimes one of these impulses had the upper hand, sometimes the other. There were even moments, on his own admission, when he thought of withdrawing the play altogether. But, as he explains in a manuscript fragment, a number of considerations held him back: a lot of money had already been spent, it

was too late to stop, the other people concerned had too
much to lose to give up, it might still be a success anyway,
and a public protest from him would wreck everything in
advance. 'I therefore resigned myself to what I declared every
evening would inevitably be a failure, in spite of everyone's
confidence.'[1] Indeed, one may wonder whether his alleged
loss of voice for three weeks was not in part a diplomatic
illness designed to provide him with an excuse in case the play
was a disaster—after all, he had originally told Marras only
that he was 'a bit hoarse'.[2] A similar suspicion arises when,
on 16 January, Christian de Trogoff noted in the *Gil Blas*, in
an article visibly inspired by Villiers himself, that 'M. Villiers
de l'Isle-Adam has only very rarely been present at the
rehearsals of his work, and does not intend to take over the
production until the dress rehearsals'.

Arnold Mortier, who certainly had inside information
about what was going on, later related Villiers's alternations
between hope and despair:

M. Villiers de l'Isle-Adam was very hard to satisfy. When anyone
reproached him with his strictness, he would reply: 'We have no
right to allow the play to be a flop!' One day, he thought the end of
the world had come because an actress wanted to suppress the word
'Madame' at the end of a sentence. Then, suddenly, he would regain
confidence. He would make fun of all the expenditure on the sets
and the costumes. 'What's the point of spending all this money?' he
would say. 'I'm absolutely sure of my play!' And in the theatre
everyone was infected by his enthusiasm.[3]

The general accuracy of this was confirmed by no less a
person than Yveling Rambaud, who wrote an article in *Le
XXᵉ Siècle artistique et littéraire* on 16 February, paying
tribute to his single-minded determination. After protesting
about the number of personal anecdotes being printed about
Villiers, Rambaud maintains that what matters is a different
aspect of the man:

The author locked in single combat with the actors, fighting scene
by scene, word by word, over the interpretation of his work, never
discouraged by any difficulty, conciliatory at first and then starting
up with the roars of a lion against the iconoclasts! The author of *Le
Nouveau-Monde* contrived to be caressing and cruel, a lapdog and

1. Villiers by Allévy, *c.* 1885

2a. Méry Laurent

2b. Judith Gautier

2c. Nina de Villard

2d. Augusta Holmès

3a. J.-K. Huysmans   3b. Stéphane Mallarmé

3c. Léon Bloy in 1887

4a. Abbé Victor de Villiers de l'Isle-Adam, Villiers's uncle

4b. Bronze medallion of Villiers by
Charles Matabon, 1863

5a. Villiers by Carjat, 1865. Villiers is wearing the type of fur-trimmed overcoat for which he had a predilection throughout his life

5b. Villiers by Nadar, *c.* 1875. For this photograph Villiers has obviously had his hair specially curled, as was his wont on ceremonial occasions

6a. Villiers by Carjat, *c*. 1875

6b. Anna Eyre, Villiers's prospective English bride

7. Portrait of Villiers by Guth, c. 1888

8a. Marie Dantine, whom Villiers married on his deathbed. The photograph was taken towards the end of her life; the baby in her arms is Marcel-Charles Longuet, son of Marcel Longuet, who edited Villiers's works for the Mercure de France

8b. Victor de Villiers de l'Isle-Adam, Villiers's son

8c. Villiers on his deathbed, by Franc Lamy

an executioner; in love with his art and his play, he suffered everything during the rehearsals, passing suddenly from the intensest heat to the iciest cold, enthusiastic at one moment about the actor he would tear to pieces the next. It was not so much the desire for glory as legitimate scruples about damaging the idea of the work that guided him during these testing times. Oh! we have seen at first hand the author, in despair, losing heart, when, after many an effort, many a repetition, many a piece of advice passed on in confidence before or after the rehearsal, he saw the actor falling back into the same error that he had battled against with all the force of his being. What diplomacy he used! I think he even forged new words in order not to offend the astonishing pride of certain actors, and, when in the evening he came away with us, feverish and discouraged, he was a pitiful sight. The poor great poet did not realize that the meticulous care he took to try to explain what he had in mind was often a waste of time. He identified the actor so much with the vision he had conceived that when the actor, through no fault of his own, fell short of the ideal, he would start to weep. Then Villiers was not playing to the gallery, there was no more destructive irony, no more posing.

Reading between the lines, it is easy enough to see what was happening. Obsessed by his inner vision, Villiers was harassing the actors unbearably, and they, already irritated by having amateurs telling them what to do, were rapidly losing patience. A gulf was opening up between those who were producing the play and those who were acting in it. But outside the theatre, Villiers's natural optimism was able to reassert itself, and he indulged in daydreams about how he was going to spend the fortune *Le Nouveau-Monde* would bring him. One of his confidants was his old friend the journalist Ed. Taine, who later recorded his impressions in *L'Étoile de France*, the title of the ressuscitated *Étoile française*.[4]

During the rehearsals of his play, Villiers was overcome with delight at seeing the dreams of his youth come true. He adored travelling, and America especially was his favourite country. He wanted to visit the scenes of the main episodes of the drama (. . .) After the dress rehearsal, he was reassured. 'There will easily be 300 performances, the average takings will be 8,000 francs, my royalties will be 12½ per cent, at least 300,000 francs, and the ruined castle of my forefathers in the Côtes-du-Nord, near Saint-Brieuc, will be magnificently rebuilt. I'll begin by paying my debts. Oh! debts are the poet's leprosy! When I've been purified, I'll be off, I'll go to see the New World, Canada above all, Quebec, Montreal. When I come back, I'll stop at

Malta, I want to write a book about the order of chivalry of that island, where my ancestor, Jean de Villiers de l'Isle-Adam, Grand Master of the Order, held in check Suliman II at the head of an army of 200,000 men'.

But he could not resist the temptation of anticipating on his good fortune, and, according to Taine, spent 1,500 francs on a smart overcoat lined with fox fur: 'For the first few days, he kept stopping to look at his reflection in shop windows; he could not recognize himself'. He also rented an attractive bachelor flat for 1,200 francs in the Boulevard Haussmann from 15 April, and started buying a suite of rosewood furniture on the instalment plan.

Meanwhile, the fatal moment of the first night was drawing near. It had originally been announced for the end of January, but successive postponements put it back to 1 February, then the seventh. Even so, the delay was insufficient because the continued success of *La Fille des chiffonniers* meant that the stage could not be used for rehearsals. So it was put off again until the thirteenth and then until the fifteenth, at which point someone realized that it would clash with the first night of a new production of *Le Juif errant*, and it was put off once more until the seventeenth. But a last-minute hitch occurred after the dress rehearsal on the sixteenth, when Mlle Rousseil peremptorily declared that she was too tired to perform the next day. Her conduct had already provoked comment in the press, and a few days earlier a journalist had written in *Le Gaulois*: 'Rumours from the rehearsals have it that the capricious artiste never had more caprices and demands than during the preparation of *Le Nouveau-Monde.*' Her latest whim forced the directors to postpone the first night until the nineteenth. The comments of Maurice Ordonneau, also in *Le Gaulois*, were acid: 'This decision, which is costing the management no less than four or five thousand francs, has been taken on account of the highly unpredictable Mlle Rousseil (. . .) If the directors of the Nations start giving in to Mlle Rousseil's whims, they are letting themselves in for a fine time.' In fact, the directors were using the extra delay to continue tinkering with the text, which was not the wisest thing to do under the circumstances.

The long wait had of course whetted the public's curiosity, and the publication of the *Contes cruels* a few days earlier had helped to draw even more attention to Villiers's name. There were not many reviews, but most of those that did appear were benevolent, and the conjunction of the book's appearance with the production of the play naturally attracted notice. *La Vie artistique*, which had had so much to do with the idea of staging *Le Nouveau-Monde*, even devoted almost all of its February number to hymning Villiers's glory—the frontispiece was a portrait of him by Teysonnières, there were two sonnets addressed to him by Alexandre Ducros and Tancrède Martel, there were long extracts from the play, there were specimens of Georges's music, and a rapturous advance notice.

At last, on 19 February, the much-heralded and much-delayed première took place, before a packed house and a full complement of critics. Considering that the actors were angry because they had not been paid, that there had been continuous discord between author, cast, and producers, that the text was still being altered at the last minute, it is perhaps surprising that the general reaction was not more unfavourable. On the whole, the public watched respectfully if without any notable enthusiasm, and even Francisque Sarcey, scarcely suspect of partiality towards Villiers, was obliged to admit that the play had not been badly received: 'It is not a failure; it is not a success either.' Émile Blémont, the one-time editor of *La Renaissance littéraire et artistique*, was prepared to go further: 'It has not been a noisy success, but it is an austere and serious success.' Whether Villiers was taken in himself no one knows. Taine went around all his usual haunts to congratulate him after the performance, but was unable to find him anywhere. Either he was celebrating privately, or he had realized that the coldness of the audience was a bad augury, and preferred to console himself in solitude.

The reaction of the critics was on the whole one of lukewarm praise. Nearly all of them paid tribute to the literary qualities of the text—'superb eruptions of style, marvellous bursts of lyricism', 'marvellously luminous style'—but expressed reservations about the play's dramatic qualities—'rather incoherent', 'confused and difficult to follow', 'a cloudy and uneven drama, but powerful'. There were a few highly enthusiastic notices, mostly from personal friends, like Louis de Gramont in *L'Intransigeant*, but even fewer outright condemnations: almost everyone found something to praise in the work. There were, however, some recurrent complaints. No one thought much of Georges's music; François Oswald declared it to be 'unbearable', and Arnold Mortier remarked sarcastically on 'interminable and obscure symphonies executed by forty musicians'. The loudest criticism was directed at the actors: 'the play is badly put over by its actors', 'M. Villiers de l'Isle-Adam has been badly served by them', 'M. Villiers de l'Isle-Adam's work has principally suffered from defective acting', 'I prefer to pass over Mlle Rousseil in silence, and Mlle Jeanne Pazza'. The main reproach was their slow and declamatory diction. Sarcey wrote: 'they officiate, they pontify; they are no longer acting a play, they are saying Mass', and Charles Martel said: 'on average they take a minute between each word'. A number of accidents caused unwanted laughter, such as Stephen Ashwell putting the wrong end of the telescope to his eye; whether these were deliberate or not is uncertain.

No author could have been entirely happy with this press, but, if Villiers read it carefully, he would have found much in it to comfort him, since the reviews generally reserved their criticisms for the presentation of the play and were benign in their treatment of the author. However, he would never have been satisfied with anything short of triumphal acclaim, and so he was doubtless extremely depressed by the coolness of the reception. If one takes the overall impression of the notices, one in fact feels that it was one of those theatrical occasions that could have gone either way, and that, with more goodwill on the part of the actors, the play might have been saved on subsequent performances. In the event, what was going on behind the scenes ensured that the outcome was disastrous. It was bad enough that on the first night Rosambeau, in the part of Vaudreuil, still brooding over the cuts in his role, should have decided on his own simply to restore some of the excised passages. What was infinitely worse was that Pop and Rambaud should have washed their dirty linen in public by protesting to the press. On 22 February Maurice Ordonneau, theatrical critic of *Le Gaulois*, published this astonishing joint letter from them:

We appeal to your impartiality to draw attention to the following strange event which has just occurred at the Théâtre des Nations; your readers will draw their own conclusions. The actor charged with interpreting the part of Vaudreuil, M. Rosambeau, in defiance of an order issued by M. Villiers de l'Isle-Adam and by the directors, took the liberty, on the first night of *Le Nouveau-Monde*, of putting back the text of the passages cut from his role.

This of course turned the simmering quarrel between the cast and the directors into open war, and from that moment all was lost. Sensing the imminence of catastrophe, several of the actors, notably Mlle Rousseil and Rosambeau, started deliberately guying the play, and the performances soon degenerated into chaos. Robert du Pontavice de Heussey claims that his brother saw Villiers amid the hubbub leading the booing himself,[5] and it is understandable: he must have hated the actors by then, and wanted to show it publicly.

Nevertheless, the play was not taken off, no doubt because Lalouette was hoping that, if he kept it on long enough, some miracle might save him from total ruin. But at the beginning of March, Pop resigned, closely followed by Rambaud. It was said that each performance was costing 1,800 francs and that the average takings amounted to only 360 francs. By 4 March the papers were announcing the end of *Le Nouveau-Monde*, and on the ninth *La Fille des chiffonniers* resumed its career of more than six hundred performances. *Le Nouveau-Monde* had had seventeen.[6] Even then, its troubles were not over. No one had been paid, and Lalouette agreed to meet the cast at five o'clock on the seventh to pay them their wages, but, when the time came, he could only produce a third of what he owed. The actors immediately issued writs against him, and, although he tried to stave off the inevitable by hanging on to the lease of the theatre and blaming Ballande for the unpaid wages, the courts on 3 April ordered him to pay the outstanding sums, at which he promptly went bankrupt.

The whole thing was a truly shattering experience for the

unfortunate Villiers. The chance for which he had been
waiting since his youth had come, and the result had been a
total disaster. A man of less character and less courage might
never have recovered from such a shock. But Villiers remained remarkably stoical. Since he had had no money to
invest in the venture, he could not lose much by it financially,
even if it was unsuccessful. His creditors naturally swooped
when they scented the possibility of prosperity, and a whole
series of lawyers took out garnishment orders on any money
he might receive from the play, to the tune of some 12,000
francs.[7] But, paradoxically, the failure of the drama saved
him from such persecution, and on 8 March he went so far as
to affirm to the long-suffering Mme Perry: 'Today I am
solvent'[8] (admittedly he was trying to borrow yet more
money from her, so his assertion is not necessarily to be taken
literally). Even so, the letter he wrote to another friend on 11
March betokened singular fortitude: 'Success or failure, the
real victory in the battle was a resurrection for me.'[9]

Certainly Villiers had no intention of taking his defeat (if
defeat it was) lying down. Almost as soon as *Le Nouveau-
Monde* closed, he started composing a counterblast to his
critics. At first his intention was simply to recount his version
of what had happened, attacking the actors for failing to
understand his intentions and criticizing the shortcomings of
the production (to this project belong some of the already-
quoted fragments). Then he evidently realized that it would
hardly do for him to turn openly on his erstwhile associates,
and decided to rewrite his article in the third person, as
though he were some independent observer, unconnected
with the production, who wanted only to arrive at an
equitable judgement of the play. A further trick was to
pretend to quote from a non-existent essay by 'M. Villiers de
l'Isle-Adam' to justify some of his opinions. It is virtually
certain that this article appeared somewhere in March or
April 1883, but so far it has proved impossible to find it. The
main arguments he presents are these: the play as acted was a
bore, but this was because the original text had been merci-
lessly truncated; in any case, the stage effects, so vital to the
impact of the whole, had been needlessly messed up; none of
the accessories had been properly provided; the actors had

adopted a hopelessly misguided style of speech. The peroration shows how ingeniously Villiers was salvaging his self-respect:

In conclusion, imagine a marvellous great tree, with all the incomparable magic of blossom, sunshine, and foliage, which someone has shorn of all these delights, even of its weightiest boughs, on the pretext of 'lightening' it. What is left? What we saw of *Le Nouveau-Monde:* a powerful trunk, dull to behold, sad, and shapeless. In short, and this is the surprising truth, there being an absolute, capital, *inconceivable* difference between the work as performed and the work as read, one may conclude that one hundred and twenty thousand francs were spent at the Nations to produce *something that had nothing to do with* Le Nouveau-Monde. No, the play has never been performed.[10]

Clearly, Villiers was still convinced that he had created a masterpiece and that it had only failed because it had been tampered with. If only the full text had been used, if only the actors had understood, if only all the stage directions had been exactly followed, all would have been well and the play would have had the success it deserved. One may be tempted to dismiss these views as the usual sophisms of a disappointed author. But there is some truth in them: the cuts, though necessary, may not have been done with enough skill; the spectacular effects could clearly have been more expertly organized; the actors undoubtedly behaved disgracefully. Whatever the rights and wrongs of Villiers's reasoning, it made it possible for him to feel that the test had not in the end been decisive, that he had yet again been the victim of circumstances, and that there was still hope for the future.

Moreover, for a brief space of time, Villiers had been a man of power and influence. He had had a great theatre at his disposal, actors had been begging him to give them parts, journalists had wanted to interview him, collectors had written in for his autograph, friends from far and wide had wanted tickets for the première, his name had been in the papers for weeks on end. He had discovered once again that he could inspire people to make the most enormous sacrifices for him—not only Marras, on whom he had relied for twenty years, but comparative strangers like d'Osmoy and Lalouette. He had also learned to distinguish true friendship from false, and it is said that when Mendès came to commiserate with him on the failure of the play, he said simply: 'How pleased you are!'[11] *Le Nouveau-Monde* had undeniably crashed, but, together with the *Contes cruels*, it had transformed his situation. Almost overnight he had gone from being a little-known eccentric to being a celebrity.

Part III

The Years of Glory

26

The publication of the *Contes cruels* on 9 February had been overshadowed by the more violent publicity around *Le Nouveau-Monde*, but it had a more durable effect on Villiers's reputation among his peers, if only because (whatever the author thought) *Le Nouveau-Monde* is a deeply flawed work, whereas *Contes cruels* is one of the outstanding collections of short stories of the century. Villiers may have derived as much pleasure from the letter Mallarmé wrote to him on receiving his copy as he did from all the flattering things that had been said about him in the press. Mallarmé had been particularly moved that Villiers, with impeccable formality, had dedicated *La Machine à gloire* to 'Monsieur Stéphane Mallarmé'.

Black and dear rascal, at every moment, for many days, I have been reading the *Contes*; I have drunk the philtre drop by drop. I cannot deny myself the joy of sending you, wherever you may be, a clasp of the hands—from over the years—which may perhaps reach you. This book, so poignant because one remembers that it represents the sacrifice of a life to everything that is noble, is fully worth (and it is no mediocre evaluation) so much sadness, the solitude, the disappointments, and the sufferings invented for you. In this work you have put an extraordinary sum of beauty! The language truly of a god everywhere! Several of the tales are of unexampled poetry, that no one will attain again; all, astonishing. And that *Annonciateur* which makes me reflect so much to see if it is not the finest piece of literature that I can call to mind . . . One can say nothing to you, you just laugh. Ah! my old Villiers, I admire you! *Monsieur* Stéphane Mallarmé thanks you specially.[1]

The depths of affection and understanding revealed in this note more than justify the words which Villiers had inscribed on the flyleaf of Mallarmé's copy: 'To my best, my only friend'.[2]

The composition of the book had undergone a forced change at the last minute. Up to the page-proof stage, it had contained *Maison Gambade Père et Fils Succ^{rs}* under the new title *Midas*, but, when Gambetta died suddenly on 31 December 1882, it was decided that it would be indecent to reprint this virulent lampoon against him, so the story had been withdrawn. What was left consisted of twenty-eight tales (including a brief cycle of poems arranged so as to form a *Conte d'amour*), originally published over a period of fifteen years, from 1867 onwards. They are remarkably diverse in nature—- prose poems, pseudo-scientific fantasies, humorous anecdotes, tales of terror, Parisian sketches, dream-like evocations of the East—and their length varies from a few paragraphs to twenty or thirty pages. The stylistic virtuosity they display runs the gamut from the stiff and formal Parnassian splendours of *L'Annonciateur* (formerly *Azraël*), through the parodistic reproduction of the vulgar exaggerations of modern advertising in works like *L'Affichage céleste*, the mock gravity of *Les Demoiselles de Bienfilâtre*, the tragic grandeur of *Impatience de la foule*, to the sombre and mysterious poetry of *Véra*.

Yet every tale, whether it be sad or gay, mocking or serious, disturbs and disorientates the reader. In *Les Brigands*, a peaceful country crossroads becomes the scene of a bloody massacre. In *Les Demoiselles de Bienfilâtre*, the terrace of a Parisian café is turned into a strange and disquieting vision. In *A s'y méprendre!*, a cunning use of linguistic devices identifies the customers of a café in the business quarter of Paris with the corpses in the Morgue. In *Virginie et Paul*, the ironic description of the conversation of two young lovers in which every sentence has a hidden pun on the word 'argent' is so subtly done that even the perspicacious Arthur Symons was misled into seeing it as an innocent idyll.[3] In *L'Inconnue*, the melancholy evocation of an impossible love suddenly ends with a bitterly misogynistic jibe. In *Le Secret de l'ancienne musique*, the comic monologue mangled by Coquelin *cadet*, beneath the jokes and the caricatures, there is a haunting sense of a symbolic meaning that constantly eludes the grasp. In *Le Convive des dernières fêtes*, the brooding suspense slowly builds up through the unrevealed presence of a sanguinary madman. In *Véra* or *L'Intersigne*, the proximity of the supernatural world gradually suffuses the world of supposed reality. Irony is present almost everywhere, and the unwary reader can easily find himself trapped in a maze of apparent contradictions, until he realizes that he has involuntarily exposed the fallibility of his own mental processes.

Sometimes one is reminded of Poe—the sinister atmosphere of the house in *L'Intersigne*, for instance, or the deliberately convoluted ratiocinating language of certain philosophical digressions, or the investigation of strange psychological aberrations in tales like *Le Désir d'être un homme*. Sometimes there are echoes of Flaubert, notably in the archaeological reconstitution of Sparta in *Impatience de la foule*. At other times the pictorial manner and rich vocabulary of Gautier seem to inspire a work like *L'Annonciateur*. Baudelaire's misogynistic sarcasms are recalled by stories such as *L'Inconnue* and *Antonie* and his aesthetic of the prose poem by *Fleurs de ténèbres* and *Souvenirs occultes*. The spirit of Heine is visible in the poems of *Conte d'amour*, with their deceptively simple versification and their progression from enthusiasm to disillusionment and hatred. But everywhere Villiers is distinctively and characteristically himself, taunting the reader, frightening him, amusing him, surprising him, disorientating him, and entertaining him. If everything that Villiers had published up to 1883 contains elements of greatness, *Contes cruels* is the first work to be indisputably and completely the work of a great writer. As Remy de Gourmont later observed, 'These tales (. . .) at last gave Villiers his proper place.'[4]

Anyone who in 1883 picked up the *Contes cruels* in the hope of learning something of Villiers's private life would have been severely disappointed. Just as he had never allowed anyone to see the sordid rooms he inhabited, so he kept the public strictly away from his personal affairs. Taine wrote of him: 'In days gone by, when I used to accompany him towards the heights of the Butte Montmartre, I always respected the mystery in which he surrounded our nocturnal separation, I never asked any questions, he never had the embarrassment of having to reply. The poor and proud poet modestly hid his domicile.'[5] The same sense of modesty precluded any confessional self-revelation in the tales. Occasionally Villiers portrays himself as an urbane narrator, drinking champagne with *demi-mondaines* in the elegant rooms of the Maison Dorée, exchanging anecdotes with actors and dramatists, flirting with a beautiful girl on a balcony looking out over a moonlit garden. But these are conventional images, disguises rather, and it is rare for the mask to be lifted. There are clear echoes of his stormy affair with Louise Dyonnet in *Antonie*, *Maryelle*, and *Conte d'amour*, but one has to know what to look for; more obvious are the embittered allusions to the misfortunes of *Le Nouveau-Monde* in *Deux Augures*, that biting satire on contemporary philistinism. Otherwise direct references to his personal circumstances are rigorously proscribed.

But there was one respect in which those who knew him could detect an individual idiosyncrasy in the *Contes cruels*, and that was the obsession with the guillotine. Many of the tales live up to the cruelty promised by the titles of the collection, none more so than *Le Convive des dernières fêtes*, where the fear and repulsion inspired by the mysterious Baron von H*** are explained when it transpires that he has a morbid fascination with executions and travels all over Europe trying to get hangmen to allow him to take their place. Villiers certainly never went as far as that, but it was well known to his friends that he could never resist turning up when a criminal was to be guillotined (executions in France were still public in those days), and the stories and articles of his later years show an increasing concentration on the macabre spectacle of judicial decapitation. In *Le Convive*, the Baron's pastime is presented as a pathological aberration, reproved by Villiers; in later works, it becomes ever more obvious that he himself is unable to repress his desire to be involved with executions.[6]

Perhaps this sadistic trait in his temperament is connected with his misogyny, so apparent in many of the tales. After having formed an impossible ideal of a woman whose genius would be equal to her beauty, Villiers had become embittered by his constant disappointments in love, and never missed the opportunity to castigate the frailty of the opposite sex. It is said that at parties he would sidle up to couples embracing as they danced and hiss: 'Never fall in love!'[7] and Henry Roujon records that he was 'more than once taken to the police station for having tried to evangelize one of those couples who, after midnight, on the outer boulevards, gracelessly discuss the temporal interests of love'.[8] His own existence with the humble Marie Dantine, tolerated more than loved, was as far from his dream as could be imagined. The only photograph of her, taken in old age, shows her to have been handsome rather than pretty; she evidently had very striking large dark eyes. She was certainly quite unlike Villiers's ideal, and no doubt, had Victor never been born, she would have passed out of his life.

Yet, as it was, Villiers showed a curious loyalty to her. After 1881 there are no more traces of those fantastic plans for rich marriages which had been such a regular feature of his life before then. Moreover, when around 1883 there was some danger of his becoming involved with another woman, he brought the affair to an abrupt end. The woman in question was a strange being. She was born in 1850, her real name was Marie-Émilie Chartroule de Montifaud, in 1865 she had married Juan-Francis-Léon de Quivogne, and she wrote semi-pornographic novels and tales under the pseudonym Marc de Montifaud. From time to time prosecutions for her works forced her to take refuge in London or in Brussels, but she was an aggressive person and wrote many pamphlets defending herself, conducted a violently libellous campaign against Francis Magnard, editor of *Le Figaro*, and gave the journalist René Maizeroy a public slap in the face at the first night of Becque's *Les Corbeaux* in 1882. She used to spend long hours reading at the Bibliothèque Nationale, dressed as a man, but she had several children and her private life was said to be above reproach. In 1883 Villiers was sufficiently close to her to have contemplated dedicating the *Contes cruels* to her (he alleged that Calmann Lévy had removed the dedication for fear of offending the powerful Magnard, but he may not have been speaking the truth).[9]

Some time later, he decided that their relationship was on the verge of becoming too intimate and wrote her a delightful letter to break it off.

We have played together, we were unhappy, that brought us together; up to now, no one can say anything against us; all we owe to each other are some entrancing moments that the most naïve birds or the most prim and proper quadrumanes would not disown. Well, things are getting hot and I smell something burning. I don't want to go on, so there!—I like you very much but, my dear and good little friend, you forget that we are very serious people.

Permit me to say to you that I am not alone in the world and that I am, just like you, in a situation for which, out of a sense of decency, I shall not use a stronger term than frightful. I have not the right, nor even the power, to create the least joy for myself. In a word, I have not the slightest desire to be a coward like so many others. If at this moment I follow my heart, we will make proper fools of ourselves, since *we will waste time being happy!*—By what right?

He continues with these ingenious arguments for a while, then suddenly reveals an old romantic dream:

Listen, I have loved enough! I am incapable of passing fancies and, if I ever fall in love again, I only want to love my wife.—Yes, with the mayor, and his sash, and the whole rigmarole.—That's definite. If I made ties for myself now, even for a short time, I have the impression that I would be deceiving her in advance. And that would be bad.

A further reason for breaking off is the effect he would have on her:

You may not know it, but I have a sinister gift for lulling people to sleep. It is a distressing speciality. You would end up by no longer seeing life as it is; I give off a disastrous languor, and it would be a kind of crime in this case. I have something of the upas-tree about me.[10]

This courteous, flattering, and tactful letter shows many things about Villiers's relations with women—his fundamental romanticism, his honesty, and his capacity for embellishing reality. It also tends to confirm Fernand Calmettes's penetrating analysis:

His action on women was purely cerebral; he persuaded them they were superior and did it in his own way, not by a direct declaration (he would have spluttered unintelligibly), but by airs, facial expressions, little insinuations. If they happened to make some very ordinary remark, he would start all sorts of antics accompanied by interjections. And the women would understand (they have a gift for understanding above all that which they are not told) that what he meant was: 'Ah! if only I could think of such witty things!' And naturally they were not displeased to discover they had a sort of genius they had never suspected.[11]

One feels that Marie de Montifaud must have been one such woman.

If Villiers possessed the power of transfiguring women by his imagination, his father had the same gift in an even higher degree. The Marquise had not been dead for long when the old man took up with a certain Louise. The only one of Villiers's friends who referred to her was Calmettes, who wrote of the Marquis: 'But for his son, who declared himself ready to go to court to accuse her of captation, he would have ended up by marrying a horrible creature who claimed to be rich and wanted the title in order to regain a little consideration in the world.'[12] Her riches were obviously fictitious, as is clear from the Marquis's letters, such as the one on 3 January 1883, in which he told his son that he and Louise would be thrown out into the street in two days' time: 'All we can do now is *find a place double quick in some boarding-house*, what would happen then to poor Louise's furniture, I can't leave her and I won't, I have been very happy to have her near me recently, she has to be saved from the situation as much as me and I am sure you agree with me about that.'[13] In fact, it is very clear that Villiers did not agree in the least, and that there was a scene every time he met Louise, of whom he disapproved strongly.

But the Marquis's faculty for dreams was indestructible, and six months later he was writing triumphantly to Villiers:

We want you to share in our happiness. Here is Louise, who now has twenty-five thousand francs and who today has in this very place a well-furnished dining-room and who is going to have in her drawing-room some magnificent pink satin curtains that I am holding in my hand, with a good piano, a superb settee, and furniture to go with it. What is more, Louise is going to have all to herself a fine estate with a magnificent feudal castle, with turrets and a park, lands, meadows, and vineyards, and a forest of several leagues and we are going to own in a perfect and regular way some mines whose riches you will be able to help us exploit with our own capital.[14]

But on other occasions he complained that Louise did not have enough to eat, that she had had to go without food for two days, that she was having to go out to work at three o'clock in the morning, that they had no money to pay the rent, that they were cold. Not even these hardships could shake his faith—indeed, his visions became even more grandiose as he gradually lost such grip on reality as had been left him by his diminishing sanity.

With his own family to support, Villiers must have found these constant plaintive demands extremely wearing—especially as he was so mistrustful of Louise. But the fuss made around *Le Nouveau-Monde* and the *Contes cruels* had conferred one considerable benefit on him: it had made his name very well known, and that was what enabled him now at last to gain a foothold in the world of the great Parisian daily papers. Two months after the production of the play, *Le Figaro* published an article by him inspired by the recent death of Louis Veuillot and relating his reminiscences of the famous editor at Solesmes in 1863 (*Louis Veuillot bénédictin*, the title under which it then appeared, was later changed to *Une entrevue à Solesmes*). Three weeks later, on 12 May, came *Le Tsar et les grands-ducs*, another set of reminiscences, about Weimar in 1870, suggested by the coronation of Tsar Alexander III, which had just taken place. There was then a six-month gap, after which a further four tales and articles appeared between March and July 1884. This may not have quite entitled Villiers to call himself a regular contributor, but it kept him in the public eye (the articles were often given front-page prominence), and, more importantly, it provided him with much-needed income, since he received two or three hundred francs for each publication. As he wrote to Marras on the day *L'Avertissement* was published: 'Now I am firmly anchored in *Le Figaro*, and with caution—mixed, naturally, with mad pleasantries (whose frivolity can be cleverly disguised in the flashes of a few whiffs of grapeshot)—the odds are, without boasting, that we shall pick up some pieces of eight, and no mistake.'[15]

Le Figaro was a right-wing newspaper, and that no doubt encouraged Villiers to give full vent to his own political opinions. They appear in his eulogy of Veuillot's militant Catholicism, in his obvious sympathy with the Tsar of Russia, and in the scepticism about popular infatuations in politics evident in *Vox populi*. But the most significant and the most committed of these articles is *L'Avertissement*, written when the Comte de Chambord was seriously ill in his exile at Frohsdorf. In this article (which, according to Villiers, had an 'enormous success'), he begins with a nostalgic evocation of his childhood in Brittany, which is one of the few overtly autobiographical passages in his work:

Once—I remember!—towards the end of a sunlit day, I was alone with one of my cousins in the avenue of a manor near Vannes. We were waiting, by the wrought-iron gate, until it was time to go indoors, and we were singing an old royalist song to greet the twilight. Above our heads, the last twitterings of a thousand birds, in the radiant foliage shot through with fire, were accompanying (for in Brittany the birds know the king's name) that air with which, twelve years earlier, our good nursemaids, once brave fighters with the Chouans, had sung us to sleep. A passer-by on the main road stopped and said sneeringly to us: 'But your king has no children!' 'And what about us?' I replied innocently. At which Tinténiac simply started picking up stones. 'What's the point? . . .' I said, holding his arm: 'just let the passers-by go on their way.'

Then he moves abruptly to a criticism of what he considers to be the defeatism of the royalists, who have compromised their cause by resigning themselves in advance to melancholy inaction. A postscript to the article was added when the news from Frohsdorf indicated that Chambord was recovering: 'So—may it please God that this Warning should be salutary for us! And may it at last be for us all, Sire, like one of those moments when one starts in one's sleep . . . and comes to life again!'[16]

In the event, the recovery proved to be only temporary, and the Comte de Chambord died on 24 August. His passing threw the legitimists into disarray, since the fact that he was childless meant that there was no longer an obvious claimant to the throne from the elder branch of the Bourbons. They could switch their support to the Orleanist pretender, the Comte de Paris; they could cling to the principle of legitimacy by turning to Don Juan of Spain; they could simply give up the struggle altogether and accept the permanence of the Republic. None of these possibilities was in the least attractive. Don Juan was remote and unpopular; the Comte de Paris was suspected of constitutionalism; the Republic was anathema. Villiers, with his deep attachment to tradition, felt these dilemmas with painful keenness, and at once started drafting an article to express them. An eloquent farewell to the dead king prefaces his reflections:

May he sleep in peace, blessed by his servants, with all the hopes that he bears away! Farewell to the glory, the strength, the greatness that, so long as he lived, the future constantly guaranteed to their faith, despite the suffering and the passage of time. Half a century of hard and sterile fidelity has vanished with one beat of the wings of death. It is well. Sleep, Sire. Glory be to God.[17]

Then he envisaged siren voices pleading with the king's men to live with the idea of a republic. The article was probably never finished, and, while one can be sure that the upholders of the Republic would have been roundly condemned, it is not clear what solution Villiers could have adopted to mitigate the total pessimism of the opening. The problem was to occupy him for years to come, but it is doubtful whether he ever found a way to elude the basic fact that the dynasty to which he had so loudly proclaimed his loyalty was extinct.

But if *Le Figaro* provided Villiers with the most regular source of income he had had for years and with a platform for his views, relations with it were by no means easy. Francis Magnard, the editor-in-chief since 1879, had been among Villiers's most venomous detractors in 1869 and 1870, when he had been a journalist on the paper, and had in return been subjected to Villiers's sarcasm in the preface to *La Révolte*. So there was no love lost between the two men, and Villiers could never be confident that what he wrote would be accepted. When, late in 1883 or early in 1884, he submitted a long political satire ridiculing republican politics, imagining that Jules Grévy, the President of the Republic, had decided to have a coronation, Magnard's reaction was brutal: 'You are probably going to find that I am a filthy bourgeois, but I prefer to say straight out that I find your lampoon absolutely incomprehensible. Fantasies of this sort must be either very short or very successful. I have the audacity to believe that your *Coronation* has neither of these qualities.' To add insult to injury, Magnard signed: 'yours very radically'.[18] Villiers was naturally hurt and indignant, and complained bitterly to Marras:

They have turned the story down and covered it with insults: 'heavy, banal, unreadable, boring, unsuitable, etc., etc.' (. . .) I've made up my mind only to skate over the surface of subjects when I write in *Le Figaro*, since that is the reward one gets for the most determined and conscientious work (. . .) Since it is *'impossible'* to be onself, I shall be the joyful amusement of others. I've given up caring.[19]

27

Though circumstances compelled him to keep on producing stories and occasional pieces for the press, and though he lavished fanatical care on them, Villiers never attributed much importance to such writings compared with his major works, and continued to devote as much time as he could to long-term projects like *Axël* and his historical studies. Since *La Vie Artistique* had published most of the Third Part of *Axël* in 1882, Villiers had been working up little by little to getting the complete drama into print, but still preferred to issue extracts first, in order to give himself more time to correct and revise, since he resolutely refused to release the work until it had assumed a form which satisfied him. Later in December 1883 he had the unexpected idea of offering a scene from it to an illustrated weekly called *Le Monde militaire*, recently founded to provide entertainment for the troops and which had already published a tale of his entitled *Sagacité d'Aspasie* (with a hypocritical dedication to Magnard). A fee was handed over, the text was set up, and Villiers announced to Mallarmé that it was about to appear ('the scene from *Axël* really isn't bad; it will amuse you').[1] Then Guy de Lonroy, the editor, decided that it was too difficult to follow out of context and in any case was out of character with the review, so returned it to the author.[2]

But Villiers was by now too set on the idea of making something of *Axël* to give up so easily, and his next device was even more surprising. In mid-February he divulged his plans to Mallarmé:

Don't ask me any questions.—I have resolved, on the twenty-eighth of this month, in a week's time, to give a *Lecture*, and the day after tomorrow there will be posters up about me as if I were any old Leconte de Lisle. Tomorrow evening, Tuesday, I'll bring your tickets, if you want to take your family to see this probable new failure of your old friend Villiers.—I am giving this Lecture (a reading from *Axël* with commentaries) to earn the two hundred francs which will at last allow me to pay off my most sacred debts.[13]

Villiers had of course long been a brilliant reader of his own works (when he was in the mood), but this was the first time he had made a formal appearance in public, and he must have approached the occasion with some trepidation. The posters that he had promised were duly put up, advertising *Axël*, a reading with commentaries by M. Villiers de l'Isle-Adam from his unpublished drama in prose, to be given in the Lecture Theatre of the Boulevard des Capucines on Thursday 28 February, at 8.30 in the evening.

Most of the text of the lecture has survived in manuscript, and it follows a strange plan. Villiers begins by emphasizing that *Axël* is not a conventional play and is not intended for the stage:

Is not the great anguish of humanity before the enigma of life, taking everything into account, a feeling . . . like any other? . . . Then why should it be forbidden to allow this constant, terrible, and distant preoccupation to show through the sombre and vibrant texture of a dramatic work? Now, could it be that the crime of thinking about profound matters is so unforgivable in the eyes of men of the world that an author accused and convicted of an offence against frivolity should have to make a hypocritical apology for having attempted to embody in a stage action a conception of a transcendental kind? . . . —No.—At least, I hope not.

But after this opening about the 'new dramatic literature' which the poster had promised, Villiers suddenly sidetracks himself by reading two of his stories, allegedly to accustom the audience to his manner. Next he comes to *Axël* and reads passages from the end of the First Part, with Sara's refusal and escape from the convent. Without any mention of the Second Part, he goes on to a brief summary of the scenes between Axël and Maître Janus, declining to enter into detail about them despite the fact that, as he says, they contain 'the guiding idea of this work'. With equal abruptness, he jumps to the last part, and reads a series of extracts from the dialogue between Axël and Sara. But, instead of relating the end of the play, he concludes without warning: 'Here begins the drama properly speaking. Unfortunately, time presses, and I cannot give you in a few words the secret of its dénouement. But, if I have not wearied your attention too much, I shall be delighted to read you the sequel on a future occasion'.[4]

This capricious performance must have been somewhat disconcerting to the audience, with the prefatory stories, the sudden leaps from one scene to another, the large gaps in the action, and the absence of any conclusion. It is a pity that not more is known about how it was received. The press seem to have ignored the occasion, and the only letter to have come to light from someone who was present was written at midnight, just after the lecture ended, by Paul Margueritte, a young novelist whose mother was a first cousin of Mallarmé (he and his younger brother Victor both later attained fame as men of letters). If one can judge by his excitement, the evening had been a great success:

Ah! Monsieur de Villiers, how beautiful it was! How you gripped us, carried us away, with the muted melancholy of your voice! What a fever of enthusiasm you have given us obscure twenty-year-olds, so much in love with ideal Art! Your thought has mysterious undercurrents, philosophical implications of a disquieting profundity. And your style, full of magnificence and majesty, has the splendour of a princely cloak![5]

Axël was not the only major work which Villiers was striving to complete at this time, nor Paul Margueritte the only young man to fall under his spell. One may suppose that he was still labouring away at intervals on the genealogy of his family and the biography of Marshal Jean which had occupied him for so long. There is no way of dating the various manuscript fragments that mark the successive stages of these two projects, but there are good grounds for thinking that they must have been in his mind in 1883, since in April of that year he was approached by a student at the École des Chartes who wanted to talk to him about the Marshal. This was Germain Lefèvre-Pontalis, son of a distinguished historian, politician, and journalist, and himself destined for a brilliant career as a diplomat and historian. He had just completed a thesis on the Marshal and wanted to discuss it with Villiers before publishing it. As was his habit, Villiers refused to allow the young man to call on him, and went instead to see him in the rue des Mathurins. Happily, Lefèvre-Pontalis too was an admirer of the Marshal and shared Villiers's view of 'the ineptitude of most of the historical judgements on his life and his deeds, so badly understood and even more badly studied by a host of self-appointed judges'.[6]

It may have been his meeting with Lefèvre-Pontalis and the publication of a summary of his thesis that made Villiers change his plans to treat the genealogy and the biography as two separate works. At some point he certainly amalgamated them into a single narrative under the title *Maison de Villiers de l'Isle-Adam*, with the subtitle *Généalogie justifiée*, which takes the story from the foundation of the family in 992 to the first capture of Paris by the Marshal in 1418.[7] The manuscript has been very carefully established by Villiers himself, but it was never published because he intended to conclude the Marshal's life (for which he had prepared numerous notes and drafts) and then trace the rest of the history of his line up to his own times. It is an extraordinarily painstaking piece of work, with masses of detailed references to scores of historians, ancient and modern, and, particularly in the early sections, a deliberate austerity in the presentation of the evidence. Villiers is no longer concerned with attacking *Perrinet Leclerc*, refuting genealogists who claim to detect lacunae in his lineage, or defending the purity of his intentions: all mention of such contemporary issues is rigorously banished, so that he gives the impression of living in the past to the total exclusion of the present. Villiers is concerned above all with the clarity, the method, the meticulousness, and the solidity of his narration.

But, as soon as Marshal Jean enters the scene, although the method remains the same, the tone changes, and the author waxes passionately eloquent. Vast as his documentation is and impressive as are the long lists of references for every statement, it soon becomes apparent that Villiers's technique as a historian is highly selective and highly tendentious. His view of the civil war is simple: the Burgundians are the saviours of the country and heroes to a man—with Marshal Jean as their most illustrious representative; the Armagnacs are without exception traitors, murderers, brigands, and criminals. All the erudite apparatus serves only to confirm the hypotheses most favourable to the Marshal: any evidence discreditable to his ancestor is dismissed out of hand, for the most part without even any discussion of its possible merits. The text is thus a work of propaganda much more than it is a work of objective historical research. It would visibly not stand up to critical analysis, so great and so evident is the bias throughout.

On the other hand, it comes close to being a masterpiece of the imaginative evocation of history. The narrative is lively, rapid, moving and extremely vivid; the language is extraordinarily expressive, with its oratorical sweep and its lapidary judgements on men and events; above all, Villiers has built a whole world of personal mythology, vibrant with passion and full of echoes of ancestral greatness, through which the gigantic figures of a past age stride, dwarfing, by their villainy or their glory, the puny bourgeois of the nineteenth century among whom the author was fated to live. Once one has read these pages, one can understand how much Villiers had come to love the Marshal as he imagined him, how much it meant for him to relive his exploits, how much it liberated him to turn aside from the mean realities around him and transport himself back into the fifteenth century. Whatever his original motives for starting the *Perrinet Leclerc* affair, it can be said to have led him, over the years, into composing one of his noblest works.

The *Maison de Villiers de l'Isle-Adam* was never published by the poet, and in 1884 it would have taken a lot of detective work to put together the different bits of *Axël* that had been published—on 12 July *La Vie militaire*, which had taken over *Le Monde militaire*, did publish the scene between Axël and Sara rejected by its predecessor, but the other fragments so far revealed had appeared in different magazines in 1872 and 1882. Much more efficacious in reinforcing Villiers's reputation was the publicity given to his work in that year by two colleagues who were themselves writers of some notoriety.

One of them was Catulle Mendès who, perhaps fired by Villiers's example, hired the Lecture Theatre of the Boulevard des Capucines to give four lectures on the *Parnasse contemporain* (later in the year they were published as *La Légende du Parnasse contemporain*). In the second lecture Mendès talked at length about his old friend:

Judged with severity and only on those works he has published, Villiers de l'Isle-Adam could be considered a half-genius. But we who know his still unpublished dramas and novels firmly believe that the time is not far distant when he will demonstrate fully and incontestably those lofty qualities of which he has so far only shown part. It will only be possible to arrive at a definitive judgement after the publication of *Axël*, the grandiose dramatic epic on which he has been working for many years. I am convinced that, after the uncertain light of the crescent, the full moon will shine out in all its glory![8]

The verdict is not unfair, but one senses in its restrictiveness that envy which Mendès was rarely able to repress in his dealings with Villiers. Had it come from anyone else, Villiers might have accepted it as a compliment, but, knowing Mendès as he did, he was furious. He had been present at the lecture and, as the audience was leaving, Léon Barracand, an acquaintance from Nina de Villard's, said to him: 'Well, you must be pleased! he says you have genius!' '"Pleased! Pleased!" he repeated, stalking up and down the courtyard outside the lecture room. "You'll see! I have a few things to say to him!"' Barracand said it was the only time he and his friends ever saw Villiers really angry.[9]

The other publicity in 1884 came from someone whom he knew much less well than Mendès, but who was to occupy an increasingly important place in his life. This was Joris-Karl Huysmans, ten years younger than Villiers, and chiefly known until then as one of Émile Zola's disciples in the *groupe de Médan*, with a number of novels and prose sketches in the Naturalist vein but with an unusually personal and pungent style. Huysmans had met Villiers in the offices of Mendès's review *La République des lettres* in 1876, and when he wrote *A Rebours*, his brilliant analysis of the decadent mentality, he decided to include Villiers among the favourite authors of his hero, the Duc Jean Floressas des Esseintes. Having been lent by Mallarmé copies of the long-defunct *Revue des Lettres et des Arts* and other early works, he was able to talk of virtually unknown writings like *Claire Lenoir, Isis, Elën*, and *Morgane*. Huysmans did not pour indiscriminate praise on everything by Villiers—he objected to the 'philosophical farrago' of the novels and to the 'romantic clichés' of the plays—but he paid tribute to his 'undeniable talent', he singled out *Véra* as a 'miniature masterpiece', and he revelled in the 'singularly inventive and acrid spirit of mockery' in the satirical tales. 'All the filth of contemporary utilitarian ideas, all the mercantile ignominy of the age were glorified in pieces whose poignant irony transported Des Esseintes.'[10] The success of *A Rebours* had a lot to do with the position Villiers rapidly came to occupy in the literary world of the 1880s, alongside writers such as Mallarmé, Verlaine, and Corbière, dissidents who provided an immensely promising alternative to both the desiccated Parnassian tradition and the oppressively materialistic world-view of the prevailing Realist and Naturalist ethos.

Another sign of Villiers's growing fame and of the change in the artistic and intellectual climate was the number of young writers who came to seek him out. One of them was Victor-Émile Michelet, a twenty-three-year-old poet and novelist immersed in occultist thought, who first met Villiers in Catulle Mendès's flat in the rue Mansart in 1884. 'He struck me as worn out': that was Michelet's immediate impression.

He was of middle height, and his movements had an innate and casual elegance. What first gripped one's attention was his forehead, very handsome, very broad, denuded on the right side by the start of the parting in his greyish hair, a lock of which, constantly falling, was constantly pushed back by the regular gesture of his very beautiful hand. His face, very wide at the top, grew very narrow at the base, the curve of his jawbone dropped sharply to the chin, from which extended the point of a little beard which Villiers would twist mechanically at times when he was deep in thought—and such times were the most frequent in his life. His eyes, lunary in quality, set far from the eyebrows, were pale and tired. And yet the gaze they cast on people and things had an extraordinary penetration.[11]

Michelet, who was a gentle, thoughtful, idealistic, young

Breton with a mystic tinge to his temperament, probably understood and appreciated Villiers as well as anyone of his generation. His description of him thus has a particular interest:

Someone like Villiers disconcerts those who look at him. People have represented a number of different Villiers. I knew two: the one who went through the crowd of 'passers-by', as he called them, and the one who appeared in private. The first, unsure under which mask he could best protect his soul and his genius, following the passers-by with uneasy glances from his flax-flower eyes, pulling at his silver-sprinkled beard with his fine pale hand, spoke reluctantly in a manner going from the loftiest eloquence down to incoherent stammering. The second was an enchanter. When he felt himself in the company of intelligent friends, the words he poured forth were winged—for one must always have recourse to the trusty epithets of Homer—and full of the magnetic power of his ardent inner life. He spoke in the same way as the phoenix rose from the ashes of its old body. He recounted his visions in a language akin to his written language, heavy with deep meanings and glittering with wit. Often I would see him in the street, with the attitude of someone feeling the cold, his head leaning ponderously on his shoulder, and I would walk with him for a long time, rejoicing in his conversation, which was as ethereal as a ghost and as firm as a rock. He felt at ease in the streets of Paris, those channels of vitality where the atmosphere is saturated with passion, with love, with grief, with joy. The hidden bubbling life of the city corresponded to his volcanic verbal power. The pavement of the boulevard was a springboard from which he soared to the supreme zones of the mind.[12]

Another young poet who turned to Villiers about the same time was Rodolphe Darzens, a friend of Michelet but a very different character. Large, athletic, aggressive, ambitious, and active, Darzens later left differing accounts of the date of his meeting with Villiers—1881 or 1882, 1883 and 1885[13]—but what is certain is that he had very soon made a place for himself in Villiers's life, helping him to organize his affairs, negotiate with publishers, and so forth. One has the feeling that the thrusting and practical Darzens came to exercise some kind of domination over the older man, who remained so remote from the day-to-day realities of life. It would be cynical to assume that Darzens was motivated by self-interest, or that his admiration for Villiers was anything but genuine. But in the event Darzens was to loom so large in everything to do with Villiers that it is difficult to believe that his motives in cultivating his friendship were entirely altruistic. A quarrelsome man with a gift for alienating people, Darzens seems to have taken good care to keep on the right side of Villiers and, whatever the services he rendered (and they were real), in the long run it undoubtedly accrued to his advantage.

Darzens was one of a group of young men who, when they had been pupils at the Lycée Condorcet (where Mallarmé taught English), had founded a little magazine called *Le Fou*. Several of them were later to become well known as poets, and they all shared a common admiration for Villiers. They included René Guilbert who, as René Ghil, was one of Mallarmé's favourite disciples and became the leader of the *École évolutive-instrumentiste*; Stuart Merrill, an American who wrote in French and was a friend and ally of Ghil; Pierre Quillard, who later moved away from imaginative literature to political activity at the time of the Dreyfus affair; and Georges Ephraïm Michel, who took the pen-name Ephraïm Mikhaël and, before his tragically early death, had developed into one of Villiers's most fervent admirers. At what stage each of them made personal contact with Villiers is not known, but probably in 1884 and certainly by 1885 they all knew him fairly well. Since the group retained a degree of cohesion for several years, it formed an important centre for the dissemination of what had by now become very markedly Villiers's influence among the young men of the rising generation.

Another centre was of course Mallarmé's *mardis*, which by 1884 had acquired a great reputation as a forum for the debate of aesthetic questions. Mallarmé's own sibylline pronouncements were naturally the main focus of attraction, and for the most part the young poets listened respectfully as the Master, standing by the stove, discoursed amid the tobacco smoke on his lofty and enigmatic conception of the nature and mission of art. But when Villiers arrived, as he frequently did, the atmosphere changed: he was one of the few people who had a recognized right to take over the proceedings, and, whether he was simply talking in his voluble way or reading from his works, his appearances always caused a stir of excitement. For the first time there was a place where people could count on meeting him, at least from time to time. His incessant changes of address, his extreme poverty, his liaison with Marie Dantine, and his reluctance to allow people to see his home circumstances had meant that, hitherto, anyone who wanted to talk to him had had to search through all the cafés of Montmartre, often with very little chance of finding him, since he had no regular haunt. Now he not only had a platform for his views and his improvisations, but he bene-fited from the additional prestige of being deeply and visibly admired and loved by Mallarmé himself—and there was no stronger recommendation in the eyes of the *mardistes*.

But it was not only among the narrower circles of the Parisian literary scene that Villiers was becoming a celebrity. His contributions to *Le Figaro* made him known to total strangers all over France and brought him a wide and varied postbag. Two pieces in particular aroused widespread inter-est. One was *Le Secret de l'échafaud*, published on 25 October 1883. In this macabre tale, in which his fascination with the guillotine is very much in evidence, Villiers relates the story of the poisoner Dr Couty de La Pommerais, who, before execution, agrees to an experiment with the surgeon Velpeau whereby, when his head is severed from his body, he will wink three times to show whether or not life persists in the brain (this was a question which greatly agitated medical and legal experts throughout the century). But, when the critical moment arrives, one eye closes with a terrible effort, and that is all: the scaffold has kept its secret. Such was the notoriety of this tale that it was at once translated into German by a Swiss called Hermann Sprecher and a little later into English by a Miss F. Simeon of Dublin, both of whom wrote to Villiers to express their admiration and to ask permission to publish their versions.[14]

Even more resounding was the success of *Les Expériences du docteur Crookes*, which *Le Figaro* published on 10 May 1884.[15] This article, which is based on Dr (later Sir) William Crookes's famous account of his spiritualist experiments, *Researches on the Phenomena of Spiritualism*, shows both Villiers's curiosity about anything which seemed to provide evidence of the existence of the supernatural and his hesitation about accepting anything disapproved of by the Church. After an admiring account of Crookes's work and a declaration that strange phenomena have undoubtedly been observed, Villiers launches into a vehement and unexpected diatribe at the end of which, having denounced this 'divinity for all', these 'sombre pieces of gossip' and 'the art of calling up the dead in twenty-five lessons', he proclaims his uncompromising allegiance to Christianity: 'As always, we abide exclusively by the Word, the Spirit of the Gospel; it is strictly, and with no possible discussion or reservations, our sole doctrine. And even if, which is impossible, an Angel of God came down from Heaven to teach us another, we would remain firm and unshakeable in our faith.'[16] In fact, these words are a quotation from the Archdeacon's sermon in *Axël* as it had been printed in 1872, and it is a measure of the shift in Villiers's opinions that what had originally been conceived as a caricature of narrow and fanatical dogmatism should now be taken to represent his own view.

The article created a sensation when it appeared and involved him in correspondence with all sorts of people—with a retired general in the Alps who had dabbled in spiritualism,[17] with a young law student who wanted to read the whole of Crookes's work,[18] and with the secretary of a brass band in the provinces, whose letter, passed on by the editor of *Le Figaro*, contained an unusual request: 'In our modest rural club a rather violent argument has arisen. Some pretty heavy bets have been laid on the article by Monsieur de Williers de l'Isle adam [*sic*]. Is it a humorous article? Does Dr Crookes exist? Can one buy his work on psychic force? I shall be glad if you would supply me with this information.'[19]

28

At the beginning of 1884 Villiers was ill for some time, and his health, weakened by years of penury, gave him increasing concern thereafter, especially in the winter, when he was liable to suffer from bronchitis. His condition cannot have been helped by the many cigarettes he smoked, but, though as far back as 1876 he had promised Victor Hugo to cut down his smoking by a third,[1] and though his private papers contain occasional injunctions to himself to 'smoke less', the habit was inveterate. Whether he was a heavy drinker, or even, as some have said, an alcoholic, is less sure. That he spent long nocturnal hours in cafés is beyond dispute, and this of course inevitably meant that there was always a drink at his elbow. It is also beyond dispute that from time to time he drank too much, since he admits as much in his letters—'I must have written you a really mad letter the other evening, we had drunk Rhine wine at Weinschenk's party' (to Fernand de Gantès in 1875);[2] 'I don't want you to think, too much or even a little, about the ghastly state I was in yesterday evening' (to Marras in 1879);[3] 'I was a bit tipsy when I wrote to you the day before yesterday: I had drunk a lot of English beer and I'm none too sure what I said in my letter' (to Mallarmé in 1884).[4] Equally, there were those among his contemporaries who regarded him as a compulsive drinker: Edmond de Goncourt, for instance, contemptuously dismissed him as a 'frequenter of beer-houses', an 'alcoholic'.[5] But Hugues Le Roux, a journalist who knew Villiers at the end of his life, is probably nearer the truth when he writes: 'Speech made him drunk like champagne, and his ideas only took shape in this intoxication.' Le Roux noted that Villiers's physical weakness was such that one glass of wine would make him talk: 'From midnight onwards, Villiers could go on in a monologue for hours, speaking as if in a dream, telling murky and terrifying stories, until his thought, emerging from a fog, suddenly took on its perfect form.'[6]

Some of the anecdotes told by Le Roux certainly suggest that, when the spirit moved him, Villiers would talk in a way that in anyone else would have indicated an advanced state of drunkenness. Maupassant was once at table with some friends including the explorer Savorgnan de Brazza, when Villiers arrived and talked so torrentially that they thought he had gone mad. It was perhaps on the same occasion that Villiers held forth for so long about places which the explorer thought he alone knew that in the end he asked in puzzlement: 'But then you must be one of my colleagues?' At another dinner, according to Le Roux, Villiers was talking

away when 'suddenly, losing his footing, he started discours-
ing, for a good quarter of an hour, in Hebrew, which he
alone understood'. His manuscripts give a similar impression
of abrupt and unforeseeable floods of inspiration: a page,
carefully begun in his well-formed, elegant handwriting, will
begin to speed up until his pen is racing illegibly across the
paper. That Villiers sometimes drank a lot is clear, but he was
nowhere near being an alcoholic in the sense that Verlaine
was. What those who did not know him well put down to the
effects of alcohol was for the most part the result of an
extreme nervous excitability and of what Le Roux calls 'one
of the most fiery imaginations a man ever possessed'.[7]

It may well have been that fiery imagination that drew him
around this time into the ambit of the Naundorff family, the
descendants of the man who, in the 1820s, had claimed that
he was in reality Louis XVII, the Dauphin otherwise presumed to have perished in prison during the Revolution.
Though Naundorff's heirs had several times taken their
claims to law in France, notably in 1874, it was only after the
death of the Comte de Chambord in 1883 that their cause
began to attract more general notice and support, since, if it
could be proved that a direct descendant of Louis XVI was
still alive, legitimism would retain the *raison d'être* which it
appeared to have lost with the passing of the childless
Pretender. No doubt it was this possibility (as well as his
irresistible penchant for everything improbably romantic)
which caused Villiers to become involved with the circles
surrounding Amélie Laprade, Naundorff's daughter, who
lived in France (the current Naundorff claimant, 'Charles
XI', was in exile). The person responsible for introducing
him into these circles was probably his own father, for the
Marquis was a convinced Naundorffist and a close friend of
Abbé Laprade, Amélie's brother-in-law, and was forever
talking in his letters about what the 'king' was going to do.
The journalist Paul Vibert recalled meeting the Marquis at
lunches given by Amélie,[8] and Charles Buet saw Villiers
himself there:

I remember, and some day I shall tell the story, the dinner at which
I was present in the rue Tronchet, with Auguste de Villiers de
l'Isle-Adam, and where the guests said *Your Royal Highness* to a

woman, likewise dead now, still very handsome in those days, very imposing, and who was exactly what Queen Marie-Antoinette, *her grandmother*, would have been like at the age of fifty.[9]

Villiers's involvement was remote from the gullible enthusiasm of his father, and his first projected article on the Naundorff question would not have gone as far as absolute affirmation—he intended it to end thus:

I know what it is to be refused justice, and I say that it is worth clarifying the matter otherwise than by an empty and cowardly sneer, and that it is difficult for a true Christian gentleman, whatever his prejudices against a cause, to give the lie direct to a king like the King of Holland and a Sovereign Pontiff like Pius VI.[10]

But this article never got beyond manuscript notes, and the only publication in which Villiers expressed sympathy for Naundorffism was *Le Droit du passé*, which appeared in *Le Figaro* on 16 July 1884 (and was subsequently reproduced in two Naundorffist papers, *La Légitimité* and *Le Légitimiste*). This article, which is obviously based on some kind of inside information and has at least some elements of truth in it, relates how, when Jules Favre went to sign the armistice with Bismarck in 1871, he sealed the document with a ring given him by Naundorff, whose lawyer he had been: the ring had at one time had the Bourbon *fleur-de-lys* engraved on it, with the result that the papers signifying the surrender of republican France were marked with the royal arms. Villiers, who had some vague acquaintance with Favre, presents this story as a symbol of atonement for the murder of Louis XVI, and does not pronounce upon the validity of Naundorff's claims, though he certainly does not dismiss them.

But it is doubtful whether he ever went much further than that, or whether his relative benevolence towards Naundorff lasted long. He himself evidently had several versions of how he severed relations with the Naundorffist clan. One which is repeated by various contemporaries is that at a dinner the Pretender was being excessively rude to a devoted old supporter who had sacrificed everything in his service, when Villiers stood up and said: 'Sire, I drink to Your Majesty. Your claims are decidedly beyond dispute. You have the ingratitude of a king!'[11] A journalist gave another reason:

'What made him part company with his "sovereign" was the annoyance of seeing the King playing bowls in his shirtsleeves in suburban café gardens.'[12] Henry Roujon produces yet another account: 'One day he broke with him and expressed himself about the prince. Why? Certain chance remarks he made indicate that Naundorff's incompetence in literature had positively nauseated him.'[13] All these more or less implausible anecdotes emanating from Villiers himself may well mask a more prosaic truth: that he became disillusioned both with the whole Naundorff story and with the mediocrity of the people who professed to believe in it.

One thing which does come across strongly is the idea that monarchs are necessarily ungrateful, and that is a theme typical of Villiers and his family. In one of the manuscript fragments on Naundorff, his resentment against Chambord's failure to take decisive action bursts out with surprising force:

Trying to be prudent, cunning, sagacious, conciliatory, and patient costs fifty-three years of exile and a lugubrious death, with the cry: 'I am the most wretched of men, with fifty millions and a whole organized party waiting for us.' I fail to see what is so 'practical' about that, and, if I as a Christian must recognize the will of God in this death, I recognize also that that will did not do much to protect the man whom it had thus tried, annulled, stricken, along with all those (whether or not they sneer) who believed in him.[14]

One may infer that, if Villiers had been in Henri V's place, he would have acted with all the boldness of a Sergius. The death of Chambord and now the disaffection with Naundorff seemed to have dealt a death blow to Villiers's royalism, and it was probably not long after this that he composed a long political dialogue under the title *Entre l'ancien et le nouveau*.[15] In this, an Orleanist Chevalier and an irreconcilably legitimist Duc debate their duty as monarchists. At first Villiers patently favours the Duc, with his sombre and noble sentiments, whereas the Chevalier is presented as a rather shallow opportunist. But, as the dialogue progresses, the Chevalier's arguments become more pressing and the Duc's obstinacy takes on a more egotistic quality, so that in the end, although no firm conclusion is reached, one is given the feeling that, eventually, all monarchists will have to overcome their scruples and rally to the Orleanist cause. That is presumably what Villiers himself did, though not without reluctance and distaste, simply in order to preserve for himself some possibility of meaningful political action.

Some of his contacts with the Naundorffists extended beyond the brief period of his personal involvement. Benjamin Daymonaz, whose patronage he had sought in 1882, was a passionate believer in the survival of Louis XVII and the author of numerous pamphlets on Naundorff. Another prominent supporter of Naundorff was the Marquis de Meckenheim, who became equerry to 'Charles XI' in 1884 and who was probably responsible for taking Villiers in hand as a potential recruit: he remained in touch with Villiers for several years and also acted as intermediary with his father. The latter's devotion to Naundorff knew no bounds:

According to recent revelations our great monarch is going to arrive with God's help, and it is doubly fortunate for human means are insufficient; I have then a very clear prophecy announcing the imminence of our happy future, which in 1836 was announced in Caen before the elite of that city by a cataleptic woman.—The ambassador of our king, de Meckenheim, left me yesterday to go and rejoin him, the king will appoint you his foreign minister and probably, president of his senate; he sends you his affectionate greetings.[16]

Among those whom Villiers frequented in the entourage of Naundorff, one stands out for the importance of the place he came to occupy in the poet's existence. This was Léon Bloy. Born in Périgueux in 1846, he had come to Paris to study as an artist, and in 1869 had been converted by Barbey d'Aurevilly. Thereafter, a series of mystical experiences provoked by and shared with Anne-Marie Roulé, a prostitute with whom he lived and who eventually went mad, had turned him into a religious writer of heterodox opinions and almost unexampled violence. The unrestrained virulence of his polemical writings and the lurid colouring of his style had made him extremely unpopular with editors and publishers alike, and, with his quarrelsome pugnacity and his touchy susceptibility, he alienated many of his potential sympathizers, so that, like Villiers, he lived in great poverty. Their paths had probably first crossed in the late 1870s, either at the Sherry Cobbler in the Boulevard Saint-Michel or at Nina de Villard's, where he was an occasional visitor, but it was not until about 1884 that the two men began to see one another regularly.[17]

It was probably at the famous cabaret Le Chat Noir that they came closer together, drawn by their shared mischance in literary matters, a hatred of the modern world and its pundits, and a certain community of interest in religion and politics. But Bloy's vigilant defence of orthodoxy (despite his own aberrations) and Villiers's idiosyncratic mixture of a simple and naïve feeling for Christianity, reminiscences of Hegelian idealism and leanings towards occultism were from the outset destined to cause friction, and, even in their muttered discussions at Le Chat Noir, there were occasional explosions. Georges Fragerolle, one of the singers there, remembered overhearing Bloy pompously telling Villiers that he had gone into the Trinité Church to say a dominical orison and an angelic salutation, at which Villiers commented: 'Couldn't you just say a *Pater* and an *Ave?*'[18] It was evidently Villiers who introduced Bloy to Meckenheim, and Bloy was fired with enthusiasm for the Naundorff cause, which fitted in with his mystical ideas on the rejection of the Lord's Anointed—indeed, he remained throughout his life a committed believer, had Meckenheim as a witness at his wedding in 1890, and wrote a book on the subject in 1900.

Not very long after they started to frequent each other, Bloy published his first book, *Christophe Colomb révélateur du Globe*, and inscribed on Villiers's copy: 'To my friend Villiers de l'Isle-Adam, in memory of our lost virginity.'[19] The virginity in question was literary, but, having lost it, Bloy was eager to go further, and Villiers soon found himself associated with his artistic enterprises, notably with *Le Pal*, a vitriolic satirical weekly that Bloy started in 1885. Bloy used one of Villiers's anecdotes in the second number, with due acknowledgement, and Villiers tried to publicize the paper and offered advice on its design.[20] Though the libellous nature of its contents doomed it to an early demise, it was only one of many schemes in which Bloy and Villiers pooled their resources to try to alleviate their desperate financial situation, and for a number of years the energetic and domineering Bloy was to push his friend into a number of more or less well-advised undertakings. At the same time, as was his wont, he was to keep a suspicious eye on Villiers's religious views, constantly and importunately chiding him for everything which he regarded as a deviation from the strictest obedience to the Church. Much of what Villiers wrote about Christianity in the latter years of his life seems designed to appease the wrath of his irascible friend—including the vehement declaration of faith at the end of *Les Expériences du docteur Crookes*, which in the 1884 *Figaro* text was prefaced by the words: 'Set your mind at rest,' almost certainly a direct address to Bloy.

The new friendship with Bloy came at the same time as Villiers's relations with Mallarmé were cemented by Mallarmé's association with Méry Laurent. For some time past, and especially since the death of their son Anatole in 1879, Marie Mallarmé had been an increasingly gloomy and austere companion for her husband, and he had come to take more and more pleasure in the company of Méry Laurent, once a nude dancer at the Châtelet, then an obscure actress, next model and mistress to Manet, and now, after an affair with Coppée, the official protégée of Dr Thomas W. Evans, a rich American dentist who had been responsible for spiriting Napoleon III out of France after the fall of the Empire. Méry was a woman of great beauty, with magnificent auburn hair; she was also cultivated, kindly, charming, and cheerful, and she brought into Mallarmé's life a light and a warmth that it had previously lacked. The exact nature of their relationship is not clear; it is no doubt best described as an amorous friendship. For Villiers, Méry soon became a tutelary deity, after Judith Gautier and Nina de Villard the third of the three women whose protective kindness meant so much to him. In March 1884 he wrote to her to make the first of many requests to which she always responded with generosity and understanding: 'To think that if, in your capacity as an angel, you would only wiggle the end of your little finger, you would quite simply force—in spite of the foolishness and injustice of possible objections—the inheritance of the post of dramatic critic on *La Patrie* to fall into my capable and legitimate hands . . .'[21] If on this occasion the request came too late for Méry to help, Villiers was rarely to turn to her in vain.

Villiers may have been unsuccessful in his desire to become Coppée's successor on *La Patrie*, but his reputation was now sufficiently well-established for him to open doors in papers other than *Le Figaro*. *La Liberté*, for instance, which had been closed to him since the unhappy experiment with *Azraël* in 1869, now welcomed him back with *Lysiane d'Aubelleyne*, on 8 August 1884.[22] The story had been announced a couple of days earlier in flattering terms: 'The renown which M. de Villiers de l'Isle-Adam has won for himself as a thinker and a man of letters, by his drama *Le Nouveau-Monde* and his *Contes cruels* as well as by his profoundly gripping articles in *Le Figaro*, dispenses us from giving any introduction to this eminent writer.' The tale itself had matured over a period of years[23] and is presented as a memory of the ball Villiers had attended at the Foreign Ministry in 1868. It tells of an encounter there with a startlingly beautiful girl who begged Villiers to meet her in a church the next day; when he went, he realized that she was taking the veil and that her presence at the ball had been a farewell to the world, imposed on her by the order she was joining. It is one of Villiers's most hauntingly beautiful evocations of spiritual love, and he was rightly proud of it. In total contrast was *L'Agence du Chandelier d'or*, a rather tasteless satire on the new law legalizing divorce, which he gave to *Gil Blas* only ten days later on 18 August. *Gil Blas*, founded in 1879, was the most Parisian of papers, famous for its witty articles and its slightly *risqué* short stories, and Villiers was obviously, if rather clumsily, trying to adapt his manner to what he thought the readers would expect.

Though for the time being neither *La Liberté* nor *Gil Blas* followed up these single publications, the fact that Villiers could make fairly regular contributions to *Le Figaro* and also get his prose accepted by two other major dailies shows that his situation had changed radically and that he was no longer beyond the pale for serious editors. Indeed, he was in demand for anthologies. Catulle Mendès persuaded him to supply three tales for a series of volumes entitled *Le Nouveau Décameron* which he was editing for the publisher Dentu, and Villiers was able to sell another to Ed. Monnier for publication in a selection of *Contes du Figaro*.[24] Also in 1884 came an abortive attempt to have *L'Ève nouvelle* published in Belgium by Albert Lacroix,[25] and a little later an offer of part of *Axël* to Charles Buet, who was running a little review called *La Minerve*. But, because Buet was dilatory about inserting it, Villiers reclaimed it in March 1885, saying that he had found another opening for what, with totally false modesty, he called 'this *very ordinary work*'.[26] Years before Villiers had averred to Mendès that what stopped him writing more was not lack of desire, but the impossibility of getting things published.[27] But by 1884 this was no longer true, and his literary activity became ever more hectic from then on.

29

Growing fame had not enabled Villiers to lead a more settled life than before, and between 1882 and 1885 he was obliged to move at least eight times—it was rare for him to remain even as long as six months in the same place, since, when the rent fell due, he usually had no alternative but to decamp. His father's situation was, if anything, worse: he had no fewer than nine different known addresses in little more than two years. Villiers was at his wits' end to know how to deal with the aged Marquis, whom senility was making even more unbearable. At one time he seems to have tried to have him certified, at which the old man was loud in his indignation:

Recognize now that providence watches over true and Christian hearts; today I know about your desires unworthy of a decent man and your horrible intentions and infamous tricks invented to satisfy them and that it is only providence that saved me from the dangers that your wicked ways made me run with the intention of having me suffer the cruellest of deaths; so, in future, do not bother to take so much trouble to prepare traps for my good faith; never again will I go to any of the perfidious meetings you arrange, but, thinking it over, taking everything into consideration, to have a quiet and Christian death I have to tell the supreme authority about your unworthy and perfidious plans and tricks so that, if you do manage to catch me by surprise and have me locked up, I can get out at the first request from my friends who are going to watch over me.[1]

This was in March 1884; in November of the same year, the Marquis was accusing his son of having taken out a writ against Louise (this was no doubt the charge of captation mentioned by Calmettes).[2]

But, although the Marquis was constantly complaining that Villiers had been rude to Louise, that he had insulted her, that she was a rich woman who would give him money to found a newspaper if he was nice to her, that she was devoted to them both, he also talked from time to time about the possibility of a rich marriage, just as his son had once done. In June 1884 it was with a woman who had in Paris 'a house worth two millions, and fifteen hundred thousand francs in *money*, with a castle, etc., etc.'[3] In July it was with 'an honourable and very rich baroness who is creating a dowry of two hundred thousand francs for me and is leaving me all her great fortune if she dies before me'.[4] In March 1885 it was 'a widow from Tours, Mme la Comtesse de St. Paul, née de Passy, she has an income of about one hundred and twenty thousand francs and her own house'.[5] Interspersed with these matrimonial delusions were equally crazy fancies about what his 'business' deals were going to bring him—sometimes it was vast sums on commissions, sometimes tangled inheritances of up to two million francs, sometimes immense riches from concessions in Peru, Bolivia, and Araucania (the Marquis was a friend of Aquilès I, who had 'succeeded' Orélie-Antoine I).

The harsh reality was very different. Almost every letter contains desperate requests for a few francs to tide him over, and in a moment of lucidity he described himself as 'absolutely stony broke, without a tosser'.[6] Police reports confirm the sad truth. Incredible as it may seem, the Marquis was officially director of a little paper called *Paris-Plaisirs*, from which he drew 100 francs a month; Villiers was paying his rent, and a few of his noble friends occasionally helped out. The room in which he was living at one time was, according to the police, 'not furnished, and contains only a mattress to serve as a bed, a table, and two chairs'.[7] Otherwise he was totally without resources. To make matters worse, he had discovered Villiers's liaison with Marie Dantine and was full of scathing sarcasm about 'your fine washerwoman'.[8] One can only conclude that Villiers was being exceptionally restrained when he told Bloy 'that *I have a father* whose sudden irruptions into my life are so unexpected and surprising that they can and must explain even that about me which is inexplicable'.[9]

But such distractions were not enough to take Villiers's mind off his main interests, which were now centred on the publication of both *Axël* and *L'Ève future*. The real reason why he had recovered *Axël* from Buet was that he had found a more lucrative outlet for it in the newly-founded *Revue contemporaine*, where the director Adrien Remacle had expressed willingness to publish it. Remacle himself relates the story of what then happened between himself, his assistant the Swiss novelist Édouard Rod, and Villiers. Having had no news of the work for some time, Remacle one day asked: 'Well, Villiers, isn't it about time you stopped your infinite corrections when your style is already so pure? When are you going to bring me your *Axël*?' Villiers replied: 'But, my friend, I've already brought it . . .' To Remacle's expression of astonishment, he explained:

'In your absence, Rod considerately said to me something like: "Oh, Villiers, you know, your *Axëls* . . .": so, you understand, without getting on my high horse as an insulted genius, I answered him, with the gravity necessary and adequate to the situation, docile, worried even about the value of my work, henceforth uncertain: "Ah! do you think so, Rod? . . . Alas! you are probably right." And I took it to Émile Michelet for his review.'[10]

Remacle was furious, but it was too late: Villiers had offered *Axël* to *La Jeune France*, a review of some standing which had been appearing since 1878. The editor was in fact Paul Demeny; Victor-Émile Michelet was only assistant editor, as was Rodolphe Darzens, and it seems to have been Darzens who was responsible for securing *Axël* for the review. This can be inferred from the letter Villiers wrote him on 12 October: 'If M. Demeny wants to publish *Axël*, all he has to do is let me know that he accepts the conditions on which we have agreed (. . .) We have said five issues with one folio of sixteen pages per issue; agreed: I've calculated very precisely and it perhaps won't quite fill the fifth folio.'[11] The next day, advised no doubt by Darzens, Villiers set out his conditions in a very official letter to Demeny: *Axël*, a work 'still in manuscript and representing years of labour', will occupy sixteen pages of five numbers of the review, at 100 francs per number—'but if that sum seems to you to exceed what you can afford on *La Jeune France*, let us forget the whole thing. I am only offering you *Axël* at that price out of friendship for your review and its readers.'[12] The next day Demeny accepted with alacrity: 'I am very honoured that you should wish to give *La Jeune France* this masterpiece called *Axël*, which I shall be proud to publish.'[13] On the eighteenth Villiers wrote again: 'I accept entirely the conditions governing the publication of *Axël* in *La Jeune France*. I have given the text to Darzens and I am at once going to see about the question of publicity in the papers, which seems to me essential in our common interest.'[14]

At the same time Darzens, who had clearly taken it upon himself to act as Villiers's business manager, opened negotiations for the publication of *Axël* in book form with Léon Vanier, well known as the publisher of the Decadent poets. On 26 October Darzens wrote to Vanier: '*La Jeune France* will be coming out on 1 November. So, if you like the idea of the *Axël* deal, go to the Alcan Lévi printing works and ask for M. Bloch, the manager, to whom I've spoken about it.'[15] Vanier however hesitated, and Stéphane Mallarmé then entered the scene to execute a stratagem he had devised with Darzens. On 11 November Mallarmé paid a call on Vanier and congratulated him on having acquired the work, 'pretending to believe that he had already bought the rights to *Axël*', and emphasizing 'how advantageous it would be for his firm to be selling a major work by Villiers'.[16] But in the end Vanier decided against it, and the book project was temporarily shelved.

That did not affect the serialization in *La Jeune France*, which duly began in the November number, and, each time Villiers had a section of the text ready, Darzens would go along and collect it from his lodgings in the rue de Maubeuge, handing over the eagerly awaited 100 francs.[17] But if Demeny had taken Villiers at his word when they had discussed the length and timing of *Axël* in *La Jeune France*, he had been very rash: the poet's inveterate habit of correcting and expanding what he wrote was never more in evidence than when it came to what he had always regarded as his life's work. Michelet has graphically described what happened when he accompanied Villiers to the printer's to check the proof corrections:

We would arrive at the printing works, where the bundles would be waiting for us on the imposing stone. The proofs were covered with a new text. Often, a whole page had been changed on proof. No sooner had I checked to see whether the author's corrections, with their clear writing covering the first proof, had all been carried out, than Villiers would seize the page, cross things out, start writing, speaking aloud the beautiful phrases as he improvized them there and then, reciting, miming, and living that extraordinary drama. And the maker-up, the male compositors, the female compositors, as sombre in their black smocks as Sara de Maupers, would stop digging around in their boxes to look at this strange character who was uttering words that were incomprehensible but as captivating as an incantation. And when Villiers stopped for a moment, one could have heard a fly in the workshop full of the greasy smell of ink.[18]

In the meantime, *L'Ève future* was also nearing fruition. On 1 February 1885 there appeared the first number of a new daily paper entitled *Le Succès*, run by Emmanuel Arène, in which were to appear several tales and articles by Villiers. From 30 May to 2 June *Le Succès* announced, in the most flattering terms, that it was going to publish *L'Ève future*: 'The fields covered by this vast and powerful conception, the ideas it contains, expressed in a masterly style, are of such an extraordinary nature that we want to leave them to surprise the readers.' But on the fourth the paper informed its readers that, because of the author's delays, it had decided not to publish the novel. These delays may have been due to Villiers's usual last-minute corrections; they may also have been a pretext to hide the fact that he had received a more profitable offer. At all events, he very soon after sold all his rights in the work to one Lèbre (Gustave or Albert—it is not clear whether they were two brothers or a single person), both for a serial publication in the illustrated weekly *La Vie moderne*, of which Lèbre was editor, and for a subsequent edition in book form. He received 600 francs for the serialization and an advance of 250 francs for the edition.[19]

But these arrangements were already second best. In April 1885 Villiers had been counting on having the novel serialized in the *Gil Blas* and then published by Monnier,[20] for whom his friend Gustave de Malherbe was working after leaving the Civil Service. Evidently these arrangements had fallen through, with the result that Villiers, in order to earn some ready cash, had been obliged to hand over the whole operation to Lèbre. Monnier, pushed by Malherbe, agreed to the new plans, and publication duly got under way in *La Vie moderne* on 18 July 1885. However, as with *Axël*, Villiers had no intention of allowing *L'Ève future* to appear in anything less than a perfect state, and from time to time the readers of *La Vie moderne* were obliged to contain their impatience while the author pondered over his latest alterations. There was even a five-week gap between 10 October and 21 November, only partly filled by an article by Bloy which Villiers succeeded in foisting on Lèbre.

With the two most ambitious works he had ever written both being serialized in the latter months of 1885, one might have thought that Villiers would have had enough to keep himself more than fully occupied. But financial necessity was so pressing that he also started negotiating for the publication of another volume of short stories. Back in 1884 he had briefly entertained the idea of an enlarged edition of *Contes cruels*,[21] and had soon realized that it would make more sense to wait until he had accumulated enough new tales to make an entirely separate collection. So, at about the same time as he was negotiating over *L'Ève future*, he also offered a volume of tales to Monnier. Terms must have been agreed during the summer, and in September Maurice de Brunhoff, who had just taken over the firm from Monnier, had in his hands the manuscript of most of the stories, though others promised were still outstanding.[22] If he had known Villiers better, he would have realized that was only half the battle. The extra tales had to be written, the title of the volume had to be decided,[23] the final choice of stories had to be fixed, the proofs had to be corrected, and Villiers, with all his other harassments, was in no hurry to get on with it. Thus 1885 came and went with the new collection still pending.

Indeed, that year was a particularly fertile one for new short pieces, in part because a number of recently founded publications were eager to have Villiers among their contributors. *Le Succès* was not only interested in *L'Ève future*: between May and November it published a short story entitled *Une profession nouvelle*, again satirizing the divorce laws; *L'Instant de Dieu*, in which Villiers's obsession with the guillotine leads him to suggest that priests should be allowed to give absolution to a severed head (this curious notion is dedicated to no less a person than the Pope); *Le Sadisme anglais*, a strange association of Swinburne's poetry with the scandal of child prostitution unearthed by the *Pall Mall Gazette*; another brief article on the guillotine, and the reproduction of an encomium of Augusta Holmès already published in *La Vie moderne*. Then there was *La Journée*, another new paper to which he contributed five stories and articles between November 1885 and January 1886. For the *Revue wagnérienne* which the young poet Édouard Dujardin had just established to spread the Wagnerian gospel among French men of letters, he was under special pressure because of his long-standing and well-known enthusiasm for the composer. Dujardin tried to get him to produce something for the first number but failed. In the end Villiers bethought himself of something he had published in 1876 at the time of the opening of the Bayreuth theatre, under the title *A propos des fêtes de Bayreuth*. Villiers had of course at the time been longing to go to Bayreuth, but shortage of funds forced him to give up the idea; a friend saw him break down in tears, so bitter was his disappointment.[24] In compensation, he had penned a fantasy in which he imagined Wagner's triumph over his detractors and persecutors, and it was this which he proposed to resurrect for Dujardin. But being unable to rediscover the original text, he rewrote it completely from memory, and it appeared as *La Légende moderne*.[25]

As for the *Revue contemporaine*, where the débâcle over *Axël* took place, Remacle was particularly anxious to have something substantial by Villiers, and begged him to write a novel, although the poet was thought to have prejudices against the genre. Villiers's response was favourable:

Well, I promise you this: I'll write a half-volume for the *Contemporaine*, not a volume, and I think it will produce a certain effect (. . .)

You see, I'm haunted by a vision . . . Why? For some time past, a vanished ancient city, Benares, has been presenting itself, urgent and demanding, like a unique and flamboyant character from the past, a living mirage. In spite of myself, I could take a photograph of that city which has risen up inside me, without any reason of previous reading or dreams, with its palaces, street scenes, shops, fully-armed royal processions and their elephants. And, do you hear, I'll give you Benares as it was, I'm certain of it, not a learned reconstitution like *Salammbô*. It will produce a certain *effect*.

Remacle not only accepted but even agreed to give Villiers regular subsidies so as to enable him to concentrate on this longer work. But Villiers took so long that in the end Remacle had to tell him the money was running out. Hurt and offended, Villiers gave him a reproachful look and said: 'I am a man of letters, Remacle . . . What you can afford or nothing at all.'[26]

The product of this lengthy preparation was *Akëdysséril*, which appeared in the *Revue contemporaine* on 25 July 1885. It is a prolix and pretentious piece, in the vein of *L'Annonciateur* (otherwise *Azraël*), in which Villiers has transposed a variation on the Wagnerian idea of the *Liebestod* into an elaborately described Indian setting. The theme itself elsewhere appears as one of his richest, notably in *Axël*, but in *Akëdysséril* he completely swamps it in a deluge of verbiage, so that most modern critics have been more keenly aware of its defects than its qualities. Yet Villiers's contemporaries were absolutely dazzled by it. Édouard Dujardin, to whom Villiers had read it before publication, wrote to him ecstatically about this 'marvel of marvels, as beautiful as a vision'[27] and extolled it in the *Revue wagnérienne*;[28] the young critic Camille Mauclair declared that 'the first fifty pages of *Akëdysséril* surpass anything Flaubert wrote';[29] Paul Valéry preferred to *Salammbô* this tale 'of an entirely free and fabulous antiquity';[30] Maurice Barrès too put Villiers 'above Flaubert in a piece like *Akëdysséril*';[31] Léon Bloy affirmed that it was 'one of the most *beautiful* and grandly beautiful things in this century';[22] Stéphane Mallarmé wrote: 'What resplendence in *Akëdysséril*: I know of nothing so fine and wish to read no more after that';[33] Maurice Maeterlinck found in it 'the most brilliant, the most sonorous French prose that has been written since Bossuet's *Oraisons funèbres* and the great pages of Chateaubriand'.[34] So, whatever later readers may think, the men of Villiers's time were unanimous: *Akëdysséril* was a masterpiece.

What with the incessant pestering from the Marquis and the intense fit of creativity that went on throughout 1885, one might think that Villiers would have had little time for leisure, but it was not so. He was still seen at Mallarmé's *mardis*, in publishers' offices, and in all his usual cafés and beer-houses. Fifty years later the writer Jean Ajalbert remembered leaving a dinner given by Dujardin with Villiers and going on to Pousset's at midnight. 'He was shivering in a thin overcoat, which hung open, clutching it round his throat, the wind blowing at it on his thin shoulders, like cast-off clothing on a dummy, a scarecrow.' But he walked quickly on, talking away, gesticulating, stopping every now and then under a gas-lamp, until they arrived at the café, where the assembled poets rose respectfully to greet him. 'Already, the atmosphere having been established in the faith of his young audience, he was speaking like an oracle, vaticinating, hovering far above the earth with which he had lost touch . . . Where was he taking us? . . . One cannot say . . . so immense, and as fleeting as a cloud.'[35] Ephraïm Mikhaël, who was present on such occasions, similarly recalled to a friend 'Villiers's conversations, the ones he used to have, the evenings when at Pousset's he would tell us so many confused, incoherent, and splendid stories. You remember? It didn't mean anything and it opened up whole worlds to us.'[36]

Because of *Axël* in *La Jeune France*, Villiers was naturally seeing a lot of Darzens and Michelet, but not all their activities were literary. Villiers was still proud of his sporting prowess, in both boxing and fencing, and his two young friends used to allow him to challenge them. Michelet noted that he was no longer anywhere near to being in training: 'Rodolphe Darzens and I several times gave him the pleasure of beating us, with the foil or with his fists, when in fact, being at that time on the top of our form, we would only have had to raise our game to make it almost impossible for him to touch us.' On the other hand, he had retained his old skill as a marksman, and, when he went to a shooting-gallery with

Michelet, he was capable of returning excellent scores. Sometimes, too, if Michelet called on him to take him to the printing-works, he would play the piano to him (in his latter years, he had somehow acquired a battered Paepe grand), and Michelet said that no one ever made him understand so well certain sections of *Lohengrin*. His voice by now was cracked and faded, but, when he was singing or declaiming, it was still capable of taking on an extraordinary, incantatory sonority.[37]

However, it was not only among the younger generation that Villiers was spending his time in 1885. For many years, there had been hostility between him and Barbey d'Aurevilly, despite all that might have been expected to bring them together—flamboyant Romanticism, contempt for the modern world, right-wing political opinions, a militant and idiosyncratic Catholicism, a love of the dramatic gesture, and a highly-coloured, swashbuckling use of language. Barbey had denounced Villiers both as poet and dramatist, in woundingly personal terms, and Villiers had riposted vigorously, so that they had always remained apart. But some time in 1885 or 1886, Bloy brought them together, they forgot their previous enmity, and thereafter admired one another in friendship. Barbey thought sufficiently well of Villiers to recommend him to his publisher, and Villiers wrote to Barbey with expressions of warm affection.[38] Michelet records that he heard each of them speak highly of the other.[39]

Apart from Marie Dantine, women now played little part in Villiers's life. No more talk of sensational marriages; no more affairs with *demi-mondaines*: only for what passed for a home life with Marie and the two children Albert and Totor. But, for one brief moment in 1885, Villiers may have revived hopes that had been dead (or dormant) for years. On the face of it, the article on Augusta Holmès which he published in *La Vie moderne* and *Le Succès* is nothing more than a well-meaning tribute to a musician whom he had known and admired for twenty years. But when one asks oneself why he decided to publish it at that particular juncture, it perhaps takes on a more significant colouring. Ostensibly, it marks her reappointment to the jury of the Musical Competition of the City of Paris. This was not however an especially newsworthy event, as the original appointment had taken place several years before, when the intrusion of a woman into a male preserve had caused a furore. Since that time Villiers had let slip various other notable occasions to speak of her, when major symphonic works had been successfully performed. Why then should he have used a not very convincing pretext to talk about her in 1885? The answer may well lie in the fact that a few months earlier she had left Mendès, unable to stand any longer his philandering, his neglect of her, and his recklessness with her money; as Mallarmé wrote sadly to a friend: 'It was no longer charming between them.'[40] Who knows but that Villiers's old love had flared up again, and that he thought that Augusta might turn to him again now that Mendès had been rejected? Such dreams, if indeed they existed, were rapidly dashed, for it was not long before Augusta, like Élisabeth in *La Révolte*, had returned home, as incapable of living without Mendès as she was of living with him.

Even so, there were occasional moments of relaxation away from Paris. It was now some time since Villiers had lost touch with such friends and relations as he still had in Brittany, and he had not visited his native province for years. Foreign travel and longer journeys were of course out of the question, and his horizons had narrowed to Paris, especially Montmartre. One of the rare exceptions to this confinement in the capital came in the summer of 1885, when he was invited to spend a week or two in Nogent-sur-Marne.[41] This invitation came from a young writer named Émile Pierre. Little is known of Pierre: he wrote stories for the *Gil Blas*, he published one or two books, he was no richer than Villiers, and he eventually became a librarian at the Chambre des Députés. Nor is it known exactly how he came into contact with Villiers, save that by 1885 Villiers was sufficiently intimate with him to agree to write a preface for his volume of stories *Le Rêve d'aimer*—and that was not a task he did willingly, since the previous year he had declined the same service for Paul Margueritte.[42] The preface itself is unexciting, since Villiers's preoccupation with his own imaginative world made it difficult for him to penetrate into that of others, but it does show his closeness to Pierre, which continued until his death. Villiers himself describes, with some embellishment, the setting of his stay at Nogent when in *Catalina* (which was perhaps written there) he evokes

my delightful isolated villa, situated on the banks of the Marne, with its paddock, its cool garden, so shady in summer, so warm in winter,—my books of German metaphysics, my pure-toned ebony piano, my dressing-gown with its faded flowers, my comfortable slippers, my peaceful study lamp,—and that whole life of profound reveries, so dear to my reflective tastes.[43]

30

On 1 December 1885 the Marquis Joseph de Villiers de l'Isle-Adam, aged eighty-three, died at 10 rue Hermel at the far end of Montmartre. His son seems to have got rid of the dreadful Louise before the end came, but even so he cannot have regarded the old man's death as anything but a happy release. He had always had mixed feelings about his father, since, although he loved him as a person, he rightly held him responsible for the family's ruin and had been unable to refrain from telling him so. Moreover, if the Marquis had always been eccentric, his oddities had in latter years almost certainly crossed the boundary into insanity, and, while Villiers had made the most devoted and unremitting efforts to keep him alive, the Marquis's unpredictable behaviour had been a constant worry, not only because of the debts he contracted but because he was at any moment liable to bring irreparable disgrace on the family name. The obituary which Villiers wrote for the royalist satirical magazine *Le Triboulet* is thus impersonal and lacking in tenderness. It consists largely of a recital of the glorious past of the family, and its only direct allusion to the Marquis's life is more striking for what it omits than for what it says: 'Despite substantial financial losses, the Marquis de Villiers de l'Isle-Adam had never solicited a post, since the death of King Charles X.'[1]

At the time when his father died, Villiers himself was ill. As early as October his bronchitis was so bad that he was threatened with pneumonia,[2] and in December he had a relapse. This bad health was at least partly responsible for the delays in all three major publications that were under way: the volume of stories with Brunhoff, *L'Ève future* in *La Vie moderne*, and *Axël* in *La Jeune France*. But one may suppose that his uncontrollable predilection for last-minute corrections also had something to do with it. The first of these works to reach completion was *L'Ève future*, the serialization of which had begun on 18 July 1885 and was concluded on 27 March 1886, after long interruptions in October and November, in December and January, and again in February and March. Lèbre, the editor of *La Vie moderne*, had in fact shown remarkable forbearance in persevering with the novel, since at one point he had been forced to suspend publication because Villiers had disappeared without leaving an address for the proofs; when Lèbre had finally decided to go ahead without waiting for the corrections, Villiers had been so enraged that when he appeared he marched off with the manuscript. It was only when Lèbre had managed to pacify him that the end of the novel could at last appear.[3]

For the volume of tales, now entitled *L'Amour suprême*, Villiers proved equally difficult to deal with. He had begun correcting the proofs in the autumn of 1885, but had still not supplied the promised tales, and indeed could not make up his mind which they ought to be. By March 1886 Brunhoff was writing him curt notes to try to get the proofs back,[4] and by May was threatening to go ahead with the printing unless Villiers sent them by return of post.[5] At the same time he was producing a separate luxury edition of *Akëdysséril*, with a photograph of the author, a facsimile of a manuscript page, and illustrations by the Belgian artist Félicien Rops; this was all that appeared of a series planned by his predecessor Monnier on *L'Amour à travers les âges*, with texts by different contemporary celebrities. But, by the time the book was ready to come out in late July, Villiers was in such a state of dudgeon over Brunhoff's real or imagined misdeeds that he dashed off an angry letter to the press, promising litigation, protesting that three tales had been included without his authorization, that he had never seen the illustrations before now and disapproved of them, that he had never had proper proofs, that it was full of misprints, and so forth.[6] But Brunhoff must have succeeded in calming him down somehow; the edition was duly put on sale, and friendly relations were restored between the two men.

If the publication of *Axël* in *La Jeune France* was attended with fewer fireworks, that was probably only because Michelet and Darzens were there to smooth things over. Certainly Villiers was just as difficult over his interminable corrections, and on two occasions the monthly instalment failed to turn up. The first time was in December, when Villiers was ill and his father had just died: the review printed only a short note from him to say that 'a persistent indisposition' prevented him from correcting the proofs, which may well have been true. The second interruption came in May. The April number had begun the publication of the last act, but in the May number there was only a note to say that the review could not yet publish the conclusion, 'which M. Villiers de l'Isle-Adam has asked us to postpone until June in order that he may carry out important modifications'.[7]

All these delays, interruptions, changes of mind, and sudden disappearances were infuriating for editors and publishers, as well as very costly in terms of proof corrections. Sometimes the alterations were purely verbal—Villiers used to say to his friends: 'my words are weighed on scales made out of spiders' webs', and his manuscripts show that he was prepared to draft and redraft a page as many as six times until it satisfied him. But sometimes he effected more drastic changes, usually additions, as he wanted to make his thought fuller and more precise. This was especially the case with *Axël*, and the story of its publication in *La Jeune France* is instructive. The manuscript he handed in was already a composite affair: for the First Part, he had used the manuscript already presented to *La Renaissance littéraire et artistique* in 1872, with new pages containing extra developments or replacing those which were too badly worn, whereas for the rest he had taken a copy made by a professional copyist, with further pages supplied by another copyist called Arnaud[8] and, no doubt, some in his own hand. The play now had no fewer than five parts, *Le Monde religieux, Le Monde occulte* and *Le Monde passionnel* corresponding to the three parts originally envisaged in 1872, but *Le Monde tragique*, the new second section necessitated by the introduction of the Commander Gaspar (or Kaspar, as he was now called), having grown so much that it had itself been divided into two. It is difficult to know how much rewriting was done

during the actual serialization, but the evidence of the manuscripts suggests that it was only shortly before that Villiers
decided to bring in another new character, Axël's page Ukko,
whose innocent and happy love for a forester's daughter
provides a contrast with the sombre love between Axël and
Sara; his irreverent wit also lightens the tone of the scenes in
which he appears with the old retainers.

But one vital correction was certainly made at the very last
minute, and explains why the final instalment had to be
postponed. Probably since the first complete version of the
play some twelve years earlier, it had ended, after the suicide
of the lovers, with the reappearance of Maître Janus, who
contemplated the corpses pensively and exclaimed: 'Oh! free
at last!' Maintained in the meantime with only minor changes
to the stage directions, this scene had clearly indicated that
the suicide had the author's approval and that Axël and Sara
had been right to liberate themselves from the shackles of life.
This was in complete conformity with the anti-Christian
ethic in which the work had originally been conceived.
Confronted with the option of the Church, Sara had refused
as firmly as Axël had refused occultism: it was logical that
both should have carried their subjective idealism to the point
of renouncing life altogether. Villiers in 1886 was however a
very different man from Villiers in 1869, when the drama had
been first mapped out, and, in particular, he had drawn very
much closer to the Church (even if he could never wholly
throw off the taint of heterodoxy). There was of course no
way in which he could change the import of the First Part,
though he did in *La Jeune France* go to some trouble to make
the Archdeacon and the Abbess less obnoxious. On the other
hand, when the end was due to be handed to the printers, the
full enormity of its implications suddenly dawned on him.
Here he was, the man who only months before had publicly
averred that always, in all circumstances, he totally accepted
the teachings of the Church, about to publish an apology for
suicide as the culmination of a work which unmistakably
spurned the Church's authority and doctrines.

At this point Villiers halted the printing and sat down to
think. The manuscript page of the last scene with Janus bears
pathetic witness to the scruples which overcame him. The

concluding stage direction before the curtain had been: '*He stands as if sunk in a mysterious melancholy.*' To this he now added a phrase, unfinished and then crossed out: 'The great sun has risen, blazes out in the clouds and illuminates all around the . . . fills the crypt with splendid . . .' Then another scrap of paper develops the same idea further,[9] until finally Villiers abandons the scene with Janus altogether, and adds this new stage direction to the preceding scene with Axël and Sara lying dead before the treasure:

Now, the sun gilds the marble tombs and the statues: the hissing of the lamp and the candle fades out in smoke in the ray of light falling from the vent.—A gold coin drops to the ground, rolls away and strikes a sepulchre with the sound of a clock striking.—And, disturbing the silence of the terrible place where two human beings have just condemned their souls to exile from HEAVEN,—there come from outside the distant murmurs of the wind in the vastness of the forests, the wakening vibrations of space, the hum of Life.[10]

This major change displaces the whole philosophical emphasis of the play. Whereas *Axël* had previously been unequivocally dedicated to death, the last word is now one of the affirmation of life, and the author, albeit somewhat reticently, indicates that he cannot condone the last and most significant action of his hero and heroine. Whether in fact such an unexpected appendix really could alter the sense of all that had gone before is very much open to doubt: nothing prepares us for it, and it stands in open contradiction to the idea which governs the play's structure and development. One tentative, belated stage direction can scarcely counteract the magnificent eloquence of Axël's savage denunciation of life in those famous lines that have passed into general currency:

Live? The servants will do that for us (. . .) Old earth, I shall not build the palace of my dreams on your ungrateful soil: I shall carry no torch, I shall strike no enemies. May the human race, disabused of its vain delusions, its vain despairs, and all the lies that dazzle mortal eyes—refusing its consent to the sport of this grim enigma,—yes, may it finish, fleeing indifferent like us, without even bidding you farewell.[11]

But if the new ending is unsatisfying both dramatically and

ideologically, it does assuage the Christian scruples which were beginning to affect Villiers more and more deeply. It is possible that his worsening health had sharpened his desire to put his conscience at rest. Henry Roujon, who knew him so intimately, well defined his worries over his religious aberrations: 'Would he be saved? The fear of hell tormented him at times.' But on the whole he thought hell was probably reserved for the importunate wine-merchant Lorbac, a few publishers, and all theatre managers.

Nevertheless he prepared carefully for the surprises of the great interrogation. Face to face with the Eternal, he would have to talk theology, as he had with Dom Guéranger, and the Adversary would be formidable. One of our habitual jokes consisted of asking him what secret thrusts he had in reserve for the terrible duel. 'Laugh away, young mockers!' he would reply. 'You'll come to it in good time. I just hope you'll manage as well as me.' But one thing troubled him. Would the supreme discussion take place in Latin, which he did not know well, or in French, which he had spent a lifetime trying to learn? At the back of his mind, he had the idea that in Paradise people talked the language of his poems; on the other hand, Latin was the idiom of the Church. To be on the safe side, he had provided himself with a few quotations from the Fathers, rightly judging that it could do no harm.[12]

The slightly flippant tone of Roujon's account should not mask its accuracy, which was later fully confirmed by Mallarmé. In his latter days Villiers became ever more anxious to ensure that he could justify his life before God, and the manifest unease which plagued him during and after the publication of *Axël* was just one manifestation of his deep-seated anxieties.

L'Ève future too had been modified since the days of *L'Étoile française*, when so much stress had been laid on the idea of a Faustian revolt against God. This aspect of the work, in which Edison had appeared as Mephistopheles to Ewald's Faust, is consistently and deliberately attenuated in the 1885–6 text; a large number of the references to earlier versions of the Faust legend are excised, the most violent expressions of rebellion against the divine world-order are toned down, and the hitherto missing ending shows the Andréïde perishing in a shipwreck before Ewald can take up his new life with her. The revolt was ordained to fail, and the shiver of fear which runs through Edison as he contemplates the starry sky betokens his recognition of the uselessness of any attempt to break the laws of God's creation. Such an ending hardly indicates a docile acceptance of the divine will, but it does at least mean that Villiers is reluctantly attempting to curb the excesses of his fractiousness.

It is within the bounds of possibility that in bestowing on his new volume of tales the title *L'Amour suprême* and in giving that story (the one previously entitled *Lysiane d'Aubelleyne*) pride of place in it, Villiers is trying to redress the balance by setting an explicitly Christian work against two others of more than dubious orthodoxy. To the interrupted taking of the veil in *Axël*, presented as a despicable example of ecclesiastical tyranny, he opposes the taking of the veil in *L'Amour suprême*, to which Lysiane d'Aubellyne freely consents in an atmosphere of radiant spirituality unequalled elsewhere in Villiers's writings. One must remember too that constantly looking over his shoulder was Léon Bloy, fiercely condemnatory of anything he regarded as an infraction of orthodoxy. Villiers's view of faith was simple. When he found Roujon reading Haeckel's *History of Creation*, he took the book out of his hands, looked at it curiously, weighed it, exclaimed at its expense, and said: 'The catechism only costs two sous, and it contains the whole of wisdom.'[13] In his ambivalent relations with priests, he was deeply affronted if one of them, after some particularly provocative tirade, called him a heretic: to quote Roujon again; 'As he pretended to orthodoxy as strictly as any inquisitor, such a misunderstanding hurt him.'[14] And since Bloy's attitude was infinitely more inquisitorial, it was inevitable that the two of them should eye one another with mutual suspicion.

This was all the more important to Villiers as he, Bloy, and Huysmans came much closer together at about the end of 1885. Their situations were strangely similar. Villiers was living with a working woman who had borne him a son. Bloy had been living with his fiancée Berthe Dumont, but she had recently died of lockjaw, and he was temporarily sheltering with her mother. Huysmans was living with an ex-prostitute, Anna Meunier, who had a child and whose mental condition was slowly deteriorating. All were technically bachelors; all were or had been involved in liaisons with working-class women; all were more or less at war with the society of their time; all were writers unpopular with the general public and suspect to publishers; all had idiosyncratic and provocative styles. There were of course differences as well, in situation, temperament, and opinion. Alone among the three, Huysmans had a job and a regular income from outside literature, since he was a civil servant in the Ministry of the Interior and was part-owner of the ailing family bindery. Bloy was volcanically irritable; Villiers lived in his dreams and translated them in his flow of conversation; Huysmans, though endowed with an extremely kind heart, outwardly practised a corrosive cynicism. Bloy and Villiers were professing Christians, despite their disagreements and their doubtful orthodoxy; Huysmans was a sceptical agnostic but felt himself drawn by everything that was strange and abnormal on the fringes of conventional religion. By 1886 the trio had banded together to form a Council of Paupers, and in effect constituted a sort of mutual aid society, as well as an unofficial club for the vituperation of all that they hated in the modern world.

31

The years 1885 and 1886 mark a decisive turning-point in French literature. It was then that the word 'Symbolism' came into fashion to designate the large group of young writers who were resolutely turning their backs on the depiction of everyday reality as the aim of art, and seeing poetry instead as the means of penetrating and expressing that ideal world of which material things were only a shadow. One of the most brilliant generations of men of letters was now reaching maturity, and they were in no doubt as to who their masters were: Mallarmé, Verlaine, and Villiers de l'Isle-Adam with, to a lesser extent, Rimbaud, about whom little was known, and, at one remove, Baudelaire. Those who for years had been what Verlaine called 'the poets with a curse on them' had now come into their own and had been adopted as the patron saints of a movement which their example had done so much to bring into being.

It is no coincidence that at the same time Villiers's major works were at last being revealed, with the publication of *L'Ève future* and *Axël*. Villiers had now become a famous man and, though he never quite formed the centre of a group in the same way as Mallarmé did, if only because the poverty and uncertainty of his domicile prevented the formation of anything like the *mardis*, there were plenty of young men who would do their best to seek him out in the cafés of Montmartre, or go specially to Mallarmé's flat in the rue de Rome on a Tuesday if they knew he was coming, or desperately try to recruit him for their little poetry reviews. Villiers's attitude to them was on the whole one of benevolent surprise. He was naturally gratified to find himself the object of so much attention after years of neglect, but he found it slightly comic that people should look reverently up to him and call him 'Master'. Moreover, the complicated aesthetic theorizing that characterized much of the Symbolist movement held little attraction for him, with the result that a whole aspect of Symbolist thought was alien to him. Adrien Remacle recorded Villiers's reactions when one day someone spoke of him as a Symbolist:

I know the symbols of the Apostles, but all I hear is cymbals! . . . The Symbolist Honoré de Balzac etches portraits of types who symbolize a whole era, a class . . . No doubt I am a Symbolist. If I wasn't Villiers de l'Isle-Adam, one of the Parnassians, I'd call myself a Romantic-Classic. I would have been a good country priest, a little bit frightening for the geese in the fields and in the congregation. God wanted me to be a poet, for my salvation.[1]

But such refusals to allow himself to be labelled or re-gimented did not blind him to the influence he now had over the minds of young authors, and he proudly stresses it in two pieces he wrote about himself in the third person, for insertion in the press by some friendly journalist. In one of them, sent to Félicien Champsaur on 14 October 1885, he claims that 'the young literary generation and even our great men of letters' have shown 'an altogether special admiration' for him, something from which he draws legitimate consolation for the years of sacrifice:

The fact of having for more than twenty years stood up to the hardships of everyday life, to all sorts of injustice, *to the indiffer-ence of the times towards works of high ambition, and that in order to forge his work in solitude, and nothing else,* seems to me too rare a thing for one lightly to criticize *the man who managed to do it.*[2]

In the other, which is a publicity notice for *L'Amour suprême,* he writes:

It is indisputable that since the *Contes cruels* the press in France and abroad has lavished on M. Villiers de l'Isle-Adam the epithets of 'unmatched stylist' and 'writer of genius', and has presented him as a sort of goldsmith working on thoughts which are unusual, disturbing, and sometimes even terrifying. It cannot be denied that, in almost all the reviews and papers of the younger French school, he is acclaimed not only as a master but as a leader.[3]

The satisfaction of knowing that he was regarded in this way (even if, for purposes of advertisement, there is some exaggeration in what he says) did not mean that he attempted to exercise leadership in any very deliberate, much less autocratic, manner. He was more than willing to hold forth in cafés to anyone who wished to listen, or to read from his works in gestation, but his monologues were much too unpremeditated and incoherent to constitute anything like a doctrine, the more so as he frequently took no notice of what others might wish to say to him. His conversation was extraordinarily rich and stimulating, it is true, as Victor-Émile Michelet testifies:

Those who frequented him all received some princely jewel from his spiritual crown. To some he opened up their own intellectual path; to others he distributed the inexhaustible riches of his ideas. From a conversation with Villiers all creative men could benefit, whatever their speciality: writers, artists, theologians, inventors, academics, businessmen, financiers, fairground barkers, etc. For he went up and down the ladder of the mind, from prophecy to buffoonery, without ever ceasing to be himself.

But he was not very interested in the theory of literature, and such advice as he gave to other writers was largely confined, after listening to someone expounding a project, to tugging his beard and saying: 'Hum! Well, if I were you, I'd do it like this . . .'[4]

Still, the prestige he enjoyed now among the Symbolist

poets was so great that it would not be wrong to speak of disciples, even if they were following a general inspiration and not a party line. The year 1886 was particularly significant for Villiers in this respect, in that it brought to Paris a whole series of young Belgians, all eager to discover what was new on the French literary scene. It was mostly through the ex-pupils of the Lycée Condorcet, who were now associated on a review called *La Pléiade*, that the Belgians were introduced to Villiers. The most famous of them was Maurice Maeterlinck, who met him at the Brasserie Pousset early in the year and saw a lot of him during the seven months he remained in Paris. He never forgot the evenings he spent in Villiers's company:

We had the impression of being the officiants or the accomplices of some piously sacrilegious ceremony, on the other side of the sky which had suddenly been revealed to us. When the café closed, we would accompany Villiers back to his uncertain domicile, then each of us would go home: some stunned, the others unwittingly matured or regenerated by the contact with genius, as if they had been living with a giant from another world. Every night, towards one in the morning, to go back to our dreary rooms, we would cross the darkened city of Paris, bent under the regal weight of the spectacle and the thoughts with which the indefatigable magician, the never-failing visionary, had overwhelmed us.[5]

In later years Maeterlinck used to evoke his admiration for Villiers in dithyrambic terms: 'all that I have done I owe to Villiers',[6] 'of all the men I have met, not one has given me so clearly the impression of genius',[7] 'when I met Villiers, I realized what the Apostles must have felt'.[8]

Villiers's impact on Émile Verhaeren was not so dramatic, but it was nonetheless significant. Verhaeren had seen him briefly in 1883, but it was only when he began making more regular visits to Paris in 1886 that he got to know him better, chiefly at Mallarmé's *mardis*. On 24 October 1886 he wrote to a friend:

Yesterday I went to Mallarmé's in the evening. Villiers was there; all the time he was dazzling with irony and verve. There is in him a mixture of the great nobleman and the old woman. Try and reconcile that. Huysmans, Villiers, Mallarmé, and Verlaine are definitely the most interesting Parisians nowadays.[9]

Verhaeren wrote an enthusiastic article on *L'Amour suprême* in the Belgian periodical *L'Art Moderne*, and he and Villiers had a fairly extensive correspondence, most of which unfortunately has not come to light.[10] Like Maeterlinck, what Verhaeren chiefly remembered in later years was Villiers's prodigious talent as a conversationalist:

Villiers de l'Isle-Adam gave—how often!—the impression of a passing prodigy. He seemed to be absent from the place where he was, he listened politely and said nothing; then, suddenly, he would start to talk himself, like someone who has been seized by the hair, and then it was as if there was in the air the movement of some great invisible thing of which he was the spokesman. We have had the privilege of seeing him like that and of having to find ourselves again and not having succeeded very quickly, minutes after the miraculous evocator of his own being had fallen silent.[11]

Georges Rodenbach was likewise introduced to him in June 1886, by Maeterlinck and his friend Grégoire Le Roy:

We went to a café in Montmartre where they used to meet, in the evenings, around the Comte Villiers de l'Isle-Adam; the author of the splendid *Contes cruels* was already seated at the table (. . .) He told us books he planned to write, the subjects of poems, all of them bearing witness to that preoccupation with the mysterious which runs through his work.[12]

Rodenbach was so impressed that almost at once he offered to organize a lecture tour for Villiers in Belgium. After a further exchange of letters,[13] it was agreed that Villiers should visit Brussels, and perhaps other cities, in December 1886 or January 1887, but at the last minute Villiers fell ill, and the tour had to be cancelled. The idea however was not dropped completely, and was later to give Villiers one of the greatest joys of his life.

The Belgians were of course not alone among the new poets in pledging their allegiance to Villiers, and many of their French contemporaries had their first meeting with him when he turned up at one of Mallarmé's *mardis*. The atmosphere of those gatherings was particularly propitious to his readings. In 1883 he read *L'Amour suprême* there[14] and in 1884 *Le Couronnement de M. Grévy*,[15] but no precise impressions of them have survived. In 1886 or 1887, on the other hand, *La Torture par l'espérance*, one of his most successful tales, produced a profound effect. Here is how Henri de Régnier, author of many novels and poems and future Academician, remembered it:

One evening I heard him read one of his finest stories: *La Torture par l'espérance*. He read in a low, profound voice, with intonations and pauses marking his intentions and emphasizing certain words to throw them into relief. The reading was also a mime, and during it a movement of his hand kept brushing back from his forehead the lock of grey hair which fell across it.[16]

No doubt it was the same occasion that André Fontainas, another Belgian poet, recalled: 'I shall never forget that evening when, for a few of us, in his very soft, well-modulated, calm voice, admirably suited to preparing and attaining the effects he wanted, he revealed, as if with mystery, the tormenting anguish of the peripeteia of a tale he was intending to write, *La Torture par l'espérance*. Can I ever judge now the value of the written text of this tale when I read it? No: I can hear that voice with its caressing intonations, its sinister cruelty, simple, right, gripping by its tone as by its expressive force, now in the joy of certain deliverance, now in the fearful horror of the suspended denouement.'[17]

René Ghil, who already knew him, heard him recite *L'Etna chez soi*, a long fantasy about the possibility of an anarchist plot to blow up Paris: 'He mimed, indeed he was the Anarchist with his methodical gestures, taking the apparatus to pieces and quietly disappearing without trace. And in his visionary eyes, there was the domination of the unknown Ideal over day-to-day stupidity.'[18] Ghil also had other memories of Villiers at the *mardis*. Once Villiers sat beside him and, after a few moments' silence, said: 'Listen to the sound of these words: *Non possumus*! I was saying them to myself on the way here: it's what the Christians said when they were pressed to burn incense to the gods of Rome ... *Non possumus*! *You* understand that: it takes root in opposition with a weight of eternity athwart the world ... *Non possumus*!'[19] On another occasion recalled by Ghil, there was some mention of Mendès, whom the *mardistes* did not much like because of his patronizing attitude to Mallarmé and Villiers. Pushing back his lock of hair, Villiers turned to his host and said:

'By the way, Mallarmé, I've just been reading an account of the exploits of that man Carrier, representative of the people, and proconsul at Nantes. His "republican marriages" have given me an idea ... You know about them? Two people, completely naked, were tied tightly together, breast to breast, mouth to mouth, and then they were thrown into the Loire. Dreadful, isn't it? And yet, just think ... to die that death, but tied to Mendès! ...'[20]

For Villiers's epigrams made him feared as well as admired. To someone who asked him mildly if Wagner's conversation was pleasant, he replied: 'Do you imagine, sir, that the conversation of Mount Etna is pleasant?'[21] Once an impertinent journalist, meeting him in the street, said: 'Hello, Villiers, still ...?' with a gesture of the finger spiralling upwards to indicate his head in the clouds. 'And you', answered Villiers, 'still ...?' with a parallel spiralling gesture, only going downwards.[22] Of Léon Bloy, when they had fallen out, he said bitterly: 'He brings dishonour on poverty.'[23] He disliked Jean Moréas, the poet of Greek origin who had arrogated to himself the titular leadership of the Symbolists and who had a noisy talent for self-advertisement, so, when Moréas fought a duel with Darzens, which ended with Moréas seizing Darzens's rapier with his left hand, Villiers was quick to express his contempt. Playing on the fact that Moréas's seconds had almost the same names as two well-known murderers, he said: 'One can understand that that sinister Greek poet should have chosen two sinister seconds. They too fought against an adversary they had previously disarmed. That's normal. But at least they weren't left-handed.'[24] Villiers had a particular trick for dealing with an importunate or insolent interlocutor. He would stare at him hard, with great and obvious attention, blinking repeatedly, stretching his head forward, and then he would say in a tone of discouragement: 'It's no use, I can't see you!'[25]

But while all that he had suffered had sharpened his sarcastic wit, Villiers was basically a kindly man, and one much more often finds him helping his friends, especially to get their works published. In 1885 he tried to persuade Brunhoff to take a novel by Marras.[26] A year later he was recommending Émile Pierre's *A plaisir!* to Savine and to the *Gil Blas*.[27] In 1887 he was writing warm references for Darzens to Gustave de Malherbe.[28] At the time

of the foundation of *Le Succès*, he did his best to get the
paper to accept articles by Huysmans and Bloy.[29] When
Meckenheim was trying to find somewhere to board out a
four-year-old child, he immediately suggested Bloy, who at
that point was living at Fontenay-aux-Roses with the mother
of his late fiancée.[30] When Michelet complained that Henry
La Luberne had plagiarized one of Villiers's stories, Villiers's
answer was characteristically generous: he explained that La
Luberne was an old friend who had talked to him about a
story he was planning and that he had advised La Luberne to
handle it differently: 'So all is for the best, and I would look
like someone taking back what he has *given* away, if I
complained about it.—Anyway, I'm delighted that he has
written it, because it was too difficult for me: it would have
taken me at least three weeks' work to draft it.'[31]

In the meantime Villiers had set about the task of getting
Axël and *L'Ève future* published in book form. With the
novel, it was comparatively simple, and Brunhoff had it in
print in May 1886, within six weeks of the end of the
serialization in *La Vie moderne*. But he had no intention of
allowing his cherished *Axël* to appear without subjecting it to
yet another wholesale revision. On 14 August 1886 he signed
a contract with the firm of Quantin, for whom Gustave de
Malherbe now worked: the agreement was that the book
would be published by the end of the following February and
that he would be paid 500 francs on handing over the
completed manuscript.[32] With deceptive speed, he delivered
the printed text of *La Jeune France*, with only minor corrections, in three bundles, the last of which arrived at the
printer's on 16 October. But this was only a device to enable
him to take possession of the advance: once he had the
money, he settled down to making all the major corrections
he wanted on the proofs. Quantin had produced the galleys
by early November, and Villiers began his delaying tactics,
asking for page proof after page proof, and requesting
postponements because he wanted a new scene, with Axël
lengthily arguing with the Commander over his right to keep
silent about the hidden treasure, to appear in a review before
it was published in the book. Since it was only in April 1887
that Dujardin's *Revue indépendante* eventually printed the

scene, under the title *Le Droit au silence*, the printer was becoming increasingly impatient, and it seems to have been agreed that a temporary suspension of the printing was in everyone's interest, if only because the unpredictable stops and starts were causing chaos in the printing-works. In the event, the interruption was to last eleven months.[33]

Part of the trouble was that Villiers's health was in danger of breaking down completely. In September 1886 Mallarmé had wanted him to come and stay in the little house he rented at Valvins, on the banks of the Seine near Fontainebleau, but Villiers had to refuse because his bronchitis was so bad that nothing would cure his cough.[34] On 16 October, when Huysmans called on him, he found him in bed, still with bronchitis. In January 1887 he was no better, and Huysmans wrote anxiously to his Dutch friend Arij Prins: 'Saw Villiers who worries me. He is still ill in bed, can't seem to get over it. The doctor, whom I saw, says he has no particular illness but that he is completely worn out, an old man years before his time—and he *has* turned into an old man in the last month or two.'[35] Bloy was equally concerned by his condition. Late in September 1886 he told Louis Montchal, a Swiss friend and benefactor, that he and Huysmans had found Villiers in bed, 'only just getting over an illness brought on by poverty and which nearly killed him'.[36] In December he thought him even worse: 'I see my very dear friend Villiers in danger of *death*. At least, that's my impression. I see him ill in a way that terrifies me.'[37]

One wonders how it was possible for a man so ill and so weakened by years of abject penury to be so productive, so lively, and so full of exuberance. Yet his mental and creative powers were not merely undimmed, they seemed to be flourishing more than ever in 1886. Not only did he complete the publication of *Axël*, *L'Ève future*, and *L'Amour suprême*, he produced a little collection of one-line humorous poems for *Le Chat noir*, the house magazine of the famous cabaret, he exhumed and rewrote *L'Évasion* for the *Revue contemporaine*, he published several short stories in different reviews and papers, and, in response to a request from Dujardin, now directing the *Revue indépendante*, he started to put down on paper *L'Etna chez soi*, the fantasy about anarchist bomb outrages that he had read out at one of Mallarmé's *mardis*. This latter enterprise nearly landed him in serious trouble. He took great pains to document himself on explosives, with the help of Huysmans,[38] whose duties at the Ministry of the Interior included the surveillance of anarchist groups, and the text eventually included a lot of details (in fact extremely boring) about the manufacture of bombs. The result pleased him greatly—'no piece of sensational news, no promotion, no advertising stunt (you'll see) can be compared to this', 'I make so bold as to count on some attention from the public this time, for *everything* is there, even if it doesn't appear'.[39] But the attention, when it came, was in the form of a visit from a police inspector who wanted to know why the *Revue* was proposing to disseminate recipes for explosives. It took Dujardin some time to convince him that the whole thing was an elaborate joke.[40]

Then there was a fresh rush of inspiration about Tribulat Bonhomet, the grotesque and sinister doctor who had first made his appearance in *Claire Lenoir* back in 1867. Though Villiers had not published anything more about him in the meantime, he had never ceased to think about him and talk about him, and he was famous among the writer's friends for all the anecdotes built around him, the sayings attributed to him, the different occupations and incarnations in which he manifested himself. These ran from Bonhomet vivisectionist ('it is a pity I was not alive when torture was allowed, since, while serving the Law, I would have advanced the cause of Science'),[41] to Bonhomet doctor (telling an injured man's wife that he would amputate his leg, even though it would not stop him dying—'one has to keep the patient happy somehow!'),[42] Bonhomet general (exhorting his troops to valiance and frightening them so much that they all panic and flee),[43] Bonhomet ermine hunter (hearing that the immaculate animals die if there is a stain on their whiteness, he goes after them with a gun loaded with ink),[44] Bonhomet composer (*The Worm*, brilliant variations for piano; *The Strappado*, fantasy for piccolo; *The Auto-da-Fé*, capriccio for piano),[45] and Bonhomet dying (arriving at the Judgement Seat, and being warned that he is to appear before God, he says: 'God? God? I'm sorry, but I have a terrible memory for names . . .').[46]

In 1886 Villiers at last started to develop some of these ideas on paper, and had *Le Banquet des Éventualistes* published in *La Journée* on 21 June, followed on 26 June by *Le Tueur de cygnes* in *Le Chat noir*—this latter story of Bonhomet strangling swans to hear their last song, a mordant satire on the bourgeois attitude to artists, is one of Villiers's finest achievements. The next month he offered a whole collection of Bonhomet stories to the publisher P.-V. Stock, who accepted with alacrity and gave him an advance of 200 francs.[47] Stock kept a clear picture of Villiers's appearance.

Villiers had fine-drawn features; his face was broad at the top and narrow at the base; he carried himself with pride and distinction; his moustache was turned up at the ends; his quite thick little beard came to a point in the style called an imperial; his long wavy hair hung down to his shoulders; he made me think of Dumas *père*'s famous Aramis. Unfortunately he lacked the magnificence of the musketeer's uniform. His modern dress was nearly always very shabby: a black suit in which he seemed awkward and ill at ease, the over-large tail-coat emphasizing the thinness of his frame. When he had removed his flat-brimmed top-hat, a frequently repeated toss of the head would throw back a recalcitrant lock of hair that kept falling in his eyes; if several locks refused to stay in place, his delicate white hand would push them back with an automatic gesture of elegant nonchalance. His very light blue eyes often had a distant look, a cigarette was eternally in his fingers; silent at first, he would suddenly become excited and then his volubility would take over the conversation as he recited and acted his tales, or, very brilliant talker as he was, related fantastic anecdotes.[48]

The small advances which Villiers received on longer works and the fees paid to him for short stories represented a much more stable income than he had enjoyed for years, particularly as he was writing with such fluency. They were nevertheless far from adequate to keep himself, Marie, Albert, and Totor fed, clothed, and housed, and Villiers was obliged to have recourse to other devices to earn a little money. As late as December 1885 he was still trying to capitalize on his skills as a boxer, according to what Bloy wrote to Louis Montchal: 'My friend, the Comte Villiers de l'Isle-Adam, owner of one of the greatest names in Europe and one of the most shining poetic minds this century has seen, is a *sparring-partner* in a gymnasium, and for wages of 60 francs a month receives about a couple of dozen blows in the face every week in order to feed his son.'[49] But as his health worsened, he had to give that up, and it was then that his friend Émile Pierre found him a more congenial sedentary occupation. Pierre knew a solicitor in Nogent called Mauroy who was an amateur poet, and he put him in touch with Villiers so that, for a consideration, he could have his verses corrected by an expert.[50]

Still, even a prolific literary lawyer was unlikely to contribute much to Villier's finances, and the temptations to cash in on whatever attributes he had must have been considerable. Huysmans was quite clear that the old notions of a rich marriage were long since buried, Villiers having become completely faithful to Marie Dantine, and told Arij Prins that since 1882 Villiers had given up thinking about women.[51] But other principles too stood in the way of his accepting money if he thought dishonour was involved. One story, which Villiers himself assiduously retailed, particularly illustrated this. In 1886 the journalist and polemicist Édouard Drumont published his long and sensational denunciation of Jewish influence in France under the title *La France juive*. The Jewish community was naturally perturbed by this substantial and apparently well-documented work of anti-semitism, which did much to fuel the fires of already existing prejudices against the Jews. It was therefore natural that they should think of bringing out some kind of refutation of Drumont, preferably by some right-wing Catholic author whom no one could suspect of undue sympathy with their interests. So much is certain; whether the particular sequel actually took place is something for which we have only Villiers's word. According to the story which he used to repeat with great relish, Arthur Meyer of *Le Gaulois* came to see him. Meyer said: 'Write something against Drumont's book, and you can name your own price.' Villiers replied that the price had been fixed from all eternity. Meyer, puzzled, asked what it was, whereupon Villiers drew himself to his full height, and said firmly: 'Thirty pieces of silver, sir. Now get out!'[52]

32

Now that Totor was five, Villiers, who was immensely proud of him, used to take him out when he went to cafés in the evenings. Baude de Maurceley met them both at Brébant's; he was already at table when Villiers burst in:

He stared round at the bench-seats in his usual suspicious way, shook hands with Brébant, whom he had nicknamed the Restorer of Letters, because he had instituted a fixed-price meal for writers; then, noticing me, came dashing over to sit at the neighbouring table, and enthusiastically, in words which were turbulent but almost rhythmically hammered out, he improvised at one and the same time a friendly greeting and the menu of his dinner—a substantial and simple meal, at the fixed price. Then, having sat the child down opposite him, he asked for an extra plate in which, with infinite care, he cut up the lion's share of his main dish (. . .)
The son resembled the father: the head and face had the same lines. He listened to his 'papa' with admiring curiosity, shyly, with his look already having something of that unease that always gleamed in the eyes, gay, sceptical, or melancholy, of the genius who wrote the *Contes cruels*. When the child had finished his meal with some little dessert, Villiers gave him a spoonful of coffee and took no more notice of him.—'Go and play now', he said, which was a paternal invitation to let us talk in peace. The child, gentle and obedient, left the table to go and 'play' by the doorway, watching the passers-by, while Villiers, with nothing on his mind, henceforth free of cares since his son had had dinner, must, on that as on every evening, have ridden some chimaera and multiplied his oratorical effects for the delight of his neighbours.[1]

Totor became a familiar figure in the cafés of Montmartre. Someone else who saw Villiers crossing the Place Blanche one rainy winter night, holding Totor by the hand and heading for some café, never forgot the sombre impression of years of suffering which his figure created.[2] People used to call Totor 'the Commodore' because of the outsize sailor's cap which he wore. He would also be taken on Sundays to the rue de Sèvres, where Huysmans lived, since it was on that evening that Huysmans usually entertained Bloy and Villiers to dinner. Huysmans described one such occasion to Arij Prins in July 1886:

Villiers came on Sunday, with his son; imagine a pretty little kid, though he is the same Kalmuk type as his father, with great big eyes that he obviously gets from his mysterious mother. The poor little devil was very nice—too intelligent—and Villiers was *maternal* more than paternal. It was really touching; in fact, it finished at midnight, as it always does. Villiers was rambling on—and Bloy had to take them home for fear of accidents, while Villiers held forth about occult sciences.[3]

Villiers was totally devoted to Totor, and in his own way was as attentive a father as he had been a son. The draft of a strange letter he sent to the Prefect of Police shows how anxiously he watched over the boy:

I have the honour to ask for a brief moment of audience with you, in order to lay before you a particular fact which it would be too long and difficult to explain in writing. On the one hand, it is concerned with an attempt to kidnap a child—my own—made by two malefactors from the outer boulevards, a kidnapping which was attempted last night in the Place de Clichy, in conditions of unbelievable audacity, and on the other hand, with the inexplicable behaviour of a policeman who was asked to help in these circumstances.[4]

There was of course in Villiers's love for Totor a strong sense of the continuance of the race, with its chivalric traditions, which occasionally led to unfortunate incidents. One day Totor came home from school and told his father that the coalman's son had attacked him. 'So you gave him a beating?' 'Oh no,' said Totor, 'he's bigger than me, but I can run faster. So I ran away and he couldn't catch me.' Villiers was furious at this dishonourable conduct and at once dragged Totor off to the coalman's, where he declared: 'Sir, your son has just brutally attacked mine. Instead of standing his ground, this child ran off. As he is just nervous and not a coward, he wants to rehabilitate himself. I approve, and our children must fight here, on the spot.' But, before the coalman could agree to the fight, his son had started hammering Totor, while Villiers shouted: 'Stop! Stop! It's my boy who's in the wrong!' By the time poor Totor had been rescued from his assailant, he was much more upset by his father's injustice than his own cowardice.[5] In fact, faithful to the family tradition, Totor, after his father's death, was to fight a real duel at the age of sixteen and came out of it with his arm in a sling.

Villiers's closeness to his son, whom he wanted everyone
to know and admire, did not extend to Marie Dantine, with
whom he was practically never seen in public. Though they
lived in the same rooms, Villiers let it be vaguely understood
that she was some kind of housekeeper, and—probably
without deceiving anyone—remained deliberately reticent
about the secret of Totor's birth. But after 1886 he managed
to stay in one place rather longer than had hitherto been
possible, with the result that, for the first time in years, he did
every now and then admit visitors. Several of them have
described what his living conditions were like. One was Jules
Destrée, a young Belgian writer who later became well
known as a politician; he was a friend of Huysmans and
wanted to write an article on Villiers, so one day, when he
was visiting Paris, Léon Bloy took him round to the rue
Pigalle, where Villiers was living. They climbed up to the
fourth or fifth floor of a wretched, dirty building, and were
eventually admitted:

The lodgings were even more chilly and more bare than I had
imagined. A bed in a corner, a desk with newspapers spread out on
it, at most ten or so books, three chairs and a table. On the walls,
the crumpled symmetry of a banal piece of tapestry-work, not a
single engraving, not a picture. Not a trinket, not a memento of
luxury on which one could look with pleasure or enjoyment. The
room of a student, the room of a pauper. I shall never forget seeing
on the bed a beige overcoat, its elegance spoilt by a large stain. And
that little detail revealed so much misfortune, such a weariness of
destitution that it made me sick at heart.

The man himself struck Destrée as a mixture.

Fairly tall, with a slim, sinewy frame, he wrapped his emaciated
body in a pitiful dressing-gown, and despair had bowed his head,
which nevertheless remained vigorous and proud. His face, care-
worn and lined, with its fine features, was framed by long greying
hair. His moustache curved aristocratically over the slightly dis-
dainful mouth, with its bitter smile, and into the eyes there would
sometimes come an almost despotic sparkle (. . .) Just as he was, I
found him superb, and I felt how much he was, literally, a prince.
In all this adversity, he had a natural, lordly simplicity, the elegant
ease of a great nobleman, a sureness in his patrician gestures, the
rhythmic movements of a creator from a great line.

Villiers talked to him of Shakespeare and Wagner, and Destrée told him how much he was admired in Belgium. As the idea of a lecture tour was still in the air, Villiers pricked up his ears: an old obsession had just re-entered his mind: 'You have a King in your country, a Court, no doubt artists are made very welcome?'[6]

Another visitor permitted to enter Villiers's sanctuary was Gustave Guiches, a young novelist who first drew attention to himself in 1887 by being one of the signatories of the famous 'Manifesto of the Five' against Zola and Naturalism. He was about twenty-six when he first met Villiers at a lunch party given by Gustave de Malherbe, and was instantly subjugated by the endless flow of fascinating conversation. Since Guiches also knew Huysmans and Bloy, he was invited to the Sunday-evening dinners in the rue de Sèvres, and became sufficiently intimate with Villiers to be allowed to visit him at home—although, according to Guiches, 'home' was scarcely an appropriate word. The furniture was sparse: a hotel clock that had lost its glass case, a vast grand piano, decrepit and out of tune, a desk near the bed, with a contraption that raised or lowered a sort of book-rest so that he could write without getting up, piles of paper and of manuscripts, books everywhere, since there were no shelves, one or two garishly-coloured vases looking like prizes in a fair. The only luxury was an ebony table inlaid with brass.

Guiches has also left one of the most vivid and detailed portraits of Villiers:

Nervous, puny, but with solid muscles and the agility of a trained gymnast, a redoubtable boxer, good with a foil and pistol, he spoke of his physical skills with surprising excitement, allowing one to glimpse his childish desire to show that he could defend himself against any attack. Loving life despite the wounds it inflicted on him, idealizing the ugly things in it, making its beauties more sublime, setting the redeeming splendours of his dreams against its sufferings, he would at first appear smiling, lavishing on everyone the marvellous fantasies of his conversation, then, at something someone said, something which was quite inoffensive but suddenly made him mistrustful, he would stop short in mid-course, harden his smile, make ironically pointed remarks, cower down defensively, exaggerating his feigned humility by a show of timidity. Then suddenly he would fling his head up with a magnetic air, brush back his hair, and his face would appear in all its intellectual beauty. His wide forehead, crossed with parallel lines, displayed the sovereign combination of spiritual faculties, like the gradual revelation of some superb page of art.[7]

But if Villiers had now usually somewhere to live, he was never safe from the consequences of the debts he and his father had accumulated over the years, and in April 1886 the bailiff's men descended on him at 31 rue de Maubeuge, armed with a writ against him from the Crédit Général des Flandres, a bank in Bruges. On 1 May his furniture was sold by auction, and the bill announcing the sale shows how summary were his possessions: desk, table, chairs, stove.[8] His collaboration on *Le Figaro* had come to an end some time previously, it is said because Magnard had finally taken offence at one of his articles,[9] and neither *La Journée* nor *Le Succès*, the two new dailies for which he had written in 1885, had survived for more than a few months, so that one of his more profitable sources of income had dried up. It was therefore of great importance for him to find some other newspaper which would regularly accept his prose, and he spent a great deal of time hanging around in waiting-rooms hoping to see editors. The Belgian novelist Camille Lemonnier used to see him in the offices of the *Gil Blas:*

I have ten times seen Villiers, slumped on a bench, waiting for someone to remember that he was there. Mendès on the other hand simply sailed in. One could feel that he was the master wherever he went: if anyone had been rash enough to try to stop him, he would have thrown them down the stairs. But Villiers, the gentle Villiers, counted for so little in the place.

Sometimes Guérin, one of the sub-editors, would look in and crook a finger at him and say: 'What, you here again, old chap?' Before anything he wrote could be accepted, he had to read it not only to the committee but to the editor-in-chief Courbouleix, who would sometimes turn it down scornfully. Lemonnier remembered one such occasion when, after a wait of two hours, Villiers was admitted to the presence, only to be told that the political colouring of the work made it unacceptable. He came out ashen and bent, because he needed the money for medical treatment: 'They don't want it!

They say the tale is royalist and they are republicans, the so-and-sos! There it is: it means death. *Dura lex sed ...* Courbouleix.'[10]

Villiers even went so far as to try to adapt his manner to the racy style characteristic of the *Gil Blas*, and told Guiches that Courbouleix had asked him for 'something spicy'.[11] The result was *Un singulier chelem!* on a rude subject borrowed from his erstwhile ladyfriend Marc de Montifaud, which appeared on 14 November 1886. Happily for him, this found favour, and for the next two years he was able to publish at least one tale or article in the *Gil Blas* every month, for which he normally received 150 francs. He even managed to establish his situation solidly enough to write more or less as he wished, and mercifully did not have to continue in the vein of *Un singulier chelem!* (though the paper, perhaps wisely, did decline to print *L'Etna chez soi*, the anarchist story which nearly got Dujardin in trouble with the police). One can well understand why, after all these difficulties and humiliations, he should have said to Michelet: 'Keep on working, you who are young. When, like me, you have worked for thirty years, you will, like me, be able from time to time to have something printed, for three sous a line, in papers that sometimes pay up.'[12]

Paradoxically, his fame as a serious writer was now growing apace, not only in France but abroad. Paul Verlaine wrote a profile of him for the series *Les Hommes d'aujourd'hui* in 1886, with a drawing by Coll-Toc; early in 1887 the Italian author Vittorio Pica wrote to ask him for information for use in his forthcoming book *Letteratura d'eccezione*;[13] the Dutch critic Van Santen Kolff wrote about him several times in German periodicals;[14] Jules Destrée published a long and enthusiastic study in *La Jeune Belgique* in January 1888; later the same year Verlaine included a substantial if gossipy essay on him in the second edition of his book *Les Poètes maudits*; a young Scotsman who wrote for the *Westminster Review* tried to get his permission to translate *L'Ève future*;[15] Arthur Symons began collecting material for the article he proposed to give Oscar Wilde for insertion in the *Woman's World*.[16]

Villiers himself often thought of returning the compliment and producing some articles on his friends and on the writers he admired—on the mystic Ernest Hello, on Léon Dierx, on Mallarmé, on Huysmans, on Verlaine, on Lactantius, and perhaps on Bloy.[17] But none of this ever saw the light of day, except that *Une soirée chez Nina de Villard*, written in 1888 on the occasion of the death of Charles Cros, may be considered in part as a tribute to Dierx. In fact, he did not read very widely and had something of a dislike for literary critics, even those who paid him compliments. Gustave Guiches noticed that he expressed his opinion about books in singularly brief comic phrases: of Huysmans's *A vau l'eau* he said: 'it's stomachic, but it's as bitter as aloes', and of Bloy's *Le Désespéré*, smacking his lips, 'it's a real lollipop! ...'[18] However, he had his own way of showing appreciation to the authors, which was to learn parts of their work off by heart—his memory remained prodigious, and he did that with some of Huysmans's *En rade*, with Mallarmé's *Le Ten O'Clock de M. Whistler*, even with some verses by Jean Ajalbert which happened to strike him in a review.[19] Indeed, with Mallarmé's poetry, he had acquired something of a reputation as an exegetist, and was one of the few, along with Téodor de Wyzéwa, to whom people turned for elucidation of its mysteries.[20] He was equally capable of reeling off strings of bad verse to show what he disliked, and was even reputed at one time to know by heart two thousand lines of Ponsard, whose platitudinous versifying he detested[21]—he also claimed that in his youth he had known all Boileau by heart.[22] Another technique he employed, if someone mentioned a fashionable writer whom he thought overrated, was to launch into a lyrical eulogy of him, feigning intense enthusiasm until, when everyone began looking astonished, he would burst out laughing.[23]

As for his own work, Stock was beginning to grow impatient over the delays on *Tribulat Bonhomet*. The contract had been signed in July 1886, and Villiers had agreed to deliver his manuscript by 15 September. But the autumn passed and the winter came, with Villiers asking for more advances and loans, still without having produced a complete text. The delays were in part caused by ill-health, in part by the necessity to keep on producing pieces for the *Gil Blas*, in part by the pressure of work on *Axël*, but perhaps most of all by Villiers's desire to rewrite *Claire Lenoir*, which was naturally to form the centrepiece of the volume. When the story had first appeared twenty years earlier, Villiers was still preoccupied with the possibility of a synthesis between Christianity, occultism, and Hegelianism, and Claire and Césaire were allies in their opposition to Bonhomet's crass materialism. But in the meantime Villiers had moved much closer to an orthodox Christianity and no longer felt the same sympathy for Hegel's philosophy (Hegel was one of Bloy's *bêtes noires*, and Villiers had been placed in an embarrassing position by constant pressure from his aggressive friend to renounce any attachment whatever to Hegelianism, which was more than he was prepared to do).[24] The result was that exhuming *Claire Lenoir* meant much careful thought and delicate adjustment.

First of all, Villiers inserted a number of passages emphasizing Claire's explicit Christianity, which in 1867 had mostly been implied rather than stated. Then he deliberately rendered Césaire's character less attractive, so that the reader would be less inclined to approve of his views. Next, he rearranged matters so as to make it clear that there was a real division of opinion between Claire and her husband. They are no longer presented as forming a united front against Bonhomet. Instead, Césaire, while still putting forward some of the arguments designed to confute the doctor, appears from time to time to be laying himself open to the criticisms which Claire had originally only directed at Bonhomet. The chapter-heading which had once identified Claire as a 'sentimental Hegelian' is removed.[25] The difficulties of incorporating all these amendments (and others concerned only with the mechanics of the action) into an already complex text were considerable, and in April 1887 Villiers was still hard at work correcting the proofs.

At that time he was living in the rue de Naples, close to Stock's own flat, and the publisher himself used to bring the proofs round and leave them with the *concierge*. But on one public holiday, Stock thought he would take them up and hand them over personally, knowing the author was ill:

I went up to the rooms where he lived, on the second or third floor, around noon. A little boy of six or seven, young Totor, opened the door to me and without further ado took me to his father, in the bedroom. Villiers, sitting up in bed, was beginning his lunch. Nearby, on a table set with a single place, there were oysters, a cold chicken, a little pot of *foie gras* and, in a cooler, a bottle of champagne. Villiers, very embarrassed by what I could see, felt obliged to supply me with an extremely confused explanation: presents from friends who, knowing he was ill, had wanted to give him a treat.[26]

In fact, Villiers was probably speaking the truth: Méry Laurent had the generous habit of sending him expensive delicacies when she knew he was unwell.

Eventually *Tribulat Bonhomet* came out in May 1887, with a note announcing a further volume of *Anecdotes et aphorismes*, and, on the fly-leaf, there is what can only be called a highly imaginative list of works which Villiers judged to be 'going to press'. This included, fairly enough, *Axël* and *Propos d'au-delà*, the title he then intended to give to his next collection of short stories. But it also included *L'Adoration des Mages*, *Le Vieux de la Montagne*, *Méditations*, and *Mélanges*. He had, it is true, done a few sketches for *Le Vieux de la Montagne* back in 1873,[27] and since 1880 at least he had intended to put together his miscellaneous articles as *Mélanges*, possibly reserving those on literary topics for *Méditations*. But probably not a word of *L'Adoration des Mages* had been written—indeed, he had explained to one of his young admirers that he had not started 'because I am not *in a state of grace*, and it is essential that I should be before I dare touch that marvel!'[28] Other works too were announced even more optimistically: two volumes of *Théâtre*, one volume of *Documents sur les règnes de Charles VI et de Charles VII* (part of the history of the family, no doubt) under the heading *Histoire*, and finally a set of *Œuvres métaphysiques*—one volume on *L'Ill-usionisme*, two entitled *De la connaissance de l'Utile*, and one on *L'Exégèse divine*. One may doubt whether anything more than the titles of these works existed, but they attest that same fertility of invention evident on the many pages of manuscript catalogues of subjects and titles which Villiers used to draw up—over a hundred such titles of tales are known, and as some of them were told orally and recorded by those present, they were certainly not all figments of his imagination.[29]

All these notebooks and manuscripts seem to have been as often in Villiers's capacious pockets as they were on his table. By carrying them round with him, he could work on them in cafés or wherever the spirit moved him, and he could test their effect by reading out from them to anyone prepared to listen. As Stock explained: 'Villiers *spoke* his work before he began writing it, not only spoke it, but *acted* it and *interpreted* it better than a first-rate actor could have done; an audience was indispensable for him to judge the effect he was seeking.'[30] But sometimes these performances were based on existing drafts, which he would alter if he felt he had not achieved his desired aim. Hence the spectacle which Anatole France found so extraordinary:

He went on writing stubbornly, and his formless, illegible, scattered manuscripts were always getting lost and found again. Sleepwalkers have faculties that we cannot understand. At night Villiers would pick up in the gutter the pages that had dropped from his masterpieces. He is said to have written on cigarette papers. What did he not use for manuscripts to scribble on? Only those who have seen them can say what they were like: nameless fragments, worn out from being carried round for years in his pockets, which fell to pieces as soon as he unfolded them, causing him a comic and profound terror when he realized how far they had disintegrated. But he reconstituted them, with obstinate patience and marvellous skill.[31]

Villiers's manuscripts do indeed offer an unbelievable sight. On all manner of different papers, from vast lined sheets to pages torn out of Totor's school exercise books, covered with inks of many different qualities and colours, some produced with the care a medieval monk might have lavished on an illuminated parchment, others hastily scrawled with a blunt pencil, they are sometimes so torn and worn that they look like a piece of lace; often they seem to have been screwed up and smoothed out again, and the variegated stains of coffee, beer, and wine that decorate them bear eloquent testimony to the sort of places in which they were produced. Mallarmé has elegantly defined the extent to which their presence on Villiers's person confirmed his sense of identity:

Fashion enjoins that a trifle of some sort of whiteness, handker-
chief, glove, I know not, or pale hothouse flower, should interrupt
the monotony of modern dress: he, a dandy of another sort, had,
once and for all and safe from variations, chosen his sign, and
straightway he had gone to that which did indeed distinguish him
from others, the page on which one writes, evocative and pure, he
half hid it, half showed it too, anxiously until he felt a friendly
question touching it and drew it out victorious. That meant: 'I am
well, thank you—and all is well. Let us not speak of anything else,'
and suppressed the empty allusions to that which 'really, when one
has the pleasure to be with one's friends, it is licit to omit'.[31]

33

The Sunday dinners with Villiers, Huysmans, and Bloy had
now become a regular event, with sometimes other guests
too—Gustave Guiches, the young novelist Lucien Descaves,
Georges Landry, a friend of Bloy, and an actor called Henri
Girard. Much of the time was taken up with lamenting the
state of the world, particularly so far as literature was
concerned, but with such verve and inventiveness that the
atmosphere was more joyous than melancholy. But Villiers
was gradually drawing closer to Huysmans, whose incisive
cynicism concealed great warmth of temperament, than to
Bloy, whose peripetual furies and imprecations were accompanied by a singularly demanding attitude to his friends. The
tone of his letters to Villiers is often hectoring and acrimonious—'I know very well that, by writing to you, I am
offering you an opportunity of not replying that you will be
only too happy to grasp',[1] 'in what milieu of fetid journalists
have you allowed your soul to grow so rotten that you have
become so profoundly, so desolatingly unable to discern
your real friends, those who will never abandon or betray
you and who are always overjoyed to see you?',[2] 'your nature
does not allow you to go in for any extra activity, even if it
was to save the life of a friend who would let himself be flayed
alive for you'.[3] Such reproaches, together with near-
hysterical and uncomprehending denunciations of Villiers's
demigods Wagner and Hegel, were putting an increasing
strain on their friendship, under which it was eventually to
break.

Yet in 1887, though there was irritation on both sides, they were much in one another's company. It was to Bloy that, one bitter winter's evening after some particularly humiliating failure with a publisher, Villiers made his famous remark: 'We won't forget this planet!'[4] It was to Bloy also, once when they were passing in front of the flower-sellers, the tombstone merchants, and the shops full of funeral articles near the Père Lachaise cemetery, that Villiers exclaimed furiously: 'Those are the people who invented death!'[5] One evening in 1887 was especially memorable. It was 14 July, and Bloy, Guiches, and Lucien Descaves decided to take Villiers to dinner in the house of Descaves's father at Montrouge. So, in the afternoon, with Huysmans, they went off to fetch him in his rooms. It was five o'clock, and he was still in bed working, but he happily accepted the invitation, on condition that he could take Totor too. So off they went, with Marie apologizing for not having had time to make the boy 'look pretty'. That evening Villiers excelled himself, and the next day Bloy wrote to a friend:

Extraordinary, fantastic evening! Saturation of art for six hours, delirium of prodigious sensations. Wagner on the piano, stories, mimicry, improvisations. Villiers, whom I thought I knew, overpowered me with stupefaction, impregnated me, intoxicated me with delight. In the end, bed for the above-mentioned Villiers with Totor at Montrouge, and early morning return for the rest of us as dawn broke.[6]

Huysmans was no less bowled over:

After the meal, Villiers sat down at the piano and, oblivious, out of this world, sang with his reedy, cracked voice pieces by Wagner among which he interpolated barrack-room songs, linking them all together with bursts of strident laughter, crazy jokes, and strange verses. No one ever had as much power to make farce surpass itself and shoot over into another world; there was always a punch-bowl flaming in his brain.[7]

Descaves remembered a few more details. The high point of the evening was the singing of two versions of Baudelaire's *La Mort des amants*, one by Maurice Rollinat, the other by Villiers, which naturally was declared superior. At three in the morning, when it was finally time for the party to break up, Villiers was prevailed upon to stay at Montrouge with Totor, and went quietly to bed, asking only for some sort of book so that he could read himself to sleep. When Descaves took him one, he was surprised to see on the bedside table an object like a scraper, with its point stuck in a cork. 'What's that?' he asked. 'Something to defend myself if I'm attacked on my way home late at night,' replied the poet.[8]

But if there were occasions when Bloy and Villiers could be together in perfect amity, there were others when, for one reason or another, the tension suddenly snapped. Once, when Bloy was developing some symbolical exegesis of the Apocalypse, he had the misfortune to say that the rhinoceros was, in his opinion, certainly meant to represent St. Joseph. At once Villiers flew at him indignantly: 'That's abominable! And the next time that in my presence you compare St. Joseph to a rhinoceros, wherever we are, I'll throw you out on your neck!'[9] Such doctrinal disagreements were however nothing to the resentments caused by Bloy's incorrigible habit of regarding other people's money as legitimately belonging to him (it is only fair to add that he was also on occasion capable of great generosity and self-sacrifice). One particularly sad incident of this kind was witnessed by J. E. S. Jeanès, who suppresses Bloy's name while identifying him clearly. Jeanès was paying Villiers for the reproduction of a short story:

One day I brought him 80 francs for a tale that I had had published for him. Being rather ill, he was keeping to his rooms. I was about to leave when there arrived a man who has remained horribly fixed in my memory, a monster of spite, pride, and savage selfishness. Shall I say who it was? People might not believe what I saw with my own eyes. He had come to borrow money from poor Villiers, and he managed to screw 75 francs out of him. After he had left, Villiers's wife appeared. What suffering and hardship were written on her face! I had never seen her. Had she been listening? She made no reproaches, but her ravaged features showed what martyrdom she had been through. 'Auguste, do you realize that I have nothing left at all?' 'Here are five francs,' he said. And she went back to the kitchen. Then he understood and, deploring his own weakness, said: 'Could you have believed that there exist creatures like the man who has just left, and beings like that woman, whom I cannot help tormenting, starving, and humiliating, despite myself, because of my incurable stupidity?'[10]

Bloy had indeed for a while some kind of strange power over Villiers, born no doubt of his overbearing technique of browbeating his friend to get what he wanted. One such case occurred in the late summer of 1887. Villiers had no doubt been boasting to Bloy of his connections with the Marquis of Salisbury, who had in 1886 become Prime Minister for the second time—in 1881, suddenly realising that the name Cecil given to one of the heroes of *Le Nouveau-Monde* was the family name of the Marquis, Villiers had sent his lordship a complimentary copy of the play and, on the strength of a polite acknowledgement, concluded that the statesman was a firm ally of his. As it happened, Lord Salisbury had a villa at Dieppe where he usually spent the summer, and Bloy took it into his head that Villiers ought to be able to extract money from him if he went there and argued his case persuasively enough (Villiers had already been in correspondence with Salisbury and there had been some question of his going to visit him in London).[11] So on 22 September Bloy wrote Villiers a comminatory letter, ordering him off to Dieppe:

You must go, and what's more go with me. That seems to me essential. It goes without saying that your lord must know nothing about me, since some day I may be called on to judge him and have him executed. But I'll be in the wings to prompt you to say things that I shall draw for you from the deep places *de abysso jacente deorsum*. And we shall come back, I take it upon myself to affirm it, with your deliverance and mine.[12]

To Louis Montchal the next day Bloy made it even clearer who was the boss of the enterprise:

Salisbury has an income of ten millions and estates as big as a kingdom. He is in a position to do whatever he is asked for Villiers, who is a count ten times over and a knight ten times over. We'll arrange things so as to make him understand that he *must* do it. I am deeply convinced that this action led by me must succeed. I have a genius for sieges and I have accomplished tougher tasks. But our friend is a very difficult weapon to handle (. . .) Anyway, my will usually overcomes his and I hope to succeed this time too.[13]

But in the event illness and perhaps resentment at being treated like a pliant agent in Bloy's hands stopped Villiers from going on this occasion, though he returned to the idea the following year when he was no longer under the thumb of the so-called Ungrateful Mendicant. In 1887 he only left Paris once, to spend a few summer days with Émile Pierre and his wife at Nogent ('It's as if I was resuscitated; I'm eating like a horse; I've slept well; the air of the woods is extraordinarily good for me; I'm not ill at all now').[14]

Another diversion in 1887 came about through the intervention of Rodolphe Darzens who, in addition to his other activities, was fencing-master at the Théâtre Libre, which was to be one of the most influential experimental theatres of the late nineteenth century, specializing chiefly in Naturalist drama. Recently founded by André Antoine, it did not seem a natural home for any of Villiers's plays, but in April 1886 the *Revue contemporaine* had published *L'Évasion*, which had as its central figure an escaped convict talking slang and could consequently just about pass muster as a Realist play. At all events, Darzens suggested to Antoine that it might be suitable for the Théâtre Libre, and Antoine, after consulting various other people, including Mendès, wrote in June 1887 to ask the author's permission to produce the play the following season.[15] Villiers was for various reasons reluctant to authorize performance—his sad experience with *Le Nouveau-Monde* had sickened him with the live theatre, and the version of *Axël* published by *La Jeune France* in 1885–6 had been explicitly designed for reading only; moreover, *L'Évasion* was an old and unrepresentative work of which he was not particularly proud. However, in the end he agreed, and rehearsals began in September with the actor Mévisto in the role of Pagnol.

By now Villiers's obsession with acting had been reawakened, and he took a more than active part in the production. Antoine himself remembered with amusement and admiration how committed he was: 'Hamming it up magnificently, with his long hair and his strange eyes, Villiers used the pretext of giving hints to the actor to take every opportunity of himself acting the part of the convict, the hero of the play, and he was so striking that, for the sheer pleasure of it, I often let him go on to the end.'[16] Once, when Antoine and Lucien Descaves were walking back to Montmartre with Villiers, Antoine asked him if he had ever seen the great actor

Rouvière. Villiers at once stopped under a gaslamp and gave an unforgettable performance of Hamlet's monologue with the gestures and intonations of Rouvière.[17] The dress rehearsal took place on 10 October, the first night on the twelfth, and a special performance for the subscribers on the thirteenth. The occasion was a resounding success, the Théâtre Libre was henceforth established on a permanent basis, and the little stage of the Passage de l'Élysée-des-Beaux-Arts became famous.

L'Évasion, it must be admitted, had little to do with this. Critics and public alike were much more interested in the adaptation of *Sœur Philomène*, the novel by the Goncourt brothers, which occupied the greater part of the programme. Perhaps that is why, when Lucien Descaves saw Edmond de Goncourt and Villiers in the foyer after the first performance, each was with his own group of friends, assiduously ignoring the other.[18] What little the press did say about L'Évasion was on the whole respectful but unenthusiastic. Villiers however took umbrage almost as violently as he had done after the attacks on *La Révolte* and *Le Nouveau-Monde*, sketched out an article defending his conception of the character of Pagnol,[19] and published in the *Gil Blas* an ill-tempered diatribe against his old enemy Francisque Sarcey, who had dismissed L'Évasion in a few contemptuous lines. *Le Cas extraordinaire de M. Francisque Sarcey* is not a reasoned justification of his play, nor a protest against the critic's narrow-mindedness: it is simply a series of not particularly amusing insults and *ad hominem* anecdotes. Villiers was as sensitive as ever to adverse criticism, but one wonders whether, on this occasion, he did not have a sneaking suspicion that the work in question scarcely deserved to be defended in detail.

In the meantime his regular contributions to the *Gil Blas* meant that he was rapidly accumulating enough material for another volume of short stories. This time he offered it to Quantin, and towards the end of September 1887 received an advance of 500 francs.[20] At that point the collection was to be entitled *Propos d'au-delà*, but this was later changed to *Histoires insolites*, after some hesitation over the alternative *Histoires semi-frivoles*[21] (it is puzzling that there never seems to have been any question of using the title *Nouveaux Contes cruels*, which had figured over most of the tales as they appeared in the *Gil Blas*). For the most part, the stories which compose the collection are briefer and more mordantly satirical in tone that those of either *Contes cruels* or *L'Amour suprême*, which is a consequence of their having been written for the *Gil Blas*. Villiers himself was conscious of the conditions of haste in which he was obliged to produce them, and would much have preferred to get on with *Axël*, his historical works, or even the revised version of *Le Nouveau-Monde* which he seems to have been working on about this time.[22] As he wrote to Huysmans: 'I'm forced to spend my time churning out exciting chit-chat for the *Gil Blas*:—all done very casually, without even having any proofs, and without their even printing my *real* text.'[23] So when he sent Mallarmé a copy, his modesty was not entirely false when he called it 'a volume of more or less entertaining anecdotes'.[24] Huysmans shared this opinion and to Arij Prins confided that he thought it 'a slightly shamefaced collection of his articles in the *Gil Blas*.—To tell you the truth, it's not good and, from the point of view of literary probity, I can't help feeling a bit indignant.'[25]

These views are unduly harsh. *Histoires insolites* perhaps does not contain any unmistakable masterpieces as *Contes cruels* and *L'Amour suprême* had done, and the subjects are on the whole treated in a simpler and more direct fashion, as befits pieces destined for a daily paper. But, among its twenty tales, there are only one or two which fail to come off—*L'Etna chez soi* is full of that tedious preoccupation with gadgetry that disfigures certain of his pseudo-scientific fantasies, *Ce Mahoin!* is no more than a slight curiosity about an execution, and *Aux Chrétiens les lions!* is a protest against cruelty to animals of which the witty title is the best part. The others are well up to Villiers's usual standard, whether it be in biting irony as in *Le Jeu des grâces*, in the spine-tingling creation of a mixture of comedy and terror as in *Les Phantasmes de M. Redoux*, in the grave poetry of *La Maison du bonheur*, or in the mysterious and moving symbols of *L'Agrément inattendu*. Taken as a whole, the volume is far from showing any diminution of Villiers' creative powers —on the contrary, his inventive verve is in some ways even better displayed here, because he passes on so quickly from one theme to another which is totally different.

Perhaps surprisingly, Villiers's political and religious opinions are less in evidence in *Histoires insolites* than they had been in *L'Amour suprême*. This may be because he had to trim his sails to the prevailing winds in the *Gil Blas*; it may also have been because his political commitment was somewhat less than it had been. Chambord was dead; Naundorff had been tried and found wanting; and, if Villiers had resigned himself to supporting the Comte de Paris, the Orleanist claimant, it was with a heavy heart.[26] But his detestation of parliamentary democracy was as lively as ever, and was given fresh vigour when scandals broke out in the highest circles of government in November 1887. It was then that it came to light that Daniel Wilson, who was a republican deputy and the son-in-law of Jules Grévy, the President of the Republic, had been plying a roaring trade in the sale of decorations and honours. When the news broke, Grévy initially tried to cling to power but in the end, deserted by all his friends, was compelled to resign. Villiers was overjoyed to learn that his worst suspicions about the corruption and venality of the republican régime had been fully justified, and bethought himself of the piece on the coronation of Grévy which he had had ready ever since 1883 or 1884. He at once took it out, extended it, rewrote it completely to take account of the new situation, and added a conclusion proclaiming that poets were the only true patriots left. But instead of offering this text to a magazine, Villiers decided to turn it into a vast practical joke and at his own expense had it printed in the format of a newspaper. This was then put on sale on the streets, with its headlines so displayed that people would think it was a genuine account of a parliamentary debate at which it had been decided to offer Grévy a presidential crown. How successful the device was is not known; the police very soon stepped in and banned the public sale of the seditious document.[27]

This brush with the police was not Villiers's only contact with the law. Apart from the forced sale of his furniture in 1886, he was expelled from his flat in the rue Pigalle in the summer of 1887 for not paying his rent, but, wherever he went, he soon found himself in trouble with the landlord. Not that he was easily intimidated by threats of legal proceedings: like his father, he believed himself to be endowed with a first-class legal brain, and in conversation made much play with terms like 'hereditary leases', 'synallagmatic contracts', and 'restrictive clauses'.[28] He was once heard declaring of a prospective adversary: 'Tomorrow I'll pulverize him in chambers!'[29] In one of the flats he occupied, he became engaged in a dispute by correspondence with the old lady on the floor below, who complained that during the night she kept hearing a noise like a roll of thunder followed by a great crash. Villiers was furious: 'That old madwoman cannot get it into her head that, if I'm too hot, I push my Chouberski stove further away from me, and, if I suddenly feel cold, I haul it straight back again. My Chouberski is not a living being and, with the best will in the world, I can't force it to wear slippers!'[30] But the last straw came when she claimed to be related to him through the Carforts. 'Madmen should be in padded cells, but impostors should be in prison!' he raged, and announced his intention of suing her. In fact litigation was far beyond his means, but the *Perrinet Leclerc* affair still rankled ('I should have taken the case myself,' he used to say),[31] and when at a dinner in the mid-1880s someone asked him if the case was still going on he replied with a sad smile: 'Perpetually'.[32]

34

Late in 1887 René Baschet, editor of a fortnightly magazine called the *Revue illustrée*, received an unexpected visit from Villiers.

One day he arrived in my office, pale and dramatic. 'My dear director,' he said to me, 'they've just exhumed the remains of my poor mother . . . Alas! I haven't enough money to have her buried again . . . Her coffin is in the open air . . . I need 800 francs . . . Can you advance them for a story of which I'll tell you the subject: Milton, blind, is dictating *Paradise Lost* to his daughters . . . Meanwhile, in the street, there happens to come past a regiment of soldiers, with the band playing . . . The daughters leave the work they are doing, and go to the window to see the handsome soldiers marching past. And while they are there, the poet continues dictating magnificent lines ... which will be lost for ever.'[1]

Such is the origin of the story entitled *Les Filles de Milton*, which was still not quite finished at the author's death, but which nevertheless represents one of his finest achievements. When he decided to write it, he knew little about Milton's life, though he had always professed to regard him as one of the sublimest geniuses, so he had to go off to the Bibliothèque Nationale to document himself. On the library staff at that time was Remy de Gourmont, then approaching thirty, essayist and novelist, later to make his name as perhaps the greatest French critic of the turn of the century, and he was delighted to have the chance of making Villiers's acquaintance.

Somewhat on edge, he waited for the books he had asked for, and no one bothered about his impatience, since for the librarians his name only gave a vague impression of historic syllables. I was able to come to his aid, but too late; as soon as he had had a quick look at the books, he had them put aside for the next day; it was not until three months later that he came back.[2]

The meeting was nonetheless an important one. Gourmont was one of Villiers's most ardent and most intelligent admirers, and almost all that he wrote in the first half of his life is profoundly marked by his contacts with the writings and conversations of the older man. They seem to have been together frequently in 1888 and the early part of 1889, and Gourmont was even invited to dinner in Villiers's rooms—he was struck by a quaint ceremonial which Villiers carried out after the meal and which consisted of pouring drops of violet essence on to the guests' fingers, with the words: 'It's the custom of the house.'. Gourmont remembered a number of Villiers's unrealized projects: a war between the English and the Arabs, in which the Arabs exhaust their enemies by making them fight against mirages; a Sermon on the Mount in which all the effects would have been oblique, with Jesus coming down a twilit road, perceptible only by the influence emanating from him; the idea of a home for prospective suicides, with a whole array of possible means for killing oneself, including crucifixion 'for those who, tired of being men, want to become gods!'³

Gourmont, a sceptic himself, was unsure how deep Villiers's Christianity went, and was impressed by the dexterity —and the pleasure—with which he skirted round blasphemy without actually committing himself. He was not the only one to notice this tendency. Anatole France produced this lapidary formula: 'His piety was terribly impious',⁴ and Henry Roujon wrote: 'While laying claim to the faith of a seminarist, he took a delight in blaspheming. He considered the right to blasphemy as his personal property, and never allowed anyone to go along with him when he was having fun with the divine. This Breton Catholic spent more time in the company of Satan than that of God.'⁵ J. E. S. Jeanès remembered one occasion when Villiers shocked even the least religious customers at Pousset's by his account of the interrogation of Christ by Caiaphas. He began by acting the part of Caiaphas asking Christ if He was the Son of God, and making everyone feel how frightened and ill at ease Caiaphas was. Then he came to Christ's reply which he thundered out majestically:

'*You have said so!* ... Miserable lackey of the basest judges, do I have to explain to you what you know as well as I do? ... what all the prophets have foretold? It is vain for you to interrogate me ... *You have said so!* What sort of a half-priest are you to think you can deceive the Son of Man ... whose destiny is being accomplished according to the Book ... under your very eyes? ... You have said so! ... And right you are, mate!'

Whereupon Villiers roared with laughter at the surprise caused by his last phrase.⁶

Disconcerting as such performances may have been, they had for Villiers a deeper significance than the mere desire to startle. They seem to have come at a time when Villiers was also thinking of writing a work on the Passion, so they indicate a greater rather than a lesser preoccupation with religion. Not much of the work on the Passion has come to light, probably because Villiers was still toying with the idea and trying to find an adequate form for it, rather than actually getting down to writing it—the co-existence of a plan for something like a miracle play under the title of *Le Fils de l'Homme*[7] and notes for what was evidently intended to be a prose narrative of the events leading up to the Crucifixion[8] indicates that he was still uncertain how to treat it. But if on the one hand Villiers was contemplating some sort of composition based on a specifically Christian inspiration, on the other hand he could not rid himself of a feeling that God had been unfair to him personally. If the deep-seated discontent that had motivated Sara's 'No' and the outright rejection of Christianity in the early versions of *Axël* had been pushed further below the surface, if Villiers managed to prevent the movements of Faustian revolt in the original *Ève future* from getting out of hand, he had not succeeded in eliminating such feelings entirely. They consequently reappeared in disguised form, coming out as blasphemy which was not quite blasphemy, disrespect which bordered on insubordination without ever quite getting there. Perhaps too as his health failed more and more completely, there was a presentiment that time was short, and that the ultimate injustice would be for God to call him away before he had accomplished his mission.

In mundane terms, and despite the continuing poverty, Villiers's situation in the literary world might in fact have seemed enviable by 1888. It was no longer difficult for him to find publishers, the editors of literary magazines were pressing him for contributions, he was offered the chance of appearing in anthologies and even in oil-paintings, he was in demand for preface-writing, he had a whole group of fervent admirers, journalists wanted to interview him, his recommendation carried a certain weight. Yet his own attitude to these outward manifestations of fame remained ambivalent and mistrustful. How could he now be satisfied with the approval of a public which had laughed at him for so long and which he had learnt to despise? Remy de Gourmont had written a novel called *Patrice*, and Villiers offered to help in having it published. The paradoxes in his behaviour did not escape Gourmont, when they went together to the offices of the *Gil Blas*:

Villiers recommended the manuscript in the most equivocal terms, affirming that it was full of high society, sensuality, perversity, elegant suppers, parties, and courtesans, which was far from the truth. With these men, he affected the strangest attitude, showering them with salutations and compliments, creeping around like a humble collaborator, happy to be allowed into the company of so many masters. It was his way of scorning them.[9]

What Villiers wanted was not the transient approval of those people who had rejected him yesterday and might reject him again tomorrow; it was something much more akin to a transcendental sense of justification, which could only come from within.

That is perhaps why Villiers was inclined to take refuge in a rather haughty refusal to participate in collective manifestations. When in August 1887 Lemerre wanted to include something by Villiers in an *Anthologie des poètes français du XIXᵉ siècle*, he received an abrupt refusal with a threat of legal action: 'My formal desire is not to appear in any anthology and to withhold my permission, as is my right, *for any page of verse signed with my name to appear in a work of that kind.*'[10] He was no less firm with Édouard Dujardin when he was invited to pose for a picture of the contributors to the *Revue indépendante*: 'With me, it is an absolutely fixed principle, that I will not infringe—although I regret it on this one occasion.'[11] Always independent, Villiers seems to have wanted to maintain his reputation for not doing what was expected of him, even when he had much greater freedom of choice.

Indeed, when Paul Alhaiza, director of the Théâtre Molière in Brussels, approached him early in January 1888 about producing *L'Évasion*,[12] his first reaction was a blank refusal, and it was only after the actor Mévisto had written a long letter pleading with him that he was persuaded to change his mind.[13] Even then, he made it clear to Mévisto that he wanted first of all to have further discussions with him about the role of Pagnol and that he intended to go to Brussels to keep an eye on the rehearsals.[14] But, once the idea of a trip to Belgium had occurred to him, he began to wonder whether he might not undertake the lecture tour that he had had to cancel the previous year because of illness. Alhaiza wanted him to give an introductory talk on *L'Évasion*, but that he declined to do, no doubt on account of the mixed feelings he continued to harbour about the play. A series of readings from his works on the lines of his 1884 lecture on *Axël* was a different matter, however, the more so as Quantin was due to publish *Histoires insolites* at any moment: if he could give some public readings from them, he might well push the sales up.

Villiers seems to have taken few steps to organize the tour: in the end, all the arrangements were made at the last minute. It was only on 13 February, the day of his departure, that Huysmans discovered his plans, and was horrified. He immediately wrote to warn Jules Destrée:

He is very excited, dreaming of lectures, piles of gold, goodness knows what else, and is riding this chimaera even more ardently than the others, if that is possible. After long discussions with him, I have become absolutely convinced that he is going off with his eyes shut and is about to waste the few measly sous that he is taking with him.

So Destrée was asked to see if something really could be fixed up: 'Please try to keep an eye on him and stop him getting into too much trouble.'[15] To Arij Prins, Huysmans was even more sceptical: 'Villiers is off to Brussels this evening. He has real attacks of madness—he even thinks the Queen of the Belgians is interested in his literature (. . .) It isn't really madness—given Villiers—it is an indescribable transport of the imagination. It's been a hard day's work trying to knock some sense into the man's head.'[16]

By this stage there was of course no stopping him, and, paying his fare with money borrowed from Bloy, he took the train for Brussels on the evening of the thirteenth, and put up at the Grand Hôtel on his arrival—the performance was only scheduled for the sixteenth, but he wanted, as usual, to interfere in the rehearsals. The journalist Gustave Vanzype came to interview him in his hotel, and Villiers wrote two pieces for him, one a carefully copied phrase from *Axël*, to be reproduced in *Le Rapide*, Vanzype's paper, the other a notice, couched in the third person which he hoped Vanzype would also insert.[17] The young reporter, very nervous at meeting the great man, could not remember very much about their interview, which lasted for two or three hours: he recalled that Villiers's movements were those of an old man but his frenetic eloquence that of a hot-headed youth.

I can hear a prophetic voice, I can hear objurgations and Olympian imprecations, acts of faith and cries of pride; I can also hear weird improvisations and fantastic incantations at the piano of that hotel sitting-room; and at the end, as I was leaving him, I can see Villiers, who had had nothing to drink, drunk, positively drunk on his speeches, on his music, on his dreams.[18]

The performance of *L'Évasion* took place at a matinée on the sixteenth along with Armand Silvestre's *Sapho* and *Le Misanthrope et l'Auvergnat* by Labiche; it was preceded by an introductory talk on Villiers's theatre by Destrée.[19] The audience was delighted, and so was Villiers—he wrote in haste immediately afterwards to Marie Dantine: '*Enormous success. Five curtain-calls. Enthusiasm ...*'[20] The reviews were somewhat less favourable when they appeared, but nevertheless appreciative; in any case, Villiers was revelling in the publicity and in the friendly welcome he was receiving from his Belgian friends, notably Destrée and Verhaeren. As for the lectures, Villiers had obviously arrived without having anything organized, with the result that he had to wait around in Brussels while people tried to arrange something. In the meantime he was constantly being fêted at dinners and receptions, and for the first time in his life found everyone treating him with the deference accorded to a great man. His mind was still on his beloved Totor, all the same, and he regretted not having brought him—Marie was urged not to let him play with his hoop in the street during his father's absence.[21] He was also irritated that *Histoires insolites* were still not ready and kept writing to ask Malherbe why the copies had not been sent.[22] His hotel expenses too were mounting up, so, amid the joyful optimism about the money the lectures would bring, the happiness of being acclaimed by everyone, and the hopes of vast advance sales of *Histoires insolites*, there is also a slight note of anxiety in his letters, and he was only able to send 15 francs to Marie.

Eventually, it was arranged that he should lecture to the Salon des XX at Brussels on the twenty-third. He gave a reading of *Le Jeu des grâces*, *La Céleste Aventure* and *La Légende moderne*, and followed it up with a kind of encore in which he improvised an account of Wagner explaining to him the conception of *Die Meistersinger*. It was a great success, both with the audience and the press, but his fee was disappointingly low—only 100 francs. Moreover, the strain of talking so much in public and in private was beginning to tell on his weakened constitution, and he was suffering badly from the intense cold—'I've never seen such a country for black, silly, paralysing cold.'[23] The fact was that Villiers had a secret ambition and was growing discouraged that it did not seem to be on the way to realization. Huysmans had been quite right: Villiers was convinced that the Queen was personally interested in him, that he would be summoned to see her, and that she would somehow bestow on him instant riches. Soon after he arrived, he told Marie that he had not yet seen the Queen,[24] and other letters contained similar obscure hints: *'tomorrow everything may change very much for the better'*,[25] *'tomorrow, or this evening, everything may change'*.[26] But if the proximity of royalty produced its usual galvanizing effect on him, he had in the end no luck in approaching the Queen: yet another royal patron had (without knowing it) failed him.

By now Villiers was no longer staying in a hotel but in the house of the publisher Edmond Deman in the rue de la Consolation. Deman knew how poor Villiers was and used the pretext of arranging for the publication of an anthology of his finest tales to ensure that he had several days of rest, comfort, and good food. The projected volume was to be entitled *Histoires souveraines*, but in the event Villiers was so dilatory in supplying the material for it that it only came out ten years after his death.[27]

The next lecture took place at the Cercle de l'Émulation in Liége five days after the first one, on the twenty-eighth. It was reasonably successful, and Villiers was able to send Marie 25 francs from his fee, after which he returned to Brussels and the Demans' hospitality. But his voice was giving out under the strain, and in Liége the public reading, which was difficult to hear, aroused less enthusiasm than his private conversations. A final lecture was arranged at Ghent on 4 March, which only required a day trip, with a fee of 200 francs. To Marie, Villiers was positively gleeful: 'I gave a lecture in the Governor's castle, where the sort of success I had was astonishing—before bankers, bourgeois and bourgeoises, five hundred icy people whom I flatter myself that I made sit up straight on their red velvet seats.'[28] To Pierre, however, he confessed some disappointment: 'Oh! it's not very argentiferous—because of the cold!' and signed himself 'your useless and lugubrious friend'.[29] Part of his discontent came from worrying about Totor, since he had heard that Paris was as cold as Belgium, and he kept thinking that the boy would be ill, or cold, or hungry.

Once he was back in Brussels from Ghent, he hung on for a few more days in Deman's house in the hope that something more would turn up. His solicitude for Totor continued unabated: 'Buy a warm suit at once for Totor, and have his hair cut, not too short, so that it completely covers his ears: otherwise he'd catch cold.' But he also wanted Marie to get new clothes for Albert and herself. By now, even from her, he could not hide the fact that he was getting tired of being in Belgium: 'I've had enough of all this noise! I've had too much of it!!'[30] The extra days in Brussels were perhaps because he hoped the copies of *Histoires insolites* would arrive before his departure, perhaps also because he could not bear to tear himself away without the expected invitation from the Queen. In the end he resigned himself to taking the train back to Paris, where he arrived on 10 March, armed with a magnificent toy for Totor as a present from the Demans.

Once Villiers was in Paris again, the miseries of the cold, the small fees, and the missed opportunities were forgotten, and a mood of euphoria took over, the more so as he had been invited to return the following year for a better-organized and more lucrative tour. 'He's come back delighted with Belgium, and I thank you for having helped to make him happy,' Huysmans wrote to Destrée.[31] Gustave Guiches had the same impression: 'He returned agog with enthusiasm and furious with the haughty stupidity of Baudelaire who did not understand Belgium.'[32] The most remarkable evocation of what Belgium meant to him comes from Mallarmé, speaking to the same Belgian audience two years later:

Know that, prolix in his serious pride, he would stop people, even those little acquainted with the facts, on his way. 'Eh! Eh! Brussels' I shall always hear him and in that apostrophe as it were a sardonic warning of *Just you here behave properly*—he would go on: 'Brussels, yes, I shall say no more.' In truth, he did say no more, then passed on;

but soon returned: 'There is also Liége, Antwerp, Bruges, Ghent', recalling cities which make the traveller attentive, and delighted, adding: 'gentlemen whom *that* (he was speaking of Genius) does not incite to a yawn, and ladies who look, I know what I'm talking about, who look as though they are beginning to appreciate it; and as for the younger generation . . .' there the term of 'ovations' was only tempered by this one other 'fraternal welcome'. In the end it was a tale in which, beneath his gesture of a sculptor of horizons (your very landscapes), everything took on an unaccustomed value, and its fixity relaxed in our conviction.[33]

Belgium in retrospect was a consecration for him, and one of the greatest satisfactions in his life.

In the excitement of his tour, Villiers had not had time to write many letters apart from those he sent to Marie and a few lines to Émile Pierre. The only other one was a brief note to Bloy, which Huysmans, with some justification, called 'the incoherent letter of a drunkard'[34] and which caused him to suspect that Villiers was drowning in floods of beer.[35] But while Huysmans was prepared to be tolerant of his friend's failings, Bloy, possessive and overbearing, was not, and, when Villiers did not get in touch with him immediately on his return, he exploded with anger in a letter to Louis Montchal:

As if all this terrible misery was not enough, I have had to suffer tortures in my dearest affections. I perhaps told you that Villiers had gone on a trip to Belgium to give some lectures. This journey, of which I had no great hopes, was made possible *by me*. I left him an hour before his departure, having completely divested myself of some money which I had got together, God knows at what cost! His trip lasted three weeks, and, against every expectation, it was a triumph. He has been back for a week already, with his pockets full of money, and I'm still waiting to hear from him. Huysmans, who has so often come to his aid and is struggling with a situation almost as frightful as my own, hasn't heard anything either. On the other hand, we have learned that Villiers has been giving superb and costly dinners at Brébant's to literary scoundrels. We think he'll come back to us as soon as he has run out of money again, which won't be long.[36]

As usual Bloy was jumping to conclusions. Villiers had not brought much money back from Belgium, the person whom he had entertained to dinner at Brébant's was Gustave de

Malherbe, with whom he wanted to discuss *Axël* and *Histoires insolites*,[38] and the wet weather, combined with exhaustion, had made him take to his bed, where he was wondering why Bloy did not come to see him.[38] But Bloy's quarrelsome nature led him to an extraordinary touchiness with his friends, and relations with Villiers never recovered from the misunderstanding.

The meeting with Malherbe had been necessary because Quantin, now that *Histoires insolites* was out of the way, was anxious to get on with *Axël* as quickly as possible. Within days of his return, Villiers had copied out and sent to Malherbe the scene *Le Droit au silence* which had appeared in the *Revue indépendante* the year before, and he added: 'The rest of *Axël* will very soon follow this time, that's for sure.'[39] In fact, as soon as he started work on it again, he was gripped by the idea of further changes and improvements, particularly to the scenes between Axël and the Commander, which had already caused him endless trouble. What bothered him was how to justify Axël's conduct in killing the Commander in order that the treasure might remain for ever in its hiding-place, when immediately afterwards Axël was to join Sara in discovering it. The problem had been with him ever since he had inserted the figure of the Commander into the original structure, and he kept on adding further tortuous explanations in the vain hope that he could somehow solve it. *Le Droit au silence* had been written in order that Axël might expound and defend (at inordinate length) his refusal to allow anyone to search for the treasure; now he embarked on another extended harangue about how the castle could be held if it were ever attacked. These tirades, which are long, cumbersome, and irrelevant to the philosophic and emotional import of the play, are a mistake on Villiers's part. One can see that his intention was to clarify certain obscurities in his drama, but in fact all he was succeeding in doing was making sections of it leaden and static.

Still, the new passage about the defences of the castle was completed on 22 May, and the packets of page proofs, which had started arriving towards the end of April, were still coming out regularly at the end of June. Then, abruptly, they stopped. Evidently the directors of Quantin had had enough of Villiers's delays and additions, which meant that publication had already been held up for almost eighteen months and that all the original estimates of production costs had been hopelessly thrown out. Faced with the threat that Quantin would abandon the project altogether, Villiers sought the advice of Darzens, who started negotiations with Vanier, the publisher already approached for *Axël* in 1886.[40] But nothing was concluded with Vanier, and for months the situation stagnated, with production suspended and no firm decision taken about the future.

At the same time, Villiers was still thinking about the possibility of a work on the Passion, and was reading around the subject among modern biblical scholars. He had always had a violent prejudice against Ernest Renan, the most eminent among them, and he was delighted when he thought he had discovered an error in the famous *Vie de Jésus*, over the question of whether or not there had been a cock in Jerusalem at the time of Peter's betrayal of Christ (in fact, Villiers was wrong: it was not Renan but the German historian Sepp who had contested the existence of the cock). Remy de Gourmont noted the effect that this supposed discovery had on him: 'one day when we were sitting at the terrace of a boulevard café, I had the illusion that I was listening to the ravings of a madman, in which the same affirmation kept recurring: "There was a cock! There was one!"'[41] To Adrien Remacle, Villiers was jubilant:

St. Renan claims, like the well-read professor he is, that at the time of Christ the cock, having been declared an unclean beast in the Hebrew world by the teaching of the high priests, was forbidden and non-existent in Jerusalem; so ... He's right: not a cock in Israel. Except *one*, one alone, a very special one, I have conclusively demonstrated it to the gentleman of the *Vie de Jésus*, who has had to give in and admit he was in the wrong. As an exception, in the very Temple of Jerusalem itself, where St. Peter was to deny the Master, in the place where the organ would be in a church, there was a *cock* in a cage, to tell the time by its crowing! The whole of Ernest twisting the Scriptures is the same sort of historical error.[42]

At first Villiers thought of producing an article to denounce Renan and sketched out a few highly insulting paragraphs.[43] Then he decided instead to write his own account of St. Peter's denial of Christ, emphasizing the presence of the cock, and composed *Le Chant du coq*, which appeared in the *Revue libre* in May 1888. J. E. S. Jeanès, who worked for the review, found him still in a state of excitement when he went to collect the manuscript: 'When he gave me *Le Chant du coq*, his main concern was to prove that there really and indubitably was a cock kept in the Temple of Jerusalem, a cock whose 'prophetic' necessity and time-keeping utility were combined so as to signal, at the appropriate moment, St. Peter's denial.'[44]

Le Chant du coq was destined to form the epilogue of Villiers's next collection of short stories, *Nouveaux Contes cruels*, which was published at the beginning of November 1888. This time, having for various reasons been in dispute successively with Calmann Lévy, Brunhoff, Stock, and Quantin, Villiers turned to a firm called the Librairie illustrée. But one of the causes of Villiers's discontent with Brunhoff had precisely been over the illustrations, and when *La Vie populaire* had reproduced *Catalina*, a suspense story about a boa constrictor in a hotel room, with a picture of the snake on the cover, he had said ruefully to the artist: 'Obviously, it's a very good drawing . . . but for a hundred and fifty lines, I try and hide from the reader that the pendulum is a boa, and you go and stick it on the front page, so that he sees it before he has even read the story . . .'[45] So this time, Villiers was adamant, with the paradoxical result that the only work of his published by the Librairie illustrée does not in fact have a single illustration.

Nouveaux Contes cruels is the shortest of Villiers's collections of short stories. It is also the least distinguished, and it is a pity that the title recalling *Contes cruels* has given it undue prominence compared to *L'Amour suprême* or *Histoires insolites*. It appeared no more than nine months after *Histoires insolites*, and it only contains eight stories, all he had produced in the meantime in the *Gil Blas* and elsewhere. Thought he reaffirms his monarchical and religious opinions with vigour, and though some of the pieces are amusing and ingenious, they are on the whole developed rather schematically, and several of them depend on borrowed subjects. Pressure of time and poor health account of course for this relative unoriginality: Villiers could not afford to neglect his regular journalistic production if he was to keep body and soul together, but in *Nouveaux Contes cruels* the effort is beginning to show. Villiers needed time for his subjects to ripen, time for his ideas to expand, time for his style to reach the peak of perfection, and that time was lacking here.

In fact, after his return from Belgium, Villiers's health gave ever-increasing cause for concern. Gustave Guiches was shocked at the frailty which caused him to collapse into a chair as soon as he made the slightest exertion.

At such times, the light from outside would fall on his face like the livid glow of an eclipse. His pallor would grow so diaphanous that it seemed like the transparence of a communion wafer, and on his face there was such an expression of suffering that in my mind's eye I could not help removing his clothes, stretching his arms wide and seeing him thus, crucified, on the granite of a Breton calvary.[46]

Forced to live in rooms which were cheap because they were so high up, he came out less and less because he was terrified at the thought of having to climb up five flights of stairs again, when only a single flight put him out of breath for ten minutes. To his chronic bronchitis had for some time been added constant stomach pains and disquieting heart symptoms. He was more bent, his hair was greyer, and his head was beginning to tremble like that of an old man, though he was barely fifty.

35

It was early in 1888 that Villiers moved into what was to be his last Parisian residence, at 45 rue Fontaine, in Montmartre near the Place Blanche. For some time past he had been hankering after a house in the country outside Paris, and had asked Lucien Descaves's father to see if he could find something suitable at Montrouge.[1] But nothing came of it, and in the end he stayed in the quarter to which over the years he had always been faithful. The rooms in the rue Fontaine were no improvement on those he had previously inhabited in the rue Blanche and the rue Pigalle. Hugues Le Roux, a journalist who went to interview him there, noted how miserable they were: 'The writer lived very near the Boulevard Clichy in a dark, airless flat where his dreams were confined in three almost bare rooms: the biggest of them was three-quarters filled by a large walnut grand piano, which left very little space for the table at which he worked.' Le Roux, who wanted some information about Villiers's ancestry for an article he was writing, had not realized what a night-bird he was, and found him in bed. Villiers received him amiably, got up, and dressed, but when he realized what Le Roux was after, said in distress: 'What! you want me to talk about Malta, like that, at nine o'clock in the morning?'[2] One disconcerting feature of his installation was the presence in the flat of a tame pigeon. According to Jeanès, the pigeon liked Wagner's music and Villiers's voice, and must have had a highly developed aesthetic sense, as it always chose a climactic moment to come flapping on to its favourite perch.[3]

Édouard Rod was as pained as Guiches by the change in Villiers's appearance when he saw him about this time: 'He was now only a shadow of his former self: his low voice had become even more hollow, echoing from the emptiness of his ravaged lungs; as he walked he was more bent than ever, in even more lamentable overcoats; he looked like a pauper, a real pauper, no longer even like a pauper in a black frock coat.'[4]

But, because he came out so little, Villiers did not see much of his friends in 1888. Mallarmé spent the summer partly at Royat taking the waters with Méry Laurent and partly at Valvins, but did not succeed in persuading Villiers to visit him there. Marras, who had been deputy curator of the palace at Fontainebleau where Villiers occasionally stayed with him, had now returned to a post in Paris, and Mallarmé joked that Villiers disdained grass and only wanted to sleep in palaces.[5] From time to time Huysmans would report to Prins that he had seen Villiers and, in a favourite metaphor, that the punchbowl was still inextinguishably flaming in his mind,[6] but the regular Sunday dinners were now a thing of the past; in any case, Huysmans spent part of the summer in Germany. As for Bloy, he was drawing apart from both of his former friends, and matters came to a head between him and Villiers early in September. Not having seen Villiers for several months, Bloy wrote to him to ask for money, having heard rumours of his prosperity; though the text of the letter is not known, there can be no doubt that it was full of those venomous reproaches of which Bloy was a past master. Irritated by the accusations, the more so as he was in fact far from being in funds, Villiers replied impatiently and ironically. The result was a letter from Bloy in effect breaking off relations, and in terms so extreme that they seem symptomatic of monstrous selfishness and incomprehension:

You are quite right to make fun of me, since I was silly and unjust enough to hope that I might get from you the only thing you are incapable of giving, that is to say, the feeling of friendship. *You have never wanted and you still don't want to have friends.* When you had the chance of some, you set about discouraging them, making no distinction between them and chance acquaintances. Terribly unwise, since SOULS are not a common commodity and it is always an iniquitous judgement to condemn oneself to die alone.[7]

After that, the breach could never be healed, though Villiers does not seem to have taken as much offence as one might have expected. He and Bloy still met several times again, and Bloy momentarily softened his anger sufficiently to write to Montchal: 'He doesn't even realize how much he hurt me. One has to take people as they are and not ask them for what they can't give.'[8] But it was not long before he informed the same correspondent that he had more or less fallen out with Villiers.[9] By this time Villiers had finally lost his temper and drafted a letter to Bloy which ended:

I count on all your intelligence to *understand* that we must not see each other again. I have no time to give you explanations which would be an insult to the Spirit that is in you. In any case, I ask you to deprive me absolutely, from now on, of your presence, as I will dispense you, I hope, from suffering mine. Please accept my regrets for having known you.[10]

These lines are so untypical of Villiers's normally easy-going nature that one wonders if the letter was ever sent. There can, however, be no doubt of the extreme anger Villiers felt with Bloy, since he drafted a page of notes about him in a very passable imitation of Bloy's own vulgar style of invective, in which he dubs his ex-friend 'the Maculator' and describes him, crudely but aptly, as 'a volcano of shit'.[11]

It may be that what had aroused Bloy's ire in the first place was hearing that Villiers had carried out on his own the plan they had jointly devised the previous year. Lord Salisbury was once again spending the summer at Dieppe, and in September Villiers took his courage in both hands and went off to seek his support. Exactly what happened is shrouded in mystery. Villiers evidently arrived on the twenty-first and took a room at the Hôtel Royal while he scouted out the lie of the land: 'I've seen the Cecil castle. I expect to see the Marquis of Salisbury *this very day*.' In the same letter to Marie, he congratulated himself on not having brought Totor because of the expense: 'He has time to wait for happy days; my only duty is to make them possible for him.'[12] On the twenty-sixth he reported to a friend that Salisbury had visited him in his hotel.[13] A day or two later he was back in Paris, with less than 25 francs in his pocket, having sent ten to Bloy.[14] So much is clear from the correspondence; the rest is obscure. A legend, put about by Villiers himself, has it that he harangued the Marquis for several hours on end, much impressed by the fact that his lordship never interrupted him once, and only discovered later that the Marquis was stone deaf.[15] But in reality the Marquis was certainly not deaf, and one must assume that Villiers invented the story to explain to his friends why he had returned to Paris empty-handed. The truth is that Villiers had sent Lord Salisbury an impeccably courteous letter to thank him for his visit, with no hint that any untoward incident had occurred. It is probable either that Villiers was too embarrassed to raise the subject of money, or that he did so in such an oblique fashion that his illustrious visitor did not realise what was expected of him.[16]

The year 1888 was not much more fertile in literature than in money-raising schemes. Apart from the handful of tales which went to make up *Nouveaux Contes cruels*, Villiers was apparently not working on any major project except perhaps the history of his family. The suspension of work on *Axël* seems to have lasted from the summer of 1888 into the spring of 1889; the titles listed on the flyleaf of *Nouveaux Contes cruels*, much the same as those in *Tribulat Bonhomet*, still seem to be no more than ideas; the possibility of a drama on the Passion seemed to have receded. Indeed, something that happened at the end of the year probably induced him to give it up for good. His young friend Rodolphe Darzens had written a one-act play entitled *L'Amante du Christ*, and in October 1888 Antoine produced it at the Théâtre Libre; a few weeks later the text was published by Lemerre, complete with a preface by the biblical scholar Eugène Ledrain and a frontispiece by Félicien Rops. The play, which retells the story of Christ and Mary Magdalen in tasteless and sentimental verse, is a mediocre piece of work, even though it did have some success, with Mévisto, Villiers's Pagnol, in the part of Christ, and the edition compounds its vulgarity—Ledrain's fulsome preface is composed in a pastiche of Renan's most ingratiating prose, and in the frontispiece Rops has even been crass enough to give Darzens's features to the face of Christ.

This was too much for Villiers, who published a denunciation of the play in the *Gil Blas* under the title 'Notre Seigneur Jésus-Christ sur les planches'. Though he reserves his severest criticisms for the author of the preface, and though he takes advantage of the occasion to work off a few anti-semitic epigrams, he does not spare Darzens, guilty in his eyes of two offences: having tried to improve on the Bible by inserting new elements into the story, and having ventured to versify the Scriptures. He tempers the harshness of his views somewhat by making it plain that he is not judging the play from a literary point of view and that his purpose is only to correct 'the grave errors of a brother in Christianity'[17]; the tenor of the article is nonetheless surprising when one considers his closeness to Darzens. It is even more surprising when one remembers that he had himself written a verse narrative about Mary Magdalen in *Premières Poésies*, had published *Le Chant du coq* only a few months before, and was contemplating some kind of dramatic version of the Passion.

In the end one is led to wonder whether Villiers is not in fact upbraiding himself as much as Darzens. Perhaps reading *L'Amante du Christ* had opened his eyes to the fact that basing works of art on the Gospels was verging on the sacrilegious; perhaps the mediocrity of the play had made him realize how heavy the penalties for failure would be in such a dangerous enterprise. At all events, it seems clear that, after his condemnation of the principle involved in Darzens's work, there could be no question of his completing his own projected Passion play. Villiers's religious sensibility had become much more acute at this time, and the notebooks from the end of his life are full of meditations on Christianity, some of them very moving, this prayer for instance: 'O God, may it please You that I should be taken in by noble and beautiful things all my life.'[18] Another note is particularly revealing of a temptation he must often have felt: 'What is the desire? Not to suffer enough for it to be possible to stop loving Jesus Christ.'[19] The strength of his faith is evident in the simplicity of this phrase: 'In death, to be eternally in that which is Jesus Christ in order to love Him with all one's being.'[20] His thoughts had turned so much to these matters that he was even capable of declaring: 'I don't give a damn about literature. I believe only in eternal life!'[21]

The fact is that his state of health was so precarious that the idea of death, which had always preoccupied him, had by now become ever-present, and the onset of the winter, which he had dreaded for several years, heightened his alarms. In September he had been well enough to bathe in the sea during his visit to Dieppe, but early in December he fell seriously ill with pleurisy and pneumonia. The strain on his heart, coupled with the persistent stomach pains from which he suffered, made him think the end might be near. One night he felt his heart giving out so rapidly that he woke Marie and asked her to bring Totor, but even then his sense of humour did not desert him: 'I want to give him my blessing! . . . It'll be better than nothing! . . .'[22] At least two doctors were called in: Dr Albert Robin, who had attended him in previous illnesses and whose literary tastes meant that he would accept an autographed book rather than money in payment, and Dr Henri Cazalis, an old friend of Mallarmé and a poet under the name Jean Lahor. In his distress, Villiers turned to both Huysmans and Mallarmé. To Huysmans he wrote: 'What can one say? You are a really good person. That's all.'[23] To Mallarmé, he said simply: 'If you have a minute, come and shake my hand.'[24] The two friends were equally solicitous, knowing that, since Villiers was incapable of writing, no money was coming into the house at all, and they quietly saw to it that he and his family lacked nothing.

By Christmas the worst seemed to be past, and, though he suffered several relapses, his lungs were gradually clearing up. On the other hand, there were fears that his heart was seriously affected, and he complained that the feeling of hollowness in his stomach was becoming intolerable, and that he was still terribly short of breath. Even so he was able to start writing again, though he was unable to satisfy Deman, who had become somewhat impatient at his long delay in doing anything about the proposed anthology *Histoires souveraines*, or Baschet, who kept wondering pointedly when *Les Filles de Milton* would be forthcoming. He was not well enough to go out yet, and had to rely on his friends to support him in the meantime. Méry Laurent, with her usual generosity, continually sent him presents and delicacies, and wanted to come and visit him in his sickroom. But Villiers refused:

You who are a sovereign, do not come to the slum in which I live, as present-day princes do. It would hurt me not to be able to welcome you with all the effects of candelabras, flowers, and sweetmeats ready served. I am one of those rather rare people for whom hardship is only a dream—from which one wakes up, even in this world. All I have to do is close my eyes and many an Élysée Palace would fade into insignificance beside the Arabian Nights of my fourth-floor rooms. But if you come, the real you, just imagine how heartrending it will be for me not to be able to project into the illusion of life the radiant palace in which I could receive you as you deserve![25]

Nevertheless she came, with yet more gifts, and Villiers was overwhelmed: 'You are too good to me and you are giving yourself a lot of trouble, for which I can't forgive myself. Just think that to have come to see me is enough, and that I shall never forget it.'[26]

By the end of January Villiers appeared to be on the mend, and Huysmans was able to tell Prins: 'Villiers is on his feet again—but seriously affected all the same. He'll do well to keep clear of pubs and nights in the open air'.[27] He was sufficiently recovered to write two stories, the last he was to complete, *Maître Pied* and *Le Meilleur Amour*. The first is a political satire, born of two events: the election of General Boulanger as deputy for a Paris constituency in January 1889, and the election, shortly before, of Félix Pyat as revolutionary socialist deputy for the Bouches-du-Rhône. Pyat was a notorious character whose previous convictions included fines amounting to 212,000 francs, 29 years of deportation, 5 months in prison, 10 years loss of civic rights, and even a death sentence. For Villiers, he was tailor-made as the typical republican parliamentarian, and, with all the Boulangist agitation against the regime and its corruption, he saw an ideal opportunity to concoct yet another of his political satires on the Third Republic and its servants. The eponymous hero of the tale is thus represented as a lawyer who cold-bloodedly decides that the only way to found a political career is to commit a gratuitous and dastardly crime. Though the story is obviously intended to take advantage of Boulanger's campaign against parliamentary government, it is not conceived as a propaganda exercise in favour of Boulanger —like many royalists, Villiers was not without sympathy for the general, but he seems to have held back from open support until he was more certain about the way in which the situation would develop.[28]

In the event, *Maître Pied* proved too inflammatory for either *Le Figaro* or *Le Gaulois*, and, when Pyat, to whom the tale openly alludes, died on 3 August 1889, it became difficult for anyone to consider publishing it. *Le Meilleur Amour* on the other hand was the last of Villiers's tales to appear during his lifetime, and it is fitting that it should be so, since it is perhaps the most poignant and in some ways the most personal he ever wrote. It tells of a young Breton, Guilhem Kerlis, who falls in love with Yvaine, a girl from his village. Their love is pure and chaste, and, when he is called away to the army, she swears to wait faithfully for his return. But as his absence in North Africa grows longer, she gradually turns to a life of pleasure and finally becomes a prostitute. Guilhem never discovers this, since a last scruple makes her continue to write to him as though she were still his virginal fiancée. Then Guilhem is mortally wounded in a skirmish with some Arabs; he dies happy, gazing at a photograph of his beloved Yvaine. Villiers prefaces the story with these words: 'Among those predestined not to conventional happiness, but to *true* happiness, we must count a young Breton named Guilhem Kerlis. One can say that few men, in their love, were more fortunate than he. Yet how simple his story was!'[29] There is an infinite sadness in this gravely told tale, but no bitterness; Villiers has achieved a masterly condensation of a whole philosophy of life in a beautifully controlled narration.

In the meantime the improvement in his health and a new agreement with the firm of Quantin meant that the printing of *Axël*, suspended since the previous summer, could be resumed. On 11 March Villiers told Malherbe that the real work on the book was finished, that he would return the remainder of the proofs of *Le Monde occulte* in a fortnight, and that the volume could appear at the end of April.[30] Another letter the following day to the director of the firm set out the fresh conditions which Villiers had accepted: the publication date would be the end of April, the format and the price would be increased to take account of all the additions and alterations, but Villiers would only claim half the extra royalties to which he would thus become entitled.[31] A few days later he signed a contract with Edmond Bailly for the publication of a selection of his articles under the title *Chez les passants*, for an advance of 500 francs:[32] this was the realization of an old project, and Villiers had already prepared his choice of pieces, which he had previously submitted to a publisher called Lavignet.[33] In fact, Bailly's acceptance of the manuscript was motivated less by commercial considerations than by the charitable desire to do something to relieve Villiers's poverty.[34] For *Chez les passants*, the proposed date of publication was 1 May. Momentarily, it appeared that Villiers's literary activity was about to get into full swing again.

He was also sufficiently recovered to take practical steps about getting out of the rue Fontaine and into more salubrious surroundings, and early in February, despite the cold, had travelled to various places near Paris to inspect possible houses to rent. For a few days he stayed in one such house at Fontenay-sous-Bois, but evidently decided against it. Then in the last week of March he had to take to his bed once again, under the care of Dr Édouard Fournier, who had been

recommended to him by Méry Laurent, in the absence of Drs
Robin and Cazalis. By the beginning of April, though, he
was about again and, with the help of Marras, was negotiating
for a house at Viroflay. One revealing phrase in the letter he
wrote to Marras on 3 April shows how seriously worried he
was about his condition, despite the brave face he was putting
on it: 'I am renting this house in the name of Mme Brégeras,
so that, in case of accident, she should be in a place of her
own.'[35] But in the end that plan too fell through.

What Villiers did not know was that his friends, led by
Mallarmé, had already rallied to his assistance, and that it was
their generosity which was making it possible for him and his
family to subsist. On 12 March Mallarmé, with the agreement
of Huysmans and Dierx, had sent out to a large number of
friends and men of letters a circular couched in these terms:

Our unfortunate friend Villiers de l'Isle-Adam is passing through a
crisis, illness, worries, of uncertain duration: some of us would like
to alleviate it for him, and I believe you would feel regret not to be
informed of this. To commit oneself to a fixed sum of five francs,
every month, handed over at regular intervals or by an advance,
with a postal draft, seems to be the simple way. We shall begin at
once, in March.

The response to this discreet appeal was remarkable, and fifty
or more friends began to subscribe. They included Baronnet,
Coppée, Deman, Dumas, Guiches, Heredia, Lavedan, Maupassant, Mendès, Sully Prudhomme, and Verhaeren, and for
the next few months Mallarmé as secretary of the subscription was to accomplish a vast amount of work in gathering in
the money and passing it on to Villiers in the guise of
pretended royalties, fees, or advances, so that the sick man
should not realize that he was in receipt of charity.[36]

Coppée and Dumas *fils* both used their influence to extract
larger sums from official bodies, with the result that the
Société des Auteurs dramatiques voted a donation of 1000
francs, the Ministère des Beaux-Arts gave 300 francs, and *Le
Figaro* 500 francs. Catulle Mendès, who was editor of *La Vie
populaire*, gave orders for the serialization of *Tribulat
Bonhomet*[37] (he had been promising to do it since 1887),[38]
which brought in a further 640 francs. This meant that, for

the time being, the financial situation was reasonably secure, and so Villiers was able to resume his search for a house outside Paris. Eventually it was his friend Émile Pierre who suggested to him that he might be able to rent the house at 15 rue de la Croix in Nogent-sur-Marne, where Pierre had previously lived and where Villiers had stayed in 1886 and 1887. It was not by any means ideal, since it had been uninhabited for nearly three years, and as Villiers himself admitted, 'was in a state that verged on the sordid',[39] but it was quiet, it had a garden, and it was surrounded by woods. So on 14 April he moved in with his family, and, once the landlord had tidied up the garden and Marie had cleaned the inside, he began to feel that the change of air and the end of the winter might restore him at least partially to health.

36

By now Mallarmé and Villiers were closer than they had ever been, even though they had for long had an almost uncanny understanding of one another, as is shown by two anecdotes related by Gustave Guiches. The first concerns a dream which Villiers recounted to Guiches. He had had a nightmare in which, taking out one of the papers in which he habitually rolled his cigarettes, he noticed that the tiny packet was labelled *Complete Works of Stéphane Mallarmé*. But when he tried to read it, page followed page, in vast quantities, yet without increasing the volume of the whole. His exasperation at the endless turning of pages grew so intense that he woke up and saw, open on his bed, that miniature masterpiece *L'Après-midi d'un faune*. 'Only a genius', said Villiers, 'can make infinity appear in such a tiny piece of finitude! . . .' Guiches's story about Mallarmé is no less expressive. He was once with Wyzéwa and Mallarmé in the offices of the *Revue indépendante*, when the lights failed while Mallarmé was reading over the latest of his highly abstruse articles on the theatre. Without hesitation Mallarmé went on reciting in the dark, then said:

Villiers de l'Isle-Adam wrote the last pages of *L'Ève future* flat on his stomach on the floor of a room emptied of its furniture and lit by the stump of a candle. Flat on his stomach, Wyzéwa! Flat on his stomach! But his spirit stood upright. For the spirit, with some people, always forms a right angle with the crushed body . . .[2]

Though Mallarmé and Villiers may never have put all their feelings for one another in words, and though in many ways they were very different, they had a deep and instinctive relationship which went far beyond any ordinary friendship or even affection. Never was that relationship stronger than in the last months of Villiers's life.

But though his arrival at Nogent had raised Villiers's hopes of recovery, his friends found him already very changed, and were pessimistic about the future. Huysmans told Prins: 'He can't get back into the saddle at all. I think that one of his lungs is damaged, as well as the heart,'[3] and Mallarmé described him to the novelist Octave Mirbeau as 'absolutely affected'.[4] Villiers himself could not but realize that he was by no means sure to live, and, though he talked cheerfully about lying in his hammock and learning by heart various of Mallarmé's works, including the prose poem *Le Nénuphar blanc*,[5] his mind was in fact on other and gloomier things. The first of them was the question of *Axël*, which was causing him much anguish. Though he had undertaken to allow Quantin to finish the printing rapidly, the religious scruples which had already dictated the modification of the end in 1886 had become even more imperious, and, as he feared death might be near, he was very reluctant to commit himself to the still distinctly unchristian message of the drama which, as he saw all too clearly, was indeed going to be his spiritual testament. The result of these agonizing doubts was the decision to adapt *Axël* in such a way as to give it a Christian sense, and it was to this desperate attempt that he devoted what remained of his waning strength.

Of the new scenes which this radical change would have necessitated, only one reached anything like a definitive form. This is a portion of the dialogue between Axël and Maître Janus, in which, to his other reasons for refusing initiation, Axël now adds fidelity to Christianity. With this insertion, *Le Monde occulte* would not otherwise have needed altering, but obviously *Le Monde passionnel* would have required extensive revision, since the lovers could no longer have been allowed to commit suicide. Only brief and fragmentary sketches for such a revision were made, and it is not possible to deduce from them exactly what Villiers's intentions were, even supposing he knew himself. No doubt the play would have concluded with a double renunciation, after remembrance of the Cross had called Axël and Sara back from the edge of the grave; he would have entered a monastery and she a convent, after the treasure had been remitted to the Church.[6] But how exactly Villiers meant to lead up to this conclusion one cannot know.

What is certain is that the decision to make *Axël* a Christian work did not come until April at the earliest, and that Villiers did not have either the time or the peace of mind to consider all its consequences. In reality, it is difficult to see how a Christian ending could have seemed anything other than illogical after Sara's firm rejection of the Church in *Le Monde religieux*. The sombrely pessimistic idealism of the drama is coherent as it stands, and it underlies the whole conception of the work; to have tried to twist it into something else at the last minute would have been to destroy it utterly. It is entirely to Villiers's honour that he should have wished to make his masterwork conform to the latest evolution of his thought, but it is unthinkable that the resultant hybrid could have been aesthetically satisfactory. Villiers had lived with *Axël* for twenty years, and it had become so much a part of him that he could not bear to see it fixed in a final, unchangeable form, detached from his being and for all time bearing witness to what he was. Had he survived, one may be sure that *Axël* would have gone through revision after revision, and just as it is unsure that the 1889 text represents any improvement on the *Jeune France* version, so it is even less sure that the Christian fragments could have led to a viable work on any level.

The second major worry that beset him at Nogent was Totor's future, and this preoccupation weighed very heavily on his mind as his health failed to improve in the way he had desired. Totor had been the almost exclusive focus of his affections ever since he was born. He hated to be separated from him, and, if they had been apart for a few hours, embraced him as though he had not seen him for months.

Everyone agreed that Totor was an unusually handsome and intelligent child, and Villiers had placed in his son all the hopes and ambitions he knew he could never realize himself. But he not only had nothing to leave Totor, he had not even any legal connection with him, since the official birth certificate made no mention of the father. In the eyes of the law, Totor was Victor Dantine, and, when Villiers died, the name Villiers de l'Isle-Adam would become extinct. With his fanatical devotion to the family glory, it can be imagined how such an idea must have tormented him. Brooding on this problem cannot have lightened the long hours of pain and weariness in the garden or in his sick-bed in the little house at Nogent.

At first Villiers had one or two visitors in Nogent. A young doctor friend, Maurice de Fleury, came out to see him, no doubt thinking of happier times when they used to wander around Paris at night together. On one such occasion, Fleury had been crossing the Pont des Arts with Villiers and Totor when a *bateau-mouche* had suddenly lit up its red and green navigation lights. Startled and delighted, Totor had asked: 'Oh, papa, what's that?' and Villiers, struck by the resemblance with the red and green bottles traditional in the windows of chemists' shops, had replied: 'It's the souls of the chemists taking wing!'[7] On this Sunday afternoon, Fleury, after talking to Villiers for some time, realized that the poet was becoming anxious lest his guest should invite himself to dinner. Knowing Villiers's circumstances, Fleury of course had no such intention, but Villiers decided he had better take no risks and, putting on an air of consternation, said: 'Oh! just imagine, we had a magnificent leg of mutton, a leg of mutton the like of which one seldom sees. But the dog, that wretched dog you see there, has eaten it all up! He even dragged off the torn remains into the gutter. It's all gone . . .' And, to lend credibility to his story, Villiers rounded on the unfortunate animal: 'You bad dog, you thief, you're the one who ate the leg of mutton!'[8]

Another visitor was the poet Georges Rodenbach, at whose wedding Villiers had been a witness in 1888. Evidently Villiers was in a bleak mood that day; looking out of the window at the chestnut trees with their white blossom, he said: 'They're carrying candles for a funeral.'[9] Rodenbach was not the only young writer who wanted to call on Villiers; on another occasion, Ephraïm Mikhaël came with a friend. But Villiers was becoming weaker, and wrote to Mallarmé in distress on 29 April: 'Visits do me harm, and it would be nice of you to say so in the way you know how to say delicate things,—Mickhaël [*sic*], who has a lot of talent, and young Mario de Saint-Ygest came, that made me talk. That kills me. I don't want to see anyone except *you and Dierx*, or Huysmans, *nobody else.*'[10] At the same time Villiers showed himself as considerate for Mallarmé as Mallarmé was for him. He even sent his friend 50 francs in case he should find himself short of money,[11] and, although he felt a desperate need for Mallarmé's company, was remorseful about making him come out to Nogent: 'My dear kind friend, Sunday is the only day when you can get on with your own work, I can't take from you what is sacred, what you have no right to give me.'[12] Literature for Villiers still took precedence over personal satisfaction.

In the early part of May Villiers's condition deteriorated sharply, and the crisis was so severe that Mallarmé thought he might be dying. Even when the sunshine and warm weather brought about some improvement, Mallarmé still felt that his chances of recovery were slight. Villiers's face was grey, he was terribly emaciated, and the stomach pains were becoming ever more intense. A local doctor called Liébaut was attending him, and Dr Fournier was giving advice, but Mallarmé thought it prudent towards the end of the month to take Dr Robin out to see him. Robin gave him a thorough examination, but what he told Mallarmé in the train on the way back to Paris was far from encouraging: the lungs were on the mend, the heart was not in too bad a state, but it seemed likely that the stomach pains were the result of cancer.[13] Villiers of course was not told, except that it was the stomach that needed attention; he was given to understand that it was some kind of dilatation that would eventually subside.[14]

There were nevertheless remissions in his suffering. The doctors advised him that it was a matter more of diet and hygiene than of medication, and banned beer and tobacco, which was a great sacrifice for him, though he was still able to drink wine provided he diluted it with water. These precautions did him some good, and early in June he even went back to Paris for the day, doubtless to be taken round the Great Exhibition in a wheel-chair. Edison had come to Paris for the Exhibition, and a copy of *L'Ève future* was sent to him by Villiers's friends, in the hope that he would consent to see the man who had made him a remarkable fictional character as well as an outstanding inventor. But nothing came of it.[15] What Villiers did get out of his trip to the Exhibition was a sight of the newly-completed Eiffel Tower, built as its centrepiece, and that gave him an idea for a story intriguingly entitled *Le Revenant de la Tour Eiffel*.[16] But the exertion left him totally exhausted, and he was bitterly disappointed that his absence from Nogent had made him miss a visit from Mallarmé. Touchingly, he sent Mallarmé the money for his fare.[17]

Throughout June his condition remained more or less stationary. The weather was hot, which helped, but the house was very damp, and he had to keep a fire burning at nights to stop his bronchial troubles recurring. As for the pain, he discovered that if he stayed in bed and kept in a certain position, it was bearable, but if he got up, his breathing was so difficult that he almost collapsed. His diet of peptone and pancreatine kept him going, and the arrival of some Malaga cheered him up—among the household expenses he calculated when he went to Nogent, a surprisingly large sum had been allocated to wine and brandy, presumably on the principle that rather more than a little of what you fancy does you good.[18] Mallarmé came to see him regularly, despite the fact that his wife was ill and that he was concerned about his daughter (Édouard Dujardin wanted to marry her, but Mallarmé disapproved, knowing from bitter experience, shared by Villiers, that one of the young writer's chief talents was extracting contributions to reviews from eminent men and then avoiding payment of the promised fees).[19] Villiers was thus able to persuade himself, with some difficulty, that he was perhaps gaining in strength and that in the autumn he might be able to go to the south of France to convalesce.

But in July it became obvious both that he needed more nursing and medical help than he could get at Nogent, and that he was obsessed with the state of the house there—

rightly, since Huysmans described it as being 'as icy as a stone cistern, totally sunless, and almost decomposed by water'.[20] So one day when he was complaining about it, Huysmans suggested that he try to get himself admitted to the Maison des Frères Saint-Jean de Dieu, a nursing-home in the rue Oudinot in Paris. Villiers, who was secretly in great anxiety about his state, gratefully snatched at the idea, which Huysmans had probably put to him because he knew that Robin had now confirmed his preliminary diagnosis of cancer.[21] For help, Villiers turned to François Coppée, who lived in the same street as the home and knew the director, and to Henry Roujon, to see if the Ministry of Public Instruction would contribute to the fees. Coppée was able to obtain a room for him on favourable terms, and Roujon persuaded the Ministry to donate enough money to pay for the first fortnight in advance.[22] So on 12 July Villiers was taken back to Paris and installed in the room where he was to die.

37

As soon as he arrived Villiers wrote to Mallarmé and Huysmans to inform them of his move; so far as is known, these were his last letters.[1] At first he was happy with the change, convinced he would get better, started making plans for the future, and resolved to give up frequenting boulevard cafés so that he could get on with his work in peace. He also talked about the alterations he wanted to make to *Axël*, and it may well be that the last of his ebbing strength was spent on sketches for the new scenes designed to give it a Christian message.[2] But the thought of death was ever-present. He must have known that it was in a room looking out on the same garden that Barbey d'Aurevilly had died only a few months earlier, and he may have heard that his uncle Victor had also died, in March 1889.[3]

Soon the euphoria of the first days disappeared, and he sank into a black melancholy, thinking both of the failure of his own life and the necessity of doing something to provide for Totor. Mallarmé was probably the only one who understood the first of these two anxieties. He alone had years ago divined the extent to which Villiers could only realize his own identity and justify himself as the scion of his illustrious family if he achieved in the field of literature some exploit comparable to the defence of Rhodes or the capture of Paris. Consequently Mallarmé alone knew how much it meant to Villiers to die before he had accomplished his self-imposed mission. Should death come now, with *Axël* still in a state that dissatisfied him, it would be as if his whole life had been in vain. This was why the old resentment against God suddenly intensified, as Mallarmé saw:

He would discuss his case, indulge in personal arguments with heaven: 'It would not be fair!' then a sigh—'You are watching' I note the funereal visitation of regret 'I would have you know' continued his face to the twilight sinking into the cleanness of white curtains 'a lawsuit between God and myself': or, one morning, frightened, and as if informed, by some sagacious nightmare, that there would be no pardon: 'during the night I have invented two or three blasphemies . . .', but he did not finish, filial; unless he was holding them back for the proper moment.[4]

The worry about Totor was more easily understandable to other friends like Huysmans, Guiches, and Malherbe, and all of them, with Mallarmé, were agreed that it was vital that something concrete should be done. Villiers himself knew this perfectly well, and on 24 July decided to make his will, which he did on official paper in these terms: 'I the undersigned Mathias de Villiers de l'Isle-Adam declare that I give and bequeath to Monsieur Philippe-Auguste Dantine, minor, born in Paris on the tenth of January eighteen hundred and eighty one, all the property that I leave on the day of my decease, making him for this purpose my universal legatee.'[5] This document, written in a firm hand, shows how great was Villiers's concern, but it solved no problems. If Totor became Villiers's sole heir, he would inherit his father's debts as well as his meagre possessions, which meant that he would end up poorer rather than richer. In any case, the will, which referred to Totor only by his mother's name, established no relationship between him and Villiers, so that his status remained unchanged. Consequently, it would be impossible to prove that he was Villiers's son, if it came to the point of seeking state help for him.

It must have been at the same time, perhaps even a day or two earlier, that Villiers broached another possibility that he had at the back of his mind, as a last resort if the worst came to the worst: he could marry Marie, which would legitimize the child.[6] But from the outset, he was adamant that he would only commit himself to this course of action at the very last moment, when it was clear that he had no hope of recovery. It was one thing to bestow his name on Marie as a dying gesture in order to try to assure his son's future and the survival of his line; it was another matter entirely to consent to spending the rest of his life married to an illiterate working-woman in the event of his recovering. This presented Mallarmé and Huysmans with a terrible dilemma. Villiers still did not know he had cancer, and Mallarmé was determined that he should not find out—with Méry Laurent's help, he had got Dr Fournier to write to Dr Mène, the doctor at the Maison des Frères Saint-Jean de Dieu, to ensure that no hint should be given to him.[7] The problem was consequently to ensure that Villiers should agree to the marriage without brutally telling him that he was dying. Dr Robin had already said to Mallarmé that he did not expect Villiers to last more than a month, if that, so the urgency was great.[8]

Villiers, having himself suggested the idea of a marriage *in extremis*, was not in principle opposed to it, but he saw that, if he married Marie Dantine, he had to die, and he was clinging to life with a fierce tenacity that made it impossible for him to give up hope. It had never been in his nature to admit defeat, and he was not going to change now. The result was that, when his friends pressed him to fix a day and send for the necessary papers, he would invent excuses, raise objections, and in the end withdraw into total silence.[9] Mallarmé, whom he called 'my good Genius'[10] and 'one of the kindest hearts that exist in the world',[11] might perhaps, in his gentle way, have succeeded in cajoling him into a decision, but, tired and ill, he went off on 23 July to spend the rest of the summer at Valvins with his wife and daughter. Though he frequently came back to Paris to see Villiers, his presence was no longer constant, and Huysmans, devoted though he was to Villiers, never quite understood what lay behind his friend's procrastinations, which he appears to have put down wholly to class prejudice, without realizing that they were essentially prompted by his desperate struggle against death.

A further complication was that Villiers was tormented by the fear of the bailiff's men. For the time being, money was not short, thanks to the subscription, which had been going on for five months, but Villiers of course knew nothing of that, since the funds had been passed on to him under various more or less plausible disguises. He had stopped writing long since, and was only too well aware that he was under contract to several publishers who were going to want their advances returned unless they soon received something from him, and that all sorts of creditors might descend on Marie and Totor if he died. Apart from that, Lemancel, the proprietor of the house at Nogent, was threatening to sue Villiers for non-payment of the rent,[12] and, since Marie and Totor were still living there, Villiers was desperate to ensure that they would somehow be protected against legal action.

In the meantime his physical condition was going from bad to worse. Since he was hardly able to take any nourishment and was suffering from constant diarrhoea, he had become frighteningly thin, and his skin was the colour of straw. As Huysmans wrote, 'in that emaciated frame, only the eyes were alive, terrifying, searching to the very bottom of your soul as soon as you came in'.[13] He had agreed with Mallarmé that, if the end should suddenly seem near, a telegram should be sent to Valvins, and, though several times the situation appeared critical, on each occasion Villiers rallied. Huysmans and Mallarmé had decided that, though it was much more likely that the Ministry of Public Instruction would help Totor if Villiers legitimized him by marrying Marie, an alternative solution was that Villiers should simply recognize Totor as his natural son, which required fewer legal formalities and—for Villiers—was less equivalent to a death sentence. In the first days of August Huysmans thought it was so urgent to do something that he persuaded Marie to collect the necessary documents such as birth certificates and the death certificate of her first husband, but, realizing that Villiers was more likely to listen to Mallarmé, begged the poet to come back to Paris and talk to the dying man.[14]

This Mallarmé did on 7 August, but with little success.

Villiers exclaimed with exceptional vehemence: 'No, no, no, not now!'[15] He averred that he would marry Marie only at the last moment and, as he put it, adding that humiliation 'to the supreme humiliation of death'.[16] In any case, Mallarmé was unable to get the medical certificate he needed to have the publication of the banns shortened for a marriage *in extremis*, because Dr Mène refused to deliver it except at Villiers's request, which was unthinkable since the certificate had to include the words 'in danger of death'. However, on Huysmans's advice, Mallarmé conferred with Père Sylvestre, the Franciscan friar who was Villiers's confessor, and together they arranged a scheme whereby the priest would suggest to Villiers that he should ask Mène for the certificate, simply in order to have it ready, pretending that it might never be needed.[17] What Mallarmé did achieve was to put Villiers's mind at rest over the possibility that all his belongings might be confiscated. This he did by improvising a fictitious contract transferring to him all the belongings of Villiers and Marie in settlement of a supposed debt of 2,500 francs: it was even antedated to 3 August to forestall possible complaints.[18] In the event, it proved not to be legally watertight, and had to be redrawn by a lawyer whom Villiers summoned to his bedside on the ninth: this time the amount was fixed at 1,150 fr. 50, and a marginal addition specified that this sum represented 'various monthly payments made to M. de Villiers de l'Isle-Adam during his illness'.[19]

On the ninth Villiers's condition seemed to improve slightly, and on the tenth he was vouchsafed what was to be the last literary joy of his life. In the literary supplement of *Le Figaro*, there appeared not only his story *Le Meilleur Amour* but also an article on his work as part of a series on contemporary French novelists. This anonymous piece was in fact the work of his young doctor friend Maurice de Fleury who, knowing how seriously ill he was, had asked for permission to have it published ahead of time. When Villiers heard who was the author, he had a characteristically ironic reaction: 'Ah! the good doctor! He's embalming me!'[20] As for *Le Meilleur Amour*, despite his weakness, he read the printed text with all his habitual meticulousness, and noticed that a detail in the final phrase had been altered without his permission. Though he could scarcely speak, he was able to whisper his indignation to Remy de Gourmont, one of the very few friends to be allowed to see him at this stage. Villiers put all the blame on to Marcade, one of the sub-editors: 'It's with corrections like that that people spoil the finest pages.'[21] However much he might have been affected physically, the spiders' webs in which Villiers weighed his words were still functioning efficiently.

But on the ninth Huysmans had at last managed to bring matters to a head over the marriage. After an hour's fruitless argument with Villiers, Huysmans had asked Père Sylvestre to intervene. 'All right, wait for me there, I'm going up to have a word with him,' the priest replied, and, five minutes later, returned to announce that he had obtained Villiers's consent to an immediate marriage.[22] However, there were insuperable legal obstacles still: the banns had to be called at least once, and on a Sunday, after which three clear days had to elapse before the wedding could take place. This meant that the banns could not be called until the eighteenth, with the wedding on the twenty-second. Sick with anxiety, Huysmans was afraid it was already too late, and tried to get Villiers at least to recognize Totor as his natural son. This met with a flat refusal. According to Huysmans, Villiers was unwilling to recognize Totor except by marrying Marie because, on Totor's birth certificate, she was described as a 'charwoman', which he wanted to have changed to 'woman of property'—and that was impossible without a court order.[23]

When he heard this, Mallarmé tried to explain to Huysmans that things were not quite as they seemed: 'Now, you know, if you put yourself in his place, one's early ideas come back at the end, and this reluctance to bring to a bad end, or to have this strident mention as an ending, the fine chimerical book of his Ancestors, which he had so perfectly completed as a pure man of letters.'[24] He also did his best to see if there was any way in which the processes of the law could be shortened, writing to Paul Beurdeley, who was Mayor of the Eighth Arrondissement, to find out if the banns could be dispensed with altogether.[25] In fact, Marie herself, aghast at the change in Villiers, had taken the initiative and had the banns published on the eleventh, which was a Sunday.[26] Both Huysmans and

Mallarmé were worried about what Villiers would think of this, and in any case they still lacked Dr Mène's certificate with the fateful words 'in danger of death', though Mallarmé knew that Villiers had already asked Méry Laurent to get a wedding-ring for him.[27] In the end, Père Sylvestre, who throughout acted with the greatest tact and humanity, went to see Villiers on the twelfth and persuaded him to ask for the certificate himself. Père Sylvestre then handed over the certificate to Huysmans,[28] who in turn passed it on to Marie, asking Malherbe to accompany her to the *mairie* to present it along with the other papers.[29] Even so, though Marie's intervention had brought matters forward by a week, Huysmans thought Villiers was sinking so fast that it would still be too late.[30]

Indeed, Villiers himself felt so ill during the night of the twelfth and thirteenth that he resigned himself to providing written evidence that Totor was his son, even though the birth certificate could not be changed. This pathetic document is no more than a scrawl, visibly written by someone so enfeebled that he could scarcely hold a pen:

Evening of 12 August two in the morning. Feeling a little ill and in case of accident I give and bequeath my books, alas, the little there is to Madame Marie Brégeras who gave me my son Victor whom I recognize by the present document in haste

Mathias de Villiers de l'Isle-Adam.[31]

Even now Villiers was determined not to admit the gravity of his state, and, despite the fact that the whole will is a tacit admission that he was dying, he persisted in saying he was 'a little ill'. It is as if he felt that the slightest wavering in his resolve would kill him.

Normally, with three clear days having to elapse after the banns, the wedding would not have taken place until the Thursday. But, as that was 15 August and a public holiday, it was agreed that it could be brought forward to the Wednesday, and on the morning of the thirteenth Huysmans sent Mallarmé a telegram to fetch him from Valvins: the wedding would be at four o'clock the next day. There were nearly last-minute hitches, because in the morning Villiers still showed signs of wanting to change his mind and because bureaucratic difficulties arose over the fact that Marie was not a French citizen.[32] It was decided that Mallarmé and Huysmans should act as Villiers's witnesses, with Dierx and Coppée for Marie. But when Huysmans went down the road to ask Coppée, Coppée refused, with the excuse that he was going away that evening, in reality because he disapproved of the marriage.[33] Villiers guessed what had happened, and said: 'We've got enough men of letters with you, Dierx, and Mallarmé; let's have a friend.' So Gustave de Malherbe was sent for.[34]

When Mallarmé arrived at the Maison des Frères Saint-Jean de Dieu, Villiers said to him: 'I'm getting married today, we're going to have some champagne, all this fuss will be the end of me.'[35] All day long Villiers remained very sombre and very wrapped up in himself, until finally he became totally exhausted. First came the civil ceremony, which took place in almost complete silence, except when the mayor, reading out the formalities, mentioned the child, at which Villiers interrupted to say: 'A legitimate child'—'Naturally'.[36] There was a moment of embarrassment when the register had to be signed and Marie, who looked piteous in her black dress and a hat with a little veil, said that she did not know how to write. Then she suggested: 'I could sign like I did with my first husband,' and someone held her hand while she traced the characters.[37] When the mayor, deferential and tactful, had concluded the ceremony, Marie produced a bottle of Veuve Clicquot sent by Méry Laurent and some glasses she had bought herself, and Villiers insisted that everyone should drink. Next came the religious wedding, conducted by Père Sylvestre. When he joined the hands of Villiers and Marie, Mallarmé had the impression that they were saying goodbye to each other.[38] At the end, the priest, realizing that Villiers was terrified of dying alone, said: 'Although women are not allowed to spend the night here, I have arranged, now that you are married, that you should not have to be separated again.' Villiers's eyes filled with tears and he sank back in exhaustion.[39] Marie was in tears too and begged Mallarmé to write to Méry Laurent to thank her for providing the ring, whose weight impressed her greatly, even though it had been too tight for her work-roughened fingers. Finally Villiers chased his guests away 'so that everyone can have dinner' and said bitterly: 'Now let my death agony start.' Totor, who seemed not to realize what was happening, poked Mallarmé in the back with a walking-stick as he left.[40]

The guests sadly went their several ways. As they left, Huysmans whispered to Mallarmé: 'Done it!'[41] But such feelings of macabre triumph were far from Mallarmé's mind. The hard-bitten Huysmans, for all his undoubted devotion to Villiers, had a certain impatience with what he regarded as the poet's unreasonable prejudices and had become immersed in the race to have the wedding performed in time, almost to the exclusion of the real aim. Mallarmé on the other hand, with his profound empathy for Villiers, had felt it his duty to hasten the marriage for the sake of Marie and above all Totor, knowing that, ultimately, that was what Villiers wanted but realizing at the same time that, by doing so, he was bringing his friend's death nearer. So his frame of mind was very black as he made his way back to Valvins.

Huysmans, who remained in Paris, went faithfully to Villiers's bedside every day. By now everyone was struck by the impression of extreme old age he gave and Mallarmé told friends that he seemed to be eighty years old. He was scarcely capable of speech, and the only nourishment he could take was a little yolk of egg, which he drank through a straw while Huysmans supported him. Villiers would hold his hand and look at him with an expression of mingled resignation and sadness: all he was able to say was: 'Oh God, is it possible?'[42] A new torment had seized him since the wedding: the idea that he was dying in the workhouse. Moreover, since Marie was still with him, he was worried about Totor, left alone with Albert at Nogent. But he still had not given up; as Huysmans told Méry Laurent: 'He is very low, is struggling furiously in the hope of getting over it, but he is sinking day by day, and his drawn features are getting so much thinner that it is frightening.'[43] On the eighteenth he received the last sacraments, and that evening realized that the end had come. Mallarmé described his last moments: 'He had no death agony, but felt himself dying, said to Marie: "Hold me tight, that I may go gently" and allowed himself to slip, in peace, into the abyss.'[44] It was eleven o'clock.

38

When Huysmans and Mallarmé heard the next day that Villiers was dead, they had to make hurried arrangements to find a cemetery where he could be buried, and it was only through the unexpected generosity of Francis Magnard of *Le Figaro* that they were able to buy a plot for five years in the Cimetière des Batignolles.[1] On 20 August Mallarmé sent a letter to Méry Laurent to tell her the circumstances of his death: 'I am writing to you beside Villiers, he has just been put in his coffin, he looked very old and handsome, a little roguish and learned, altogether one of his ancestors.'[2] One or two friends came to pay their respects, notably Henri Lavedan and Franc-Lamy, who made a sketch of Villiers on his death-bed, and many others sent flowers. The funeral took place on the twenty-first, in pouring rain, with the mourners led by Totor, carrying in his hand a lily given by the *Gil Blas* and not really comprehending what was happening. Huysmans, Dierx, and Mallarmé took turns at sheltering him under their umbrellas. After the service at the church of Saint-François-Xavier, the procession set off for the distant cemetery, but the weather was so bad that Leconte de Lisle, who had been going to pronounce a graveside eulogy, had to go home. Instead, it was Jean Marras who made a short speech, much to the indignation of Huysmans, who had never met him and did not realize that he was one of Villiers's oldest friends.[3]

Just before he died Villiers had designated Huysmans and Mallarmé as his literary executors and the only people allowed to touch his papers. Both *Chez les passants* and *Axël* were still at the proof stage, and, when Huysmans went to the house at Nogent, he was appalled at the confused mass of manuscripts, galley proofs, and page proofs that he discovered. For *Chez les passants* there was no great problem, the proof correction having reached an advanced stage, and Bailly was able to bring it out in December 1889. But with *Axël* the situation was chaotic. If the first two Parts were ready for printing, *Le Monde occulte* was only half revised, and *Le Monde passionnel* not at all. Moreover, there was the question of the projected Christian amendments, so that it took Huysmans and Gustave de Malherbe between them the rest of the summer to sort things out, with the director of Quantin becoming ever more impatient. In the end the work appeared in January 1890, with the text as Villiers had left it and an appendix giving those Christian fragments that had been composed: a note jointly written by Huysmans and Mallarmé explained their significance.

In the meantime they had also had to take steps to find money for Totor's education, and a petition was sent to the Ministry of Public Instruction in October, signed by Leconte de Lisle, Théodore de Banville, François Coppée, Paul Bourget, Alexandre Dumas, Edmond de Goncourt, and Émile Zola among others.[4] This was favourably received and it was arranged that Totor should be given an allowance by the state until he reached the age of twenty-one. But that was not by any means the end of their troubles. Villiers's death had created a vast stir in the world of journalism, with scores if not hundreds of obituary articles, most of them written by people who suddenly claimed to have been friends and admirers ('how much gossip! how much disrespect! how many invented last words!' commented Mallarmé),[5] and publishers naturally wanted to take advantage of the publicity. It then transpired that Villiers had taken on all sorts of contradictory contractual obligations with different firms. Moreover, Marie proved singularly difficult to deal with. Having fallen into the hands of an unfrocked priest who had invented some sort of hair oil, she did her best to get Mallarmé and Huysmans to hand over at once all the money they had set aside for Totor, which they refused to do, knowing that she was being manipulated by unscrupulous confidence tricksters. By the end of the year she had become so impossible that Mallarmé and Huysmans were forced more or less to wash their hands of her.[6]

In the early stages of handling Villiers's papers, they had had the help of Rodolphe Darzens, and it was he who gradually replaced them as the widow's literary adviser. Throughout the 1890s Darzens acted as her representative with publishers, newspaper editors, and theatre managers, and he was able to produce a number of unpublished works and new editions that brought in a certain amount of money. Totor came to regard him as a friend and guardian, and there is no doubt that he devoted a great deal of time and trouble to Villiers's complex and difficult affairs. On the other hand, he was an irascible and aggressive man, whose unpredictable demands were liable to indispose those who might otherwise have done more for Villiers's memory. *Axël* was given three successful performances in 1894, at great expense, by the young actor Paul Larochelle, son of the theatre manager who had been one of the co-defendants in the *Perrinet Leclerc* case, and *Elën* was respectfully received in 1896,[7] as was *La Révolte*. But difficulties over copyright and Darzens's awkward character meant that a planned edition of Villiers's complete works never saw the light of day.

Totor's half-brother Albert Brégeras died of tuberculosis in 1892. Totor himself attended the Lycée Chaptal and had dreams of following in his father's footsteps as a writer. He spent a lot of his spare time composing juvenile novels and diaries, and also acted the part of Pagnol in an amateur production of *L'Évasion* in 1899.[8] Together with some of his schoolfellows, he founded a little review entitled *L'Idée*, and even had printed visiting-cards on which he described himself as a 'journalist on *L'Idée*'. He had something of Villiers's chivalrous character and managed to get himself involved in a duel before he left school. But his health, like that of Albert, was undermined by tuberculosis, and, though there were plans to send him to North Africa in the hope that the climate would help him, he died before he could go, on 28 April 1901.[9] Before his death he had become friendly with a boy of about the same age, Marcel Longuet, the grandson of Karl Marx and the nephew of a socialist minister. Longuet seems to have persuaded him, perhaps rightly, that Darzens was not the man to manage his mother's affairs, and, after Totor died, Longuet was entrusted with the job of taking over. It was consequently Longuet who, between 1914 and 1931, was responsible for the publication of Villiers's complete works by the Mercure de France.

In 1895 the grant of the plot of land at the Cimetière des Batignolles ran out and, thanks to Rodolphe Darzens and Lucien Descaves, enough money was raised to transfer

Villiers's remains to the Père Lachaise, where they still rest, under a great slab of Breton granite, bearing the arms of the Villiers de l'Isle-Adam family and their motto: *Va oultre!* In 1901 his beloved Totor was interred beside him. When Villiers himself was reburied there, in pouring rain as on the day of his funeral in 1889, a journalist asked Mallarmé if he would say 'a few words'. His only reply was: 'One does not say "a few words" about Villiers de l'Isle-Adam.'[10] In fact, in 1890 Mallarmé had gone on a lecture tour in Belgium where, in a funeral oration that more than stands comparison with Bossuet's, he had magnificently summed up the life and achievement of Villiers, 'the man who never was, save in his dreams'.[11]

Marie herself lived until 1920, as poor as ever. When she died, Marcel Longuet happened to be away in North Africa, and, by the time he returned, she had been buried in a pauper's grave. Such of Villiers's papers as remained in her hands had disappeared, carried off by Frédéric Brou the sculptor, a friend of Bloy, and a gentleman called Lefiblec, who identified himself as a former magistrate.[12] A number of manuscripts had already vanished at the time of the poet's death, pocketed by more or less well-meaning friends in search of 'souvenirs'; most of the others had been kept by Rodolphe Darzens even after his dismissal. Over the years many of them have come to light; it may be that others have been irrevocably lost or are lying somewhere awaiting discovery. No doubt Villiers would not be unhappy that, even after his death, he should continue to be elusive and mysterious.

CONCLUSION

'Admirable but mad': that is how Sartre summed up Villiers.[1] Certainly Villiers's grandfather was eccentric and his father positively certifiable, at least by the end of his life. In his own case, there are undoubted elements of abnormality—a pronounced tendency to mythomania, violent changes of mood, a frequent lack of coherence in his conversation, an inability to recognize or adapt to the realities of a situation, distinct hypochondria, perhaps a degree of alcoholism, maybe even a hint of paranoia. But the truth about his personality is much too complex to be so summarily defined, and, in any case, it is hard to believe that the man who wrote some of the most brilliant and original works in nineteenth-century French literature, who was supported and encouraged by Baudelaire, Gautier, Flaubert, Hugo, and Wagner, who was the intimate friend of men as eminent and diverse as Mallarmé, Verlaine, Huysmans, Bloy, and Remy de Gourmont, who was an inspiration and an exemplar to a whole generation of men of letters, was a lunatic.

It is, of course, clear that Villiers was very unlike most other people, especially those people who formed the majority of the society in which he lived. An unrepentant aristocrat in an age of parliamentary democracy, a fervent idealist in a time of often sordid materialism, a high-minded poet in a period when prosaicism reigned supreme, he was in diametrical opposition to almost all the values which surrounded him, and, far from attempting to conform to them, he set out to flout them, to ridicule them, and to subvert them. This inevitably involved his appearing as a rebel, an outsider carrying his differences with the rest of the world to the point where the rest of the world had difficulty in recognizing him as a kindred being, and that was a challenge which he readily accepted. As Henri de Régnier said, he was 'a living protest against the positivist and realist spirit of his times',[2] and it is the fact that he lived that protest as much as he wrote it that determined so much of his behaviour.

For in Villiers's eyes being a writer was something that filled and dominated the whole of his existence. Not for him the Flaubertian maxim of living like a bourgeois and thinking like a demigod, or the Mallarméan solution of outwardly accepting the constraints and conventions of social norms while attempting secretly to save the world through poetry. Villiers was crystal clear from childhood onwards that he was a writer, and only a writer, and that everything else about him must be subservient to that exclusive and tyrannical vocation. It was, as he used to say to Mallarmé, 'the only really worthwhile glory of our day',[3] and his duty to his ancestors commanded him to conquer it. Hence the unshakeable singlemindedness with which, for over thirty years and in the teeth of appalling hardships, he pursued a calling which won him far more derision than respect.

But this compulsive dedication to being a writer led to innumerable complications not only in his relationship with a society which was uninterested in or hostile to such values, but also in his own sense of identity. Villiers seems to have begun as much with a desire to *be* a writer as with a desire actually to write, and when he was still at school had already contracted the habit of behaving in the way in which he thought a writer ought to behave—the inspired airs, the careless dress, the long hair, the fits of melancholy, the unhappy love affairs. Encouraged by his doting family, who made no effort to bring him to a sense of more mundane activities, he soon found himself living out the part he had created for himself, and this was something he was to continue doing for the rest of his life. The nature of the part changed frequently, but the impulse to act never left him, and, paradoxically, one of the constants of his personality was the need to adopt a whole range of different personae for himself. His obsessive admiration for great actors and his preoccupation with the stage were no accidents; they corresponded to a deep-seated urge of his whole being.

This playing of roles (and roles often unrelated to any concrete reality) is something one can trace back to the earliest known facts about him. At school he was the Great Writer, the Bereaved Brother, the Kidnapped Infant, the Duellist. In later years his repertoire was enormously extended: the Betrayed Lover, the Ironic Dandy, the Misunderstood Genius, the Profound Philosopher, the Sad Clown, and so forth. Sometimes, abetted by a real talent for mimicry, it actually took the form of wanting to perform on the stage:

his involuntary imitation of the actor Dumaine, his purchase of the costume for Hamlet, his demonstrations to professionals of the way in which his dramas should be acted, his electrifying readings from his own works, are all evidence of an innate ability to act and a persistent ambition to do so. According to Judith Gautier, he had it in him to be a great actor, and as good a judge as Antoine was fascinated by his performances.

But Villiers very soon discovered that the parts he played were liable to enter into conflict with what others insisted on regarding as what was true or right. He had not lost a brother, he was not allowed to fight a duel, he was forbidden to while away his time in lessons by penning interminable novels. Such interferences with the free play of fantasy have been experienced by all children, and most of them sooner or later learn that it is wise to control the fantasy and accommodate it to the rude exigencies of everyday life. With him, however, the fantasy was so strong that there could be no question of subordinating its demands to those of common sense. Besides, whatever the ambivalence of their relations, there was always the powerful example of his father to remind him that even grown-ups did not always see the world as a dull and predictable place in which the expected inevitably happens. So the role-playing went on with unabated zest, and, where reality threatened it, reality was ignored.

Of course, reality repeatedly took its revenge, as is its inconvenient way when people ignore it, and, especially after Villiers left the shelter of the backwoods of Brittany for the harsher climes of Paris, he was continually being exposed to mockery, to cynicism, to jealousy, to exploitation, to downright trickery. It became more and more difficult to persuade others to take his roles seriously, and at the same time the hope of incarnating them so fully that they would indeed turn into reality receded. Theatre managers rejected his plays, critics ignored his poetry, his mistress proved to be unfaithful, the dreams of 'reigning' were ignominiously shattered. Worst of all, the supply of money, that indispensable adjunct to any successful dramatic production, began to dry up as his father's extravagances ran through Tante Kerinou's fortune. It was around this period that Villiers started to develop irony and self-parody as a means of defending himself against attack and misfortune. If he was the first to laugh at himself, he would forestall the sneers of others; if he kept on changing masks, he would elude their sarcasms and their insults. So one finds him deliberately propagating implausible stories about himself, kowtowing obsequiously to philistine publishers, engaging in wildly incongruous occupations such as comptroller of waggonage, sparring partner, and cured madman, and generally behaving in a way that made it impossible for others to know whether he was being serious or not.

The same evolution is perceptible in his art. *Premières Poésies*, *Isis*, *Elën*, and *Morgane*, all written wholly or partly in Brittany, are in deadly earnest; *Claire Lenoir*, the first major work composed after he had finally settled in Paris, is extraordinarily ambivalent in its mixture of burlesque and tragedy, the more so as it is presented from the point of view of Villiers's antithesis, Tribulat Bonhomet. From then on, Villiers cultivated more and more the wiles of ironic ambiguity, feigning to be serious when he was joking, and to be speaking in jest when he was in deadly earnest. Mallarmé was quite right to see a secret correspondence in his work between the twin poles of Laughter and the Dream.[4] Remy de Gourmont too understood this mechanism: 'Villiers realized himself both in dreams and in irony, ironizing about his dreams when life disgusted him with them.'[5]

No doubt the suspicion with which he often viewed others springs from a similar source. Many memoir-writers have recorded the way in which he would look mistrustfully at others, fall silent at a chance word, carry strange weapons in case he was attacked. He was too used to ill-luck, to disappointments, to being duped, ever to feel that people were on his side, and in the course of time came to adopt an attitude of excessive circumspection towards them. Yet he also had a compulsive need for applause and approval, which led him to perorate endlessly before chance audiences in cafés, when he could give vent to his histrionic impulses. Hence a constant though unpredictable alternation between expensiveness and withdrawal, gregariousness and solitude. He was one of the most brilliant conversationalists in Paris in the 1880s—Huysmans, not an indulgent critic, called him 'the most astonishing talker of this age'[6]—but he would disappear for weeks on end, and no one would know what had become of him. In fact, he was usually alone in a squalid garret, devoting himself entirely to the fabrication of some new masterpiece.

The fact is that Villiers remained a solitary figure nearly all his life.[7] He used the familiar 'tu' to half the journalists in Paris, but no one ever fully shared his existence. He was an only child, and there can have been little real communication with either his flibbertigibbet father or his timid and down-trodden mother; as for Tante Kerinou, one has the impression that she asserted her will without paying much attention to what anyone said to her. He made one or two close friendships that lasted until his dying day, notably with Mallarmé and Marras, and to a lesser extent with Mendès (though there storms were forever arising, because Villiers, with some reason, suspected Mendès of being essentially concerned for himself). With Mallarmé and Marras, the relationship was one of total trust, and the letters he wrote bear eloquent witness to the closeness of his ties with both men. At different times, others too were taken into his confidence—Huysmans, Fernand de Gantès, Robert du Pontavice de Heussey, and some of the young Symbolists such as Rodolphe Darzens and Remy de Gourmont. But while many people knew him superficially, few were welcomed into his intimacy: one or other of his multiple masks would always be worn.

That he never had a home of his own had of course something to do with this. His family changed its domicile with bewildering frequency, even when money was no problem; he himself was shuttled around from school to school, and later had more than thirty known addresses in Paris, never staying more than a few months in the same place. He owned practically nothing, and, until the last years of his life, hardly ever allowed anyone to visit him in whatever rooms he inhabited. When he was in the same flat as his parents, he wanted to keep his friends well out of their way; when he was on his own, he was too ashamed of the sordid dwelling-places poverty forced him to accept for him to want anyone to see them. So, though he was a dutiful and devoted son, he never had any secure background into which he could retire. He spent an enormous amount of time in cafés but did not even have a regular haunt, though he was rarely to be found outside the general region of Montmartre. Such rootlessness must inevitably have contributed to the lack of stability in his character.

Nor did Villiers ever have a fixed or permanent relationship with a woman: quite the contrary. He is reputed to have had one or more tragic love-affairs in his adolescence; there was the violent liaison with Louise Dyonnet in the early 1860s; then occurred the broken engagement with Estelle Gautier; finally came the time with Marie Dantine, culminating in his deathbed marriage. And of course there was the whole incredible string of intended matches with fabulously rich and lovely heiresses, of which the most extraordinary was the adventure with Anna Eyre in 1873. One can well understand that, for his friends, this long catalogue of tragi-comic delusions should have been the subject of merriment. But Villiers took each one just as much to heart as its predecessors, and the last disappointment was just as bitter as the first. Alongside these near-marriages or more significant affairs, there were certainly other transient encounters—Clarisse, Marianne, Mathilde Leroy, Marc de Montifaud, to mention only those which have left the memory of a name—but they served only to satisfy his sexual needs without involving his emotions. Three feminine presences, those of Judith Gautier, Nina de Villard, and Méry Laurent, provided him with friendship, affection and something approaching maternal solicitude at different times of his life. One looks in vain however for any durable bond of love in his existence.

Léon Bloy thought that the centre of Villiers's life was 'his truly unexampled need for a restitution of Woman'.[8] Certainly his feminine ideal as it appears in his early works—Hermosa, Tullia Fabriana, Morgane—is a *Machtweib* of superhuman intelligence and beauty, and that was evidently what he was looking for in everyday reality too. Whenever he met a woman whom he thought attractive, he would start spinning round her a web of purely imaginary qualities plucked from his own brain, and, when it became apparent that these invented attributes were alien to her, he would become bitterly disillusioned. His impossibly lofty dreams led to traumatic awakenings; the only wonder is that the dreams always reformed. But, as real women obstinately (and understandably) failed to live up to them, so he increasingly took refuge in a biting and cynical misogyny. It is perhaps no accident that the writing of *L'Ève future*, his most vehemently anti-feminine work, should have coincided with the beginning of his liaison with Marie Dantine, who was in so many ways the antithesis of his ideal—humble, poor, plain, uncultured, unintelligent, unassertive. It is as if he had chosen to insult an ethereal image that he could no longer hope to attain.

Yet once Villiers had thrown in his lot with her, and however reluctantly he may have done it, he remained surprisingly faithful to her. For, if he was often capricious and changeable, he also possessed remarkable stubborness in maintaining a line of conduct he had chosen for himself. He was clearly ashamed of having Marie as a companion, tried to pretend that she was only his charwoman, and was never seen in public with her, but, once she started to live with him, he gave up his ambition of marrying an heiress and even renounced the transitory affairs that had previously punctuated his life. In the end he consented to marry her on his deathbed, and this, for a man so fanatically attached to the dignity of his name, was nothing less than the supreme sacrifice.

Of course it was not simply or even mainly attachment to Marie that kept Villiers faithful to her and led him to make such a sacrifice: he patently never treated her as an equal and to some extent at least regarded his connection with her as a humiliation. It was primarily his profound love for the son she gave him. Villiers unexpectedly proved to be an extraordinarily affectionate and solicitous father, constantly concerned for the welfare and happiness of Totor—much more than he was for his own or for Marie's. By all accounts, Totor was indeed an attractive child, pretty, precocious, and intelligent, but that was not what accounted for the fierceness of Villiers's love for him. What he saw in his child was the continuance of the line of the Villiers de l'Isle-Adams, which he had believed was destined to end with him. If he himself had not succeeded in fulfilling the ancestral duty of blazoning the name of Villiers de l'Isle-Adam abroad in the modern world, perhaps his son could do it for him. As Mallarmé so clearly saw, the obligations which Villiers believed his lineage laid upon him were felt just as keenly at the end of his life as they had been at the beginning—maybe even more so, since he had long ago given up thinking that it conferred any privileges on him.

Indeed, the main theme of the tragic drama that played itself out in Villiers's last days was the question of whether he had been able to be what his ancestors would have wished him to be. As he grew older and his health disintegrated, Villiers became ever more anxious lest his life should turn out to have been a failure. Remy de Gourmont noted this: 'He felt he had had a destiny and that he had missed it.'[9] But as always it is to Mallarmé that one must turn for the most subtle and penetrating analysis of what was going on in Villiers's mind as he lay in his hospital bed,

with anguish seeking in himself the personification of one of the eternal human types. What! had existence so much slipped between his fingers that he himself could distinguish no clear trace of it; had he been tricked, was that it? so invincible hope still visited his bedside. Consumption, perhaps? disorder of the heart, but one forgets a certain virus left by the fury of having seemed superfluous to his times; and there is, propped against the sick man's pillows, in his look, as it were an interdiction, to that part of him which had already vanished and which the eyes found again, on judging inequitably the spectre lying there of the early hopes: with the reconstitution of the intimate pride before the obvious fact that everything possible, in that milieu, had been attempted by him and that his life, so disseminated, omitted almost, exists![10]

In the end, Villiers's quest for a sure identity resolved itself, as it was always bound to, into the assessment of the validity of what he had written, above all *Axël*, which in a peculiarly poignant sense was his life's work. That he himself was not satisfied with it is sadly clear, but it could not have been otherwise. How could he have given a definitive form to something that was intended to sum up the sense of a whole life, as yet unfinished? It is also true that his work did not bestow on him the incomparable place in the hierarchy of literary reputations which alone would have seemed worthy in his own eyes. His youthful ambition to supplant Victor Hugo was never accomplished. If one were to judge the work by those impossibly high standards that Villiers would have wished to apply to it, one would be forced to conclude that he did not achieve what he set out to do.

But clearly it would be nonsensical to take Villiers's impossible dreams as the basis for our valuation of his success or failure. As an author, he had an incalculable impact on the course of French and indeed European literature, so much so that Edmund Wilson was moved to take Axël's castle as the archetypal symbol of the mood of a whole generation of men of letters. Writers as diverse and as considerable as Valéry, Claudel, Gide, Stefan George, and Yeats have declared their debt to him. His *Contes cruels* are probably as much read as any single volume of short stories in any language; *La Révolte* is regularly performed at the Comédie Française and elsewhere; *Le Nouveau-Monde* was enthusiastically received when Jean-Louis Barrault revived it in 1977; television has successfully premièred *Le Prétendant*; *Axël*, though it still awaits the production it deserves, has met with acclaim on its various appearances on stage, radio, and television. As a writer, Villiers is very much a live presence today, and he is assured of a permanent and prominent position in the hierarchy of literary values.

That alone would be more than enough to justify anyone's existence. But when one takes into account the disasters which studded Villiers's life, any one of which would have been enough to shatter the spirit of a lesser man, one cannot but admire him for having set such a unique and shining example of true courage and true nobility. The history of literature provides few if any comparable cases of such unshakeable devotion to the highest ideal of art in the teeth of the most fearsome adversity, and the flame was burning as brightly at the end as it had done at the beginning—one wonders indeed how he can possibly have survived so many unimaginable misfortunes. The two mottos of the Villiers de l'Isle-Adam family were *Va oultre* and *La main à l'oeuvre*. No one could more faithfully have obeyed these twin injunctions to adventure and to perseverance; the shades of his ancestors surely know that he was marvellously worthy of his line.

NOTES

1 (pp. 3–11)

1. On the more distant forebears of the poet, see Joseph Bollery, *La Bretagne de Villiers de l'Isle-Adam*, Saint-Brieuc, Les Presses bretonnes, 1961, and Théophile Janvrais, *Le Berceau des Villiers de l'Isle-Adam*, Saint-Brieuc, Prudhomme; Paris, Champion, 1913. The most fully documented challenge to the continuity of Villiers's supposed lineage came from Max Prinet, 'Les Ancêtres parisiens de Villiers de l'Isle-Adam', *Mercure de France*, 1ᵉʳ août 1928. Alain Néry, re-examining the question in his Sorbonne thesis on 'Les Idées politiques et sociales de Villiers de l'Isle-Adam', recognizes the force of Prinet's arguments but concludes that, while the descent probably did not follow the line traced by Villiers himself, one cannot exclude the possibility that it is nevertheless continuous by some other route.

2. Most of the information about Lilly is to be found in J. Baudry, *Etude généalogique et biographique sur les ascendants du poète Villiers de l'Isle-Adam*, Paris, Champion, 1905. It derives essentially from a series of letters addressed to the Comte and Comtesse Jégou du Laz between 1782 and 1790 and discovered in the castle of Trégarantec.

3. J. Baudry, p. 35.

4. Ibid., p. 36.

5. He wrote to complain about this to his aunt in July 1784: J. Baudry, p. 41.

6. Ibid., pp. 61–2.

7. Ibid., p. 63.

8. These details about Lilly's later career were mostly discovered by Pierre Reboul ('Le Grand-père de Villiers de l'Isle-Adam', *Le Divan*, juillet-septembre, 1954).

9. This document was discovered in the Pimodan archives by Louis Tiercelin (*Bretons de lettres*, Paris, Champion, 1905, p. 171).

10. The evidence for his arrest was first produced by Pierre Reboul ('Le Grand-père'), but he did not realize that it was a case of mistaken identity. Hence the dismissive note in J. Bollery, *La Bretagne*, pp. 51–2. But while Reboul may have been misled on that point, it seems clear that the rest of his information is accurate, and it is a pity that Bollery did not see fit to take account of it.

11. J. Bollery, *La Bretagne*, p. 51.

12. L. Tiercelin, p. 169.

13. Ibid., p. 170.

14. The story of the confusion and quarrels brought about by this change of name has been recounted and fully documented by Émile Drougard in two important articles: 'Villiers de l'Isle-Adam défenseur de son nom', *Annales de Bretagne*, t. 62, 1955, and 'Pour le nom: Villiers de l'Isle-Adam et ses homonymes', *Revue des Sciences humaines*, octobre-décembre 1957.

15. The letter is reproduced in both of the above-mentioned articles by É. Drougard.

16. The question is complicated by the fact that the sum Lilly hoped to get as indemnity for the loss of the estates was 26,400 francs, almost the same as the sum allocated from the 'milliard des émigrés'. An official document relative to the latter sum was published by Édouard de Rougemont in his *Villiers de l'Isle-Adam*, Paris, Mercure de France, 1910, p. 34, so there is no doubt about its existence. Villiers alleged many years later that the San Domingo money had been paid in error to the wrong Villiers de l'Isle-Adam and that Lilly had recovered it through legal action. But É. Drougard was unable to discover any evidence of the truth of this assertion and was inclined to think that Villiers had confused the two indemnities. It would indeed have been very difficult for Lilly to have had himself indemnified under both heads, since, to qualify for a share of the 'milliard des émigrés', it was necessary to prove that one had emigrated, whereas, to qualify for the San Domingo money, it was necessary to prove that one had remained in France.

17. This was discovered by Remy de Gourmont at the Bibliothèque Nationale ('Notes sur Villiers de l'Isle-Adam', *Mercure de France*, août 1890). Gourmont first attributed it to Villiers and then to his father (*Promenades littéraires*, 2ᵉ série, Paris, Mercure de France, 1906). But Joseph Bollery (*La Bretagne*, p. 76) suggests, with much more plausibility, that the author is really the uncle.

18. On the Abbé Victor, see, in addition to Joseph Bollery's book, Chanoine J. Raison du Cleuziou, 'Le Chanoine Yves-Marie-Victor Villiers de l'Isle-Adam et le conte de *L'Intersigne*', *Mémoires de la Société d'émulation des Côtes-du-Nord*, t. 83, 1954.

19. L. Tiercelin, pp. 175–6.

20. The brief by which this was done, dated 15 August 1840 and signed by the Grand Master Carlo Candida, was one of the family's treasured possessions. But it is not among the masses of family papers preserved in the Fonds Bollery in the Bibliothèque Municipale of La Rochelle.

21. L. Tiercelin, p. 178.

22. On this aspect of Joseph-Toussaint-Charles's activities, see Comte H. Le Noir de Tournemine, *Autour de Villiers de l'Isle-Adam*, Saint-Brieuc, Guyon, 1906.

23. The most reliable and well-documented study of this remarkable enterprise is 'L'Agence "Villiers de l'Isle-Adam"' (*Mémoires de la Société d'émulation des Côtes-du-Nord*, t. 91, 1962), by J. Raison du Cleuziou.

24. So he is described by Charles Le Goffic, quoted by J. Raison du Cleuziou, 'L'Agence'.

25. According to É. de Rougemont (p. 220, n. 2), the Marquis lost a lot of money in this affair.

26. In 1853 he published a brochure on this with a certain Edmond de Genoux (Rougemont, p. 45, n. 1).

27. In an article published in *Paris-Journal* on 29 September 1909, Paul Vibert, who had lunched with him in his old age, noted: 'One looked with respect on this man who had about his person something like a

last reflection of the Middle Ages.' (Quoted by J. Raison du Cleuziou, 'L'Agence'.)

28. On this side of the family, see Léon Dubreuil, 'A propos de Villiers de l'Isle-Adam: du côté de la tante Kerinou', *Annales de Bretagne*, t. 65 (1958).
29. According to the accounts picked up by H. Le Noir de Tournemine, op. cit.
30. See the marriage contract, drawn up on 31 May 1837, and quoted by J. Bollery, *La Bretagne*, p. 82.

2 (pp. 11–18)

1. These reminiscences were collected by H. Le Noir de Tournemine (pp. 18–19).
2. According to the census returns quoted by H. Le Noir de Tournemine (p. 20).
3. The address figures on various documents in the Fonds Bollery. See J. Bollery, *La Bretagne*, p. 88.
4. Noted by H. Le Noir de Tournemine.
5. A vast pile of documents relating to this case is preserved in the Fonds Bollery. Joseph Bollery wrote of it: 'We have before us the dossier of this unimaginable jigsaw puzzle, and we would advise anyone who cared about his mental stability against reading it. The summary alone of the heads of the case is composed of no less than 38 foolscap pages of small handwriting.' (*La Bretagne*, p. 89.)
6. These papers too are in the Fonds Bollery. See J. Bollery, *La Bretagne*, p. 88.
7. Villiers de l'Isle-Adam, *Correspondance générale*, edited by Joseph Bollery, Paris, Mercure de France, 1962 (hereafter abbreviated to *C.G.*), vol. I, p. 23.
8. Ibid., p. 25.
9. The odyssey of Villiers's education has been patiently traced by Émile Drougard, 'Les Études de Villiers de l'Isle-Adam', *Annales de Bretagne*, t. 65, 1958. See also Joseph Bollery, 'Documents biographiques inédits sur Villiers de l'Isle-Adam', *Revue d'Histoire littéraire de la France*, janvier-mars 1956, and Dr H. de Sallier Dupin, 'Villiers de l'Isle-Adam', *Les Échos de Saint-Vincent*, octobre 1955.
10. These details are given by H. Le Noir de Tournemine, and, although É. Drougard was unable to confirm them, he regarded them as too circumstantial to be without foundation.
11. Quoted by le R. P. Marsille, 'Les Cent Jours vannetais de l'éducation de Villiers de l'Isle-Adam', *Bulletin mensuel de la Société polymathique du Morbihan*, juin 1962.
12. Recorded by H. Le Noir de Tournemine, p. 31.
13. Again, these views were collected from his schoolfellows by H. Le Noir de Tournemine, p. 23.
14. The details of the duel are recorded by H. Le Noir de Tournemine.
15. H. Le Noir de Tournemine, p. 32.
16. Robert du Pontavice de Heussey, *Villiers de l'Isle-Adam*, Paris, Savine, 1893.

17. According to Paul Ginisty, quoted by H. Le Noir de Tournemine.
18. Her memories were noted by H. Le Noir de Tournemine, p. 25.
19. Ibid., p. 26.
20. Courcoux's memories too were recorded by Le Noir de Tournemine, p. 29.
21. H. Le Noir de Tournemine, p. 27.
22. According to H. Le Noir de Tournemine.
23. Robert du Pontavice de Heussey, pp. 30–4.
24. Louis Tiercelin, p. 180. All subsequent biographers have examined these two assertions by Pontavice and Tiercelin with some puzzlement, since two similar shattering experiences seem too much to be readily believed. Pontavice is well known to be unreliable about anything of which he was not an eye-witness, whereas Tiercelin was certainly relying on the evidence of Amédée Le Menant des Chesnais, who knew Villiers well as an adolescent. But one cannot exclude the possibility that Villiers had confided later in Pontavice, and indeed Tiercelin appears to accept that there were two disastrous love-affairs. The idea that his enigmatic reference to a fate worse than death means incarceration in a convent is suggested by some of the peculiarities of the convent scenes in *Axël*, where there is an attempt to force Sara to take vows against her will.

3 (pp. 18–24)

1. For a long time there was a legend, fostered by Pontavice de Heussey, that Villiers's family had suddenly decamped to Paris in either 1855 or 1857 in order to allow him to pursue his literary career there. The assertion is repeated by Rougemont, p. 62, by Fernand Clerget, *Villiers de l'Isle-Adam*, Paris, Louis-Michaud, n. d. [1913], pp. 22–3, by Max Daireaux, *Villiers de l'Isle-Adam, l'homme et l'œuvre*, Paris, Desclée de Brouwer, 1936, pp. 40–1. Even recent historians have continued to propagate it—for instance Jacques-Henry Bornecque, *Villiers de l'Isle-Adam créateur et visionnaire*, Paris, Nizet, 1974, pp. 29–30. But Joseph Bollery's researches clearly established that there was no such single occasion, rather a series of more or less long stays, with no definitive transfer of domicile until late in the 1860s. He also demonstrated that the gradual move to Paris had nothing to do with Villiers's poetic ambitions but resulted from the father's business activities (*La Bretagne*, p. 90).
2. The letter is reproduced by Lemercier de Neuville himself in his *Souvenirs d'un montreur de marionnettes*, Paris, Bauche, 1911, p. 88; he also tells the whole story of *La Muselière* and his friendship with Villiers. See also *C.G.*, vol. I, p. 30.
3. H. Le Noir de Tournemine, who is very well informed on Villiers's youth, makes the claim.
4. Villiers talks about both these projects in an undated letter to Lemercier de Neuville (*C.G.*, vol. I, p. 31). In another letter to Lemercier, this one unpublished (in the Clayeux Collection), he discusses his drama and says: 'By the way, I forgot to tell you that the end of *Faust*

has been completely changed.—A born idiot could have done something just as good as the one you have.'

5. *C.G.*, vol. I, pp. 31–2.
6. Lemercier de Neuville, p. 87.
7. Ibid., p. 90.
8. Joseph Bollery, *La Bretagne*, p. 89.
9. See H. Le Noir de Tournemine.
10. *C.G.*, vol. I, p. 34. The letter was first published by Émile Drougard, 'Villiers de l'Isle-Adam à Solesmes', *Revue de la Méditerranée*, mars-avril 1947.
11. H. Le Noir de Tournemine records that, when the conscripts for 1858 were called up at Saint-Brieuc, 224 young men were eligible but only 153 were needed; since they were chosen by lot and Villiers had drawn the number 220, he escaped. His occupation was given as 'dramatist' (p. 43).
12. *La Causerie*, 11 décembre 1859.
13. All that is known about Villiers's relations with Le Menant is recorded by Louis Tiercelin (op. cit.), who heard it from Le Menant himself.
14. There are hints that they may not have spent all their time quite so innocently. Jean de La Varende ('Villiers de l'Isle-Adam,' *Revue des Deux Mondes*, novembre 1938) wrote: 'By chance, one of my old great-uncles had a house on the village square next to Le Menant's. No doubt Le Menant was pious; however, it certainly does not seem that the occupations of the preacher and the preached-at were all that orthodox.'
15. The passport was found and published by J.-H. Bornecque, p. 35.
16. *C.G.*, vol. I, p. 110.
17. So Villiers told a friend (*C.G.*, vol. I, p. 36). The letter is reproduced in facsimile in R. du Pontavice de Heussey, pp. 59–62.
18. This article and those few others that appeared were discovered and analysed by Luc Badesco, *La Jeunesse des deux rives. La Génération poétique de 1860*, Paris, Nizet, 1971, pp. 679–80.
19. One wonders how Villiers came into contact with Soulary. Joseph Bollery suggests (*C.G.*, vol. I, p. 39) that, as Villiers went several times to Lyon, he could have met Soulary there. The truth is more likely to be the other way round: that he went to Lyon because someone had put him in touch with Soulary. That might well have been Albert Glatigny, who appears to have been a friend of his.
20. *C.G.*, vol. I, p. 38.
21. These two articles were exhumed by Marcel Longuet, 'Deux critiques musicales de Villiers de l'Isle-Adam', *Mercure de France*, 15 mars 1932.
22. The most substantial study of *Premières Poésies* is to be found in Luc Badesco, *op. cit.* There are also some interesting remarks in William T. Conroy Jr, *Villiers de l'Isle-Adam*, Boston, Twayne, 1978.
23. *C.G.*, vol. I, p. 170.

4 (pp. 24–37)

1. This has been many times reproduced.

382 Notes

2. *C.G.*, vol. I, pp. 40–1. In the same letter he announced that *Les Assomptions humaines,* his second volume of poetry, would be ready in a few months and that he was meditating on various dramas.
3. On Hyacinthe du Pontavice de Heussey, see his son's book on Villiers; Jacques Vier, 'Une grande amie de la Bretagne, la comtesse d'Agoult (Daniel Stern)', *Annales de Bretagne,* t. 64, 1957; P.-G. Castex and J.-M. Bellefroid, introduction to *Tribulat Bonhomet,* Paris, Corti, 1967; and the 'Note des éditeurs' (in fact his sons Jules and Robert) in his *Œuvres complètes,* Paris, Quantin, 1887.
4. For many years it was supposed, following Robert du Pontavice de Heussey's claims, that he exhorted Villiers to idealism. But the truth, as established by P.-G. Castex and J.-M. Bellefroid, is the exact opposite. The confusion probably arose from the fact that Robert deliberately obscured his father's opinions because they were so contrary to his own. In an unpublished letter belonging to J.-M. Bellefroid, Jules admits the truth: 'We are royalists and conservatives, and he was a socialist and a freethinker: all his work proves it.'
5. Jacques Vier, op. cit.
6. See for instance Max Daireaux, p. 53. But Émile Drougard had already contested this notion ('Villiers de l'Isle-Adam et Éliphas Lévi', *Revue belge de philologie et d'histoire,* t. 10, no. 3, 1931).
7. See the relevant chapter in A. W. Raitt, *Villiers de l'Isle-Adam et le mouvement symboliste,* Paris, Corti, 1965.
8. On Villiers and Baudelaire, see the chapter in A. W. Raitt.
9. *C.G.*, vol. I, pp. 44–5.
10. Ibid., p. 47.
11. So Robert du Pontavice de Heussey said (p. 66).
12. 'Villiers would jump with indignation and cry that I was drowning in stupid prejudice': thus Robert du Pontavice de Heussey's account of Villiers's reactions when he expressed reservations about Baudelaire (p. 155).
13. Henry Roujon, *La Galerie des bustes,* Paris, Rueff, 1909, p. 118.
14. Ibid., p. 117.
15. Gustave Guiches, 'Villiers de l'Isle-Adam intime', *Le Figaro,* 31 août 1889. But the anecdote is suspect: some years later, Guiches repeated it (*Au banquet de la vie,* Paris, Spes, 1925, p. 172), attributing it to Léon Cladel rather than Villiers. However, one may suppose that the earlier attribution, being nearer the time, is more likely to be right. Robert du Pontavice de Heussey records a number of other stories he says Villiers used to tell about Baudelaire, but some of them are so manifestly impossible that one is forced to blame either Pontavice's notoriously defective memory or Villiers's habitual fantasizing.
16. Henry Roujon, p. 118.
17. *C.G.*, vol. I, p. 40.
18. Ibid.
19. Ibid., p. 41.
20. Ibid., p. 45. The letter, to Baudelaire, is dated from 4 rue St. Gouëno at Saint-Brieuc, and according to H. Le Noir de Tournemine that house belonged to the Séberts.

21. Ibid., p. 48.
22. Robert du Pontavice de Heussey, pp. 71–2. Though this was his first visit to the rue Saint-Honoré flat, Pontavice had met Villiers in 1858 when the poet had burst into their house at Fougères, where the child had been left alone as a punishment.
23. Fernand Calmettes, *Leconte de Lisle et ses amis*, Paris, Librairies-Imprimeries Réunies, n.d. [1902], p. 199.
24. Quoted by Louis Tiercelin, p. 165.
25. F. Calmettes, p. 157.
26. Calmettes (p. 200) records that Tante Kerinou's usual partner was an elderly noble and former lifeguard, who was incapable of losing without pulling a long face.

He would begin by complaining courteously to the old lady, putting on an *ancien régime* air, but, as his temper rose, the tone fell.
– Madame la marquise, you are not paying attention.
– I do beg your pardon, monsieur le marquis.
– Have you forgotten how to play, marquise?. . .
– Pardon, marquis . . .
– Well, what the hell are you up to, madame?
– I forbid you to swear, monsieur.
And the old lifeguard, laying the cards down with the gesture of a violent man resigning himself to the worst, would mutter into his beard a term of supreme disdain:
– Woman . . .

27. Accurate information on Mendès is not easy to come by, but see notably the many references in Luc Badesco, op. cit.
28. For instance, Edmond de Goncourt in his brutal diary entry for 10 September 1870: 'He has just the face of Christ with the clap.' (*Journal*, edited by Robert Ricatte, Paris, Fasquelle-Flammarion, 1956, vol. II, p. 599.)
29. There were of course other aspects to his anti-semitism, but in an unpublished page of anti-semitic reflections entitled 'Sentences occultes' (Castex Collection), some of the remarks are clearly specific references to Mendès.
30. Notably Édouard de Rougemont, who expresses himself very violently about Mendès, even calling him a 'venomous toad' (p. 222).
31. Again, not much information is available about Marras, but see Joseph Bollery's note in *C.G.*, vol. I, pp. 54–5; Louis Barthou, 'Jean Marras et Leconte de Lisle', *Revue des Deux Mondes*, 15 novembre 1933; and Mme C. Lefèvre-Roujon, *Correspondance inédite de Stéphane Mallarmé et Henry Roujon*, Geneva, Cailler, 1949, pp. 45–8.
32. The print order was discovered in the F18 file in the Archives Nationales by Dr D. M. Bellos, who was kind enough to draw my attention to it.
33. *C.G.*, vol. I, pp. 50–1.
34. *C.G.*, vol. II, p. 138.

35. Henry Laujol (pseudonym of Henry Roujon), 'Villiers de l'Isle-Adam', *La Revue bleue*, septembre 1889.
36. Henry Roujon, *La Galerie*, p. 138.
37. These two reviews were brought to light by Luc Badesco, op. cit.
38. F. Calmettes, p. 158.

5 (pp. 37–48)

1. Robert du Pontavice de Heussey, pp. 74–87.
2. F. Calmettes, pp. 195–6; H. Roujon, *La Galerie*, p. 118; Émile Bergerat, *Souvenirs d'un enfant de Paris*, Paris, Fasquelle, 1911–12, vol. II, p. 226.
3. So at least Bergerat suggests, and Pontavice's descriptions might well apply to Mendès.
4. Stéphane Mallarmé, *Œuvres complètes*, Paris, Bibliothèque de la Pléiade, 1945, p. 489.
5. Edmond and Jules de Goncourt, vol. II, p. 78. They add that Villiers looked as though he was descended from the Templars by way of the Funambulists.
6. *C.G.*, vol. I, p. 69.
7. Ibid., pp. 69–71.
8. Ibid., pp. 71–2.
9. Ibid., pp. 72–4.
10. Ibid., p. 61.
11. The first part of this letter was published by P.-G. Castex and J. Bollery in the second volume of their edition of *Contes cruels* (Paris, Corti, 1956), p. 274. The second part, in the Castex Collection, is unpublished. Though the signature has vanished, there can be little doubt that it is from Louise Dyonnet.
12. The story of Villiers's visits to Solesmes was first told by Émile Drougard, 'Villiers de l'Isle-Adam à Solesmes'. His account has been completed by Jacques Raison du Cleuziou, 'L'Entrevue à Solesmes de Louis Veuillot et d'A. Villiers de l'Isle-Adam', *Mémoires de la Société d'émulation des Côtes-du-Nord*, t. 98, 1969 (dealing mainly with the second visit). The secretary's notes are quoted by E. Drougard.
13. *C.G.*, vol. I, p. 57.
14. So at least he said to Tante Kerinou, according to her above-mentioned letter to Dom Guéranger.
15. *C.G.*, vol. I, pp. 58–60.
16. Ibid., p. 60.
17. Ibid.
18. Ibid., pp. 62–3.
19. Quoted by J. Raison du Cleuziou, 'L'Entrevue'.
20. *C.G.*, vol. I, p. 63.
21. These memories were set down in *Une Entrevue à Solesmes*, written in 1883 and collected in *Histoires insolites, Œuvres complètes*, Paris, Mercure de France, 1914–31, vol. VI—hereafter referred to as *O.C.*
22. Quoted by J. Raison du Cleuziou, 'L'Entrevue'. Mentioning their visit to Marras—without comment—Villiers refers to Taine as 'Henri',

which at first sight seems odd, since the philosopher's first name was Hippolyte. But he was also sometimes known as Henri. The secretary's notes put his identity beyond question.

23. *C.G.*, vol. I, pp. 51–4. The letter contains a draft of a prose poem which Villiers wanted Baudelaire to develop. Villiers later told Baudelaire that while he was at the abbey he had said to one of the monks that Baudelaire might go there for retreat, and the monk had replied: 'Well, if he comes, we shall receive him. We would even receive convicts.' (Baudelaire, *Correspondance*, edited by Claude Pichois, Paris, Bibliothèque de la Pléiade, 1973, vol. II, p. 281.)

24. Ibid., p. 62.

25. Mallarmé for instance talks about 'the retreat in many an abbey consulted by a juvenile science' (p. 490), and a recent editor of *Axël* even writes: 'After somewhat disordered schooling, Auguste-Mathias had the good fortune to be entrusted for several years to the care of the Benedictines of Solesmes who gave him a sound classical training and, no doubt, the love of belles-lettres.' (*Axël*, edited by Pierre Mariel, Paris, La Colombe, 1960, pp. 8–9.)

26. *O.C.*, vol. VI, p. 217.

27. *C.G.*, vol. I, p. 52.

28. Quoted by Luc Badesco, p. 725, n. 249, from the *Petite Revue* of 5 December 1863. At the same banquet, Villiers sang his own setting of Baudelaire's *Le Vin de l'assassin*.

29. Letter from Eugène Lefébure to Mallarmé, quoted in *C.G.*, vol. I, p. 80.

30. See Remy de Gourmont, *Promenades littéraires*, 2ᵉ série, p. 32. A letter sent jointly to Villiers in May 1875 by Henry Roujon, Catulle Mendès, and Augusta Holmès urges him to return from Brittany, where he was staying, with, among other things, '*Isis* reconstituted', which shows that he had claimed to have lost the sequel (*C.G.*, vol. I, p. 199).

31. See Joseph Bollery, *La Bretagne*, pp. 106–10. Luc Badesco later discovered two other texts of the same poems, unexpectedly published in *La France hippique* in August 1860 and January 1861 (pp. 693–711 and 1379–85). *La France hippique* was a journal about horses run by Baron Ephrem Houel du Hamel, a friend and relative of Villiers, who occupied an important post in the administration of the French National Stud. Villiers was close to him at the time, as is attested by the letter he sent him in 1860 (*C.G.*, vol. I, pp. 40–2).

32. This article does not figure in *O.C.* as published by the Mercure de France, but part of it was included in *Nouveaux Contes cruels et Propos d'au-delà*, Paris, Crès, 1923, also edited by Marcel Longuet, who reprinted only the general doctrinal section and omitted all that deals directly with Mendès, against whom he had a violent prejudice. The other part, which is substantial, has never been reproduced, though it has been examined by Luc Badesco (pp. 982–91).

33. *C.G.*, vol. I, p. 91. The letter, along with several others, is wrongly dated by Joseph Bollery, who thought they were written in 1866. See below, chapter 6, note 26.

6 (pp. 49–59)

1. Quoted by Henry Roujon, *La Galerie*, p. 107.
2. Catulle Mendès, *La Légende du Parnasse contemporain*, Brussels, Brancart, 1884, p. 194.
3. Article signed Henry Laujol in *La Jeune France*, 1ᵉʳ avril 1883.
4. Henry Roujon, *La Galerie*, p. 113.
5. Adolphe Racot, *Portraits d'aujourd'hui*, Paris, Librairie illustrée, 1887, p. 286.
6. Stéphane Mallarmé, pp. 489–90.
7. François Coppée, in *La Patrie*, 26 février 1883.
8. Louis-Xavier de Ricard, *Petits Mémoires d'un Parnassien*, edited by M. Pakenham, Paris, Lettres Modernes, 1967, p. 103.
9. Quoted by Miodrag Ibrovac, *José-Maria de Heredia*, Paris, Presses Françaises, 1923, p. 125.
10. According to Catulle Mendès (*La Légende*, p. 223), it was Louis Ménard who took him, Villiers, and Coppée to Leconte de Lisle's, where they met Heredia and Dierx.
11. M. Ibrovac, p. 109. In August 1870 Leconte de Lisle gave an unsuccessful reading of *La Révolte* to some ladies at Paramé, but apart from that and the fact that he was prepared to deliver a graveside eulogy at Villiers's funeral in 1889 (he was prevented by rain), there is little evidence that he had much regard for him. Their relations are discussed by F. Calmettes (op. cit.).
12. Letter in J.-M. Bellefroid, 'Villiers de l'Isle-Adam en Bavière (1869)', *Revue d'Histoire littéraire de la France*, octobre-décembre 1963.
13. *C.G.*, vol. I, p. 67. Villiers sent Flaubert copies of *Isis* and the 1866 edition of *Morgane*, with signed dedications (Lucien Andrieu, 'Les Dédicaces des livres envoyés à Flaubert et conservés à l'Hôtel de Ville de Canteleu', *Bulletin des Amis de Flaubert*, no. 24, 1964). There is no mention of Villiers in Flaubert's correspondence.
14. Some time before September 1864 Villiers copied a draft of one of Samuel's speeches into Mallarmé's autograph album (Henri Mondor, *Mallarmé plus intime*, Paris, Gallimard, 1944, p. 125). Mallarmé noted early in 1865 that Villiers had been working on the play for three years (*Correspondance*, edited by Henri Mondor and Jean-Pierre Richard, Paris, Gallimard, 1959, p. 154; subsequent volumes are edited by Mondor and L. J. Austin). In a letter written in September 1864, alluding to one of the characters in the plays, Villiers compared himself to his 'Andréas of yesteryear' (*C.G.*, vol. I, p. 73). So it seems likely that in 1864 he was writing up something first sketched out earlier.
15. *O.C.*, vol. VIII, p. 284.
16. The play was produced in 1896 by Paul Larochelle, the man responsible for producing *Axël* in 1894. But it was not a success, and he later admitted that it had been an error of judgement (Paul Larochelle, *Trois hommes de théâtre*, Paris, Éditions du Centre, 1961, pp. 270–2).
17. Villiers was very proud of this passage, and resurrected it in 1888 for separate publication in the periodical *La Vie pour rire*. In his *Biblio-*

iconographie de Villiers de l'Isle-Adam (Paris, Mercure de France, 1939, p. 56), Joseph Bollery assigned to the number in which it appeared the date 6 October, but Alain Néry has recently discovered that Bollery's dating was incorrect for this periodical, which did not date its numbers. However, the correct date for this particular issue is not known.

18. Mallarmé, *Correspondance*, vol. I, pp. 153–4.
19. Ibid., p. 158, n. 1.
20. Ibid., p. 159, n. 1.
21. Paul Verlaine, *Œuvres complètes*, Paris, Messein, 1926, Vol. V, p. 307.
22. The question of the date of *Morgane* has been much discussed. A whole row of critics and biographers (Le Noir de Tournemine, Rougemont, Clerget, Daireaux, Bollery) have all declared that it was written in 1855. This belief presumably originates with the 1880 edition of *Le Nouveau-Monde*, on the flyleaf of which the date opposite *Morgane* does indeed appear as 1855. But, as the works are listed there in chronological order, that is manifestly a misprint for 1865. Gustave Kahn has argued convincingly that *Morgane* is a later work than *Elën* ('Villiers de l'Isle-Adam', *Mercure de France*, 15 juillet 1922).
23. *C.G.*, vol. I, p. 97, where the letter is assigned to 1866. J.-M. Bellefroid (reviewing the edition in the *Revue d'Histoire littéraire de la France*, octobre-décembre 1963) has pointed out that it should be 1865, since the Société des Lectures to which it refers only existed in that year.
24. This letter does not figure in *C.G.* Extracts from it were published in 1972 in a catalogue of the Librairie des Argonautes.
25. *C.G.*, vol. I, p. 83.
26. Ibid., where the letter is assigned to 1866. In the review quoted above, J.-M. Bellefroid has demonstrated that a whole series of letters to Marras and Heredia which J. Bollery placed in 1866 were in fact written in November or December 1865.
27. These misadventures are recounted in the misdated letters in *C.G.*, vol. I, pp. 85–94.
28. *C.G.*, vol. I, p. 92. See J. Raison du Cleuziou, 'Le Chanoine'.
29. J. Bollery, *La Bretagne*, p. 89.
30. Unpublished letter in the Sickles Collection.
31. F. Calmettes, p. 199.
32. Ibid.
33. *C.G.*, vol. I, p. 63.
34. Ibid., p. 84.
35. Ibid., p. 101.
36. Ibid., p. 84.
37. F. Calmettes, p. 188.

7 (pp. 59–70)

1. *C.G.*, vol. I, pp. 96–8.
2. Joanna Richardson, *Théophile Gautier*, London, Reinhardt, 1958, p. 206.

3. F. Calmettes, p. 193.
4. Ibid., p. 194.
5. See R. Pichard du Page, *Une musicienne versaillaise. Augusta Holmès*, Versailles, Dubois; Paris, Fischbacher, 1921.
6. Henri Mondor, *Vie de Mallarmé*, Paris, Gallimard, 1941, p. 151.
7. Stéphane Mallarmé, *Correspondance*, vol. I, p. 177, n. 1.
8. *C.G.*, vol. I, p. 113.
9. Ibid., pp. 103–4.
10. Mallarmé, *Œuvres complètes*, p. 498.
11. H. Mondor, *Vie de Mallarmé*, p. 668.
12. *C.G.*, vol. I, p. 80.
13. Ibid., p. 97.
14. Ibid., p. 99.
15. Ibid.
16. Ibid., p. 97.
17. This was Adolphe Le Nepvou de Carfort, who died young of typhoid.
18. *C.G.*, vol. I, p. 83.
19. These were 'A celle qui est morose' and 'El Desdichado', which he later expanded into *Souvenirs occultes* in the *Contes cruels*. They were discovered by Auriant (*Fragments*, Brussels, Nouvelle Revue Belgique, 1942, pp. 81–6.)
20. There is a complete unpublished manuscript draft of the article in the Taylorian Library in Oxford and a fragment of a corrected version in the Castex Collection. Villiers listed it among his writings on the flyleaf of *Le Nouveau-Monde* in 1880, but there is no clue as to where it had appeared.
21. *Mémoires d'un veuf*, in *Œuvres posthumes*, Paris, Messein, 1927, vol. II, p. 348.
22. Gustave Guiches, 'Villiers de l'Isle-Adam intime'.
23. This is the only music by Villiers of which a transcription has survived. Judith Gautier's version of it figures in Fernand Clerget, op. cit., p. 71.
24. *C.G.*, vol. I, p. 112.
25. Ibid., pp. 82–3.
26. Ibid., p. 83.

8 (pp. 70–77)

1. According to Baude de Maurceley ('La Vérité sur le salon de Nina de Villard', *Le Figaro*, 3 avril 1929), he had bought it with some money he had inherited.

Villiers's carriage stood all day long outside the Café de Madrid, where his Parnassian friends Mendès and Dierx hung out. Sometimes, it would be taken across the boulevard to stand outside the Café des Variétés. Finally, after three months, the small fortune having disappeared, it became necessary to sell the carriage and the horses. The day before the sale, Villiers decided to make use of it. But what trip could he undertake? He couldn't think of anything. Then the coachman, with gentle familiarity, said simply: 'Monsieur le comte, supposing we went to the Bois de Boulogne?' Villiers hadn't thought of the '*drive round the lake*', since replaced by the '*Allée des Acacias*'. And that was the solitary occasion on which the grand carriage was put to real use.

2. On Armand Gouzien, see Émile Drougard's edition of *Les Trois Premiers Contes*, Paris, Belles Lettres, 1931, vol. I, pp. 13–16.
3. *C.G.*, vol. I, pp. 105–7.
4. See the letters in *C.G.*, vol. I, pp. 104, 107, 109–11, 115–18.
5. *C.G.*, vol. I, p. 117.
6. The article on *Hamlet* was collected in *Chez les passants*; the other was not preserved by Villiers but figures in *O.C.*, vol. XI.
7. Mendès, *La Légende*, p. 9.
8. In *Le Nain jaune*, 1866.
9. Fernand Clerget (p. 38) quotes Adrien Remacle's unpublished memoirs to this effect, and in his novel *La Femme pauvre* (Paris, Mercure de France, 1947, p. 163) Léon Bloy makes a similar allusion. But Villiers was probably in Brittany at the time, and these belated reminiscences are doubtless fictitious compensations.
10. Much has been written about Wagner in France, but see above all Léon Guichard, *La Musique et les lettres en France au temps du wagnérisme*, Paris, P.U.F., 1963.
11. The claim has been made for *L'Esprit Nouveau*, by Maxime Leroy in *Les Premiers Amis français de Wagner*, Paris, Michel, 1925.
12. *C.G.*, vol. I, p. 113.
13. Ibid., p. 112.
14. Louis de Gavrinis, 'Les Hommes de plume. Auguste Villiers de l'Isle-Adam', *La Comédie française*, 2 janvier 1875. The article includes a note apologizing to Henry Roujon who, Gavrinis thought, was sure to find it disrespectful.
15. At the time of his edition of *Les Trois Premiers Contes*, Émile Drougard had been unable to find any information about *La Fronde*. But it has now been studied in detail by Alain Néry in his thesis on 'Les Idées politiques et sociales de Villiers de l'Isle-Adam'.

9 (pp. 77–87)

1. See the article by Willy Garcias in *La Table ronde*, 25 novembre 1920; also *C.G.*, vol. I, pp. 120–8, In another article, in *Le Goéland*, août 1938, Willy Garcias explains the circumstances: his father, a banker who had fallen on hard times, had opened a high-class boarding house in Paris, where Catulle Mendès and Judith Gautier took lodgings. They introduced Villiers there, and Mme Garcias, taking pity on his poverty, decided to marry him off to a rich but ugly South American girl who was also a boarder. Villiers sat next to her one evening, but was so horrified that the next day he wrote to Garcias to say he would not be dining that evening and asking him to move Catulle's chair next to that of the girl.
2. *C.G.*, vol. I, p. 100.
3. Ibid., pp. 127–8.
4. He had in fact in 1864 appeared in the long-established and distin-

guished salon of Mme Virginie Ancelot, which years before had been frequented by men like Stendhal and Mérimée. That was where Xavier de Ricard saw him for the first time, 'looking rather lost in that solemn company of academicians, poets, artists' (*Petits Mémoires d'un Parnassien*, p. 48). But he does not seem to have been a regular visitor.

5. F. Calmettes, pp. 191–2.

6. Léon Barracand, 'Souvenirs d'un homme de lettres', *Revue des Deux Mondes* (15 août 1937).

7. F. Calmettes, p. 192.

8. Ibid., p. 128.

9. '*La Tentation*, scènes inédites', published by P.-G. Castex, *Revue d'Histoire littéraire de la France*, janvier-mars 1956. A curious and hitherto unnoticed feature of *La Tentation* is that it is unmistakably based on the same plot as Jean Marras's play *La Famille d'Armelles*, written about 1872, produced in 1883, and published in 1891. An unpublished letter from Villiers to Marras, written on 31 December 1882, contains a renunciation by Villiers of any further share in the elaboration of Marras's drama: 'Circumstances outside my control deprive me of the pleasure of collaborating on the play we had spoken about under the provisional title *Le Père et le fils*' (copy belonging to J. Bollery). The nature of the subject makes it clear that *Le Père et le fils* is the same thing as *La Famille d'Armelles*. There are several puzzling features about the letter, not least the fact that rehearsals of the play had started at the Odéon and then been suspended, which makes the idea of 'collaboration' by Villiers enigmatic. Most probably Villiers wrote the letter in order that Marras could demonstrate to the management of the Odéon that he really was entitled to call the work his own.

10. On Cros (and Nina) see Louis Forestier, *Charles Cros, l'homme et l'œuvre*, Paris, Minard, 1969.

11. *C.G.*, vol. I, p. 223.

12. Baude de Maurceley, 'La Vérité sur le salon de Nina de Villard', *Le Figaro*, 2–8 avril 1929.

13. Collected in *Chez les passants*, *O.C.*, vol. XI.

14. George Moore, *Memoirs of my Dead Life*, London, Heinemann, 1936, p. 67. Moore met Villiers several times, but did not have a particularly high opinion of him. It was he who said of Villiers: 'He has no talent whatever, only genius, and that is why he is a *raté*.' (p. 75.)

15. Unpublished letter; a copy was in the possession of Joseph Bollery.

16. All that is known about this curious affair is to be found in Joseph Bollery, 'Une descendance inconnue de Villiers de l'Isle-Adam au Congo ex-belge,' *La Fenêtre ouverte*, décembre 1961 (the letter mentioned in the previous note only came to light after the publication of the article).

17. This letter does not figure in *C.G.*, but extracts from it are quoted in Auriant, p. 89.

18. *C.G.*, vol. I, pp. 127–8.

19. See Léon Guichard, *La Musique et les lettres*, and Judith Gautier's own memoirs, *Le Troisième Rang du collier*, Paris, Juven, 1909.

10 (pp. 87–99)

1. Émile Bergerat, *Souvenirs d'un enfant de Paris*, Paris, Fasquelle, 1911–12, vol. I, p. 128.
2. See *C.G.*, vol. I, pp. 137–44.
3. Villiers confused the question of dating this journey by writing '1868' in his article *Souvenir* (*O.C.*, vol. XI, p. 96). But Émile Drougard was able to show that this was an error ('Richard Wagner et Villiers de l'Isle-Adam', *Revue de Littérature comparée*, avril-juin 1934).
4. *C.G.*, vol. I, p. 130.
5. Ibid., p. 131.
6. Ibid., pp. 136 and 138.
7. Ibid., p. 133.
8. Ibid., p. 135.
9. Ibid., p. 132.
10. The story is told by Judith Gautier (op. cit.) as though the incident had occurred in 1869. But one may deduce from Villiers's correspondence (*C.G.*, vol. I, pp. 156–7) that it more likely took place in 1870.
11. Quoted by Émile Drougard, 'Villiers de l'Isle-Adam et Richard Wagner', *Revue musicale* (février 1936). Cosima's diaries have only recently been published in full (*Die Tagebücher*, edited by M. Gregor Dellin and D. Mack, Munich, Piper Verlag, 1976–7); see vol. I, p. 130.
12. J. Gautier, pp. 161–2.
13. Cosima Wagner, vol. I, p. 131.
14. Léon Guichard, *Lettres de Richard et Cosima Wagner à Judith Gautier*, Paris, Gallimard, 1964, pp. 104–5. Judith Gautier used this letter in reconstructing the conversation with the Wagners the previous evening, and a good deal of what she reports Wagner as saying is in fact taken from it.
15. Judith Gautier, p. 124.
16. *C.G.*, vol. I, p. 139.
17. Discovered and published by J.-M. Bellefroid, 'Villiers de l'Isle-Adam en Bavière (1869)'.
18. Discovered and published by Joseph Bollery, *Mercure de France* (1er novembre 1939).
19. Discovered and published by Émile Drougard, '*L'Or du Rhin* et *L'Exposition universelle des Beaux-Arts à Munich*', *Nouvelles littéraires*, 29 juillet and 5 août 1939. Parts of the article were included by Judith Gautier in *Le Troisième Rang du collier*, where she mistakenly asserted that Villers had never bothered to send it in. Evidently he had kept an early draft which somehow found its way into Judith's possession.
20. *C.G.*, vol. I, p. 140.
21. Ibid.
22. From a letter not in *C.G.*, published by J.-M. Bellefroid, 'Villiers de l'Isle-Adam en Bavière'.
23. The story is told by Judith Gautier (op. cit.). It is interesting to note that Édouard de Rougemont, anxious to establish that Villiers was a

serious-minded man, only quotes the first part of Judith's account and omits the sequel (p. 147).

24. Judith Gautier records that there was much ill-will against them in Munich because they were regarded as responsible for the post-ponement of the performance. This is confirmed by François Oswald, writing in *Le Gaulois* on 7 September 1869:

> Here's a good joke: as I called a short time ago at the Café de l'Opéra to say goodbye to the little Wagnerian clan that meets there every evening, Catulle Mendès, his wife Mme Judith Gautier, Villiers de l'Isle-Adam, Servais, etc., I learnt that they have just received an anonymous warning. They are threatened with a hostile demonstration by Wagner's enemies, who intend, after having beaten them up, to force them to leave the city (. . .) Mendès is going to write to the minister of police to inform him that from tomorrow he will only go out armed with revolvers.

25. This too was published by Émile Drougard in the article quoted above. None of the pieces published by Villiers during the 1869 journey figures in *O.C.*

26. So he says in the letter to Marras published by J.-M. Bellefroid (see note 22).

27. R. Escholier, *Victor Hugo: un amant de génie*, Paris, Fayard, 1953, pp. 41–2.

28. In *C.G.* (vol. I, pp. 151–3), Joseph Bollery has assigned this letter, which is undated, to March 1870, because it was known that Mendès and his wife were in Belgium then. But the contents of the letter make it clear that it relates to the earlier journey, which Bollery did not know about.

29. *C.G.*, vol. I, pp. 147–8.

30. This letter has never been reproduced; it explains an otherwise enigmatic reference to Dumas's 'violent intervention' in Villiers's preface to the play (*O.C.*, vol. VII, p. XII).

31. *C.G.*, vol. I, p. 149.

32. Ibid., pp. 153–4. But the date suggested by Joseph Bollery—March or April 1870—is too late: there is a reference to 'the letter from M. Dumas *fils*', which suggests that it was written only a few days after 20 January, when the letter was published.

33. On this episode, see A. W. Raitt, '*Lohengrin* raconté par Villiers de l'Isle-Adam', *Revue des Sciences humaines* (juillet 1956).

34. Léon Barracand, op. cit.

35. Quoted by Luc Badesco, p. 1003.

36. *C.G.*, vol. I, p. 150.

37. Remy de Gourmont, *Épilogues I*, Paris, Mercure de France, 1963, p. 47.

38. On the evolution of the text of *La Révolte*, see Émile Drougard, '*La Révolte* de Villiers de l'Isle-Adam: le texte original', *Bulletin du bibliophile* (novembre 1948), and F. Cipriani, '*La Révolte*, dramma di Villiers de l'Isle-Adam, note con frammenti inediti', *Annali della Facoltà di Lettere e Filosofia dell'Università degli Studi di Milano* (settembre-dicembre 1975). There are in fact in the Bibliothèque de

l'Arsenal other unpublished manuscripts of the play which have not
been studied by either of these authors.

39. The information comes from the printer's declaration in the F 18 file in
    the Archives Nationales, discovered by Dr D. M. Bellos.

11 (pp. 99–105)

1. *O.C.*, vol. VII, pp. 26–7.
2. Ibid., p. 46.
3. Maurice Descotes, *Le Public de théâtre et son histoire*, Paris, P.U.F.,
   1964, p. 308.
4. *O.C.*, vol. VII, p. 11.
5. See Dorothy Knowles, *La Réaction idéaliste au théâtre depuis 1890*,
   Paris, Droz, 1934.
6. In *Le Temps*, 9 mai 1870.
7. Magnard is only displaying his ignorance: it means 'without frontiers'.
8. *Le Figaro*, 7 avril 1870.
9. On these events, see J.-M. Bellefroid, 'Une chronique de Villiers de
   l'Isle-Adam sur Victor Noir', *Revue des Sciences humaines*, juillet-
   septembre 1965.
10. In *Le Journal*, 2 décembre 1896.
11. Henry Roujon, *La Galerie*, p. 116.
12. In *Le National*, 9 mai 1870.
13. In *Le Diable*, 7 mai 1870.
14. In *La Vogue parisienne*, 13 mai 1870.
15. The article signed 'Un Passant' in *Le Rappel*, 8 mai 1870, may be by
    Pelletan, who is one of the people Villiers thanks in his preface.
16. D'Hervilly's article has not been traced, but he too is thanked by
    Villiers in the preface.
17. In *Le Journal officiel*, 9 mai 1870.
18. In *La Marseillaise*, 10 mai 1870.
19. In *L'Opinion nationale*, 9 mai 1870.
20. In *Le Gaulois*, 8 mai 1870.
21. According to Catulle Mendès, quoted in Stéphane Mallarmé, *Corre-
    spondance*, vol. I, p. 328.
22. In *Le Parlement*, 11 mai 1870.
23. *O.C.*, vol. VII, p. XV.
24. Ibid., p. XXII.
25. According to Remy de Gourmont, 'its failure had been so brutal and so
    flagrant that Villiers, after the invective of the preface, became sickened
    with the work and affected to despise it.' (*Épilogues I*, p. 44.) In fact,
    he republished a slightly revised version of it in 1877 in an ephemeral
    review called *La Quinzaine*, as was recently discovered by Alain Néry.
    The play was not produced again during Villiers's lifetime, though a
    fictitious performance of it forms one of the central scenes of Remy de
    Gourmont's novel *Sixtine* (1890). In 1894 Antoine wanted to put it on
    at the Théâtre Libre with Sarah Bernhardt as Élisabeth, but was refused
    permission by Villiers's widow or her representative (unpublished
    letter belonging to Henri Leclercq). He did, however, succeed in

staging it in 1896, when it was moderately well received, but what had seemed audacious and shocking in 1870 appeared relatively innocuous after Ibsen's *Doll's House*. There were several more productions in the 1890s by Antoine and others, and in 1903 it was accepted at the Comédie Française, where it was first produced in 1914, with revivals in 1930, 1942, and 1955. There have also been broadcast versions of it and more than one recent production in Paris outside the Comédie Française.

26. *C.G.*, vol. I, p. 148.
27. L.-X. de Ricard, p. 91.

12 (pp. 105–117)

1. In *Le Tzar et les grands-ducs*, *O.C.*, vol. V, pp. 198–9.
2. Pontavice de Heussey, pp. 241–4. There are obvious errors in this account, since Pontavice avers that the reading took place in Bayreuth at Wagner's request.
3. Cyprien Godebski, quoted in *L'Art moderne*, 22 septembre 1895.
4. In *Le Tzar et les grands-ducs*, written in 1883.
5. As has been suggested by Marilyn Gaddis Rose, 'Villiers de l'Isle-Adam's Commander: a possible prototype', *Romance Notes*, 11, 1970.
6. Henry Roujon, *La Galerie*, p. 119. Roujon spells the name Lorbach, but the person in question is undoubtedly Charles de Lorbac, who had published a brief biography of Wagner in 1861. Baude de Maurceley (op. cit.) heard Villiers tell the same story.
7. *C.G.*, vol I, p. 155.
8. This letter is not in *C.G.* It was published by Jean Mistler, 'Notre ami Wagner', *Nouvelles littéraires* (24 octobre 1963).
9. *C.G.*, vol. I, p. 156.
10. For the full story of this visit, see A. W. Raitt, 'Villiers de l'Isle-Adam in 1870', *French Studies*, October 1959, where further references are given.
11. *C. G.*, vol. I, p. 156.
12. This article is not in *O.C.* It was published by A. W. Raitt, 'Villiers de l'Isle-Adam in 1870'.
13. *C.G.*, vol. I, p. 157.
14. Ibid., pp. 157–8.
15. Published by Roger Lhombreaud, 'Deux âmes qui s'entendent si merveilleusement . . .', *Revue de Paris*, juillet 1955; *C.G.*, vol. I, p. 159.
16. *C.G.*, vol. I, pp. 157–8.
17. This article is not in *O.C.* It was published by Émile Drougard, 'Les Premiers Jours de la guerre de 1870', *Nouvelles littéraires*, 6 mai 1939.
18. Cosima Wagner, vol. I, p. 262.
19. Quoted by Otto Strobel, *Neue Urkunden zur Lebensgeschichte Richard Wagners 1864–1882*, Karlsruhe, 1939, pp. 214–15.
20. Henry Roujon, 'Lorsque Villiers de l'Isle-Adam nous jouait du Wagner . . .', *Le Journal*, 28 février 1904.
21. *C.G.*, vol. I, pp. 160–1, 163 and 164.

22. Catulle Mendès, *Rapport sur le Mouvement poétique français de 1867 à 1900*, Paris, Imprimerie Nationale, 1903, pp. 107–8.
23. *C.G.*, vol. I, pp. 158–9.
24. Villiers did not have much contact with this aunt (or indeed with any of the brothers and sisters of his parents, except the Abbé Victor), but he did draft a letter to *Le Figaro* about her when she died early in the 1880s (unpublished document belonging to J.-M. Bellefroid). It is, in fact, another proclamation of his right to the name; it is not known whether it was sent or published.
25. *C.G.*, vol. I, pp. 162–3.
26. Ibid., p. 164.
27. Ibid., p. 163.
28. Quoted by Miodrag Ibrovac, p. 560.
29. According to the ex-Madame Paul Verlaine, *Mémoires de ma vie*, Paris, Flammarion, 1935, pp. 129–30. But Cros specialists are sceptical about this story; see Charles Cros, *Œuvres complètes*, edited by Louis Forestier and Pascal Pia, Paris, Pauvert, 1964, p. 562, and Louis Forestier, p. 377.
30. Pontavice de Heussey, p. 200.
31. Henry Roujon, *La Galerie*, p. 121.
32. Léon Deffoux, *Les Derniers Jours de Villiers de l'Isle-Adam* (Paris, Bernard, 1930), pp. 17–18; the book is mainly based on Malherbe's recollections.
33. *C.G.*, vol. I, p. 166. Another title he used was 'Captain General of the Horsemen of the Republic', which, according to *L'Artiste* of juillet-août 1871, was how he had signed the register of a boarding house in the Quartier Latin (see E. de Rougemont, p. 151).
34. *O.C.*, vol XI, 110–11.

13 (pp. 117–124)

1. Bergerat, vol. I, pp. 226–7.
2. *C.G.*, vol. I, pp. 171–2. The original note appeared on 9 October 1871 and Villiers's reply on the twelfth. Both were exhumed by Daniel A. de Graaf in *Mercure de France*, 1er octobre 1953.
3. Unpublished letter belonging to the late Mme Aline Pasquet, Jean Marras's daughter.
4. Mallarmé, *Correspondance*, vol. I, p. 350. It might be inferred from this that Cazalis had told Mallarmé that Villiers was detained in Paris against his will. But the letter from Cazalis to which Mallarmé was replying makes it clear that this is not so (see C. P. Barbier and L. Joseph, *Correspondance avec Henri Cazalis 1862–1897*, Paris, Nizet, 1977, pp. 463–4). Nevertheless Mallarmé's opinion carries weight.
5. *C.G.*, vol. I, pp. 167–8.
6. Ibid., pp. 168–9.
7. The story of the proposed attribution to Villiers is complicated, and the quarrel over it was long and acrimonious. It was J.-H. Bornecque, in the *Mercure de France*, 1er août 1953, who first republished these articles as Villiers's work. In an article already mentioned, D. A. de

Graaf appeared to support his position, but it was strongly contested in subsequent issues of the *Mercure* by W. M. Blows (1er novembre 1953 and again on 1er février 1954) and by André Lebois (1er avril 1954). The most circumstantial and persuasive refutation came from Émile Drougard, who, in the *Mercure* of 1er décembre 1953, adduced all kinds of historical and stylistic arguments for thinking that the articles were not by Villiers, and suggested that the author might be Mendès. J.-H. Bornecque rejected them all and maintained his original view. There the matter rested for several years until, in the *Mercure* of mars 1958, É. Drougard produced the evidence of Lepelletier's *Histoire de la Commune*, not hitherto mentioned, and reluctantly accepted that J.-H. Bornecque had been right. The latter has naturally restated his opinion in his recent book on Villiers (pp. 76–8). But it is by no means sure that the issue is beyond dispute, and in his thesis Alain Néry expresses serious doubts: 'In all honesty one must admit that the whole business remains obscure. It is possible that "Marius" is Villiers, or that he is not.' (p. 182.) He also envisages the possibility that Marras and Villiers may have collaborated on the articles. But when one takes all the evidence into account, including a letter to Jules Favre not known in the 1950s, the odds against 'Marius' being Villiers seem very high indeed. E. Drougard's original objections retain all their force; the suspect coincidence in dates between Michelet and Lepelletier removes some of the weight from the latter's testimony (produced more than forty years after the event), even if E. Drougard did not realize this; and there can be no doubting Villiers's involvement with the Versaillais. As always, absolute proof of a negative is difficult to attain, but the balance of probabilities is strongly against Villiers having written *Tableau de Paris*.

8. Not in *C.G.* Published by André Billy in *Le Figaro littéraire*, 24 mars 1966.

9. Here is the passage in question: 'During the insurrection in Paris, I was one of the first associates of M. Langeron, the official representative of Versailles. I shared with him the perils which threatened all those who, having put their names on his lists, were ready, at a word from the executive power, to join with the army in saving the cause of order, religion, justice, and society.' Since Favre was in a position to check with Langeron, it seems inconceivable that Villiers could have been inventing, and, if this letter had been known sooner, the whole debate about *Tableau de Paris* would necessarily have been very different. J.-H. Bornecque does not mention it in his recent book.

10. *C.G.*, vol. I, p. 170.

11. For a long time, as a result of an erroneous affirmation by Pontavice de Heussey (p. 87), it was thought that she had died several years earlier. Her death certificate was discovered by Joseph Bollery, 'Villiers de l'Isle-Adam. Documents biographiques inédits', *Mercure de France*, 1er octobre 1938.

12. *C.G.*, vol. I, p. 172.

13. Ibid., p. 172. The letter is dated 14 November 1871; it is curious that Villiers should have waited three months before writing it.

14. See Joseph Bollery, *La Bretagne*, p. 85.

14 (pp. 127–136)

1. Joseph Bollery, 'Villiers de l'Isle-Adam. Documents biographiques inédits'.
2. That is the address given on the above-mentioned letter to Dom Guéranger.
3. Unpublished document in the Fonds Bollery.
4. Léon Barracand, op. cit.
5. Unpublished letter; a copy of an extract from it is in the Fonds Bollery.
6. See above, chapter 9, note 9.
7. F. Calmettes, pp. 179–80.
8. Ibid., p. 190.
9. Ibid.
10. Louis de Gavrinis, op. cit.
11. J. Gautier, pp. 119–20.
12. Henry Roujon, *La Galerie*, p. 122.
13. Ibid., p. 119. There is a fuller discussion of Villiers's involvement with Orélie-Antoine I in Alain Néry's thesis.
14. This story was related to several different people by Villiers's son Victor, notably to Marcel Longuet (quoted by Édouard de Rougemont, p. 153) and to Georges Casella, who retails it in *Pèlerinages*, Lausanne, Payot, 1918, p. 73.
15. *O.C.*, vol. VII, p. 78.
16. Reproduced under the title *Marthe* in *Nouvelles Reliques*, edited by P.-G. Castex and J.-M. Bellefroid, Paris, Corti, 1968.
17. Unpublished manuscript formerly in the Leclercq Collection.
18. One was published by Judith Gautier herself in the *Mercure de France*, avril 1893, with an account of its genesis. The other figures in *Reliques*, edited by P.-G. Castex, Paris, Corti, 1954; it apparently includes the prose poem *Le Miroir*, also collected in *Reliques*.
19. Henry Roujon, *La Galerie*, p. 116.
20. R. de Gourmont, *La Culture des idées*, Paris, Mercure de France, 1900, pp. 63–4.
21. Xavier de Ricard remembered hearing Villiers read *Axël* in Leconte de Lisle's salon (p. 91).
22. See chapter 12.
23. Quoted by É. Drougard, 'L'*Axël* de Villiers de l'Isle-Adam', *Revue d'Histoire littéraire de la France*, octobre-décembre 1935.
24. Unpublished letter quoted by Mlle M. A. Schreiner in her 1953 Sorbonne thesis on 'Émile Blémont et la "Renaissance littéraire et artistique" '.
25. See the above-mentioned article by É. Drougard (note 23) and the same writer's 'Fragments manuscrits d'*Axël*', *Revue des Sciences humaines*, janvier-mars 1955.
26. *O.C.*, vol. IV, p. 29.
27. Henry Roujon, *La Galerie*, p. 128.
28. Quoted by Fernand Clerget, pp. 70–1.

15 (pp. 136–145)

1. Recollected by Verlaine's former wife, p. 115.
2. Quoted by É. de Rougemont, pp. 162–3.
3. This can be deduced from a copy of the first edition of *Morgane*, belonging to P.-G. Castex, which had been sent by Villiers to Carvalho and subsequently to other managers. See Villiers de l'Isle-Adam, *Le Prétendant*, edited by P.-G. Castex and A. W. Raitt, Paris, Corti, 1965.
4. In the story *L'Amour suprême*, *O.C.*, vol. V, p. 13.
5. Unpublished manuscript in the Fonds Bollery.
6. *C.G.*, vol. I, p. 145.
7. Ibid., pp. 174–5.
8. Calmettes, p. 189.
9. *C.G.*, vol. I, p. 173.
10. Ibid., pp. 176–7.
11. The letter is only summarized in *C.G.* (vol. I, p. 178). Its full text is printed in J.-H. Bornecque, p. 74.
12. As is noted by É. Drougard, 'Villiers de l'Isle-Adam défenseur de son nom'.
13. The Bodleian Library in Oxford has a copy of *Elën* inscribed by Villiers to his 'cousin' the Comtesse de La Houssaye. This does not prove any real relationship, since Villiers made exceedingly free use of the term.
14. *C.G.*, vol. I, p. 180.
15. Quoted by Henri Mondor, *Vie de Mallarmé*, p. 548.
16. As transpires from Villiers's letter to Mallarmé on 5 January 1874, where he says he left precipitately for London on receipt of a note from the young lady (*C.G.*, vol. I, p. 183).
17. At least the entries for the family in Burke's *Landed Gentry of Ireland* suggest that she may have been connected with it in some way. Her name was discovered by an inscription on a bound copy of *La Révolte*, dedicated, very formally, to 'Miss Anna Eyre Powell' (see Joseph Bollery, 'Documents biographiques inédits sur Villiers de l'Isle-Adam'). The name Powell has been carefully erased, no doubt because the lady later used the name Anna Eyre in her operatic and Journalistic enterprises. See also the edition of *L'Ève future* by J. Bollery and P.-G. Castex, Paris, Le Club du Meilleur Livre, 1957. The fact that under treatment the erased name showed up as 'Powells' is presumably due to the misreading of a flourish of handwriting as an extra letter. So far as can be seen from directories of the period, the name Anna was fairly common in various branches of the Eyre Powell family, but none of the Annas identified there would have been of the right age to be Villiers's fiancée. There does not seem to be any trace of the birth of Anna Eyre Powell, at the appropriate period, in Somerset House, but she may well have been born in Ireland. It is also possible that she was illegitimate: so Villiers intimates apropos of the heroine of an unpublished early version of *L'Amour suprême*, in which he clearly had Anna Eyre in mind.

18. These details were all discovered by J.-M. Bellefroid whose researches on the subject are still unpublished. Anna Eyre made her début as an opera singer in Paris at the Théâtre des Italiens in 1876 as Leonora in *Il Trovatore*; the press reported unfavourably on her performance and insinuated that she had only been engaged because of support from highly-placed friends. She also sang in a matinee at the Italiens in March 1877. Thereafter she disappears from view until March 1880 when she becomes editor of the *Journal des jeunes mères*, retitled *Journal des mères* in October of the same year. The magazine published a biographical note about her in its number of 17 November 1880, which is probably highly fanciful. It claims that she was born in Ireland of a family with royal and ancient blood; that she was brought up in a French convent from the age of three until the age of twenty, when she had an annual income of £75,000; that she and the nuns had to flee from the Prussians in 1870; that the war ruined her family; that she then studied singing at Milan Conservatoire for eighteen months; that in 1875 she sang in opera in Milan, Cagliari, and Naples; that she had medals from the Société de Sauvetage and the Roman Academy as well as the title of canoness. J.-M. Bellefroid has found no evidence to support any of these contentions, other than that there was a Fondation de Notre-Dame des Arts in the rue du Rocher at Neuilly, founded in 1855 to give a religious education to artistically gifted girls. J.-H. Bornecque (pp. 85–6) has disputed the identification of Anna Eyre with Villiers's fiancée, but his reasons are tenuous: there can be little doubt that the identification is valid, and it is only a pity that so little solid information about her has come to light.

19. *C.G.*, vol. I, p. 185.
20. Ibid., p. 184.
21. Ibid., p. 182.
22. Ibid.
23. Ibid., p. 184. That is also where Villiers situates the seat of Alicia Clary's family in *L'Ève future*.
24. Ibid., pp. 184–5.
25. Ibid., pp. 186–7.
26. Ibid., p. 182.
27. Ibid., pp. 183–5.
28. Ibid., p. 183.
29. Henry Roujon, *La Galerie*, pp. 117–18.
30. Gustave Kahn, 'Villiers de l'Isle-Adam', *Mercure de France*, 15 juillet 1922. Henri de Régnier also heard the story from Mallarmé and mentions it, but more vaguely than Kahn, in more than one of his volumes of memoirs.'
31. It may be that there was some kind of sequel to the sorry events. J.-H. Bornecque (p. 92) has found a passport issued to Villiers on 12 February 1875 to enable him to go to London 'on business'. Whether the journey actually took place, and if so why, is not known.
32. *C.G.*, vol. I, pp. 187–8.
33. This letter is not in *C.G.*; it was published by F. Boux de Casson, a

descendant of Gantès, in 'Cinq lettres inédites de Villiers de l'Isle-Adam', *Aspects*, 7 juillet 1944 (the article in fact contains the text of six letters, some of them highly important).

16 (pp. 146–157)

1. Some of these fragments were published by É. Drougard ('Fragments manuscrits d'*Axël*') and by P.-G. Castex and J.-M. Bellefroid (*Nouvelles Reliques*). One or two others, still unpublished, are in the Castex Collection.
2. See P.-G. Castex's edition of *Contes cruels* (Paris, Garnier, 1968), p. 442.
3. Quoted by F. Clerget, p. 124.
4. Quoted by André Lebois, p. 116.
5. G. Guiches, 'Villiers de l'Isle-Adam', *La Nouvelle Revue*, 1er mai 1890.
6. C. Mendès, *Rapport sur le mouvement poétique français*, pp. 126–7.
7. F. Clerget, p. 92.
8. Ibid., pp. 92–3.
9. *C.G.*, vol. I, p. 189; the letter is however wrongly dated there—the correct date is 29 December, not 20 December.
10. Unpublished letter belonging to the present writer. This letter made possible the discovery of the notes in Oswald's column, not known at the time when *Le Prétendant* was published in 1965. In fact, Oswald's notes as printed in *Le Gaulois* are anomalous, in that the first one calls the play *L'Aventurier* and the second *L'Aventurière*. The latter designation is more likely to be the correct one, since the term applies more accurately to Morgane than to Sergius.
11. The letter is not in *C.G.*, but it was published in the edition of *Le Prétendant*.
12. The letter is not in *C.G.*; it is one of those published by F. Boux de Casson, op. cit.
13. This is another letter not in *C.G.*, but published by F. Boux de Casson.
14. So E. de Goncourt claimed, vol. IV, p. 838.
15. The story was related by Suzanne Meyer-Zundel, a friend of Judith, to Léon Guichard, who recorded it in *Lettres à Judith Gautier par Richard et Cosima Wagner*, p. 369.
16. See S. Mallarmé, *Correspondance*, vol. IV, p. 386.
17. Baude de Maurceley, 3 avril 1929.
18. Mallarmé, *Correspondance*, vol. II, p. 47.
19. Quoted by Edmond de Goncourt, vol. IV, p. 838.
20. This letter is not in *C.G.*; it was published by F. Boux de Casson.
21. Quoted by Edmond de Goncourt, vol. IV, p. 838.
22. Henry Roujon, *La Galerie*, p. 171.

17 (pp. 157–166)

1. *C.G.*, vol. I, p. 191.

2. For all these details, see the previously quoted article by F. Boux de Casson.
3. *C.G.*, vol. I, pp. 196–7.
4. See the 1965 edition of *Le Prétendant*.
5. Villiers's letter to Roujon has not survived, but its tenor is clear from Roujon's reply (*C.G.*, vol. I, pp. 200–1).
6. The letter is published in part in Louis Forestier, p. 137.
7. Franc-Lamy, quoted by F. Clerget, p. 93.
8. The article the journalist wrote is reproduced in Charles Cros, *Œuvres complètes*, pp. 334–8.
9. The affair, long and immensely complicated, is of course recounted more or less accurately in all the books about Villiers. But two very detailed articles by Émile Drougard sum up all that is known about it: 'Villiers de l'Isle-Adam défenseur de son nom', and 'Pour le nom: Villiers de l'Isle-Adam et ses homonymes'.
10. Curiously, everyone seems to have taken for granted the accuracy of Villiers's own view of the play and its portrayal of his ancestor. But a study of the text shows how far he has exaggerated in claiming that it is particularly hard on the Marshal.
11. *C.G.*, vol. I, pp. 202–3.
12. Quoted by E. Drougard, 'Pour le nom'.
13. F. Calmettes, p. 197.
14. Henry Roujon, *La Galerie*, p. 120.
15. *C.G.*, vol. I, p. 204.
16. Sarcey himself told the story when reviewing *Le Nouveau-Monde* in *Le Temps*, 26 février 1883.
17. *C.G.*, vol. I, pp. 206–7.
18. Sarcey hints at it, and critics like Daireaux have presented it as a certainty. Pontavice de Heussey produces a highly suspect anecdote about Villiers going off to protest angrily to Hugo about the fact that his play had never been produced and being reprimanded by an acolyte of the poet: 'Honesty is not a matter of age, sir!' to which Villiers allegedly replied: 'Nor is stupidity!' and stalked out. Apart from the inherent improbability of Villiers making such a scene in front of his demigod, the same story is retailed by Calmettes about Jean Marras in a different connection (p. 144).
19. Here, for instance, is an anonymous letter published by *Le Gaulois* on 4 October 1876:

Theatrical matters interest me greatly, so I take the liberty of asking you a question. It is about M. Michaëlis. What has become of the works awarded prizes in the famous 1875 competition, which set so many dramatists by the ears and which overnight transformed the inventor of this colossal but costfree publicity stunt into a little Maecenas of French literature? Please be good enough to let me know 1, what motto decorated the 1,000 franc gold medal; 2, what subject was depicted in the Barbedienne bronze; 3, in what American cities, during the Philadelphia Exhibition, the prizewinning plays were put on by those good old Yankees so dear to M. Michaëlis's heart. In our opinion, it is wrong of M. Michaëlis to seek to avoid the gratitude which is due to him for faithfully carrying out the programme he set himself, and the public will thank you, sir, for bringing him out of this modest attitude.

> Given Villiers's friendship with François Oswald, *Le Gaulois*'s theatrical correspondent, it is not impossible that he is himself behind this missive.

20. The contract is in *C.G.*, vol. I, pp. 207–10.
21. According to the 'Gossip' by his friend Mallarmé which appeared in the London *Athenaeum* on 6 February 1876: see *Les 'Gossips' de Mallarmé*, edited by H. Mondor and L. J. Austin, Paris, Gallimard, 1962, p. 67.
22. This letter has never been reproduced.
23. Several unpublished letters to Villiers from the Committee are in the Fonds Bollery.
24. *C.G.*, vol. I, p. 218. On all this episode, see A. W. Raitt, 'Les Déboires d'un auteur dramatique: Villiers de l'Isle-Adam à l'Ambigu', *Cahiers d'Histoire et de Folklore*, octobre-décembre 1955.
25. *C.G.*, vol. I, pp. 219–20.
26. Ibid., p. 220.

18 (pp. 167–177)

1. *C.G.*, vol. I, pp. 213–14.
2. Ibid, p. 205. See also the letter on pp. 220–21.
3. These latter two publications have only been discovered recently and are not mentioned in any of the Villiers bibliographies.
4. The story is recounted by a former assistant of Lacroix quoted by F. Clerget, pp. 96–8. The articles were collected under the title *Trois Portraits de femmes*, Paris, Bernard, 1929.
5. That these fantastic projects were public knowledge is shown by this note published in several newspapers—*Le Pays*, *L'Opinion*, and *Le Gaulois*—early in October 1876 (it has never been reproduced):

M. Villiers de l'Isle-Adam, the prize-winner of the Michaëlis competition, Parnassian though he may be, is going to settle down, like so many others: there is a rumour that he is going to get married very shortly. His bride is a poor American girl afflicted with a dowry of several millions. It is through the good offices of Victor Hugo that she offered her hand to the poet Villiers, the happiest of mortals, in anticipation of his becoming immortal.

6. *C.G.*, vol. I, pp. 178–9.
7. Ibid., p. 215.
8. On all this, see the introduction to the 1965 edition of *Le Prétendant*.
9. Pontavice de Heussey, pp. 94–5.
10. *C.G.*, vol. I, p. 222.
11. Analysed by P.-G. Castex, 'Villiers de l'Isle-Adam historien de sa maison', *Revue du Nord* (avril-juin 1954).
12. Reproduced in É. Drougard, 'Villiers de l'Isle-Adam défenseur de son nom'.
13. Henry Roujon, p. 121.

14. The only full and reliable account of the case is to be found in É. Drougard, 'Villiers de l'Isle-Adam défenseur de son nom'.
15. Mentioned in É. Drougard's article.
16. F. Calmettes, p. 197.
17. Reproduced as an appendix to É. Drougard's article.
18. *C.G.*, vol. I, pp. 231–3. The text of the letter was first quoted by Pontavice de Heussey, pp. 116–19, but Émile Drougard was unable to find it in any of the newspapers of the time. Several drafts of it are reproduced in his article.
19. On the whole business of Villiers's contacts with Georges de Villiers de l'Isle-Adam, see Émile Drougard's article 'Pour le nom'. Once again, this constitutes the only full and accurate account of what happened.
20. This letter is not in *C.G.*; it is reproduced in É. Drougard's 'Pour le nom'.
21. *C.G.*, vol. I, pp. 224–5.
22. Ibid., pp. 228–9.
23. See Drougard, 'Pour le nom' and *C.G.*, vol. I, pp. 227–8.
24. See, for instance, Fernand Baldensperger, 'Un Villiers de l'Isle-Adam vagabond et agitateur', *Mercure de France*, 1er juillet 1934.
25. For instance by H. Bernès, 'Villiers de l'Isle-Adam sous la Commune', *Mercure de France*, 1er novembre 1910.
26. See, for instance, É. de Rougemont, p. 190, n. 1.

19 (pp. 177–185)

1. Pontavice de Heussey, pp. 123–4.
2. See the long letter to a friend in *C.G.*, vol. I, pp. 233–6.
3. According to Pontavice, it was at Le Pin-Galant that 'one of the most marvellous scenes of the work (2nd Part, *Le Monde tragique*, scene VIII)' was written (pp. 158–9). But the scene in question is just a brief transitional episode. Either Pontavice was careless over identifying it or the numbering was changed later.
4. In *Paris à l'eau-forte*, the review edited by Lesclide, the publisher noted on 20 August 1876: 'Villiers de l'Isle-Adam left me, promising to let me have *Axël*, for which I am still waiting.'
5. Pontavice de Heussey, p. 140.
6. Ibid., pp. 141–9.
7. *C.G.*, vol. I, p. 233.
8. Ibid.
9. This manuscript belongs to P.-G. Castex and is described, with extracts, in his article 'Villiers de l'Isle-Adam historien de sa maison'.
10. Also in the Castex Collection.
11. *C.G.*, vol. I, pp. 237–8.
12. R. du Pontavice de Heussey, p. 149. Pontavice says Villiers intended to offer it to Chabrillat of the Ambigu, but that only came later. That it was presented to Duquesnel is shown by a later letter of Villiers (*C.G.*, vol. I, p. 276). There is no record at the Odéon of its having been rejected there; presumably Villiers withdrew it himself.
13. Georges Duval, *Mémoires d'un Parisien*, Paris, Flammarion, n.d. [1913], pp. 222–3.

14. *C.G.*, vol. I, p. 247.
15. The press notices in 1876 make it clear that the play was then in four acts. A sketch for an interpolated second act, by someone other than Villiers, used to form part of the Leclercq Collection.
16. This manuscript is preserved in the Fonds Bollery.
17. These letters are in *C.G.*, vol. I, pp. 239–46. They were originally published, and the story told, by P.-V. Stock in *Mémorandum d'un éditeur*, 2e série (Paris, Stock, 1936).
18. For instance in the letters to Mme Tresse.
19. Gustave Le Rouge, 'Verlainiens et décadents', *Les Nouvelles littéraires* (11 août–15 décembre 1928).
20. Mallarmé, *Œuvres complètes*, p. 482.
21. Baude de Maurceley, 3 avril 1929.
22. Ibid., 4 avril 1929.
23. E. de Goncourt, vol. III, p. 548.

20 (pp. 185–195)

1. These details about the origins of 'Ave Mater victa' were discovered by J.-M. Bellefroid.
2. This remark, attributed to a certain V***, is quoted by Jules de Clerville (alias Godefroy van der Dussen d'Herpent) in *Le Spectateur*, 30 December 1875.
3. The full text of the poem has never been found; only the first three stanzas are known from a manuscript (*C.G.*, vol. I, pp. 248–50).
4. *C.G.*, vol. I, pp. 252–3. But J. Bollery's suggestion that the letter was addressed to Villiers's father is most unconvincing: in view of the mention of the Church, it is more likely to have been meant for his uncle the Abbé.
5. Ibid., p. 253. The text is in fact ambiguous, since it is unclear whether the Marquis is referring to 'commerce' in general or to a newspaper called *Le Commerce*, to which there are allusions elsewhere (ibid., p. 250).
6. Ibid., pp. 251–2.
7. See P.-G. Castex, 'Villiers de l'Isle-Adam historien de sa maison'.
8. This was one of the three portraits of women he wrote for Albert Lacroix. Lacroix had originally only commissioned two, but Villiers added the study of Isabeau on his own initiative.
9. The evidence about this is the presence of the title on a list of tales he had published up to about 1878 (see P.-G. Castex's edition of *Contes cruels*, Paris, Garnier, 1968, p. xiv). It cannot have been written much before the spring of 1878, since it was only then that Edison suddenly became famous in France as a result of his invention of the phonograph. On the origins of *L'Ève future*, see not only the edition of the novel by J. Bollery and P.-G. Castex but also the relevant chapters of Jacques Noiray's 1979 Sorbonne thesis on 'Le Thème de la machine dans le roman français de la seconde moitié du dix-neuvième siècle'.
10. Gustave Guiches, 'Villiers de l'Isle-Adam intime'. It is worthwhile noting that Pontavice's long story about *L'Ève future* originating in the

suicide of an English lord (p. 166) is totally implausible: it bears all the marks of having been constructed to fit the circumstances of the novel.

11. Remy de Gourmont, *Promenades littéraires*, 2ᵉ série, p. 30.
12. C.G., vol. I, pp. 261–3.
13. G. Duval, p. 223.
14. These pages have been published in *Nouvelles Reliques*.
15. C.G., vol. I, p. 256.
16. This obscure story has been studied by Joseph Bollery, 'Un problème bibliographique résolu par la mort d'un académicien', *Livrets du mandarin*, 4ᵉ série, janvier 1942.
17. Pontavice du Heussey, pp. 188–91. But Pontavice is wrong to assert that Villiers always wrote with a pencil: on the contrary, nearly all his manuscripts are in ink, and he seems only to have used a pencil when there was no pen to hand.
18. Ibid., p. 197.
19. Ibid., pp. 190–1.
20. Ibid., pp. 189–90. In fact, Pontavice later pretends (p. 264) that this person was someone other than Marie Dantine. But this is evidently no more than a matter of discretion.
21. A recent article by Tony Bourg ('Marie Dantine—Luxembourgeoise par erreur', *d'Letzeburger Land* [4 Mai 1979]) has established a number of interesting facts about Marie. Technically, she was not a citizen of Luxembourg, as is usually supposed, but of Belgium, since she was born near Vielsalm, just north of the border, in a region which had been ceded to Belgium in 1839. Her date of birth was 15 August 1845, and her father was a village cobbler. In January 1869 she went into domestic service in Verviers, and presumably went from there to Paris, where, at the Mairie of the VIIᵉ Arrondissement on 26 September 1874, she married Joseph Brégeras, a coachman from Florenville in Belgium.
22. Pontavice de Heussey, pp. 167–8.
23. The question of Villiers's status in *La Croix et l'épée* has been very carefully studied by Alain Néry in 'Les Idées politiques et sociales de Villiers de l'Isle-Adam'.
24. C.G., vol. I, p. 250.
25. Ibid., pp. 270–1.
26. Ibid., pp. 269–70.
27. Léon Deffoux, p. 26.
28. Henri de Régnier, *De mon temps*, Paris, Mercure de France, 1933, p. 52.
29. Ibid., p. 51.
30. Léon Deffoux, p. 27. The story is also told by J. E. S. Jeanès, *D'après nature*, Besançon, Granvelle, 1946, pp. 176–7.

21 (pp. 195–203)

1. C.G., vol. I, pp. 276–8.
2. Ibid., pp. 275–6.
3. Unpublished letter from Edmund Gerson to Villiers, dated 16 February 1880, in the Fonds Bollery.
4. C.G., vol. I, pp. 236–7, where the letter is wrongly assigned to 1877.

Internal evidence makes it clear that it must have been written in the spring of 1880.

5. Ibid., p. 280.
6. P.-V. Stock, p. 185.
7. It has often been alleged that these three plays are all parts of a trilogy. But Émile Drougard has adduced decisive arguments against such a supposition ('L'*Axël* de Villiers de l'Isle-Adam').
8. *C.G.*, vol. I, pp. 284–5.
9. Édouard Rod, 'Mes Débuts dans les lettres', *La Semaine littéraire* (Geneva), 17 septembre 1910.
10. F. Calmettes, p. 201.
11. *C.G.*, vol. I, p. 189.
12. Ibid.
13. Ibid., p. 195.
14. Ibid., p. 221.
15. Ibid., p. 239. Fuller quotations from this letter have since appeared in the Catalogue Charavay no. 735 (décembre 1969).
16. Ibid., p. 261.
17. Ibid., p. 262.
18. See S. Mallarmé, *Œuvres complètes*, p. 502.
19. Henry Roujon, writing as Henry Laujol, 'Villiers de l'Isle-Adam', *La Jeune France*, 1er avril 1883. Admittedly, Roujon casts doubt on the story.
20. Several pages of this story were published by Émile Drougard under the title *L'Ombre de Meyerbeer* in *L'Arche* (juillet 1946). A number of others, under the alternative title *La Séance du docteur Muller*, figure in the Castex-Bollery edition of *Contes cruels*.
21. *C.G.*, vol. II, pp. 8 and 9. The story of the 'cured madman' is related by Edmond de Goncourt (among others) in his diary entry for 4 February 1882 (vol. III, p. 147).
22. The story is told both by Le Noir de Tournemine, following a Comte Harscouet (p. 49), and by Fernand Calmettes (p. 195). There is probably some connection between that and an unpublished letter belonging to J.-M. Bellefroid dated 27 August 1878, from the Vice-Rector of the Académie de Paris inviting Villiers to call on him.
23. *C.G.*, vol. I, p. 253.
24. Louis Forestier, p. 228, n. 11.
25. Gustave Kahn, *Silhouettes littéraires*, Paris, Montaigne, 1925, p. 14. A year or two later, Mallarmé lent the album to Verlaine with stern words of caution: 'It goes without saying that it's extremely precious to me! Those are things one can't get hold of any more.' (*Correspondance*, Vol. II, p. 304.)
26. Pontavice de Heussey, pp. 252–3.
27. The anecdote is retailed by one of Villiers's friends.
28. The circumstances of Villiers's candidature have been most fully investigated by Alain Néry in his thesis.
29. Fragment of *Augusta Holmès* in *Chez les passants* (Crès edition), p. 278.

30. Pontavice de Heussey, p. 255.
31. In the fragment of *Augusta Holmès*, quoted above.
32. Pontavice de Heussey, p. 255.

22 (pp. 203–215)

1. *C.G.*, vol. I, p. 283.
2. F. Calmettes, pp. 200–1.
3. *C.G.*, vol. I, p. 286.
4. Ibid., p. 288.
5. Joseph Bollery, 'Documents biographiques inédits sur Villiers de l'Isle-Adam'.
6. Léon Deffoux, p. 14.
7. J.-M. Bellefroid, 'Une chronique de Villiers de l'Isle-Adam sur Victor Noir', *Revue des Sciences humaines* (juillet-septembre 1965).
8. This announcement was overlooked by J. Bollery and P.-G. Castex in their edition of *L'Ève future*, where it is wrongly stated (p. 336) that there was no further mention of the novel after the instalment of 4 February.
9. The statement by J. Bollery and P.-G. Castex (p. 336) that there were still three chapters to come is erroneous: the order of the chapters in 1881 is not the same as in 1886, and the announcement of 5 February makes it clear that the editor expected only one more instalment, hence probably only one more chapter.
10. *L'Andréïde paradoxale d'Edison* seems to have had no conclusion, and the interruption of serialization in 1886 just before the the end suggests that even then Villiers's mind was not made up. A manuscript fragment dating from some time between 1881 and 1885 shows part of a rather different conclusion from the one eventually published (in the Bollery–Castex edition, pp. 388–9).
11. *C.G.*, vol. I, pp. 285–6.
12. Ibid., p. 287.
13. This unpublished document is in the Taylorian Library, Oxford.
14. Only a few phrases of this letter are to be found in *C.G.*, vol. II, p. 9. Joseph Bollery subsequently obtained a copy of the complete text. In *C.G.* the name of the addressee is wrongly given as Bretonneau de Moydin, his signature on the letters he sent to Villiers being difficult to decipher. Alain Néry's researches have established that the name is in fact Moydier.
15. *C.G.*, vol. II, p. 11.
16. Ibid., p. 12.
17. Ibid., p. 10. The addressee's name is wrongly spelled there as Luppé. Again, the circumstances surrounding this letter have been established by Alain Néry.
18. In the introduction (under the pseudonym Henry Laujol) to Villiers's contribution to *Le Nouveau Décaméron*, an anthology of tales published in 1884.

23 (pp. 215–225)

1. Edmond de Goncourt, vol. III, p. 1052.

2. At any rate, he appears to have used her address to pick up his mail in 1883—see *C.G.*, vol. II, p. 46 and the letter to Mallarmé in *Baudelaire to Beckett*, Humanities Research Centre, Austin, Texas, 1972.

3. Quoted by F.-A. Cazals, *Paul Verlaine, ses portraits*, Paris, Bibliothèque de l'Association, 1896.

4. J. E. S. Jeanès, pp. 178–9.

5. *O.C.*, Vol. VII, p. 25.

6. Henri Lavedan, 'Courrier de Paris', *L'Illustration*, 17 avril 1909.

7. Léon Deffoux, pp. 19–21.

8. In the letter quoted on p. 55.

9. *C.G.*, vol. I, p. 219 (the letter is not at its right place there).

10. See the letter from Glatigny to Mallarmé quoted in Mallarmé, *Correspondance*, vol. I, p. 100. Villiers evidently did not distinguish himself: 'My first pair of seconds, Catulle and Villiers, made a complete mess of things, and, if I hadn't been lucky enough to meet Launay and Derey straightaway, there would have been nothing left for me but to blow my brains out.'

11. *C.G.*, vol. I, p. 149. See also above, p. 127.

12. Ibid., pp. 266–7.

13. J.-M. Bellefroid, 'Une chronique de Villiers de l'Isle-Adam sur Victor Noir'.

14. A. W. Raitt, *Villiers de l'Isle-Adam et le mouvement symboliste*, pp. 351–2, and *C. G.*, vol. II, p. 187.

15. Unsigned article in *Le Journal*, 27 février 1894.

16. A number of titles of such pieces are known from various sources: *Requête de quelques lions*, *Complainte du Minotaure*, *A Geneviève Mallarmé*, *Réflexions diplomatiques*, and *L'Humble Modèle*. These texts remain unknown. In other cases, tales have been collected without any known previous publication, but one can be sure that they had in fact appeared in some paper or other.

17. Unpublished report in the archives of the Comédie Française discovered by Mme Sylvie Chevalley. In 1883 Villiers had evidently still some idea of publishing *Le Prétendant*. In the article about him published in *La Jeune France* on 1 April of that year, Henry Roujon writes of *Elën* and *Morgane*: 'We dare not analyse them here, since they are soon to be republished, after having been completely recast (. . .) we shall see the main theme of *Isis* develop in the fierce soul of that Morgane who remains up to the present the poet's favourite daughter.'

18. *C.G.*, vol. II, p. 28, where Villiers says he remembers only her kindness and not her suspicions.

19. *C.G.*, vol. vol. I, p. 188 and vol. II, p. 15.

20. *C.G.*, vol. II, pp. 17–19.

21. Ibid., pp. 19–21.

22. Ibid., pp. 13–14.

23. Ibid., p. 19.

24. Ibid., p. 16.

25. Anatole France, *La Vie littéraire*, vol. III, Paris, Calmann Lévy, 1891, p. 126.

24 (pp. 225–236)

1. R. de Gourmont, *Promenades littéraires*, 4e série (Paris, Mercure de France, 1920), p. 73.
2. *C.G.*, vol. II, p. 22.
3. See P.-G. Castex's edition of *Contes cruels*, p. xvi.
4. J. E. S. Jeanès, pp. 167–9.
5. *C.G.*, vol. II, pp. 22–3.
6. In the Fonds Bollery there are two such unpublished letters, one, undated, from the actress C. Meyer, and the other, dated 20 December 1882, from J. Renot, making a determined plea to be given the part of Stephen Ashwell.
7. Unpublished manuscript belonging to P.-G. Castex.
8. Ibid.
9. *C.G.*, vol. II, p. 24.
10. Auriant, pp. 89–90.
11. É. de Rougemont, p. 243.
12. *C.G.*, vol. I, p. 275.
13. Unpublished manuscript belonging to P.-G. Castex.
14. Ibid.
15. Unpublished letter in the Fonds Bollery.
16. *C.G.*, vol. II, p. 32.

25 (pp. 237–246)

1. Unpublished manuscript belonging to P.-G. Castex.
2. *C.G.*, vol. II, p. 24.
3. Arnold Mortier, *Les Soirées parisiennes de 1883*, Paris, Dentu, 1884, p. 69.
4. The article is actually signed Daniel Grégoire, but this is almost certainly a pseudonym of Taine, who produced most of the paper himself.
5. Pontavice de Heussey, p. 268.
6. And not five, as Joseph Bollery writes in *C.G.*, vol. I, p. 18.
7. Unpublished document in the Fonds Bollery.
8. *C.G.*, vol. II, p. 39.
9. Ibid., p. 40.
10. Unpublished manuscript in the Fonds Bollery.
11. Max Daireaux, p. 174.

26 (pp. 249–259)

1. *C.G.*, vol. II, p. 41.
2. Henri Mondor, *Vie de Mallarmé*, p. 441.
3. In his article on Villiers which appeared in the *Woman's World*, October 1889.
4. R. de Gourmont, *Promenades littéraires*, 4e série, p. 77.
5. In the previously quoted article in *L'Étoile de France*, 4 mars 1883.
6. On this subject, see Robert Laulan, 'La Hantise de l'échafaud chez Villiers de l'Isle-Adam', *La Presse médicale*, 25 et 26 décembre 1959.

7. Henry Roujon, *La Galerie*, p. 134.
8. Ibid., p. 125.
9. *C.G.*, vol. II, p. 40.
10. *C.G.*, vol. I, pp. 272–3. Joseph Bollery has tentatively assigned this undated letter to 1880, but that seems too early, since Villiers was demonstrably still in close touch with her in 1883.
11. F. Calmettes, pp. 189–90.
12. Ibid., p. 201.
13. *C.G.*, vol. II, p. 25.
14. Ibid., p. 45.
15. Ibid., p. 44.
16. *O.C.*, vol. XI, p. 219.
17. Unpublished manuscript in the Fonds Bollery.
18. *C.G.*, vol. II, p. 202. Joseph Bollery thought the letter was written in 1887: 1883 is however much more likely. In addition, there is a misreading. Magnard did not sign 'very cordially', as is transcribed here—the original, which is in the possession of the present writer, clearly reads 'very radically'.
19. Ibid., pp. 53–4.

27 (pp. 259–269)

1. *C.G.*, vol. II, p. 48.
2. Ibid., pp. 50–1.
3. This letter is not in *C.G.*; it was published by J.-M. Bellefroid, 'Deux lettres inédites de Villiers de l'Isle-Adam à Mallarmé et à Méry Laurent', *Revue d'Histoire littéraire de la France*, avril–juin 1965.
4. Some of the text of the lecture can be found in J.-H. Bornecque, pp. 122–3: the remainder of it, still unpublished, was formerly in the Leclercq Collection.
5. *C.G.*, vol. II, pp. 63–4.
6. Ibid., pp. 42–4.
7. This important unpublished manuscript is in the Taylorian Library, Oxford.
8. C. Mendès, *La Légende du Parnasse contemporain*, p. 123.
9. Léon Barracand, op. cit.
10. J.-K. Huysmans, *À rebours*, Paris, Charpentier, 1947, pp. 255–8. On the relations between Villiers and Huysmans, see Robert Baldick, *The Life of J.-K. Huysmans*, Oxford, Oxford University Press, 1955.
11. V.-É. Michelet, *Figures d'évocateurs*, Paris, Figuière, 1913, pp. 184–5.
12. Ibid., pp. 186–7.
13. See A. W. Raitt, *Villiers de l'Isle-Adam et le mouvement symboliste*, p. 351.
14. These two unpublished letters are in the Castex Collection. It is worth recording that, if Pontavice is to be believed (pp. 70–1), Villiers had particular reasons for remembering the trial of Couty de La Pommerais in 1864, since one of the documents produced by the defence was a certificate signed by the Marquis, attesting that Couty had a right to the title of count.

15. See Margaret Groves, 'Villiers de l'Isle-Adam and Sir William Crookes', *French Studies*, April 1975.
16. *O.C.*, vol. V, pp. 174–6.
17. *C.G.*, vol. II, pp. 67–8.
18. Ibid., p. 65.
19. Unpublished letter belonging to the present writer.

28 (pp. 269–278)

1. *C.G.*, vol. I, p. 206.
2. F. Boux de Casson, op. cit.
3. *C.G.*, vol. I, p. 270.
4. *C.G.*, vol. II, p. 50.
5. E. de Goncourt, vol. IV, pp. 278 and 724.
6. Hugues Le Roux, *Portraits de cire*, Paris, Lecène, 1891, p. 24.
7. Ibid., p. 27.
8. Quoted by J. Raison du Cleuziou, 'L'Agence'.
9. Charles Buet, 'Les Morts royales', *Le Magasin littéraire de Gand*, 15 octobre 1894.
10. Unpublished manuscript in the Fonds Bollery.
11. See, for instance, R. du Pontavice de Heussey, pp. 246–7.
12. Jean Raulet, 'Villiers de l'Isle-Adam', *Le Voltaire*, 22 août 1889, quoted in Alain Néry's thesis, where there is a full discussion of Villiers's relations with the Naundorffist party.
13. Henry Roujon, *La Galerie*, p. 110.
14. Unpublished manuscript in the Fonds Bollery.
15. This was published after Villiers's death by Rodolphe Darzens in the *Revue de l'évolution* (1er mai 1892), with the claim that it had never previously been printed. But the presence of the title on various manuscripts where Villiers lists his published works proves that this claim is false, though the original publication has never been located.
16. *C.G.*, vol. II, p. 81.
17. See Joseph Bollery, *Léon Bloy*, Paris, Albin Michel, 1947–54.
18. Quoted by Joseph Bollery, *Léon Bloy*, vol. II, p. 73.
19. *C.G.*, vol. II, p. 83.
20. Ibid., pp. 81–2.
21. Ibid., p. 58.
22. This publication has only recently been discovered: it had hitherto been supposed that the story was unpublished until it appeared in the volume to which it gave its title (*L'Amour suprême* in 1886).
23. A voluminous series of unpublished manuscripts of the story is in the Taylorian Library, Oxford. The original drafts were almost completely different from the final version.
24. *C.G.*, vol. II, p. 75.
25. Ibid., p. 76.
26. Ibid, p. 83.
27. *C.G.*, Vol. I, p. 147.

29 (pp. 278–289)

1. *C.G.*, vol. II, p. 62.

2. Ibid., p. 78. See p. 255.
3. Ibid., p. 69.
4. Ibid., p. 72.
5. Ibid., p. 84.
6. Ibid.
7. Quoted by J.-H. Bornecque, p. 113.
8. *C.G.*, vol. II, p. 62.
9. Ibid., p. 81.
10. Adrien Remacle's unpublished 'Cahiers de ma vie', quoted by F. Clerget, pp. 130–1.
11. *C.G.*, vol. II, p. 98.
12. Ibid., p. 99.
13. Unpublished letter in the Sickles Collection.
14. *C.G.*, vol. II, pp. 100–1.
15. Letter published in *L'Intransigeant*, 8 janvier 1928.
16. Mallarmé, *Correspondance*, vol. II, p. 298.
17. Unpublished document by Darzens, formerly in the Leclercq Collection.
18. V.-É. Michelet, *Figures*, pp. 231–2.
19. *C.G.*, vol. II, p. 97.
20. Ibid., pp. 85 and 113–15.
21. There exists in the Fonds Bollery an unpublished list of titles drawn up by Villiers in 1884, under the title *Contes cruels*, and containing all the tales included in the 1883 volume, as well as those which had appeared in the press in the meantime.
22. As appears from an extract from a letter not in *C.G.*, quoted in the Catalogue D. Janvier, août 1938.
23. *C.G.*, vol. II, p. 95.
24. Henry Roujon, 'Lorsque Villiers de l'Isle-Adam nous jouait du Wagner . . .'.
25. *C.G.*, vol. II, pp. 84–5.
26. Quoted in F. Clerget, pp. 131–2.
27. *C.G.*, vol. II, p. 93.
28. On 8 August 1885.
29. In *La Revue*, 15 avril 1907.
30. Paul Valéry, *Œuvres*, Paris, Bibliothèque de la Pléiade, 1957, vol. I, p. 615.
31. Quoted in *Le Goéland*, 1er août 1938. The poetry journal of the late Théophile Briant is full of information about Villiers.
32. Unpublished letter to René Martineau in the Fonds Bollery.
33. Mallarmé, *Correspondance*, Vol. II, p. 293.
34. M. Maeterlinck, *Bulles bleues*, Monaco, Éditions du Rocher, 1947, pp. 198–99.
35. Jean Ajalbert, *Mémoires en vrac*, Paris, Albin Michel, 1938, pp. 191–2.
36. Quoted by Henri Perrin, 'Entre Parnasse et Symbolisme: Ephraïm Mikhaël', *Revue d'Histoire littéraire de la France*, janvier-mars 1956.
37. V.-É. Michelet, *Figures*, pp. 188 ff.
38. Jacques Petit, *Barbey d'Aurevilly critique*, Paris, Les Belles Lettres,

1963, p. 604. Villiers's letter of thanks, published in this work, is not in
C.G.

39. V.-É. Michelet, *Figures*, p. 206.
40. Mallarmé, *Correspondance*, vol. II, p. 297.
41. As is clear from the letter quoted above in note 23.
42. C.G., vol. II, pp. 53–4.
43. O.C., vol. V, p. 131.

30 (pp. 289–296)

1. This article, which appeared on 10 January 1886, has never been
   reproduced. Though it is unsigned, the attribution to Villiers is proved
   by the letter to him from the editor of the magazine in C.G., vol. II,
   pp. 108–9.
2. C.G., vol. II, p. 101.
3. See the letter from Lèbre in C.G., vol. II, pp. 113–15.
4. Unpublished letter belonging to the present writer.
5. C.G., vol. II, p. 121.
6. Ibid., pp. 123–4. It is not known whether the letter was actually
   published in any newspaper.
7. On the history of the publication of *Axël*, see Émile Drougard,
   'Documents relatifs à l'impression d'*Axël* en volume', *Bulletin du
   Bibliophile*, nos. 2 and 3 (1955).
8. See the letter in C.G., vol. II, p. 92. J. Bollery tentatively placed the
   letter in 1885: the reference to 'the *Liberté* of the 8th' alludes to the
   publication of *Lysiane d'Aubelleyne* (*L'Amour suprême*) in that paper
   on 8 August 1884, so that the letter must date from the second half of
   that month. One might be tempted to suppose that there was only a
   single copy, dating from 1884, but that cannot be so: textual evidence
   proves that there was a copy in existence by 1882. Evidently Villiers
   wanted Arnaud to copy out those pages containing new material or so
   drastically altered that they were illegible. Most of the manuscript
   drafts of *Axël* known to have survived were in the Leclercq Collection;
   others belong to P.-G. Castex.
9. See Émile Drougard, 'Fragments manuscrits d'*Axël*'. The proof that
   the change was made at the very last minute derives from the fact that
   the altered copy of the original ending has affixed to it, by way of
   signature, a piece of paper bearing Villiers's name in print and torn
   from the April number of *La Jeune France*.
10. O.C., vol. IV, p. 271.
11. Ibid., pp. 261 and 270.
12. Henry Roujon, *La Galerie*, p. 127.
13. Ibid.
14. Ibid., p. 128.

31 (pp. 296–307)

1. Quoted by F. Clerget, pp. 149–50.
2. C.G., vol. II, pp. 99–100.
3. Unpublished document in the Taylorian Library, Oxford.

4. V.-É. Michelet, *Figures*, pp. 191–2.
5. M. Maeterlinck, p. 199.
6. Quoted in Jules Huret, *Enquête sur l'évolution littéraire*, Paris, Charpentier, 1893, p. 128.
7. 'Villiers de l'Isle-Adam', *Comoedia*, 27 janvier 1927.
8. Letter published in *Le Goéland*, août 1938.
9. Quoted in A. Mabille de Poncheville, *Vie de Verhaeren*, Paris, Mercure de France, 1953, p. 153.
10. See *C.G.*, vol. II, pp. 230–1.
11. Emile Verhaeren, *Impressions*, Paris, Marpon et Flammarion, 1928, vol. III, p. 33.
12. Georges Rodenbach, *Évocations*, Brussels, La Renaissance du Livre, 1924, pp. 165–6.
13. *C.G.*, vol. II, pp. 147–9.
14. See the letter to Mallarmé mentioned in chapter 23, note 2.
15. J.-M. Bellefroid, 'Deux lettres inédites de Villiers de l'Isle-Adam à Mallarmé et à Méry Laurent'.
16. Henri de Régnier, *Nos Rencontres*, Paris, Mercure de France, 1932, p. 56.
17. André Fontainas, *Mes Souvenirs du Symbolisme*, Paris, Nouvelle Revue critique, 1928, p. 88.
18. René Ghil, *Les Dates et les œuvres*, Paris, Crès, 1925, p. 107.
19. Ibid., p. 106.
20. Ibid., p. 5. In A. W. Raitt, *Villiers de l'Isle-Adam et le mouvement symboliste*, p. 359, it is wrongly stated that this is the only reference to Villiers in the book.
21. Max Daireaux, p. 27.
22. F. Clerget, quoting Michelet, p. 116.
23. Remy de Gourmont, *Promenades littéraires*, 2e Série, p. 13.
24. J. E. S. Jeanès, p. 208.
25. Jacques Maritain, 'Le Témoignage d'un ami de Léon Bloy', *Revue des Jeunes*, 10 janvier 1925.
26. *C.G.*, vol. II, p. 87.
27. Ibid., pp. 145–46.
28. Ibid., p. 199.
29. Joseph Bollery, *Léon Bloy*, vol. II, pp. 170–1.
30. *C.G.*, vol. II, p. 102.
31. Ibid., pp. 133–4. On this episode, see Émile Drougard, 'Une réplique française de *La Légende du Grand Inquisiteur*', *Revue des Études slaves*, 2, 1934.
32. *C.G.*, vol. II, pp. 128–30.
33. Émile Drougard, 'Documents relatifs à l'impression d'*Axël*'.
34. *C.G.*, vol. II, pp. 134–5.
35. J.-K. Huysmans, *Lettres inédites à Arij Prins 1885–1907*, edited by Louis Gillet, Geneva, Droz, 1977, pp. 65 and 74.
36. Léon Bloy, *Lettres aux Montchal*, Paris, Bernard, 1947–8, p. 242.
37. Ibid., p. 272.
38. As is shown by the letter of which only a part is in *C.G.* (vol. II,

p. 140); the full text was published later by Joseph Bollery, 'Une lettre inédite de Villiers de l'Isle-Adam à Huysmans', *Bulletin de la Société J.-K. Huysmans*, 50, 1966.

39. *C.G.*, vol. II, pp. 141 and 152.
40. The story is told by Dujardin himself in F. Lefèvre, 'Une heure avec Édouard Dujardin', *Les Nouvelles littéraires*, 4 juin 1932. It is confirmed by Marcel Longuet, 'Villiers de l'Isle-Adam', *Comoedia*, 31 mars 1931.
41. *Reliques*, p. 73.
42. *Tribulat Bonhomet*, edited by P.-G. Castex and J.-M. Bellefroid, p. 247.
43. R. du Pontavice de Heussey, p. 240.
44. Ibid.
45. Unpublished manuscript formerly in the possession of Max Daireaux.
46. H. Le Roux, p. 16.
47. *C.G.*, vol. II, pp. 124–5.
48. P.-V. Stock, pp. 181–2.
49. L. Bloy, *Lettres aux Montchal*, pp. 105–6.
50. *C.G.*, vol. II, pp. 110, 125, and 173.
51. J.-K. Huysmans, *Lettres inédites à Arij Prins*, p. 105.
52. The story is recounted by every biographer of Villiers. It exists in various versions among Villiers's own papers.

32 (pp. 307–318)

1. Baude de Maurceley, 8 avril 1929.
2. Quoted by F. Clerget, p. 7.
3. J.-K. Huysmans, *Lettres inédites à Arij Prins*, pp. 50–1.
4. *C.G.*, vol. II, p. 49.
5. Gustave Guiches, *Le Banquet*, Paris, Spes, 1926, pp. 35–6.
6. Quoted by Gustave Vanwelkenhuyzen, *Villiers de l'Isle-Adam vu par les Belges*, Brussels, Palais des Académies, 1959.
7. Gustave Guiches 'Villiers de l'Isle-Adam', *La Nouvelle Revue*.
8. Joseph Bollery, 'Documents biographiques inédits sur Villiers de l'Isle-Adam'.
9. According to Gustave Kahn, 'Trente ans de Symbolisme', an article which appeared in *Les Nouvelles littéraires* at a date impossible to specify (there is a cutting in the Fonds Bollery):

Villiers, having written under the title *Les Perroquets* a satire on the press, had the idea of offering it to *Le Figaro*. No doubt there were no direct or indirect criticisms of Magnard in it, and the sub-editor certainly saw none. But Magnard thought he detected some, and, as he was the absolute master of the situation, that was the end of Villiers's contributions to *Le Figaro*.

10. Quoted by Gustave Vanwelkenhuyzen. Another story about Villiers and Courbouleix is told by Paul Ginisty, *Souvenirs de journalisme et de théâtre*, Paris, Éditions de France, 1930, p. 67:

One day, at a lunch given by the *Gil Blas*, Villiers de l'Isle-Adam, in especially good form, developing the themes of his *Tribulat Bonhomet* (. . .) had literally stupefied this former shirt-maker who had retired from business once he had made his fortune. 'I'm prepared to admit', he had said, 'that that gentleman may be a genius, but, next time, don't put me next to him!'

11. Gustave Guiches, *Le Banquet*, p. 29.
12. V.-É. Michelet, *Figures d'évocateurs*, p. 225.
13. *C.G.*, vol II, pp. 158–9.
14. Ibid., p. 153.
15. Ibid., p. 210.
16. This letter is not in *C.G.* It was published by Roger Lhombreaud, *Arthur Symons*, London, Unicorn Press, 1963, pp. 45–6. Symons subsequently translated a number of works by Villiers into English and wrote an appreciative essay on him in *The Symbolist Movement in Literature*. When he got no reply from Villiers, Symons enlisted Gourmont's help (*C.G.*, vol. II, p. 249).
17. *C.G.*, vol. II, p. 161.
18. Gustave Guiches, *Le Banquet*, p. 53.
19. Jean Ajalbert, pp. 197–8.
20. According to Henri Mondor, *Vie de Mallarmé*, p. 475, who is perhaps basing his affirmation on F. Calmettes, pp. 241–2.
21. Gustave Guiches, 'Villiers de l'Isle-Adam intime'.
22. Henry Roujon, *La Galerie*, p. 131.
23. Remy de Gourmont, *Promenades littéraires*, 2ᵉ série, pp. 9–10.
24. There are numerous echoes of these arguments in Léon Bloy's *roman à clef La Femme pauvre* and in his *Résurrection de Villiers de l'Isle-Adam*.
25. On this revision, see É. Drougard's critical edition of *Les Trois Premiers Contes* and A. W. Raitt, *Villiers de l'Isle-Adam et le mouvement symboliste*, pp. 240–3.
26. P.-V. Stock. pp. 190–1.
27. *C.G.*, vol. I, p. 177. Some of his rough sketches were published by Remy de Gourmont in *Promenades littéraires*, 2ᵉ série, others by J.-H. Bornecque, and in *Nouvelles Reliques*. But they are very fragmentary, and it is impossible to take seriously Pontavice's claim (p. 24) that he had 'held in his hands the thick manuscript, entirely completed' of the play.
28. The remark was made to the poet Saint-Pol-Roux, quoted by René de Berval, 'Hommage à Villiers de l'Isle-Adam', *Mercure de France*, septembre 1938.
29. See for instance the list in *Nouvelles Reliques* and the chapter on 'Les Contes parlés' in André Lebois, *Villiers de l'Isle-Adam révélateur du verbe*, Neuchâtel, Messeiller, 1952.
30. P.-V. Stock, p. 191.
31. A. France, vol. II, pp. 124–5.
32. Mallarmé, *Œuvres complètes*, p. 485.

33 (pp. 318–326)

1. *C.G.*, vol. II, p. 117.
2. Ibid., p. 172.

3. Ibid., p. 241.
4. Quoted by, among others, J. E. S. Jeanès, p. 179.
5. As told by Bloy to René Martineau, quoted in *Le Goéland*, septembre 1937.
6. Joseph Bollery, *Léon Bloy*, vol. II, pp. 244–5.
7. Letter from Huysmans published by R. du Pontavice de Heussey, p. 285.
8. Lucien Descaves, *Souvenirs d'un ours*, Paris, Éditions de Paris, 1946, p. 71.
9. Gustave Guiches, *Le Banquet*, p. 85.
10. J. E. S. Jeanès, p. 179.
11. On the relations between Villiers and the British statesman, see A. W. Raitt, 'The poet and the Prime Minister: Villiers de l'Isle-Adam and the Marquess of Salisbury', *French Studies*, October 1980. There are two letters from Villiers to Lord Salisbury in the archives of Hatfield House; I am most grateful to the archivist, Mr R. H. Harcourt Williams, for his help in finding them. The first, which accompanied a copy of *Le Nouveau-Monde*, is dated 20 August 1881; the second was written on 26 September 1888, the day after the two men met at Dieppe. Their tone is extremely ceremonious, and it is clear that contacts were irregular and formal. There exists, in the possession of J.-M. Bellefroid, a curious document which has, on one side, in Villiers's hand, a series of his one-line poems, and on the other, in someone else's hand, a draft of a letter evidently dictated by Villiers. Though this has been very carefully inked over, it is possible to make out that it is addressed to his benefactress Mme Perry and that he is attempting to borrow money from her so that he can go to London. The first sentence appears to read: 'I have received a letter from Lord Salisbury who is expecting me in London on Friday.' The letter probably dates from 1885 or 1886. Another document belonging to J.-M. Bellefroid is a list of people to whom he wished to send copies of *L'Amour suprême*: Lord Salisbury is one of them.
12. *C.G.*, vol. II, pp. 190–1.
13. L. Bloy, *Lettres aux Montchal*, pp. 364–5.
14. *C.G.*, vol. II, p. 184.
15. Ibid., p. 178.
16. André Antoine, *Mes Souvenirs sur le Théâtre Libre*, Paris, Fayard, 1922, p. 59.
17. A. Antoine, p. 71.
18. Ibid., p. 98.
19. Unpublished manuscript belonging to J.-M. Bellefroid.
20. L. Bloy, *Lettres aux Montchal*, p. 364, and *C.G.*, vol. II, p. 189.
21. *Reliques*, pp. 73 and 97. It is not certain that it was to this volume that Villiers was thinking of giving that title, but it seems likely.
22. '*Le Nouveau-Monde*, new version' is mentioned on a list of his works he drew up towards the end of his life, and substantial fragments of the revised text are in the Castex Collection.
23. *C.G.*, vol. II, p. 161.

24. Ibid., p. 229.
25. J.-K. Huysmans, *Lettres inédites à Arij Prins*, p. 113.
26. That he did so resign himself is shown by the letter (*C.G.*, vol. II, p. 287) in which, on the grounds of ill-health, he declines an invitation to a reception celebrating the Comte de Paris's silver wedding.
27. É. Drougard, 'Une originale peu connue de Villiers de l'Isle-Adam', *Bulletin du Bibliophile*, janvier 1948.
28. Gustave Guiches, *Le Banquet*, p. 40.
29. Léon Deffoux, p. 23.
30. Gustave Guiches, *Le Banquet*, pp. 93–4.
31. Henry Roujon, *La Galerie*, p. 121.
32. Quoted in H. Le Noir de Tournemine, p. 32.

34 (pp. 326–339)

1. Interview with Baschet published in *Toute l'édition*, 12 octobre 1935.
2. Remy de Gourmont, *Promenades littéraires*, 2ᵉ série, pp. 15–16. See also *C.G.*, vol. II, p. 210, where Gourmont reminds Villiers that the books are still waiting for him. The list of works that Gourmont recommended to him is to be found in Alexis von Kraemer, *Villiers de l'Isle-Adam. En literatur-historisk Studie*, Helsinki, Akademisk Afhandling, 1900, p. 33, n. 2. Villiers did make some notes on Milton's life (an unpublished page of perfunctory annotations is in the Castex Collection), but does not seem to have used them in the story.
3. Remy de Gourmont, *Promenades littéraires*, 2ᵉ série, pp. 26–7.
4. A. France, p. 121.
5. Henry Roujon, 'Villiers de l'Isle-Adam', *Revue bleue*, septembre 1889.
6. J. E. S. Jeanès, pp. 174–5.
7. Unpublished document belonging to Max Daireaux.
8. É. de Rougemont, pp. 410–13.
9. Remy de Gourmont, *Promenades littéraires*, 2ᵉ série, p. 8.
10. *C.G.*, vol. II, p. 183.
11. Ibid., p. 201.
12. Ibid., pp. 212–13. The spelling given there is Althaiza, which is a mistake.
13. Ibid., pp. 212–13. This letter should obviously be placed after Alhaiza's letter and not before it.
14. Letter not in *C.G.* It was published by A.-S. Dufief, 'Villiers, le Théâtre Libre et l'acteur Mévisto', *20th—l'Avant-Siècle*, 2, 1976.
15. J.-K. Huysmans, *Lettres inédites à Jules Destrée*, edited by Gustave Vanwelkenhuyzen, Paris, Droz/Minard, 1967, pp. 138–9.
16. J.-K. Huysmans, *Lettres inédites à Arij Prins*, p. 110.
17. First published in facsimile in *Empreintes*, 10–11, 1952, pp. 40–1.
18. Quoted by Gustave Vanwelkenhuyzen, op. cit.
19. The story of Villiers's visit to Belgium has been most fully told by Émile Drougard, 'Villiers de l'Isle-Adam et la Belgique', *Collection*, 23 octobre-11 décembre 1937.
20. *C.G.*, vol. I, p. 215, where the words 'five curtain-calls' have inadvertently been omitted.

21. Ibid, p. 217.
22. Ibid., pp. 216, 218, and 220.
23. Ibid., p. 221.
24. Ibid., p. 217.
25. Ibid., p. 219.
26. Ibid., p. 227.
27. See Émile Drougard, 'Les *Histoires souveraines* de Villiers de l'Isle-Adam', *Annales de Bretagne*, t. 55, 1948. In this article, as in 'Villiers de l'Isle-Adam et la Belgique', É. Drougard suggests that this stay with Deman was separate from the lecture tour and took place late in 1887. But this belief depends on the fact that M. Drougard had been misinformed about the date of the letter in which Huysmans tells Destrée that Villiers has returned delighted with Belgium. M. Drougard believed it to have been written on 1 December 1887, but it is clear from the full text, which has since been published in Huysmans's *Lettres inédites à Jules Destrée*, that it in fact dates from late April 1888. As there is no other evidence to support the idea of a journey to Belgium in 1887, the hypothesis falls to the ground.
28. *C.G.*, vol. II, p. 226.
29. Ibid., p. 225.
30. Ibid., p. 228.
31. J.-K. Huysmans, *Lettres inédites à Jules Destrée*, p. 142.
32. G. Guiches, *Le Banquet*, p. 53.
33. Mallarmé, *Œuvres complètes*, p. 509.
34. *C.G.*, vol. II, pp. 222–3.
35. J.-K. Huysmans, *Lettres inédites à Arij Prins*, p. 111.
36. L. Bloy, *Lettres aux Montchal*, p. 407.
37. *C.G.*, vol. II, p. 229.
38. Ibid., p. 232.
39. Ibid.
40. Letters exchanged between Darzens and Vanier, published in *L'Intransigeant*, 5 janvier 1928.
41. Remy de Gourmont, *La Culture des idées*, pp. 63–4.
42. Quoted by F. Clerget, p. 163.
43. Unpublished document formerly in the Leclercq Collection.
44. J. E. S. Jeanès, p. 173.
45. Article by unidentified author in *La Volonté* (10 juillet 1936).
46. G. Guiches, *Le Banquet*, p. 56.

35 (pp. 339–349)

1. *C.G.*, vol. II, p. 178.
2. H. Le Roux, *Portraits de cire*, p. 22. Because Pontavice de Heussey in his book (p. 185) attributes the story to Anatole France, many other writers have followed him.
3. J. E. S. Jeanès, p. 176.
4. É. Rod, op. cit.
5. *C.G.*, vol. II, p. 242.
6. J.-K. Huysmans, *Lettres inédites à Arij Prins*, pp. 120, 133, 147, and 148.

7. *C.G.*, vol. II, p. 242–3.
8. L. Bloy, *Lettres aux Montchal*, p. 410.
9. Ibid., p. 417.
10. The last phrase of the latter has been published in *Nouvelles Reliques*, p. 44. The remainder is from the unpublished manuscript in the Castex Collection.
11. Unpublished manuscript formerly in the Leclercq Collection.
12. *C.G.*, vol. II, pp. 244–5.
13. Ibid., p. 245.
14. Ibid.
15. The story seems first to have been told in the gossipy and indiscreet obituary article which Georges Rodenbach published in *Le Figaro* on 20 August 1889. The anecdote was evidently retailed by Villiers himself, since it is repeated in *La Galerie des bustes*, pp. 122–3, where Roujon adds that Villiers would conclude: 'That's just my luck!' as though Salisbury had suddenly taken it into his head to lose his hearing.
16. Villiers's letter was published in A. W. Raitt, 'The poet and the Prime Minister: Villiers de l'Isle-Adam and the Marquess of Salisbury'.
17. *O.C.*, vol. XI, pp. 94–5.
18. *Reliques*, p. 78.
19. G. Guiches, *Le Banquet*, p. 44.
20. Ibid., p. 45.
21. Ibid.
22. Ibid., p. 95.
23. *C.G.*, vol. II, p. 252.
24. Ibid., p. 257.
25. Ibid., p. 259.
26. Ibid., p. 260.
27. J.-K. Huysmans, *Lettres inédites à Arij Prins*, p. 156.
28. In P.-G. Castex's edition of *Contes cruels*, p. 367, note f, it is stated that in 1888 Villiers became a member of the Central Committee of the League of Patriots, the pro-Boulanger organization. Once again this appears to be a confusion with Georges de Villiers de l'Isle-Adam, a committed Boulangist, one of whose works, published in 1887, is entitled *Vive Boulanger! Quand même! Debout!*
29. *O.C.*, vol. XI, p. 37.
30. *C.G.*, vol. II, p. 264.
31. Ibid., pp. 264–5.
32. Unpublished letter from Villiers to Lavignet in the Mariémont Collection.
33. *C.G.*, vol. II, pp. 270–1.
34. So Mallarmé later told Villiers's widow (*Correspondance*, vol. IV, p. 553).
35. *C.G.*, vol. II, p. 274.
36. See Mallarmé, *Correspondance*, vol. III, pp. 292–4, and vol. IV, pp. 631–3.
37. *C.G.*, vol. II, p. 272.
38. According to that letter (ibid., p. 204), Villiers had provided a copy with

pencil alterations. But the text eventually published by *La Vie populaire* was identical to the 1887 edition.
39. *C.G.*, vol. II, p. 278.

36 (pp. 349–355)

1. G. Guiches, *Au banquet de la vie*, p. 201.
2. Ibid., p. 210.
3. J.-K. Huysmans, *Lettres inédites à Arij Prins*, p. 160.
4. Mallarmé, *Correspondance*, vol. III, p. 305.
5. *C.G.*, vol. II, p. 277.
6. As has been suggested by Drougard, 'L'*Axël* de Villiers de l'Isle-Adam'.
7. In *Le Goéland*, août 1938.
8. Quoted by Léon Deffoux, pp. 41–2.
9. Georges Rodenbach, 'Villiers de l'Isle-Adam', *Le Figaro*, 20 août 1889. According to Remy de Gourmont (*Promenades littéraires*, 2ᵉ série, p. 14), Rodenbach had had this article ready for several days and called at the hospital twice daily to find out if Villiers was still alive, in order to make sure of getting in first.
10. *C.G.*, vol. II, p. 280.
11. Ibid., p. 277.
12. Ibid., p. 280.
13. Mallarmé, *Correspondance*, vol. IV, p. 542.
14. Letter from Huysmans quoted by Pontavice de Heussey, p. 286.
15. See *C.G.*, vol. II, p. 289.
16. Ibid., pp. 288 and 295. In *Nouvelles Reliques* (p. 40) there is a brief sketch which is perhaps a draft of this tale.
17. Ibid., p. 283.
18. This list has been published by J.-H. Bornecque, p. 190.
19. See the chapter on Dujardin in A. W. Raitt, pp. 338–49.
20. In the letter to Pontavice, p. 286.
21. *C.G.*, vol. II, p. 291.
22. See Mallarmé, *Correspondance*, vol. III, p. 324.

37 (pp. 355–363)

1. *C.G.*, vol. II, p. 292. The letter to Huysmans is not in *C.G.*; it has been published by J.-H. Bornecque, p. 192.
2. See Huysmans's letter to Pontavice, pp. 286–7.
3. It is possible that the news never reached him, since as late as 18 August Huysmans was intending to write to the Abbé to ask for help (Mallarmé, *Correspondance*, vol. III, p. 347, n. 1).
4. Mallarmé, *Œuvres complètes*, p. 497.
5. *C.G.*, vol. II, p. 292.
6. A vast amount of nonsense has been written about this marriage, most of it originating from the deformed version put about by Léon Bloy in the *roman à clef La Femme pauvre*. According to this tale, Huysmans forced Villiers, against his will, to marry Marie, either in order to humiliate him and satisfy some obscure desire for vengeance, or

because of his misplaced zeal as a new convert, as Max Daireaux claimed (pp. 221–7). In reality, it was not Huysmans's idea at all and Mallarmé was at least as active in trying to make the arrangements: neither of them was actuated by religious motives, and Huysmans was not converted until several years later. As long ago as 1954 it was demonstrated that it was Villiers who first raised the possibility of a deathbed marriage (A. W. Raitt, 'The Last Days of Villiers de l'Isle-Adam', *French Studies*, July 1954), but the old version continued to circulate for a long time afterwards (for instance in Pierre Mariel's edition of *Axël*, p. 16; there are even echoes of it in J.-H. Bornecque's recent book on Villiers).

7. Mallarmé, *Correspondance*, vol. III, p. 326.
8. Ibid., p. 329.
9. So Huysmans told Pontavice, pp. 288–9.
10. *C.G.*, vol. II, p. 272.
11. In a letter to Méry Laurent, not in *C.G.*, but published by J.-M. Bellefroid, 'Deux lettres inédites de Villiers de l'Isle-Adam à Mallarmé et à Méry Laurent'.
12. See *C.G.*, vol. II, p. 295, and Mallarmé, *Correspondance*, vol. IV, p. 635.
13. In R. du Pontavice de Heussey, p. 288.
14. Mallarmé, *Correspondance*, vol. III, p. 333, n. 1.
15. J.-H. Bornecque, p. 194.
16. Mallarmé, *Correspondance*, vol. III, p. 333.
17. Ibid., pp. 333–4.
18. See *C.G.*, vol. II, p. 293, and *Correspondance*, vol. III, p. 334, n. 2.
19. Document reproduced in *Empreintes*, 10–11 (1952), p. 39.
20. In Léon Deffoux, p. 43.
21. Gourmont, *Promenades littéraires*, 2ᵉ série, pp. 13–14. A similar story is told by Georges Rodenbach in his obituary article on Villiers in *Le Figaro*.
22. See Huysmans's letter in R. du Pontavice de Heussey, p. 289.
23. Mallarmé, *Correspondance*, vol. II, pp. 337–8, n. 1.
24. Ibid.
25. Ibid., p. 339.
26. Ibid., p. 340.
27. Ibid., p. 338.
28. *C.G.*, vol. II, pp. 298–9.
29. See A. W. Raitt, 'The Last Days of Villiers de l'Isle-Adam'.
30. See the letter from Huysmans to Méry Laurent in É. de Rougemont, p. 323, and Mallarmé, *Correspondance*, vol. III, p. 340, n. 1.
31. *C.G.*, vol. II, p. 298.
32. And not a Luxembourgeoise, as was thought at the time: see Tony Bourg, op. cit.
33. Mallarmé, *Correspondance*, vol. III, p. 345.
34. Léon Deffoux, p. 16.
35. Mallarmé, *Correspondance*, vol. III, p. 343.
36. Léon Deffoux, p. 13.
37. It has always been said, following Huysmans's account, that Marie only

signed with a cross, which someone helped her to trace. But Tony Bourg (op. cit).), having studied the certificates of Marie's marriages to both Brégeras and Villiers, has established that Marie signed both of them with the same signature, though on the second there is a cross as well. Presumably, though she could not write, she knew how to sign her own name, but was so nervous and overcome with emotion that she first made a cross and then needed her hand held to produce the signature. In fact, it is only Huysmans who quotes her as saying: 'I can make a cross like I did for my first husband.' According to Mallarmé, what she said was: 'I'll sign like I did at my first wedding.'

38. Mallarmé, *Correspondance*, vol. III, p. 344.
39. J.-K. Huysmans, in R. du Pontavice de Heussey, p. 292.
40. Mallarmé, *Correspondance*, vol. III, p. 344.
41. Ibid., p. 342.
42. É. de Rougemont, p. 323.
43. Ibid.
44. Mallarmé, *Correspondance*, vol. III, p. 348.

38 (pp. 364–367)

1. R. du Pontavice de Heussey, p. 294.
2. Mallarmé, *Correspondance*, vol. III, p. 348.
3. A. W. Raitt, 'The Last Days of Villiers de l'Isle-Adam'.
4. Mallarmé, *Correspondance*, vol. IV, p. 548.
5. Mallarmé, *Œuvres complètes*, p. 488.
6. See a whole series of letters in Mallarmé, *Correspondance*, vols. III and IV.
7. On these performances, see Paul Larochelle, *Trois hommes de théâtre*.
8. According to an unidentified newspaper in the Fonds Bollery.
9. On Totor, see Georges Casella, op. cit.
10. Quoted in the *Revue biblio-iconographique*, 21 décembre 1895.
11. Mallarmé, *Œuvres complètes*, p. 496.
12. According to Édouard de Rougemont in conversation with the present writer.

Conclusion (pp. 368–376)

1. Quoted in a 1964 autograph catalogue of the Maison Charavay, Paris.
2. Régnier, *Portraits et souvenirs*, Paris, Mercure de France, 1913, p. 23.
3. Mallarmé, *Œuvres complètes*, p. 489.
4. Ibid., p. 503.
5. Remy de Gourmont, *Le Livre des masques*, Paris, Mercure de France, 1921, p. 91.
6. To Pontavice de Heussey, p. 284.
7. Pontavice de Heussey (p. 69) says that a few years before his death Villiers wrote this to him: 'I have always felt alone, even beside a beloved woman or a friend, even in the intimacy of my family circle, so enthusiastic and so affectionate.'
8. L. Bloy, *La Résurrection de Villiers de l'Isle-Adam*.
9. Remy de Gourmont, *Promenades littéraires*, 4ᵉ série, p. 73.
10. Mallarmé, *Œuvres complètes*, pp. 496–7.

BIBLIOGRAPHY

(Place of publication Paris unless otherwise stated.)

1. WORKS BY VILLIERS DE L'ISLE-ADAM

i. First editions

Deux essais de poésie, Tinterlin, 1858.

Premières Poésies, Lyon, Scheuring, 1859.

Isis, Dentu, 1862.

Elën, Poupart-Davyl, 1865.

Morgane, Saint-Brieuc, Guyon Francisque, 1866.

La Révolte, Lemerre, 1870.

Le Nouveau-Monde, Richard, 1880.

Maison Gambade Père et Fils Succ^{rs}, Éditions de la Comédie humaine, 1882.

Contes cruels, Calmann Lévy, 1883.

L'Ève future, Brunhoff, 1886.

L'Amour suprême, Brunhoff, 1886.

Akëdysséril, Brunhoff, 1886.

Tribulat Bonhomet, Tresse et Stock, 1887.

Histoires insolites, Quantin, 1888.

Nouveaux Contes cruels, Librairie illustrée, 1888.

Chez les passants, Comptoir d'édition, 1890.

Axël, Quantin, 1890.

L'Évasion, Tresse et Stock, 1891.

Nouveaux Contes cruels et Propos d'au-delà, Calmann Lévy, 1893.

Trois Portraits de femmes, Bernard, 1929.

Reliques, edited by P.-G. Castex, Corti, 1954.

Correspondance générale, edited by J. Bollery, 2 vols., Mercure de France, 1962.

Le Prétendant, edited by P.-G. Castex and A. W. Raitt, Corti, 1965.

Nouvelles Reliques, edited by P.-G. Castex and J.-M. Bellefroid, Corti, 1968.

ii. Complete works

The *Complete Works* of Villiers de l'Isle-Adam were published by the Mercure de France between 1914 and 1931 under the direction of Marcel Longuet.

I *L'Ève future* (1914).

II *Contes cruels* (1914).

425

III *Tribulat Bonhomet; Nouveaux Contes cruels* (1922).

IV *Axël* (1923).

V *L'Amour suprême; Akëdysséril* (1924).

VI *Histoires insolites* (1924).

VII *La Révolte; L'Évasion; Le Nouveau-Monde* (1925).

VIII *Morgane; Elën* (1927).

IX *Isis* (1928).

X *Premières Poésies* (1929).

XI *Propos d'au-delà; Chez les passants; Pages posthumes* (1931).

A new edition of the complete works is being prepared for the Bibliothèque de la Pléiade by P.-G. Castex, J.-M. Bellefroid, and the present writer.

iii. Annotated editions

Les Trois Premiers Contes, edited by É. Drougard, 2 vols., Belles Lettres, 1931.

Contes cruels, edited by P.-G. Castex and J. Bollery, 2 vols., Corti, 1954 and 1956.

L'Ève future, edited by J. Bollery and P.-G. Castex, Le Club du Meilleur Livre, 1957.

Œuvres, edited by J.-H. Bornecque, Le Club du Livre français, 1957.

Axël, edited by P. Mariel, La Colombe, 1960.

Contes cruels et Nouveaux Contes cruels, edited by A. Lebois, Union générale des éditions, 1963.

Contes cruels et Nouveaux Contes cruels, edited by P.-G. Castex, Garnier, 1968.

Tribulat Bonhomet, edited by P.-G. Castex and J.-M. Bellefroid, Corti, 1967.

Contes et récits, edited by J. Chupeau, Bordas, 1970.

L'Ève future, edited by P. Citron, L'Âge d'Homme, 1979.

Contes cruels, edited by P. Citron, Garnier-Flammarion, 1980.

iv. English Translations

The Revolt and the Escape, translated by Lady Theresa Barclay, London, Duckworth, 1901.

Claire Lenoir, translated and introduced by A. Symons, New York, Boni, 1925.

Queen Ysabeau, translated by A. Symons, Chicago, The Pembroke Press, 1925.

Axël, translated by H. P. R. Finberg, with an introduction by W. B. Yeats, London, Jarolds, 1925.

Sardonic Tales, translated by H. Miles, London, Blue Jade, 1927.

Cruel Tales, translated by R. Baldick, with an introduction by A. W. Raitt, London, O.U.P., 1963.

Axël, translated and introduced by Marilyn Gaddis Rose, Dublin, Dolmen Press, 1970.

v. Correspondence

Correspondance générale, edited by J. Bollery, Mercure de France, 1962.

2 BOOKS ON VILLIERS DE L'ISLE-ADAM

Baudry, J.: *Étude généalogique et biographique sur les ascendants du poète Villiers de l'Isle-Adam*, Champion, 1905.

Bloy, L.: *La Résurrection de Villiers de l'Isle-Adam*, Blaizot, 1906.

Bollery, J.: *Biblio-iconographie de Villiers de l'Isle-Adam*, Mercure de France, 1939.

—: *La Bretagne de Villiers de l'Isle-Adam*, Saint-Brieuc, Les Presses bretonnes, 1961.

Bornecque, J.-H.: *Villiers de l'Isle-Adam créateur et visionnaire*, Nizet, 1974.

Bürgisser, P.: *La Double Illusion de l'or et de l'amour chez Villiers de l'Isle-Adam*, Berne, Lang, 1969.

Chapoutot, H.: *Villiers de l'Isle-Adam*, Delesalle, 1908.

Clerget, F.: *Villiers de l'Isle-Adam*, Louis-Michaud, n. d. [1913].

Conyngham, D.: *Le Silence éloquent. Thèmes et structures de 'L'Ève future' de Villiers de l'Isle-Adam*, Corti, 1975.

Conroy, W. T. Jr: *Villiers de l'Isle-Adam*, Boston, Twayne, 1978.

Daireaux, M.: *Villiers de l'Isle-Adam, l'homme et l'œuvre*, Desclée de Brouwer, 1936.

Deenen, M.: *Le Merveilleux dans l'œuvre de Villiers de l'Isle-Adam*, Courville, 1939.

Deffoux, L.: *Les Derniers Jours de Villiers de l'Isle-Adam*, Bernard, 1930.

Demant, W.: *Elemente der Epik bei Villiers de l'Isle-Adam*, Bonn, 1916.

Du Pontavice de Heussey, R.: *Villiers de l'Isle-Adam*, Savine, 1893.

Gourevitch, J.-P.: *Villiers de l'Isle-Adam ou l'univers de la transgression*, Seghers, 1971.

Habrekorn, D. (ed.): *Bloy, Villiers, Huysmans: Lettres*, Editions Taot, 1980.

Janvrais, T.: *Le Berceau des Villiers de l'Isle-Adam*, Saint-Brieuc, Prudhomme; Champion, 1913.

Jean-Aubry, G.: *Une amitié exemplaire: Villiers de l'Isle-Adam et Stéphane Mallarmé*, Mercure de France, 1942.

Kraemer, A. von: *Villiers de l'Isle-Adam. En litteratur-historisk Studie*, Helsinki, Akademisk Afhandling, 1900.

Lanfredini, D.: *Villiers de l'Isle-Adam*, Florence, Le Monnier, 1940.

Lebois, A.: *Villiers de l'Isle-Adam révélateur du verbe*, Neuchâtel, Messeiller, 1952.

Le Noir de Tournemine, H.: *Autour de Villiers de l'Isle-Adam*, Saint-Brieuc, Guyon, 1906.

Mallarmé, S.: *Villiers de l'Isle-Adam*, Librairie de l'Art indépendant, 1890.

Michelet, V.-É.: *Nos Maîtres: Villiers de l'Isle-Adam*, Librairie hermétique, 1910.

Palgen, R.: *Villiers de l'Isle-Adam auteur dramatique*, Champion, 1925.

Pierredon, G.: *Notes sur Villiers de l'Isle-Adam*, Messein, 1939.

Raitt, A. W.: *Villiers de l'Isle-Adam et le mouvement symboliste*, Corti, 1965.

Rougemont, É. de: *Villiers de l'Isle-Adam*, Mercure de France, 1910.

Schmidt, M.: *Formen der Angst bei Villiers de l'Isle-Adam*, Zurich, Leemann, 1934.

Testu, Dr C.: *Essai psycho-pathologique sur Villiers de l'Isle-Adam*, Jouve, 1931.

van der Meulen, C. J. C.: *L'Idéalisme de Villiers de l'Isle-Adam*, Amsterdam, H. J. Paris, 1925.

Vanwelkenhuyzen, G.: *Villiers de l'Isle-Adam vu par les Belges*, Brussels, Palais des Académies, 1959.

3 MAIN ARTICLES ON VILLIERS DE L'ISLE-ADAM
(not including newspaper articles published during Villiers's lifetime or obituary articles published on his death).

Albertsen, L. L. and Rose, M. G.: 'Villiers de l'Isle-Adam's *Axël*: what's in a name?', *Romance Notes*, Spring 1979.

Bellefroid, J.-M.: 'Villiers de l'Isle-Adam en Bavière (1869)', *Revue d'Histoire littéraire de la France*, octobre–décembre 1963.

—: 'Deux lettres inédites de Villiers de l'Isle-Adam à Mallarmé et à Méry Laurent', *Revue d'Histoire littéraire de la France*, avril–juin 1965.

—: 'Une chronique de Villiers de l'Isle-Adam sur Victor Noir', *Revue des Sciences humaines*, juillet–septembre 1965.

Berval, R. de: 'Hommage à Villiers de l'Isle-Adam', *Mercure de France*, septembre 1938.

Besnier, P.: 'L'Entre-deux Mondes des *Contes cruels*', *Annales de Bretagne*, t. 76, 1969.

—: 'A propos des *Contes cruels*', *Bulletin de l'Association Guillaume Budé*, mars 1970.

—: 'Le Double dans les *Contes cruels*', *Mémoires de la Société d'émulation des Côtes-du-Nord*, t. 99, 1970.

—: 'De la révolte au désespoir: Villiers de l'Isle-Adam en 1870', *Annales de Bretagne*, t. 77, 1970.

—: 'Félicien David ou le fantôme de l'Opéra', *Mémoires de la Société d'émulation des Côtes-du-Nord*, t. 102, 1973.

—: 'J.-K. Huysmans et Villiers de l'Isle-Adam', in *Mélanges Pierre Lambert consacrés à Huysmans*, Nizet, 1975.

Bollery, J.: 'Villiers de l'Isle-Adam. Documents biographiques inédits', *Mercure de France*, 1er octobre 1938.

—: '*Le Dragon impérial*', *Mercure de France*, 1er novembre 1939.

—: 'Un problème bibliographique résolu par la mort d'un académicien', *Livrets du mandarin*, 4e série, janvier 1942.

—: 'Deux pré-originales inconnues de Villiers de l'Isle-Adam', *Revue des Sciences humaines*, janvier–mars 1955.

—: 'Documents biographiques inédits sur Villiers de l'Isle-Adam', *Revue d'Histoire littéraire de la France*, janvier–mars 1956.

—: 'Villiers de l'Isle-Adam et la Bretagne', *Mercure de France*, septembre 1961.

—: 'Une descendance inconnue de Villiers de l'Isle-Adam au Congo ex-belge', *La Fenêtre ouverte*, décembre 1961.

—: 'Au sujet de *Un Dilemme*', *Bulletin de la Société J.-K. Huysmans*, 50, 1966.

—: 'Une lettre inédite de Villiers de l'Isle-Adam à Huysmans', *Bulletin de la Société J.-K. Huysmans*, 50, 1966.

Bornecque, J.-H.: '*Tableau de Paris*', *Mercure de France*, août 1953.

Boudet, G.: 'Sur un des *Nouveaux Contes cruels* de Villiers de l'Isle-Adam: *L'Enjeu*', *Revue d'Histoire littéraire de la France*, janvier–mars 1961.

Bourg, T.: 'Marie Dantine—Luxembourgeoise par erreur', *d'Letzeburger Land*, 4 Mai 1979.

Boux de Casson, F.: 'Cinq lettres inédites de Villiers de l'Isle-Adam', *Aspects*, 7 juillet 1944.

Castex, P.-G.: 'Villiers de l'Isle-Adam au travail', *Revue des Sciences humaines*, avril–juin 1954.

—: 'Villiers de l'Isle-Adam historien de sa maison', *Revue du Nord*, avril–juin 1954.

—: 'Histoire d'un *Conte cruel*', *Revue des Sciences humaines*, janvier–mars 1955.

—: '*La Tentation*, scènes inédites', *Revue d'Histoire littéraire de la France*, janvier–mars 1956.

—: 'Maître Fulcran', Mercure de France, 1er avril 1956.

Castex, P.-G. and Raitt, A. W.: 'De Morgane au Prétendant', Revue des Sciences humaines, janvier–mars 1955.

Chambers, R.: '"De grands yeux dans l'obscurité." Regard scientifique et vision occulte dans Claire Lenoir et L'Ève future', Australian Journal of French Studies, 3, 1972.

Cipriani, F.: 'La Révolte, dramma di Villiers de l'Isle-Adam, note con frammenti inediti', Annali della facoltà di Lettere et Filosofia dell'Università degli Studi di Milano, settembre–dicembre 1975.

Decottignies, J.: 'Baphomet ou la fiction', Revue des Sciences humaines, juillet–août 1974.

—: 'L'Histoire et le secret: Villiers de l'Isle-Adam et Richard Wagner', Revue des Sciences humaines, 1978–4.

Di Scanno, T.: 'L'esoterismo e la morte in Axël di Villiers de l'Isle-Adam', in Il Superuomo e i suoi simboli nelle letterature moderne Bologna, La Nuova Italia, 1971.

Drougard, E.: 'Le Vrai Sens d'Axël', Grande Revue, avril 1931.

—: 'Villiers de l'Isle-Adam et Éliphas Lévi', Revue belge de Philologie et d'Histoire, t. 10, 3, 1931.

—: 'Villiers de l'Isle-Adam et Théophile Gautier', Revue d'Histoire littéraire de la France, octobre–décembre 1932.

— : 'L'Art de Villiers de l'Isle-Adam', Grande Revue, juillet 1933.

—: 'Une réplique française de La Légende du Grand Inquisiteur', Revue des Études slaves, 2, 1934.

—: 'Richard Wagner et Villiers de l'Isle-Adam', Revue de Littérature comparée, avril–juin 1935.

—: 'Villiers de l'Isle-Adam et Hoffmann', Revue de Littérature comparée, avril–juin 1935.

—: 'L'Axël de Villiers de l'Isle-Adam', Revue d'Histoire littéraire de la France, octobre–décembre 1935.

—: 'Villiers de l'Isle-Adam et Richard Wagner', Revue musicale, février 1936.

—: 'Le Fondement historique d'Axël', Nouvelle Revue, février 1936.

—: 'Les Sources d'Axël', Revue d'Histoire littéraire de la France, octobre–décembre 1936.

—: 'Villiers de l'Isle-Adam et Björnstjerne Björnson', Revue de Littérature comparée, octobre–décembre 1937.

—: 'Villiers de l'Isle-Adam et la Belgique', Collection, 23 octobre–11 décembre 1937.

—: 'Les Premiers Jours de la guerre de 1870', Nouvelles littéraires, 6 mai 1939.

—: 'L'Or du Rhin et L'Exposition universelle des Beaux-Arts à Munich', Nouvelles littéraires, 29 juillet and 5 août 1939.

—: 'L'Ombre de Meyerbeer', L'Arche, juillet 1946.

—: 'Les Débuts de Villiers de l'Isle-Adam', *Cahiers de la Lucarne*, mai 1947.

—: 'Villiers de l'Isle-Adam à Solesmes', *Revue de la Méditerranée*, mars–avril 1947.

—: 'Villiers de l'Isle-Adam et Ibsen', *Revue de Littérature comparée*, avril–juin 1947.

—: 'Les *Histoires souveraines* de Villiers de l'Isle-Adam', *Annales de Bretagne*, t. 55, 1948.

—: 'Une originale peu connue de Villiers de l'Isle-Adam', *Bulletin du Bibliophile*, janvier 1948.

—: 'La Pré-originale de *L'Ève future*', *Bulletin du Bibliophile*, juillet 1948.

—: '*La Révolte* de Villiers de l'Isle-Adam: le texte original', *Bulletin du Bibliophile*, novembre 1948.

—: 'Villiers de l'Isle-Adam défenseur de son nom', *Annales de Bretagne*, t. 62, 1955.

—: 'Fragments manuscrits d'*Axël*', *Revue des Sciences humaines*, janvier–mars 1955.

—: 'Documents relatifs à l'impression d'*Axël* en volume', *Bulletin du Bibliophile*, nos. 2 and 3, 1955.

—: 'Pour le nom: Villiers de l'Isle-Adam et ses homonymes', *Revue des Sciences humaines*, octobre–décembre 1957.

—: 'Les Études de Villiers de l'Isle-Adam', *Annales de Bretagne*, t. 65, 1958.

Dubreuil, L. 'A propos de Villiers de l'Isle-Adam: du côté de la tante Kerinou', *Annales de Bretagne*, t. 65, 1958.

Dufief, A.-S.: 'Villiers, le Théâtre Libre et l'acteur Mévisto', *20th-L'Avant-Siècle*, 2, 1976.

Dumesnil, R.: 'Villiers de l'Isle-Adam et Richard Wagner', *Revue de Paris*, juillet 1959.

Garcias, W.: 'Lettres de Villiers de l'Isle-Adam', *La Table ronde*, 25 novembre 1920.

—: 'Une page inconnue de la vie de Villiers de l'Isle-Adam', *Le Goéland*, 1er août 1938.

Gavelle, E.: 'Une source d'*Axël*', *Revue des Sciences humaines*, janvier–mars 1955.

Goldgar, H.: '*Axël* de Villiers de l'Isle-Adam et *The Shadowy Waters* de W. B. Yeats', *Revue de Littérature comparée*, octobre–décembre 1950.

Gourmont, R. de: '*Les Filles de Milton*', *Écho de Paris*, 17 février 1891.

—: 'Notes sur Villiers de l'Isle-Adam', *Mercure de France*, août 1890.

Graaf, D. A. de: 'Une source de *L'Ève future*', *Synthèses*, avril 1961.

Groves, M.: 'An early version of Villiers de l'Isle-Adam's *La Maison du bonheur*', *Romance Notes*, 10, 1969.

—: 'Villiers de l'Isle-Adam and Sir William Crookes', *French Studies*, April 1975.

—: 'Villiers de l'Isle-Adam, *Aux Chrétiens les lions!* and the Porte Saint-Martin Theatre', *Romance Notes*, 16, 1975.

Hachelle, M.-J.: 'Villiers de l'Isle-Adam pamphlétaire', *Collection*, 2 décembre 1939.

Jean-Aubry, G.: 'Villiers de l'Isle-Adam et la musique', *Mercure de France*, 15 novembre 1938.

Kahn, G.: 'Villiers de l'Isle-Adam', *Mercure de France*, 15 juillet and 1er août 1922.

Kies, A. and Bandy, W. T.: 'Villiers de l'Isle-Adam: lettre inédite à Asselineau', *Bulletin baudelairien*, avril 1971.

Latil-Le Dantec, M.: 'Villiers de l'Isle-Adam ou l'homme double', *Table ronde*, 212, 1965.

Laulan, R.: 'La Hantise de l'échafaud chez Villiers de l'Isle-Adam', *La Presse médicale*, 25 and 26 décembre 1959.

La Varende, J. de: 'Villiers de l'Isle-Adam', *Revue des Deux Mondes*, 1er novembre 1938.

Lebois, A.: 'En relisant *L'Ève future*', in *Admirable XIXe siècle*, Denoël, 1958.

Le Braz, A.: 'Villiers de l'Isle-Adam et l'Ordre de Malte', *Le Fureteur breton*, juin–juillet 1912.

Le Dantec, Y.-G.: '*Conte d'amour*', *La Muse française*, 15 novembre 1938.

Lhombreaud, Roger: 'Deux âmes qui s'entendent si merveilleusement . . .', *Revue de Paris*, juillet 1955.

Longuet, M.: 'Villiers de l'Isle-Adam', *Comœdia*, 31 mars 1931.

—: 'Deux critiques musicales de Villiers de l'Isle-Adam', *Mercure de France*, 15 mars 1932.

Maeterlinck, M.: 'Villiers de l'Isle-Adam' *Comœdia*, 27 janvier 1927.

Marsan, J.: 'Villiers de l'Isle-Adam', in *Autour du Romantisme*, Toulouse, Éditions de l'Archer, 1937.

Marsille, le R. P.: 'Les Cent jours vannetais de Villiers de l'Isle-Adam', *Bulletin mensuel de la Société Polymathique du Morbihan*, juin 1962.

Mistler, J.: 'Notre ami Wagner', *Nouvelles littéraires*, 24 octobre 1963.

Miyauchi, Y.: 'Déplacement stylistique de l'épithète chez Villiers de l'Isle-Adam', *Études de Langue française*, mai 1959.

Mombello, G.: 'A proposito dell'amicizia letteraria tra Villiers de l'Isle-Adam e Verlaine', *Studi francesi*, settembre-dicembre 1960.

Mont, D.: 'Genèse et sources d'un conte de Villiers de l'Isle-Adam, *La Légende de l'éléphant blanc*', *Revue d'Histoire littéraire de la France*, juillet-août 1974.

Picard, M.: 'Notes sur le fantastique de Villiers de l'Isle-Adam', *Revue des Sciences humaines*, juillet-septembre 1959.

Prinet, M.: 'Les Ancêtres parisiens de Villiers de l'Isle-Adam', *Mercure de France*, 1er août 1928.

Przyboś, J.: 'La foi du récit: étude sur *Véra* de Villiers de l'Isle-Adam', *French Review*, February 1980.

Raison du Cleuziou, Chanoine J.: 'Le Chanoine Yves-Marie-Victor Villiers de l'Isle-Adam et le conte de *L'Intersigne*', *Mémoires de la Société d'Émulation des Côtes-du-Nord*, t. 83, 1954.

—: 'L'Agence "Villiers de l'Isle-Adam",' *Mémoires de la Société d'Émulation des Côtes-du-Nord*, t. 91, 1962.

—: 'A la recherche d'un trésor perdu: notes de lecture en marge d'*Axël*', *Mémoires de la Société d'Émulation des Côtes-du-Nord*, t. 96, 1967.

—: 'L'Entrevue à Solesmes de Louis Veuillot et d'A. Villiers de l'Isle-Adam', *Mémoires de la Société d'Émulation des Côtes-du-Nord*, t. 98, 1969.

Raitt, A. W.: 'The Last Days of Villiers de l'Isle-Adam', *French Studies*, July 1954.

—: 'Autour d'une lettre de Mallarmé', *Revue des Sciences humaines*, janvier–mars 1955.

—: 'Les Déboires d'un auteur dramatique: Villiers de l'Isle-Adam à l'Ambigu', *Cahiers d'Histoire et de Folklore*, octobre–décembre 1955.

—: 'Etat présent des études sur Villiers de l'Isle-Adam', *L'Information littéraire*, janvier–février 1956.

—: '*Lohengrin* raconté par Villiers de l'Isle-Adam', *Revue des Sciences humaines*, juillet 1956.

—: 'Villiers de l'Isle-Adam in 1870', *French Studies*, October 1959.

—: 'Villiers de l'Isle-Adam et l'illusionnisme des Symbolistes', *Cahiers de l'Association internationale des Études françaises*, 1960.

—: 'Villiers de l'Isle-Adam et le fantastique', *Cahiers de l'Association internationale des Études françaises*, 1980.

—: 'The poet and the Prime Minister: Villiers de l'Isle-Adam and the Marquess of Salisbury', *French Studies*, October 1980.

Randal, G.: 'Le Mariage *in extremis* de Villiers de l'Isle-Adam', *Mercure de France*, 1er juillet 1948.

Reboul, P.: 'Autour d'un conte de Villiers de l'Isle-Adam', *Revue d'Histoire littéraire de la France*, juillet–septembre 1949.

—: 'Villiers de l'Isle-Adam et le *Melmoth* de Maturin', *Revue de Littérature comparée*, octobre–décembre 1951.

—: 'Le Grand-père de Villiers de l'Isle-Adam', *Le Divan*, juillet–septembre 1954.

Rose, M. G.: 'Villiers de l'Isle-Adam's Commander: a possible prototype', *Romance Notes*, 11, 1970.

—: 'Milton, Chateaubriand and Villiers de l'Isle-Adam: *Paradise Lost and Axël*', *Studies in Romanticism*, 9, 1970.

Roujon, H.: 'Lorsque Villiers de l'Isle-Adam nous jouait du Wagner . . .', *Le Journal*, 28 février 1904.

Rouzet, G.: 'Villiers de l'Isle-Adam à Bruxelles', *Mercure de France*, 15 août 1938.

Sallier Dupin, Dr H. de: 'Villiers de l'Isle-Adam', *Les Échos de Saint-Vincent*, octobre 1955.

Taillade, N.: '*Claire Lenoir* et le grotesque', *Les Annales*, 9, 1973.

Valéry, P.: 'Villiers de l'Isle-Adam', *Tel quel*, 4, 1961.

4 OTHER WORKS QUOTED IN THIS BOOK

Ajalbert, J.: *Mémoires en vrac*, Albin Michel, 1938.

Andrieu, L.: 'Les Dédicaces des livrés envoyés à Flaubert et conservés à l'Hôtel de Ville de Canteleu', *Bulletin des Amis de Flaubert*, no. 24, 1964.

Auriant: *Fragments*, Brussels, Nouvelle Revue Belgique, 1942.

Badesco, L.: *La Jeunesse des deux rives. La Génération poétique de 1860*, Nizet, 1971.

Baldensperger, F.: 'Un Villiers de l'Isle-Adam vagabond et agitateur', *Mercure de France*, 1er juillet 1934.

Baldick, R.: *The Life of J.-K. Huysmans*, Oxford, Oxford University Press, 1955.

Barracand, L.: 'Souvenirs d'un homme de lettres', *Revue des Deux Mondes*, 15 août 1937.

Barthou, L.: 'Jean Marras et Leconte de Lisle', *Revue des Deux Mondes*, 15 novembre 1933.

Baschet, R.: interview in *Toute l'édition*, 12 octobre 1935.

Baude de Maurceley: 'La Vérité sur le salon de Nina de Villard', *Le Figaro*, 2–8 avril 1929.

Baudelaire, C.: *Correspondance*, edited by C. Pichois, Bibliothèque de la Pléiade, 1973.

Bergerat, É.: *Souvenirs d'un enfant de Paris*, Fasquelle, 1911–12.

Bernès, H.: 'Villiers de l'Isle-Adam sous la Commune', *Mercure de France*, 1er novembre 1910.

Billy, A.: 'Propos du samedi', *Le Figaro littéraire*, 24 mars 1966.

Bloy, L.: *La Femme pauvre*, Mercure de France, 1947.

—: *Lettres aux Montchal*, Bernard, 1947–48.

Bollery, J.: *Léon Bloy*, Albin Michel, 1947–54.

Buet, C.: 'Les Morts royales', *Le Magasin littéraire de Gand*, 15 octobre 1894.

Calmettes, F.: *Leconte de Lisle et ses amis*, Librairies-Imprimeries Réunies, n.d. [1902].

Casella, G.: *Pèlerinages*, Lausanne, Payot, 1918.

Cazals, F.-A.: *Paul Verlaine, ses portraits*, Bibliothèque de l'Association, 1896.

Cros, C.: *Œuvres complètes*, edited by Louis Forestier and Pascal Pia, Pauvert, 1964.

Descaves, L.: *Souvenirs d'un ours*, Éditions de Paris, 1946.

Descotes, M.: *Le Public de théâtre et son histoire*, P.U.F., 1964.

Du Pontavice de Heussey, Hyacinthe: *Œuvres complètes*, Quantin, 1887.

Duval, G.: *Mémoires d'un Parisien*, Flammarion, n.d. [1913].

Escholier, R.: *Victor Hugo: un amant de génie*, Fayard, 1953.

Fontainas, A.: *Mes Souvenirs du Symbolisme*, Nouvelle Revue critique, 1928.

Forestier, L.: *Charles Cros, l'homme et l'œuvre*, Minard, 1969.

France, A.: *La Vie littéraire*, vol. III, Calmann Lévy, 1891.

Gautier, J.: *Le Troisième Rang du collier*, Juven, 1909.

Ghil, R.: *Les Dates et les œuvres*, Crès, 1925.

Ginisty, P.: *Souvenirs de journalisme et de théâtre*, Éditions de France, 1930.

Goncourt, E. and J. de: *Journal*, edited by Robert Ricatte, Fasquelle-Flammarion, 1956.

Gourmont, R. de: *Promenades littéraires*, 2e série, Mercure de France, 1906.

—: *Promenades littéraires*, 4e série, Mercure de France, 1920.

—: *La Culture des idées*, Mercure de France, 1900.

—: *Le Livre des masques*, Mercure de France, 1896.

—: *Épilogues*, I, Mercure de France, 1903.

Guichard, L.: *La Musique et les lettres en France au temps du wagnérisme*, P.U.F., 1963.

—: *Lettres de Richard et Cosima Wagner à Judith Gautier*, Gallimard, 1964.

Guiches, G.: *Au banquet de la vie*, Spes, 1925.

—: *Le Banquet*, Spes, 1926.

Huret, J.: *Enquête sur l'évolution littéraire*, Charpentier, 1893.

Huysmans, J.-K.: *A rebours*, Charpentier, 1947.

—: *Lettres inédites à Jules Destrée*, edited by G. Vanwelkenhuyzen, Droz/Minard, 1967.

—: *Lettres inédites à Arij Prins 1885–1907*, edited by L. Gillet, Geneva, Droz, 1977.

Ibrovac, M.: *José-Maria de Heredia*, Presses Françaises, 1923.

Jeanès, J. E. S.: *D'après nature*, Besançon, Gravelle, 1946.

Kahn, G.: *Silhouettes littéraires*, Montaigne, 1925.

—: 'Trente ans de Symbolisme', *Les Nouvelles littéraires*, date unknown.

Knowles, D.: *La Réaction idéaliste au théâtre depuis 1890*, Droz, 1934.

Larochelle, P.: *Trois hommes de théâtre*, Éditions du Centre, 1961.

Lavedan, H.: 'Courrier de Paris', *L'Illustration*, 17 avril 1909.

Lefèvre, F.: 'Une heure avec Édouard Dujardin', *Les Nouvelles littéraires*, 4 juin 1932.

Lefèvre-Roujon, Mme C.: *Correspondance inédite de Stéphane Mallarmé et Henry Roujon*, Geneva, Cailler, 1949.

Lemercier de Neuville: *Souvenirs d'un montreur de marionnettes*, Bauche, 1911.

Le Rouge, G.: 'Verlainiens et Décadents', *Les Nouvelles littéraires*, 11 août–15 décembre 1928.

Le Roux, H.: *Portraits de cire*, Lecène, 1891.

Leroy, M.: *Les Premiers Amis français de Wagner*, Michel, 1925.

Lhombreaud, Roger: *Arthur Symons*, London, Unicorn Press, 1963.

Mabille de Poncheville, A.: *Vie de Verhaeren*, Mercure de France, 1953.

Maeterlinck, M.: *Bulles bleues*, Monaco, Éditions du Rocher, 1947.

Mallarmé, S.: *Œuvres complètes*, edited by H. Mondor and G. Jean-Aubry, Bibliothèque de la Pléiade, 1945.

—: *Les 'Gossips' de Mallarmé*, edited by H. Mondor and L. J. Austin, Gallimard, 1962.

—: *Correspondance*, edited by H. Mondor and J.-P. Richard for Vol. I and H. Mondor and L. J. Austin for the remainder, Gallimard, 1959–.

—: *Correspondance avec Henri Cazalis 1862–1897*, edited by C. P. Barbier and L. Joseph, Nizet, 1977.

Maritain, J.: 'Le Témoignage d'un ami de Léon Bloy', *Revue des Jeunes*, 10 janvier 1925.

Mendès, C.: *La Légende du 'Parnasse contemporain'*, Brussels, Brancart, 1884.

—: *Rapport sur le mouvement poétique français de 1867 à 1900*, Imprimerie Nationale, 1903.

Michelet, V.-É.: *Figures d'évocateurs*, Figuière, 1913.

Mondor, H.: *Vie de Mallarmé*, Gallimard, 1941.

—: *Mallarmé plus intime*, Gallimard, 1944.

Moore, G.: *Memoirs of my Dead Life*, London, Heinemann, 1936.

Mortier, A.: *Les Soirées parisiennes de 1883*, Dentu, 1884.

Perrin, H.: 'Entre Parnasse et Symbolisme: Ephraïm Mikhaël', *Revue d'Histoire littéraire de la France*, janvier–mars 1956.

Petit, J.: *Barbey d'Aurevilly critique*, Les Belles Lettres, 1963.

Pichard du Page, R.: *Une musicienne versaillaise. Augusta Holmès*, Versailles, Dubois; Paris, Fischbacher, 1921.

Racot, A.: *Portraits d'aujourd'hui*, Librairie illustrée, 1887.

Régnier, H. de: *Nos Rencontres*, Mercure de France, 1932.

—: *Portraits et Souvenirs*, Mercure de France, 1913.

—: *De mon temps*, Mercure de France, 1933.

Ricard, L.-X. de: *Petits Mémoires d'un Parnassien*, edited by M. Pakenham, Lettres Modernes, 1967.

Richardson, J.: *Théophile Gautier*, London, Reinhardt, 1958.

Rod, É.: 'Mes Débuts dans les lettres', *La Semaine littéraire* (Geneva), 17 september 1910.

Rodenbach, G.: *Évocations*, Brussels, La Renaissance du Livre, 1924.

Roujon, H.: *La Galerie des bustes*, Rueff, 1909.

Stock, P.-V.: *Mémorandum d'un éditeur*, 2e série, Stock, 1936.

Strobel, O.: *Neue Urkunden zur Lebensgeschichte Richard Wagners 1864–1882*, Karlsruhe, 1939.

Tiercelin, L.: *Bretons de lettres*, Champion, 1905.

Valéry, P.: *Œuvres*, Vol. I, Bibliothèque de la Pléiade, 1957.

Verhaeren, E.: *Impressions*, vol. III, Marpon and Flammarion, 1928.

Verlaine, P.: *Œuvres complètes* and *Œuvres posthumes*, Messein, 1925–7.

Verlaine, ex-Mme P.: *Mémoires de ma vie*, Flammarion, 1935.

Vier, J.: 'Une grande amie de la Bretagne, la comtesse d'Agoult (Daniel Stern)', *Annales de Bretagne*, t. 64, 1957.

Wagner, C.: *Die Tagebücher*, edited by M. Gregor-Dellin and D. Mack, Munich, Piper Verlag, 1976–7.

INDEX

Index